P9-CDE-178

MIKE MEYERS' CERTIFICATION
Passport ✦

CompTIA

DISCARD

Network+®

Fifth Edition
(Exam N10-006)

COMPUTERS

MIKE MEYERS

JONATHAN S. WEISSMAN

FEB 1 9 2016   New York   Chicago   San Francisco   Athens
London   Madrid   Mexico City   Milan
New Delhi   Singapore   Sydney   Toronto

Library of Congress Cataloging-in-Publication Data

Meyers, Michael, 1961-
Mike meyers' CompTIA network+ certification passport, (exam N10-006) /
Mike Meyers, Jonathan S. Weissman, Scott Jernigan. — Fifth edition.
    pages cm
Includes index.
ISBN 978-0-07-184796-4 (set) — ISBN 978-0-07-184191-7 (book) — ISBN 978-0-07-184798-8 (cd) —
ISBN 0-07-184796-0 (set) — ISBN 0-07-184191-1 (book) — ISBN 0-07-184798-7 (CD)
    1. Computer networks—Examinations—Study guides.   2. Telecommunications
engineers—Certification.   3. Computer technicians—Certification—Study guides.
    4. Microcomputers—Maintenance and repair—Examinations—Study guides.
    I. Weissman, Jonathan S.   II. Jernigan, Scott.   III. Title.
TK5105.5.M4837 2016
004.6076—dc23   2015034054

McGraw-Hill Education books are available at special quantity discounts to use as premiums and sales promotions, or for use in corporate training programs. To contact a representative, please visit the Contact Us pages at www.mhprofessional.com.

Mike Meyers' CompTIA Network+® Certification Passport, Fifth Edition (Exam N10-006)

1 2 3 4 5 6 7 8 9 0 DOC/DOC 1 0 9 8 7 6 5

ISBN: Book p/n 978-0-07-184191-7 and CD p/n 978-0-07-184798-8
of set 978-0-07-184796-4

MHID: Book p/n 0-07-184191-1 and CD p/n 0-07-184798-7
of set 0-07-184796-0

Sponsoring Editor Tim Green	**Technical Editor** Total Seminars, LLC	
		Production Supervisor James Kussow
Editorial Supervisor Jody McKenzie	**Copy Editor** Bart Reed	
		Composition Cenveo Publisher Services
Project Manager Anupriya Tyagi, Cenveo® Publisher Services	**Proofreader** Paul Tyler	
		Illustration Cenveo Publisher Services
	Indexer James Minkin	
Acquisitions Coordinator Amy Stonebraker		**Art Director, Cover** Jeff Weeks

I dedicate this book to my acquisitions editor at McGraw-Hill, Tim Green, who's been such an instrumental part of my success over the years.

—Mike Meyers

To the three most important people in my life: My beautiful wife, Eva Ann, and my amazing sons, Noah Harrison and Jacob Meir. Thank you for being the best family a guy can have! I love you all so much!

—Jonathan S. Weissman

To my one and only Katie. Always and forever.

—Scott Jernigan

About the Authors

Mike Meyers, lovingly called the "AlphaGeek" by those who know him, is the industry's leading authority on CompTIA Network+ certification. He is the president and co-founder of Total Seminars, LLC, a provider of PC and network repair seminars, books, videos, and courseware for thousands of organizations throughout the world. Mike has been involved in the computer and network repair industry since 1977 as a technician, instructor, author, consultant, and speaker. Author of numerous popular PC books and videos, including the best-selling *CompTIA Network+ Certification All-in-One Exam Guide*, Mike is also the series editor for the highly successful *Mike Meyers' Certification Passport* series, the *Mike Meyers' Computer Skills* series, and the *Mike Meyers' Guide To* series, all published by McGraw-Hill. As well as writing, Mike has personally taught (and continues to teach) thousands of students, including U.S. senators; U.S. Supreme Court justices; members of the United Nations; every branch of the U.S. Armed Forces; most branches of the U.S. Department of Justice; and hundreds of corporate clients, academic students at every level, prisoners, and pensioners.

E-mail: michaelm@totalsem.com
Facebook: Mike Meyers (Houston, TX)
Twitter/Skype/Most IMs: desweds
Web Forums: www.totalsem.com/forums

Jonathan S. Weissman has always listed teaching as his number-one passion, since his very first class on September 4, 2001.

He is a tenured Associate Professor and IT Program Coordinator in the Computing Sciences Department at Finger Lakes Community College. For FLCC, in addition to teaching, Jonathan rewrote the IT degree, to keep it current with the industry, and designed the Networking Lab. He also is a full-time Lecturer in the Computing Security Department at Rochester Institute of Technology, teaching both graduate and undergraduate courses. The highlight of his career came in May 2014, when he was awarded the RIT Outstanding Teaching Award for Non-Tenure Track Faculty 2013–2014. Jonathan also is a Lecturer in the School of Management at Nazareth College, and teaches IT courses at Naz.

Jonathan has a master's degree in computer science from Brooklyn College. He has 34 industry certifications, including

- **Cisco**   CCNP Routing and Switching, CCNA Routing and Switching, CCNA Security, CCENT

- **CompTIA**   Security+, Network+, A+, Linux+, i-Net+
- **EC-Council**   Certified Ethical Hacker, Computer Hacking Forensic Investigator
- **IPv6 Forum**   Certified Network Engineer (Gold), Certified Trainer (Gold)
- **Committee on National Security Systems**   NSTISSI-4011 National Training Standard For Information Systems Security Professionals
- **Oracle**   OCA Java SE 7
  …and many more.

Jonathan does computer networking and cybersecurity industry consulting for area businesses and individuals, and also serves as technical editor for many industry textbooks. This is the second book he has co-authored with Mike Meyers, following the recently published *Mike Meyers' CompTIA Network+ Guide to Managing and Troubleshooting Networks Lab Manual, Fourth Edition.*

Jonathan has taught over four dozen courses in networking, routing and switching, cybersecurity, systems administration, ethical hacking, forensics, malware reverse engineering, programming, web design and scripting, database design, and many more.

LinkedIn: https://www.linkedin.com/pub/jonathan-s-weissman/9b/b64/58

Scott Jernigan wields a mighty red pen as editor in chief for Total Seminars. With a master of arts degree in medieval history, Scott feels as much at home in the musty archives of London as he does in the crisp IPS glow of Total Seminars' Houston HQ. After fleeing a purely academic life, he dove headfirst into IT, working as an instructor, editor, and writer.

Scott has edited and contributed to dozens of books on computer literacy, hardware, operating systems, networking, and certification, including *CompTIA Strata IT Fundamentals All-in-One Exam Guide* (with Mike Meyers) and *Computer Literacy: Your Ticket to IC³ Certification.* He has taught computer classes all over the United States, including stints at the United Nations in New York and the FBI Academy in Quantico, Virginia.

About Total Seminars

Total Seminars provides certification training services to thousands of schools, corporations, and government agencies. Total Seminars produces the #1 selling *CompTIA A+* and best-selling *CompTIA Network+* certification books, and develops training materials such as the Total Tester for superior exam preparation. You can find Total Seminars on the Web at www.totalsem.com.

Becoming a CompTIA Certified IT Professional Is Easy

It's also the best way to reach greater professional opportunities and rewards.

Why Get CompTIA Certified?

Growing Demand

Labor estimates predict some technology fields will experience growth of more than 20% by the year 2020. (Source: CompTIA 9th Annual Information Security Trends study: 500 U.S. IT and Business Executives Responsible for Security.) CompTIA certification qualifies the skills required to join this workforce.

Higher Salaries

IT professionals with certifications on their resume command better jobs, earn higher salaries, and have more doors open to new multi-industry opportunities.

Verified Strengths

91% of hiring managers indicate CompTIA certifications are valuable in validating IT expertise, making certification the best way to demonstrate your competency and knowledge to employers. (Source: CompTIA Employer Perceptions of IT Training and Certification.)

Universal Skills

CompTIA certifications are vendor neutral—which means that certified professionals can proficiently work with an extensive variety of hardware and software found in most organizations.

Learn

Learn more about what the exam covers by reviewing the following:

- Exam objectives for key study points.

- Sample questions for a general overview of what to expect on the exam and examples of question format.

- Visit online forums, like LinkedIn, to see what other IT professionals say about CompTIA exams.

Certify

Purchase a voucher at a Pearson VUE testing center or at CompTIAstore.com.

- Register for your exam at a Pearson VUE testing center.

- Visit pearsonvue.com/CompTIA to find the closest testing center to you.

- Schedule the exam online. You will be required to enter your voucher number or provide payment information at registration.

- Take your certification exam.

Work

Congratulations on your CompTIA certification!

- Make sure to add your certification to your resume.

- Check out the CompTIA Certification Roadmap to plan your next career move.

Learn More: Certification.CompTIA.org/networkplus

Disclaimer

Contents

Acknowledgments

The team at McGraw-Hill managed the process and kept us moving, jumping, skipping (and other assorted mobility words that should be substituted for "writing"). So a big salute to Tim Green and Amy Stonebraker. Project manager Anupriya Tyagi, copy editor Bart Reed, proofreader Paul Tyler, and the compositors at Cenveo did a fabulous job turning text into a printed book. It was great working with you.

Our team at Total Seminars' Orbital HQ once again demonstrated creativity, professionalism, and self-deprecating humor during the usual tough process of creating a book. Thank you—Dave Rush and Michael Smyer—for the great work on writing, editing, illustrating, and photographing.

Check-In

May I See Your Passport?

What do you mean, you don't have a passport? Why, it's sitting right in your hands, even as you read! This book is your passport to a very special place. You're about to begin a journey, my friend: a journey toward that magical place called certification! You don't need a ticket, you don't need a suitcase—just snuggle up and read this passport. It's all you need to get there. Are you ready? Well then, let's go!

Your Travel Agent: Mike Meyers

Hello! I'm Mike Meyers, president of Total Seminars and author of a number of popular certification books. On any given day, you'll find me stringing network cable, setting up a website, or writing code. I love every aspect of this book you hold in your hands. It's part of a powerful new book series called the *Mike Meyers' Certification Passports*. Every book in this series combines easy readability with a condensed format—in other words, the kind of book I always wanted when I went for my own certifications. Putting a large amount of information in an accessible format is certainly a challenge, but I think we've achieved our goal, and I'm confident you'll agree.

I designed this series to do one thing and only one thing: to get you the information you need to achieve your certification. You won't find any fluff in here. I packed every page with nothing but the real nitty-gritty of the Network+ Certification exam. Every page has 100 percent pure concentrate of certification knowledge! But I didn't forget to make the book readable, so I hope you also enjoy the casual, friendly style.

My personal e-mail address is mikem@totalsem.com. Please feel free to contact me directly if you have any questions, complaints, or compliments.

Your Destination: CompTIA Network+ Certification

This book is your passport to CompTIA's Network+ Certification, the vendor-neutral industry-standard certification for basic networking skills. CompTIA Network+ Certification can be your ticket to a career in all-around networking or simply an excellent step in your certification pathway. This book is your passport to success on the CompTIA Network+ Certification exam.

Why the Travel Theme?

The steps in gaining a certification parallel closely the steps in planning and taking a trip. All of the elements are the same: preparation, an itinerary, a route, even mishaps along the way. Let me show you how it all works.

This book is divided into 12 chapters. Each chapter begins with an "Itinerary" section, which lists the objectives covered in that chapter, and an "ETA" section to give you an idea of the time involved in learning the skills in that chapter. Each chapter is organized by the objectives, which are either drawn from those officially stated by the certifying body or reflect our expert take on the best way to approach the topics. Also, each chapter contains a number of helpful items to highlight points of interest:

Exam Tip

Points out critical topics you're likely to see on the actual exam.

Travel Assistance

Lists additional sources, such as books and websites, to give you more information.

Local Lingo

Describes special terms in detail in a way you can easily understand.

Travel Advisory

Warns you of common pitfalls, misconceptions, and downright physical peril!

The end of each chapter gives you two handy tools. The "Checkpoint" reviews each objective covered in the chapter with a handy synopsis—a great way to review quickly. End-of-chapter "Review Questions" (and answers) test your newly acquired skills.

CHECKPOINT

But the fun doesn't stop there! After you've read the book, take advantage of the free electronic practice questions (see Appendix B)! Use the full practice exam to hone your skills, and keep the book handy to check your answers.

When you find yourself acing the practice questions, you're ready to take the exam.

Go get certified!

The End of the Trail

The IT industry changes and grows constantly, *and so should you*. Finishing one certification is only one step in an ongoing process of gaining more and more certifications to match your constantly changing and growing skills. Read Appendix A, "Career Flight Path," at the end of the book, to find out where this certification fits into your personal certification goals. Remember, in the IT business, if you're not moving forward, you're way behind!

Good luck on your certification! Stay in touch!

Mike Meyers
Series Editor
Mike Meyers' Certification Passport

Network Fundamentals

ETA	NEWBIE	SOME EXPERIENCE	EXPERT
	4 hours	2 hours	1 hour

When you link computers together to share files and communicate and do all the things we like to do, you create a *network*. Networks range in size from the smallest and simplest network—two computers connected together—to the largest and most complex network of all—the Internet.

This chapter begins with an overview of all the pieces that come together to make a computer network, including the hardware needed to make the physical connections. The chapter then dives into two network models techs use to discuss network components and functions.

Objective 1.01   Overview of How Networks Work

Networks come in many sizes and vary widely in the number of computers attached to them. Some people connect two computers in their house so that they can share files or play games together—the smallest network you can have. Compare this to companies that have thousands of employees in dozens of countries and need to network their computers together to get work done. Network folks put most networks into one of two categories: LANs and WANs. You'll find a few other groupings as well.

A *local area network (LAN)* covers a small area and contains a modest number of computers (see Figure 1.1). A LAN is usually in a single building or group

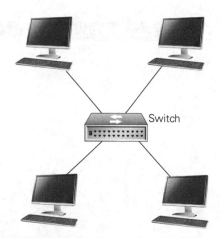

| **FIGURE 1.1** | A local area network (LAN) |

of nearby buildings. Typical LANs include home and school networks. A LAN is simply a single network or a broadcast domain that represents nodes that can hear each other's broadcast transmissions. Routers never forward broadcasts.

A *wide area network (WAN)* covers a large area and can have a substantial number of computers (see Figure 1.2). A WAN is composed of two or more LANs connected together. All of the LANs in all of the schools in a city school district, for example, link together to form a WAN. Computers in a WAN usually connect through some type of public network, such as a telephone system, leased lines, or satellites. The largest WAN in existence is the *Internet,* which is a worldwide network that connects millions of computers and networks.

An *intranet,* in contrast, is essentially a private TCP/IP network that is a scaled-down version of the Internet for a very specific group of users. Just like the Internet, an intranet will offer various network services, such as websites, FTP access, Voice over IP, and so on. The key difference is that it's private rather than public.

Another similar term, *extranet,* is used to denote a private intranet that is also made accessible to a select group of outsiders using the Internet.

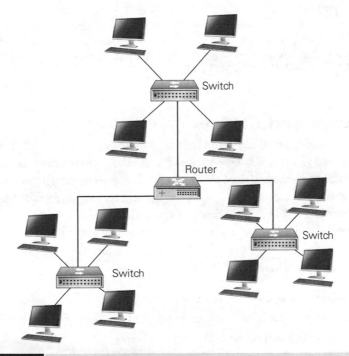

FIGURE 1.2   A wide area network (WAN)

Here are a few other *xANs* in use in various networks:

- A *campus area network (CAN)* is a group of interconnected LANs within a small geographical area, such as a school campus, university, hospital, or military base.

- A *metropolitan area network (MAN)* is a group of networks with a sociopolitical boundary, such as a network of district authority offices in a town or city. MANs can range in size from a few city blocks to entire cities. Sites on a MAN are usually interconnected using fiber-optic cable or some other high-speed digital circuit, and the MAN itself may carry voice as well as data traffic.

- A *global area network (GAN)* is a single network with connection points spread around the world. GANs are used mostly by large corporate organizations and consist of a series of networked, orbiting satellites. Note the subtle difference between a WAN and a GAN. The latter is a single network, not a number of interconnected networks.

Travel Advisory

The terms CAN and GAN don't exist as official standards, but their use and definitions have become generally accepted over time. A MAN, however, is an official standard of the Institute of Electronics and Electrical Engineers (IEEE), known as the IEEE 802.6 standard.

Servers and Clients

People use two types of devices in networks these days: servers and clients. In a nutshell, *servers* share things—such as files, folders, and printers—and *clients* request access to those shared things. Let's get one thing straight: almost any personal computer can act as a server or a client (or both)! Even at the same time! A lot of it has to do with how you set up the computer.

Computers running Windows 7/8/8.1/10, Mac OS X, and the many varieties of Linux make up the vast majority of clients. You'll also find other devices that are clients, though, such as the following examples:

- Game consoles, such as the Xbox One
- Smartphones and tablets, such as the iPad
- DVRs, such as TiVo and other set-top boxes

FIGURE 1.3   A server sharing network resources

Server computers come in all shapes and sizes, but they serve—if you'll pardon the pun—a similar purpose. Servers manage *network resources* (such as printers and e-mail—all the stuff that makes a network valuable), provide central storage of files, and provide services for users (such as the printer server telling the printer to print, or the e-mail server sending your e-mail). See Figure 1.3.

Client computers enable you to access the shared resources, programs, and services on server machines (see Figure 1.4). Most users access servers via clients, although there's no law that says you can't access a server from another

FIGURE 1.4   A client accessing network resources

server machine. The latter machine, in that case, would be *acting* as a client, regardless of the firepower of the box!

Networks are traditionally classified into *client/server* and *peer-to-peer* designations, depending on the role played by each computer in the network. In a client/server network, one or more computer systems act as a server, while the remaining computers are clients that access resources from the server. On some home or small office networks, however, there may not be a separate dedicated server. Instead, every computer on the network acts as both a client and a server. Such networks are called peer-to-peer networks.

> **Exam Tip**
>
> The CompTIA Network+ exam uses the terms *client/server topology* and *peer-to-peer topology* to describe these two network arrangements. A topology more commonly refers to the way computers connect together rather than the roles they play on a network, but be prepared for the unusual use of the word on the exam. Chapter 3 covers the more commonly described network topologies.

Every operating system (OS) today can operate as a client, a server, or both, and many networks employ a mix. My network, for example, has a set of dedicated servers, and each employee has one, two, or more computers in his or her office. Many of the office computers have shared folders, such as for music or games, so they function as both clients and servers. This nice mishmash of machine roles creates a *hybrid* network.

Network Components

Whether you want to put together a LAN or connect a couple of LANs into a WAN, you need connectivity between the PCs and a way to handle communication. Computers connect to a network in one of two ways:

- Directly to a LAN via a cable from the computer to a LAN port
- Wirelessly to the LAN

A typical network client has a *network adapter,* also known as a *network interface card (NIC),* that connects via a cable to a central network box called a switch. Figure 1.5 shows a typical NIC.

Every NIC has a unique identifier called a *media access control (MAC) address.* I'll go into more detail on these addresses in Chapter 4. For now, just know that a MAC address acts like a name for a computer on a LAN.

FIGURE 1.5   A network interface card

To make this into a nicely configured network, add another network client, throw in a server, turn on network sharing—and voilà!—you have a network. Each machine attaches to a network cable that then connects at the other end to the switch. Any device attached to a network—client, server, printer, or whatnot—is called a *node*.

Ethernet

You might be wondering how you can tell what sort of cable to use for this network and how to determine the type of switch required for a network. Networking means communicating; the computers need to be able to speak the same language and follow the same technology.

The *Ethernet* standard defines everything about modern network hardware. Ethernet cables have standard connectors—for example, the *RJ45 connectors* shown in Figure 1.6. Ethernet defines electrical signaling as well. That way, the sending NIC will break data down into little pieces and the receiving NIC will know exactly how to put them back together.

If two machines do not have the same kind of networking technology—a common problem in the early days of computer networks—then they can't be networked together. I won't bore you with a list of all the networking technologies that have had a brief moment of glory and market share in the past. Suffice it to say that today, Ethernet is, and has always been, king of the LAN, since knocking Token Ring off the map with 10BaseT.

FIGURE 1.6   RJ45 connectors

Most modern Ethernet networks employ one of three technologies (and sometimes all three): *100BaseT, 1000BaseT,* and *10GBaseT.* As the numbers in the names suggest, 100BaseT networks—called *Fast Ethernet*—run at 100 Mbps; 1000BaseT networks—called *Gigabit Ethernet*—run at 1000 Mbps, or 1 Gbps; and 10GBaseT networks—called *10 Gigabit Ethernet*—run and 10,000 Mbps, or 10 Gbps. *10BaseT*—simply called *Ethernet*—has long been obsolete.

Each Ethernet technology requires a specific kind of cabling that can handle its top speed. 100BaseT networks use Category 5 (CAT 5) or better Ethernet cables, whereas Gigabit Ethernet runs on Category 6 (CAT 6) or Category 6a (CAT 6a) Ethernet cables (see Figure 1.7).

FIGURE 1.7   Category 6 (CAT 6) cable

Hubs and Switches

Switches sit at the very center of networking, handling the tasks of receiving and sending packets of data to the connected computers.

Before switches, hubs were the central devices that linked nodes together. A *hub* flooded the frame down every network cable connected, hoping one of the computers connected was the recipient machine (see Figure 1.8).

A *switch,* in contrast, learns the physical address of every machine connected to it, reads the recipient address on the frames, and sends those frames along only on the appropriate connection (see Figure 1.9).

The radically more efficient switches now have completely replaced hubs on all modern networks.

Software

Of course it takes both hardware and software to make network communication work well. If Jacob's computer requests an MP3 file from Noah's computer, Noah's operating system and other software take that MP3 file and break it into smaller pieces of data, and then place the data in IP *packets* that contain

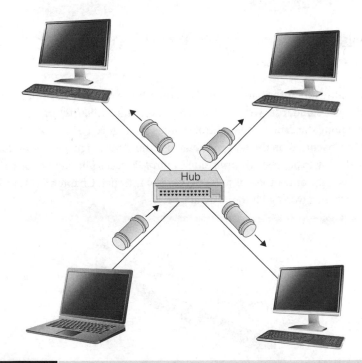

FIGURE 1.8 A hub repeating frames down every network cable

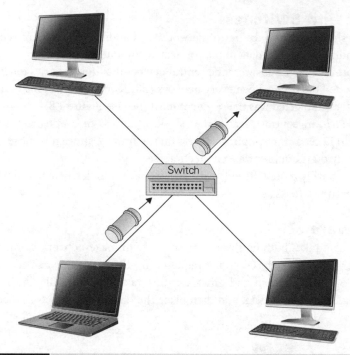

FIGURE 1.9   A switch sending frames only to the recipient

logical addressing information. The NIC then takes the packets and, following the Ethernet standards, wraps up those packets into *Ethernet frames* that get sent out along the cable to the central switch (see Figure 1.10).

All the machines on the network must use the same language—or *protocol*—for any sharing to happen. *Transmission Control Protocol/Internet Protocol (TCP/IP)* has been the only protocol suite used by the Internet. Chapter 5 covers TCP/IP in depth, so I won't go into the details here.

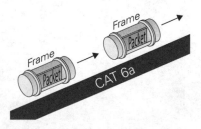

FIGURE 1.10   Packets wrapped in frames sent along an Ethernet CAT 6a cable

Applications

Finally, you need network-aware applications to accomplish things like accessing a shared file over a network. A commonly used network application is the web browser, such as Mozilla Firefox (see Figure 1.11) or Google Chrome.

Connecting LANs

Enabling communication between two or more LANs requires several other pieces. First, you need a physical connection through cabling or radio frequency waves. Second, you need special-purpose boxes to provide the intelligent direction so that data can properly flow either within a LAN (via switches) or between the LANs (via routers). Finally, devices need an address that goes beyond the LAN and applies WAN-wide. That address is an *IP address,* because everyone uses TCP/IP to communicate. Chapter 5 covers IP addresses.

Travel Advisory

All nodes on a TCP/IP network have two addresses. The MAC address is the physical address of a computer on a LAN. The IP address enables communication across routers and thus between LANs as well as within LANs.

FIGURE 1.11 Firefox web browser

Objective 1.02 The OSI Seven-Layer Model

The *International Organization for Standardization (ISO)* created a framework, into which the major network hardware and software components and protocols could be placed, to give every item a common reference point. This framework, a seven-layer model called *Open Systems Interconnection (OSI)*, provides a means of relating the components and their functions to each other and a way of standardizing components and protocols.

Travel Advisory

The letters used for the International Organization for Standardization—ISO—don't map to the initials in English, French, or Russian, the three official languages used by the body. ISO is not an acronym for the organization, but a Greek word that means equality, which all standards bodies look to promote.

The OSI model provides a critical common language that network hardware and software engineers can use to communicate and ensure that their equipment will function together. Each layer of the model represents a particular aspect of network function.

Exam Tip

The CompTIA Network+ exam expects you to know the layers by name, how they function in relation to each other, and what they represent.

As well as helping to standardize the design elements of network components, the OSI model helps describe the relationships between network protocols. As you'll see, more than one protocol or action is needed to get your data onto a network.

The Layers and What They Represent

Let's run through the layers and an overview of their tasks and responsibilities. Figure 1.12 summarizes the layers and their functions.

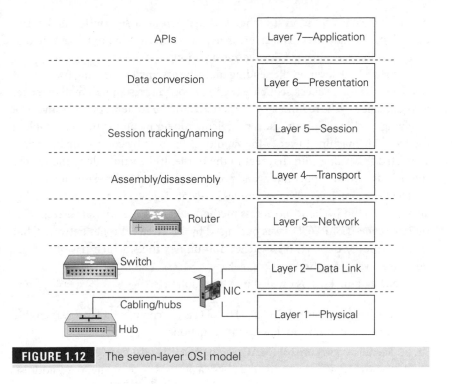

FIGURE 1.12 The seven-layer OSI model

Layer 1: Physical Layer

Layer 1 of the OSI model, the *Physical layer,* defines the network standards relating to the electrical signals that travel the network cables, the connectors, and the media types (cables) themselves. The Physical layer also determines the way that data is placed on the network media.

For the CompTIA Network+ exam, you need to know examples of components that run at each layer of the OSI model. Cables are an example of a network component that is considered part of the Physical layer. Hubs also operated at this layer in their heyday.

Layer 2: Data Link Layer

Layer 2, the *Data Link layer,* defines the rules for gathering and completing all the elements that make up a data frame and putting the whole thing together, so that it can be passed to a Physical-layer device and on to the network. Switches exist at layer 2, and carefully read frames, learning the port or ports to send frames to, unlike the layer 1 hubs that sent all frames to all connected ports (except the port the frame originated on). The exact contents of the frame will vary, but Ethernet frames will include the physical address of the receiving machine, the physical address of the sending machine, a description of the data being sent, the data itself, and an error-detection mechanism to make sure that no part of the data changed during transmission.

The Data Link layer on the sending machine assembles outgoing frames and calculates the frame check sequence (FCS) by applying a standard mathematical formula called cyclic redundancy check (CRC) to the contents of the frame. The receiving machine performs the same calculation for incoming frames, enabling the receiving machine to verify the validity of the data by comparing its locally generated FCS value with that sent in the frame. If the values don't match, the frame is discarded. Upper layers and protocols deal with retransmissions.

The Data Link layer also determines how data is placed on the wire by using an access method. The wired access method, *carrier sense multiple access/collision detection (CSMA/CD)*, was once used by all wired Ethernet networks, but is automatically disabled on switched full-duplex links, which have been the norm for a very long time.

The Data Link layer is divided into two sublayers:

- **Logical link control (LLC)** ∼The LLC is the component layer responsible for error-control and flow-control functions.
- **Media access control (MAC)** The MAC is responsible for addressing network devices by using the physical address—that's the MAC address burned in to the ROM chip of each network card. This physical address is placed in the layer-2 header for both the sending and receiving systems.

Exam Tip
For the CompTIA Network+ exam, know that layer 2 is divided into two sublayers and is responsible for physical addressing. The device that works with a physical address (that is, the switch) runs at this layer.

Figure 1.13 shows the layer-1 and layer-2 components.

Layer 3: Network Layer

Layer 3, the *Network layer,* is responsible for routing functions and logical addressing. The Network layer addresses identify not only a system, but also the network on which the system resides. The router uses this information to determine how to send data to the destination network. The IP address in a TCP/IP network is a layer-3 address; routers use this address to determine to which network and node to send a packet.

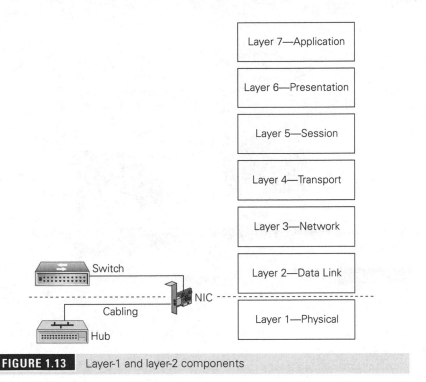

FIGURE 1.13 Layer-1 and layer-2 components

If the data being sent is bigger than the maximum transmission unit (MTU) allowed by the layer-2 protocols (for Ethernet, it's 1500 bytes), the Network layer breaks the packet into smaller ones that will fit inside two or more frames. Breaking up data into smaller chunks at layer 3 is known as *fragmentation*.

Exam Tip
Examples of layer-3 components are Internet Protocol (IP), IP addresses, and routers. An IP address is a layer-3 address; a MAC address is a layer-2 address.

Layer 4: Transport Layer

Connection-Oriented vs. Connectionless Communication Some protocols, such as the Simple Mail Transfer Protocol (SMTP) used for sending e-mail messages, require that the e-mail client and server verify that they have a good connection before a message is sent (see Figure 1.14). This makes sense

FIGURE 1.14 Connection between e-mail client and server

because you don't want your e-mail message to be a corrupted mess when it arrives.

Alternatively, a number of protocols simply send data without first waiting to verify that the receiving system is ready (see Figure 1.15). When Voice over IP (VoIP) is used, for example, the call is made without verifying first whether another device is there.

FIGURE 1.15 Connectionless communication

The connection-oriented protocol is called *Transmission Control Protocol (TCP)*. The connectionless protocol is called *User Datagram Protocol (UDP)*.

Travel Assistance	

Chapter 5 covers TCP, UDP, and all sorts of other protocols in detail.

Everything you can do on the Internet—from browsing the Web, to making Skype calls, to playing *World of Warcraft*—is predetermined to be either connection-oriented or connectionless.

Segments within Packets and Datagrams within Packets   To see the Transport layer in action, strip away the IP addresses from an IP packet. What's left is a chunk of data in yet another container called a *TCP segment* or a *UDP datagram*.

TCP segments have many fields that ensure the data gets to its destination in good order. These fields have names such as Checksum, Flags, and Sequence and Acknowledgment numbers. Chapter 5 goes into more detail on TCP segments, but for now, just know that TCP segments have fields that ensure the connection-oriented communication works properly. Figure 1.16 shows a TCP segment.

Data comes from the Application-layer applications. If TCP is used, the Transport layer breaks that data into chunks, adding port numbers and sequence numbers, creating the TCP segment. The Transport layer then hands the TCP segment to the Internet layer, which in turn creates the IP packet that encapsulates the segment.

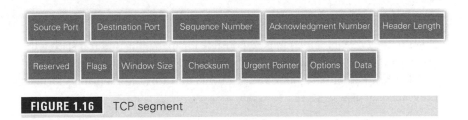

FIGURE 1.16   TCP segment

Travel Advisory

Discussed more in Chapter 5, port-numbering is a form of addressing that gives each application (both source and destination) a unique number between 1 and 65,535. Some of these port numbers are very well known. HTTP, the protocol that makes web pages work, uses port 80, for example.

UDP also gets data from the Application-layer programs and adds port numbers to create a container called a *UDP datagram.* A UDP datagram lacks most of the extra fields found in TCP segments, specifically the sequence number, acknowledgment number, and flags, simply because UDP doesn't care if the receiving computer gets its data. The UDP datagrams are not broken into chunks, like TCP segments are, before being handed down to the layer below. Figure 1.17 shows a UDP datagram.

Just like with TCP segments, when the Transport layer hands the UDP datagram to the Network layer, it in turn creates the IP packet that encapsulates the datagram.

Exam Tip

Examples of layer-4 protocols are Transmission Control Protocol (TCP) and User Datagram Protocol (UDP).

Layer 5: Session Layer

Layer 5, the *Session layer,* is responsible for the session setup. The Session layer also manages and terminates the data connections (called *sessions)* between programs on networked devices. These sessions enable networked systems to exchange information.

Layer 6: Presentation Layer

Layer 6, the *Presentation layer,* is responsible for managing and translating the information into an understandable format that the Application layer can process further, taking datagrams and segments and turning them into formats programs can use.

| Source Port | Destination Port | Length | Checksum | Data |

FIGURE 1.17 UDP datagram

Layer 7: Application Layer

Layer 7, the *Application layer,* represents the network-related program code and functions running on a computer system that either initiate the request (on the sending system) or service the request (on the receiving system).

Note that the Application layer does not refer to applications such as Microsoft Outlook. Instead, it refers to the protocols or application programming interfaces (APIs) on which those programs rely. For example, Internet Message Access Protocol (IMAP) and Simple Mail Transfer Protocol (SMTP) are important Application-layer protocols for e-mail, but many different end-user applications use those protocols (such as Outlook and Mozilla Thunderbird).

Using the Seven-Layer Model

The seven-layer model is only a theoretical representation of how networks function. Although knowing it inside-out won't change your life, it should help you pass the CompTIA Network+ exam. The conceptual use of the model assumes that an event on one computer system (for example, a user pressing ENTER on a login screen) creates some data that sets off a chain of events. The data runs down through the layers on the sending machine and then leaves the system, traveling across the network and then up through the layers on the receiving machine, until the data arrives intact at the Application layer and is processed by the receiving system. Later chapters in this book point out where certain key protocols and hardware fit into the model, and this can be useful stuff to know for both the CompTIA Network+ exam and for real life.

 ## The TCP/IP Model

The OSI model was developed as a reaction to a world of many different protocols made by different manufacturers that needed to play together. ISO created the OSI seven-layer model as the tool for manufacturers of networking equipment to find common ground between multiple protocols, enabling them to create standards for interoperability of networking software and hardware.

The adoption of TCP/IP as the sole protocol suite used in modern networks has rendered the OSI seven-layer model somewhat obsolete at the layers specific to TCP/IP. Many techs use a model specifically tailored to TCP/IP networks called, appropriately, the *TCP/IP model.*

Local Lingo

Internet model   A lot of techs and tech sites call the TCP/IP model the *Internet model*.

The TCP/IP model consists of four layers:

- Link/Network Interface
- Internet
- Transport
- Application

It's important to appreciate that the TCP/IP model doesn't have a standards body to define the layers. Because of this, there are a surprising number of variations on the TCP/IP model. Some authors even have it as five layers, rather than four!

A great example of this lack of standardization is the Link layer. Without a standardizing body, we can't even agree on the name. Although "Link layer" is extremely common, the term "Network Interface layer" is equally popular. A good tech knows both of these terms and understands that they are interchangeable. Notice also that, unlike the OSI model, the TCP/IP model does not identify each layer with a number.

CompTIA has chosen one popular version of the TCP/IP model for the CompTIA Network+ competencies and exam. That's the version you'll learn right here. It's concise, having only four layers, and many important companies, including Cisco and Microsoft, use it (although with a few variations in names, as just described). The TCP/IP model gives each protocol in the TCP/IP protocol suite a clear home in one of the four layers.

The clarity of the TCP/IP model shows the flaws in the OSI model. The OSI model couldn't perfectly describe all the TCP/IP protocols. The TCP/IP model fixes this ambiguity, at least for the TCP/IP protocol suite.

The Link Layer

The TCP/IP model lumps together the OSI model's layer 1 and layer 2 into a single layer called the *Link layer* (or *Network Interface layer*).

A nice way to separate layers in the TCP/IP model is to think about packets and frames. Any part of the network that deals with frames is in the Link layer.

The moment the frame information is stripped away from an IP packet, we move out of the Link layer and into the Internet layer.

Travel Advisory

At the Link layer, just about every network tech reverts back to the OSI model for troubleshooting. It's important to distinguish between problems happening at the Physical layer (with cabling, for example) and problems that reflect the Data Link layer (with switches and MAC addresses, for example). That's why accomplished techs know both models!

The Internet Layer

The *Internet layer* maps directly to OSI's Network layer in function. It should really be called the "IP packet" layer. Any device or protocol that deals with pure IP packets—getting an IP packet to its destination—sits in the Internet layer. IP addressing itself is also part of the Internet layer, as are routers and the magic they perform to get IP packets to the next router. IP packets are created at this layer.

The Transport Layer

The *Transport layer* maps directly to OSI's Transport layer in both function and name.

The Application Layer

The TCP/IP *Application layer* combines features of the top three layers of the OSI model (see Figure 1.18). Every application, especially connection-oriented applications, must know how to initiate, control, and disconnect from a remote system. No single method exists for doing this. Each application uses its own method.

Travel Advisory

In reality, when looking at documentation nowadays, or even troubleshooting, the OSI model is the one that's almost always referenced. You'll hear "It's a layer-1 issue," "a layer-2 VPN," "a layer-3 device," or even "a layer-4 switch," and in all of those cases the OSI model is being referenced. The TCP/IP protocols themselves should not be confused with the TCP/IP model. The protocols in the TCP/IP suite (which includes both the TCP/IP protocols and the TCP/IP model) have essentially been mapped to the existing layers of the OSI model.

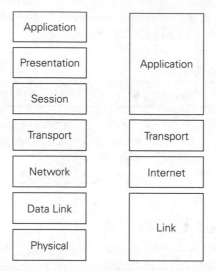

Application	
Presentation	Application
Session	
Transport	Transport
Network	Internet
Data Link	Link
Physical	

FIGURE 1.18   TCP/IP Application layer compared to OSI layers 5–7

CHECKPOINT

✔**Objective 1.01: Overview of How Networks Work**   The most obvious pieces of network hardware are the computers on the network. These are divided into client and server systems, unless they are desktop systems that are sharing resources, in which case they are known as peer-to-peer systems. Corporate networks generally use dedicated servers because they offer higher performance, greater stability, and better security than peer-to-peer options. Your network won't be complete without some media—such as copper wiring, fiber optics, wireless, or infrared—to interconnect your systems, as well as network interface cards (NICs) to connect your systems to the media. Other devices on the network—such as switches and routers—enable you to expand the system locally or to other sites.

✔**Objective 1.02: The OSI Seven-Layer Model**   The OSI seven-layer model describes how data flows from one networked system to another. It's a theoretical model into which many of the standards, components, and functions of a network fit. The model promotes the use of recognized network standards and helps ensure compatibility between network hardware and software from different manufacturers.

✓**Objective 1.03: The TCP/IP Model** The TCP/IP model describes how data flows from one networked system to another, specifically for TCP/IP networks. Every TCP/IP protocol and application fits into one of the four layers in the model, making the TCP/IP model ideal for troubleshooting modern networks.

REVIEW QUESTIONS

1. What name is given to a network in which computers act as both clients and servers?
   A. A multitasking network
   B. A mainframe network
   C. A peer-to-peer network
   D. A LAN network

2. What standard defines the hardware technology of modern LANs?
   A. ARPANET
   B. Ethernet
   C. OSI
   D. TCP/IP

3. Which is the modern device that connects nodes of the same network together?
   A. Modem
   B. Switch
   C. Frame
   D. Hub

4. What device enables LANs to connect and direct packets to the correct LAN?
   A. Hub
   B. Frame
   C. Router
   D. Switch

5. A protocol operating at which layer of the OSI model is responsible for logical addressing and routing?
   A. Transport
   B. Network
   C. Session
   D. Application

6. A protocol operating at which layer of the OSI model handles the formatting of data so upper or lower layers can work with it further?
   A. Application
   B. Presentation
   C. Session
   D. Transport

7. Layer 3 is the _____ layer of the OSI model.
   A. Session
   B. Application
   C. Data Link
   D. Network

8. At which layer of the TCP/IP model are UDP datagrams created?
   A. Link/Network Interface
   B. Internet
   C. Transport
   D. Application

9. Which type of communication requires the client and server to acknowledge the transmission?
   A. ACK request
   B. Connectionless
   C. Connection-oriented
   D. Session

10. At which layer of the TCP/IP model do cables fit?
    A. Link/Network Interface
    B. Internet
    C. Transport
    D. Application

REVIEW ANSWERS

1. **C**   A network with computers acting as both clients and servers is a peer-to-peer network.

2. **B**   Ethernet is the standard.

3. **B**   Switches replaced hubs as the connecting device for a single network.

4. **C**   A router connects LANs and directs packets to the correct LAN.

5. **B**   A protocol operating at the Network layer provides addressing and routing functions.

6. **B**   A protocol operating at the Presentation layer handles the formatting of data (among other functions).

7. **D**   Layer 3 of the OSI model is the Network layer.

8. **C**   The Transport layer is where datagrams can be found.

9. **C**   Connection-oriented communication requires the client and server to acknowledge the transmission.

10. **A**   Cabling is in the Link/Network Interface layer of the TCP/IP model.

Network Media

	NEWBIE	SOME EXPERIENCE	EXPERT
ETA	2 hours	1 hour	30 minutes

Techs use the term network *media* rather than *cabling* because some parts of a network's data highway can be made up of materials other than physical cable. A laser or microwave link might connect local area networks (LANs) in two buildings, for example, or a wireless device might connect laptops to your main network. Inside the building, you'll find connectors, adapters, wall ports, and other such parts.

Local Lingo

bounded media   Physical network cabling (copper and fiber).
unbounded media   Radio frequency (RF), microwave, infrared, and satellite network links.

As you might imagine, a number of different network media types are available. Some are faster than others, some will work over relatively long distances, and some don't require a physical connection to the main network. This chapter covers all the major media types and their characteristics, uses, and key features.

Exam Tip

Network media and connectors and the electrical signals traveling over them are represented by standards at layer 1 (the Physical layer) of the OSI seven-layer model.

Objective 2.01   Coaxial Cabling

Coaxial cable, better known as "coax," is the granddaddy of all mainstream network media types. Coax was very much associated with the original designs of the popular Ethernet networking standard, developed in 1973, although today you'll only see it used with broadband Internet solutions.

Travel Advisory

baseband vs. broadband   The coaxial cable used in early Ethernet networks carried only a single digital signal (baseband). The coaxial cable used for cable Internet and television, in contrast, carries many analog signals at once (broadband). These cables use an **F connector** that screws on, making for a secure connection.

Coaxial cable has a central conducting core surrounded by a protective, insulating layer; an outer metal screen made of a woven copper mesh; a metal-covered plastic or foil (or both); and an overall insulating jacket (see Figure 2.1). The metal screen helps shield the data traveling down the central core from being corrupted by external signals, such as radio waves, and other sources of electromagnetic interference (EMI), such as high-current power cables, cell phones, electric motors, fluorescent tubes, and local electrical storms. The screen also reduces the amount of data signals that can radiate from the cable to become another source of EMI and thus cause problems for other data cables and systems. The cable is referred to as *coaxial* (or simply *coax*) because both the center wire and the braided metal shield share a common axis, or centerline.

Coax is considered old technology and isn't used these days for new LANs, except in fairly specialized settings such as elevator shafts. Coax will crop up for connecting a LAN to an Internet connection provided by your local cable company, because high-speed Internet through the cable lines has become a popular broadband solution.

Exam Tip

Coax is often preferred when connections need to run through elevator shafts because it's resistant to radio noise and is much cheaper than fiber (discussed later in this chapter).

FIGURE 2.1   Coaxial (coax) cable

Coaxial Cable Types

A mind-boggling number of different types of coax are available, each one suitable for a specific purpose, such as audio, video, TV, satellite, cable, radio, or data. Each coax type has its own characteristics, closely matched to the type of signal that cable is designed to carry. These coax types are called *radio-grade (RG)*. Table 2.1 shows the RG baseband coax types used for data networking that you might see on the Network+ exam.

The nominal impedance—a measure of the wire's resistance that shows how much the cable impedes or resists the flow of electric current—is one of the factors that determines the RG type. As you can see, the nominal impedance of cable TV coax is different from that of Ethernet coax. This difference is the main reason why the cable types should not be used in conjunction with the wrong technology. The differences between Thick Ethernet and Thin Ethernet are explained in the next chapter.

Coaxial Connectors

Coaxial cables have used many types of connectors over the years. Ancient Ethernet networks used a thin cable with a bayonet-style connector called a *BNC connector*. The BNC refers to both the connection mechanism and the creators—Bayonet Neill-Concelman. You'll still find these connectors, but only as potential answers on CompTIA Network+ exams. Modern coaxial cables use screw-on *F connectors* (see Figure 2.2).

| FIGURE 2.2 | Coaxial cable with the common F connector |

| TABLE 2.1 | Coax Cable Types for Networking |

Coax Type	Most Common Use	Nominal Impedance
RG-58	Thin Ethernet baseband (10Base2)	50 ohms
RG-8	Thick Ethernet baseband (10Base5)	50 ohms
RG-59	Early cable TV broadband	75 ohms
RG-6	Later cable TV broadband	75 ohms

Objective 2.02 # Twisted-Pair Cabling

Many modern networks use a telephone-type cable known as *unshielded twisted-pair (UTP)*. UTP network cables, as shown in Figure 2.3, have four pairs of twisted wires. The twists in the cable pairs reduce crosstalk and also act as a partial shield. As you might have guessed from the name, UTP has no overall metal screen—just the cable pairs inside the covering. UTP cable is popular because it is relatively cheap and simple to install. Better still, the same wiring infrastructure can be used for data and voice/telephony. That means when you install UTP cable as part of a building's infrastructure, the same cabling system can be used for many of the building's services, such as computer networks, security systems, telephones, and so on.

> ### Local Lingo
> **crosstalk**   An unwanted interaction, or interference, between two electrical signals.

Although UTP cable provides a low-cost solution, it supports some fairly high-tech, high-spec, high-price kits to create very sophisticated, high-performance networks.

Shielded twisted-pair (STP) cable has a screen covering the wire pairs and a ground wire running the length of the cable. STP is intended for use in electrically noisy environments. In most cases, moving network cabling away from interference is cheaper than installing shielded cabling.

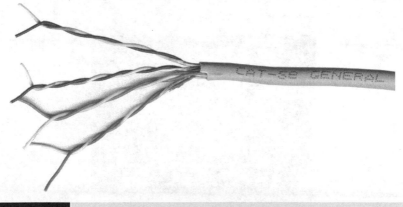

FIGURE 2.3   Four-pair UTP cable

UTP Cable Types

UTP comes in a variety of grades, called *categories,* numbered Category 1 through Category 6a, as summarized in Table 2.2. These categories define the maximum supported data speed of the cable, and they have been developed over the years to cater to faster and faster network designs.

It might have caught your eye in Table 2.2 that UTP cable is used for Ethernet networks, since a few paragraphs ago, you learned about Ethernet and *coax* cable. Well, UTP replaced coax many years ago, as Ethernet was one of the first networking standards to be reengineered to work on this media type. In addition, most new cabling installations will use Category 6 (CAT 6) or Category 6a cabling, because they support all current (and planned) data speeds and standards. The category level of a piece of cable will normally be written on the cable itself, as shown in Figure 2.3, or on the box, as shown in Figure 2.4.

TABLE 2.2	UTP Cable Categories	
Category	**Maximum Rated Speed**	**Typical Use**
Category 1	1 Mbps	Voice only—regular analog phone lines; not used for data communications
Category 3	10 Mbps	Ethernet over UTP at 10 Mbps (10BaseT)
Category 5	100 Mbps	Ethernet over UTP at 100 Mbps (100BaseT)
Category 5e	1 Gbps (1000 Mbps)	Ethernet over UTP at 1000 Mbps (1000BaseT)
Category 6	10 Gbps	10 Gigabit Ethernet (10GbE)
Category 6a	10 Gbps	10 Gigabit Ethernet (10GbE)

| FIGURE 2.4 | Category 6 UTP cabling |

All cable accessories, such as the wall- or pillar-mounted data ports, must also match the category of the cable being used. Mixing CAT 6a cable with CAT 3 wall sockets, for example, could cause that part of the network not to work properly. The post-installation network testing should pick up this type of mismatch, but it is better to get things right the first time rather than find out later you need to replace all your data outlets!

> ### Exam Tip
> For the exam, be sure to know the UTP category cable types and their associated transfer rates.

Variations in Core Wires and Sheath Materials

UTP varies in both the construction of the individual internal copper wires and in the material of the protective sheath on the outside of the cable. You need to use the proper variety of cable in a specific area of a building.

Most UTP cables have core strands that are single copper wires. These are called *solid-core* cables. A typical eight-wire UTP cable would have eight copper wires inside a protective sheath. Solid-core cable has superb electrical characteristics but tends to fail in places where there are tight turns or lots of handling.

In specific spaces where cables need to make a lot of tight turns or where you tend to move the cable quite a bit, you would use a type of UTP with the conductive core of each wire made from fine strands of copper. This type of cable is called *stranded-core* or just *stranded*. Many folks use stranded cables to connect computers to wall plates. (See also "Patch Panel" later in this chapter for the most common use of stranded cabling.) Figure 2.5 shows solid- and stranded-core cables.

The sheaths on UTP cabling come in two varieties, called PVC and plenum. *PVC cable* is named for the sturdy sheath made of polyvinyl chloride (PVC) that's great for protecting the internal wires but bad if it burns, because the PVC gives off toxic fumes.

There are spaces in buildings, such as between a drop ceiling and the true ceiling, designed to facilitate air flow. That's where air conditioning and heating returns typically run. This space is called the *plenum*. The sheath on *plenum cable* is made of some low-fume material, such as a fluorinated ethylene polymer (FEP), to reduce the risk of smoking, in the event of a fire. The sheath is often reinforced as well to facilitate pulling across long stretches.

FIGURE 2.5   Solid- and stranded-core UTP cables

Local Lingo

plenum   A fancy name for the gap between the real ceiling
(or the bottom of the next floor up, if you want) and the suspended tiles.

UTP Connectors

UTP network cabling uses an eight-pin contact connector type known as an
RJ45, as shown in Figure 2.6 (the RJ stands for *registered jack*). Whereas network cables use an eight-pin connector, note that the telephone cable uses a
four-pin connector known as the RJ11 connector.

Local Lingo

8P8C   Technically, the term RJ45 defines the wiring scheme and
the mechanical interface of the plug. What almost every tech in the
world calls an RJ45 is officially known as an 8P8C connector, for eight
positions and eight contacts. So now you know.

All UTP networking standards, except 100BaseT4, before Gigabit Ethernet
use only two of the four UTP cable pairs, but Gigabit Ethernet uses all four pairs.

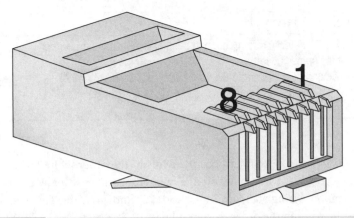

FIGURE 2.6   An RJ45 connector

Travel Assistance
Chapter 3 gives you the scoop on the various Ethernet standards.

UTP Wiring Standards

It probably won't come as a surprise to know that UTP connectors and wiring have associated color codes and wiring schemes. Each wire inside a UTP cable must connect to the proper pin on the connector at each end of the cable. The wires are color-coded to assist in properly matching the ends; each pair of wires has a solid-colored wire and a striped wire: blue/blue-white, orange/orange-white, brown/brown-white, and green/green-white. Two industry organizations, the Telecommunications Industry Association (TIA) and the Electronic Industries Alliance (EIA), developed a variety of standard color codes to facilitate installation. EIA disbanded in 2011, moving the standards to TIA, but you will still hear the term TIA/EIA or EIA/TIA used by technicians.

T568A and T568B Wiring Standards

Two major wiring standards, *T568A* and *T568B,* determine the order of the wires placed in the RJ45 connector. Using an established color-code scheme ensures that the wires match up correctly at each end of the cable. This consistency makes troubleshooting and repair easier.

Travel Advisory

TIA/EIA   Most techs refer to the two popular wiring standards either without the preceding letter, such as 568B, or with the full initials of the two groups that created the standards, such as TIA/EIA568A. The CompTIA Network+ competencies use the form in this book, with just the T.

The T568A wiring standard has the wires in the order white/green, green, white/orange, blue, white/blue, orange, white/brown, and finally brown. The most common wiring standard in use today is known as the T568B standard and has the wires in the order shown in Figure 2.7.

Straight-through and Crossover Cables

When crimping a UTP cable, you can create two types of cables—a straight-through cable or a crossover cable. The typical *straight-through cable* for CAT 5/5e, for example, uses only four wires—wires 1, 2, 3, and 6. With a straight-through cable, pin 1 of the RJ45 connector on one end follows the wire to pin 1 on the other end, and as a result, pin 1 on both ends of the wire are connected.

Figure 2.8 shows a device containing an RJ45 crimper, wire stripper, and wire snips.

This straight-through cable works great for connecting a workstation to a switch because the network interface card on the computer uses pins 1 and 2 as the transmit pins, while pins 3 and 6 are the receive pins. On the switch, pins 1 and 2 are the receive pins, while pins 3 and 6 are the transmit pins. When you use straight-through cable, the transmit pins of the workstation will connect to the receive pins on the switch (via the straight-through cable), allowing data to be sent. Likewise, the receive pins on the workstation are connected to the transmit pins on the switch via the straight-through cable, allowing the workstation to receive data.

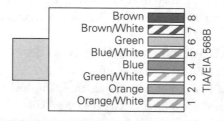

FIGURE 2.7   The T568B wiring standard

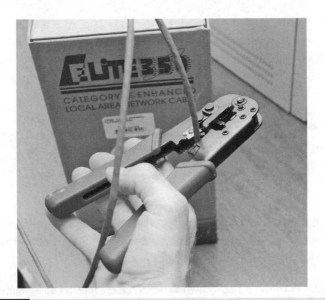

FIGURE 2.8   A useful tool

If you try to connect two computers directly (NIC to NIC) with a straight-through cable, the systems will not be able to communicate because the transmit pins (pins 1 and 2) on one system will be connected to the transmit pins on the second system, so neither system can receive data.

The transmit pins have to be connected to the receive pins at the other end, which is what the crossover cable creates. With a *crossover cable,* wires 1 and 2 (transmit) from one end of the cable are switched to the receive wire placeholders (wires 3 and 6) at the other end of the cable (shown in Figure 2.9).

When you use a crossover cable to connect two computers, two routers, or two switches, the crossover cable will connect the transmit pins on one computer to the receive pins on the second computer using wires 1 and 2 in the cable.

Gigabit Ethernet, however, uses a modified scheme. Because Gigabit Ethernet cables use all eight wires, in addition to wires 1 & 3 and 2 & 6 being crossed,

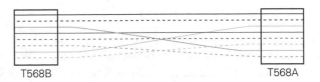

T568B   T568A

FIGURE 2.9   A crossover cable connecting two computers

wires 4 & 7 and 5 & 8 are crossed. Furthermore, because all Gigabit Ethernet devices have an automatic crossover detection feature called *auto MDI-X*, which automatically detects signals and determines how to send them down the wires (straight or crossed), there are folks in the industry who believe that the Gigabit Ethernet crossover cable is not necessary.

Exam Tip

For the exam, know the order of wires in the T568A and T568B standards and also know which wires are switched in a crossover cable.

Rollover and Loopback

In the networking world, you will come across a number of other cable types, including rollover cables and loopback cables.

- **Rollover cable**   Also known as the console cable, it's used to connect the administrator's system to the console port of a Cisco router or switch. The administrator connects the console cable to his or her Universal Serial Bus (USB) port through an adapter and then to the console port of the switch or router to administer the device and change its configuration. They call this a *rollover* cable because the wires are rolled over from one end to the other—wire 1 on one end becomes wire 8 on the other end, 2 becomes 7, 3 becomes 6, 4 becomes 5, and 5 becomes 4.

- **Loopback cable**   This special cable is used for self-diagnostics and typically has the wires connecting the transmit pins to the receive pins on the same system, keeping the communications local. This cable type is used only as a testing tool and is not used for network communication.

 **Objective 2.03**   ## Optical Fiber

Optical fiber is relatively expensive to purchase and install because it requires specialized handling and connection techniques. For this reason alone, fiber is not usually installed for desktop network connections unless a

special need exists, such as locations with high levels of electromagnetic interference. In general, fiber will be used where one or more of the following apply:

- Long distances need to be covered; depending on the type of fiber optic,
  this can be in the tens of kilometers.
- A link is needed between buildings, and other options, such as
  microwave and laser, are impractical (no line of sight, for example), too
  expensive, or electrically unworkable.
- High speeds (10 Gigabit Ethernet and beyond) are required.
- Security is a concern. Optical fibers don't radiate signals that can
  be picked up by listening equipment, and it is difficult to tap a fiber
  without being detected.
- The general environment is electrically unfriendly to data—that is, full
  of EMI, such as in a factory or in a radio/TV/radar transmitter room.
- Any potential for an electrical spark must be eliminated, such as in a
  laboratory using flammable gases and other volatile chemicals.

Data can be sent down an optical fiber cable as either infrared or laser light,
according to the system in use and the maximum distances involved. Each type
of system requires a specific type of media; infrared LED systems use *multimode fiber (MMF)*, whereas laser-diode-based systems (mainly used for high-
speed, long-haul data and telecom links) use *single-mode fiber (SMF)* cable.

Exam Tip

The wavelength of a particular signal (laser, for example) refers to
the distance the signal has to travel before it completes its particular
shape and starts to repeat. The different colors of the laser signals
feature different wavelengths.

Travel Advisory

Infrared and laser-diode light sources can cause eye damage if you stare
at them directly, so never look down a fiber cable to see if it's working.
Professional testing kits use optical sensors and/or cameras.

If you don't have the proper equipment available, test for faults
by replacing suspect fiber leads with known good ones.

An optical fiber cable has three components: the fiber itself; the cladding, which actually makes the light reflect down the fiber; and the insulating jacket. Fiber cabling is specified by its mode of operation and a two-number designator representing the core and cladding diameter in microns (mm, or millionths of a meter). The most common size used for general networking is multimode 62.5/125 mm, which can be used for cable runs of up to 275 meters. Almost all fiber networking standards require two fibers, and a pair is often connected together as duplex optical fiber cabling (see Figure 2.10). Longer cable runs are possible with other types of fiber-optic cabling (up to 80 km as of this writing, though not through an IEEE 802.3 standard).

As alluded to earlier, two types of fiber-optic cables are available:

- **Single-mode fiber (SMF)**   Uses a single cohesive frequency (ray) of laser light, known as a *mode,* to carry the transmission over long distances (up to as much as around 40 km).
- **Multimode fiber (MMF)**   Uses multiple rays of light (modes) simultaneously, with each ray of light running at a different reflection angle to carry the transmission over short distances (under 2 km). MMF is cheaper than SMF and is typically used within a building or between buildings of a campus, due to the short distances required.

Exam Tip
Remember that SMF is used to reach long distances whereas MMF transmits over shorter distances.

FIGURE 2.10   Duplex optical fiber cabling

Optical Fiber Connectors

Because they are optical rather than electrical, fiber cables have their own series of connector types.

The two most common types of fiber-optic connectors are the *ST* (stick and twist) and *SC* (stick and click) types (see Figure 2.11). ST connectors *do* look a bit BNC-ish, but be careful, because unlike a BNC connector, which can be impaled on its socket and twisted with total abandon until the locking guides engage with the fixing lugs, ST connectors have a keying mechanism to stop just this kind of youthful exuberance. If you do get carried away, you can snap the ceramic connector body—so easy does it!

You'll also find other fiber connectors, such as the fiber local connector (LC), ferrule connector (FC), and mechanical-transfer registered jack (MT-RJ). These connectors are similar to other connector types, such as the RJ and fiber SC shape. The fiber LC is the preferred connector of the two for communications exceeding 1 Gbps due to its small form factor.

Mechanical Connection Variations

Aside from the various connection types (LC, MT-RJ, and so on), fiber connectors vary in the connection point. The standard connector type today is called a Physical Contact (PC) connector because the two pieces of fiber touch when inserted. These connectors replace the older flat-surface connector that left a little gap between the connection points due to imperfections in the glass.

FIGURE 2.11   ST and SC fiber connectors

PC connectors are highly polished and slightly spherical, reducing the signal loss at the connection point.

Two technologies have dropped in price and have replaced PC connectors in some implementations: UPC and APC. Ultra Physical Contact (UPC) connectors are polished extensively for a superior finish. These reduce signal loss significantly over PC connectors. Angled Physical Contact (APC) connectors add an 8-degree angle to the curved end, lowering signal loss further. Plus, their connection does not degrade from multiple insertions, unlike earlier connection types.

Uses for Fiber

Although the entire works of Shakespeare can be transmitted down a single fiber many times per second across a transatlantic phone link, that's not the primary use for fiber cable. Most of the fiber you are likely to encounter provides interlocation links on Ethernet-based networks. Table 2.3 gives descriptions and speeds for some of the fiber-optic standards. The highest-rated Ethernet standards, added to the mix in 2010, are 40 Gigabit Ethernet (for servers) and 100 Gigabit Ethernet (for backbones).

1905.1-2013

The "IEEE Standard for a Convergent Digital Home Network for Heterogeneous Technologies," otherwise known as 1905.1-2013, deals with a bunch of technologies used for home networking, including IEEE 1901 over power lines.

TABLE 2.3   Common Fiber-optic Cabling Standards

Standard	Cabling	Cable Details	Connectors	Length
1000BaseSX	Multimode	850 nm	Variable, commonly LC	220–500 m
1000BaseLX	Single-mode	1300 nm	Variable, commonly LC and SC	5 km
10GBaseSR	Multimode	850 nm	LAN	26–300 m
10GBaseSW	Multimode	850 nm	SONET/WAN	26–300 m
10GBaseLR	Single-mode	1310 nm	LAN	10 km
10GBaseLW	Single-mode	1310 nm	SONET/WAN	10 km
10GBaseER	Single-mode	1550 nm	LAN	40 km
10GBaseEW	Single-mode	1550 nm	SONET/WAN	40 km

Transmitting and receiving Ethernet over power lines, as well as transmitting and receiving Ethernet over HDMI cables, are unique ways to set up a home network.

Implementing Multiple Types of Ethernet

Because Ethernet packets don't vary among the many flavors of Ethernet, network hardware manufacturers have long built devices capable of supporting more than one flavor right out of the box. Ancient hubs supported 10Base2 and 10BaseT at the same time, for example.

You can also use dedicated *media converters* to connect any type of Ethernet cabling together. Most media converters are plain-looking boxes with a port or dongle on either side. They come in all flavors:

- Single-mode fiber (SMF) to UTP/STP
- Multimode fiber (MMF) to UTP/STP
- Fiber to coaxial
- SMF to MMF

Exam Tip
The CompTIA Network+ exam competencies erroneously describe some media converters as single-mode fiber to *Ethernet* and multimode fiber to *Ethernet*. It's all Ethernet! Don't be surprised if you get one of those terms on the exam, however. Now you'll know what they mean.

The Gigabit Ethernet folks created a standard for modular ports called a *gigabit interface converter (GBIC)*. With many Gigabit Ethernet switches and other hardware, you can simply pull out a GBIC module that supports one flavor of Gigabit Ethernet and plug in another. You can replace an RJ45 port GBIC, for example, with an SC GBIC, and it'll work just fine. Electronically, the switch or other gigabit device is just that—Gigabit Ethernet—so the physical connections don't matter. Ingenious!

The *small form-factor pluggable (SFP)*—also known as a *mini-GBIC*—and the *SFP+* transceivers work in a similar fashion as GBICs and include connectors for the 10 Gigabit standards, among others. SFPs are smaller than GBICs so manufacturers can pack more slots onto a networking device, and they're backed by many different manufacturers.

Objective 2.04 # Wireless Media Types

There have been multiple wired and wireless ways to connect computers into networks over the years, and more continue to be created all the time. The vast majority of networks use UTP cabling, with fiber to interconnect LANs and wide area networks (WANs). The CompTIA Network+ exam even expects you to know that you can link two computers together directly using a cable that plugs into a serial port with its DB-9 or RS-232 connector, something we haven't used for decades because the serial connection supports only transfer rates of 150 KB per second (KBps).

Couplers are small devices with two female ports that enable you to connect two pieces of cable together to overcome *distance limitations.* UTP couplers are most common, but you can find couplers for every type of network: fiber couplers, even coaxial or BNC couplers. The plastic UTP couplers are relatively easily broken if exposed to humans.

Parallel connections are as ancient as serial ports. Parallel can run up to around 2 Mbps, although when used for networking, they tend to be much slower. Parallel is also limited to point-to-point topology but uses a 25-pin female (rather than male) DB-type connector, commonly called a *DB-25.*

802.11 Wireless Networks

Wireless connections are arguably are the hottest growth area in networking. The Institute of Electrical and Electronics Engineers (IEEE) 802.11 committee supports six standards for wireless local area networks (WLANs): 802.11a, 802.11b, 802.11g, 802.11n... and the latest and greatest, 802.11ac and 802.11ad (the latter is not covered on the new CompTIA Network+ exam).

Each of these wireless standards uses radio links to provide network connectivity to PCs and laptop computers through a transmitter/receiver unit (transceiver), generally known as an *access point (AP)* or *wireless access point (WAP),* which transmits and receives signals to and from the wireless network adapters (see Figure 2.12). By installing a number of strategically placed transceivers, you can achieve coverage over a wide area of floor space.

FIGURE 2.12 Wireless network equipment for the office

Wireless Basics

Before we get into the wireless networking details, let's take a look at the different methods to carry radio frequency (RF) traffic that are used on a wireless network:

- **Direct Sequence Spread Spectrum (DSSS)**   DSSS is a modulation technique that transfers data using the full bandwidth of a frequency. 802.11b wireless networks use DSSS. This method sends extra bits for resisting interference and providing the ability to recover data that didn't reach the destination. (More on the 802.11 standards in a bit.)

- **Frequency Hopping Spread Spectrum (FHSS)**   As the name implies, with frequency hopping, FHSS transmits radio signals by switching frequencies at a high rate. The benefit of FHSS is that it is harder for someone to tap into the data as the frequency continues to change.

- **Orthogonal Frequency-Division Multiplexing (OFDM)**   With OFDM, the data is delivered by being spread across multiple parallel channels. This helps overcome some of the inherent problems in Wi-Fi networking, such as signal bounce. 802.11g, 802.11n, 802.11ac, and 802.11ad wireless networks use OFDM transmission.

Travel Advisory
See Chapter 10 for a discussion of bounce problems.

802.11 networks can operate in one of two modes: ad hoc or infrastructure. In an *ad hoc mode* network, the wireless nodes communicate directly with each other; you don't need a WAP for two hosts to communicate. Although this might be handy for transferring files between two laptops in the train station, ad hoc 802.11 networking doesn't help you connect to your corporate network or the Internet.

To connect to an existing wired network, you need to use *infrastructure mode,* which uses a WAP device. The WAP is connected to the wired network and sends data between the wireless clients and systems on the wired network.

A single WAP servicing a given area is called a *Basic Service Set (BSS).* This service area can be extended by adding more access points. This is called, appropriately, an *Extended Service Set (ESS).*

BSSID, SSID, and ESSID

Wireless devices connected together into a network, whether ad hoc or infrastructure, require some way to identify that network. Frames bound for computers within the network need to go where they're supposed to go, even when you have more than one Wi-Fi network overlapping. The jargon gets a little crazy here, especially because marketing has come into the mix.

The *Basic Service Set Identifier (BSSID)* defines the most basic infrastructure mode network—a BSS of one WAP and one or more wireless nodes. With such a simple network, the Wi-Fi folks didn't see any reason to create some new numbering or naming scheme, so they made the BSSID the same as the Media

Access Control (MAC) address for the WAP. Simple! Ah, but what do you do about ad hoc networks that don't have a WAP? The nodes that connect in an ad hoc network, known as an Independent Basic Service Set (IBSS), randomly generate a 48-bit string of numbers called an Independent Basic Service Set Identifier (IBSSID) that looks and functions just like a MAC address, which goes in every frame.

You could, if required, discover the MAC address for the WAP in a BSS and manually type that into the network name field when setting up a wireless computer. But that causes two problems. First, people don't want to remember strings of 48 digits, even if translated out as six hexadecimal octets, like A9–45–F2–3E–CA–12. People want names. Second, how do you connect two or more computers together into an IBSS when the BSSID has to be randomly generated?

The Wi-Fi folks created another level of naming called a *Service Set Identifier (SSID),* a standard name applied to the BSS or IBSS to help the connection happen. The SSID—sometimes called a *network name*—is a 32-bit identification string that's inserted into the header of each frame processed by a WAP. Every Wi-Fi device must share the same SSID to communicate in a single network.

So let's take it one step further into a Wi-Fi network that has multiple WAPs, an ESS. How do you determine the network name at this level? You just use the SSID, only you apply it to the ESS as an *Extended Service Set Identifier (ESSID).*

Unfortunately, most Wi-Fi devices just use the term *SSID,* not *ESSID.* When you configure a wireless device to connect to an ESS, you're technically using the ESSID rather than just the SSID, but the manufacturer often tries to make it simple for you by using only the term *SSID.*

Exam Tip

The CompTIA Network+ certification exam uses the two terms— *SSID* and *ESSID*—interchangeably. Concentrate on these two terms for the exam.

Wireless Standards

Like all technologies, wireless has improved over the years, and as a result, different versions of wireless networking standards exist. Let's look at each of the wireless standards—and definitely make sure you know these for the CompTIA Network+ exam!

- **802.11b**   Has a throughput of 11 Mbps and runs at the 2.4 GHz frequency. 802.11b was the second wireless standard ever. Interestingly enough, the first was simply 802.11 without any letters after it.
- **802.11a**   Has a throughput of 54 Mbps and operates at the 5 GHz frequency. This wireless standard is incompatible with 802.11b/g, which runs at the 2.4 GHz frequency.
- **802.11g**   Improves upon the 802.11b standard by increasing the transfer rate to 54 Mbps, while staying compatible with 802.11b by running at the 2.4 GHz frequency.
- **802.11n**   Designed to run at both 2.4 GHz and 5 GHz so that it is compatible with 802.11b and 802.11g. An 802.11n-only network can take advantage of the less cluttered 5 GHz space for better coverage. The theoretical throughput jumps to 600 Mbps.
- **802.11ac**   Added in 2013, and only uses the 5 GHz frequency band. Theoretical throughput jumps to a whopping 3.2 Gbps, and is aimed for the home media environment.
- **802.11ad**   Also added in 2013, using a new frequency band of 60 GHz, the theoretical throughput of 7 Gbps is geared for a possible mobile office of the future!

The 802.11n standard brought several improvements to Wi-Fi networking, including faster speeds and new antenna technology implementations.

The 802.11n specification requires all but handheld devices to use multiple antennas to implement a feature called *multiple in/multiple out (MIMO),* which enables the devices to make multiple simultaneous connections. With up to four antennas, 802.11n devices can achieve amazing speeds. They also can implement *channel bonding* to increase throughput even more, where the devices use multiple radio signals simultaneously. (The official standard supports throughput of up to 600 Mbps, although practical implementation drops that down substantially.)

Many 802.11n WAPs employ *transmit beamforming,* a multiple-antenna technology that helps get rid of dead spots—or at least make them not so bad. The antennas adjust the signal once the WAP discovers a client to optimize the radio signal.

Table 2.4 summarizes the key features of the main 802.11 networking standards. Keep in mind that the distance limitations specified in the table assume

TABLE 2.4	802.11 Wireless Network Standards					
Standard	**802.11a**	**802.11b**	**802.11g**	**802.11n**	**802.11ac**	**802.11ad**
Maximum throughput	54 Mbps	11 Mbps	54 Mbps	Up to 600 Mbps	3.2 Gbps	Up to 7 Gbps
Maximum range	~150 feet	~300 feet	~300 feet	~300 feet	~100 feet	~15 feet
Frequency	5 GHz	2.4 GHz	2.4 GHz	2.4/5 GHz	5 GHz (and 2.4 GHz for backward compatibility)	60 GHz (and 2.4 GHz and 5.0 GHz for backward compatibility)
Backward compatibility			802.11b	802.11a/b/g	802.11a/b/g/n	802.11a/b/g/n/ac

perfect conditions. In the real world, walls, plumbing, and other factors will often limit your wireless network to much smaller coverage areas. Be sure to know these specs for the CompTIA Network+ exam.

Exam Tip

Make sure you know the IEEE 802.11 wireless standards and their associated characteristics for the CompTIA Network+ exam.

Wireless Frequency Ranges

I have mentioned that the different wireless standards run at either the 2.4 GHz frequency, the 5 GHz frequency, or the 60 GHz frequency. It is important to note that these frequencies are actually a *range* of frequencies, and each frequency range is known as a *channel*. If you want, you can change the channel that your wireless devices use, which will change the frequency being used by your wireless network. This is important because you may have a wireless network running on the same channel (frequency) as some of your household devices (such as a cordless phone), which will cause them to interfere with one another. In this case, you can change the channel of the wireless network to prevent the interference from occurring. Table 2.5 shows the different frequencies used by the 2.4 GHz Wi-Fi channels. You do *not* need to memorize this chart for the exam. I just included it to aid in setting up a Wi-Fi network.

TABLE 2.5	Wi-Fi Channels and Their Associated Frequencies
Channel	**Frequency Range**
1	2.3995 GHz–2.4245 GHz
2	2.4045 GHz–2.4295 GHz
3	2.4095 GHz–2.4345 GHz
4	2.4145 GHz–2.4395 GHz
5	2.4195 GHz–2.4445 GHz
6	2.4245 GHz–2.4495 GHz
7	2.4295 GHz–2.4545 GHz
8	2.4345 GHz–2.4595 GHz
9	2.4395 GHz–2.4645 GHz
10	2.4445 GHz–2.4695 GHz
11	2.4495 GHz–2.4745 GHz
12	2.4545 GHz–2.4795 GHz
13	2.4595 GHz–2.4845 GHz

Notice in Table 2.5 that the frequencies overlap from one channel to another. In fact, in the United States, only channels 1, 6, and 11 *don't* overlap! It's important that if you need to change the channel, you do so by a difference of at least two. For example, if you are running on channel 6 and you are experiencing problems, try changing all your wireless devices to channel 1 or 11.

Travel Advisory

latency   Wireless networks experience much higher *latency*—the time delay between sending and receiving signals—than wired networks, so you might run into problems with latency-sensitive applications, such as Skype or Google Hangouts, which feature streaming voice and video.

Although the CompTIA Network+ competencies suggest different latencies among the various Wi-Fi standards, there doesn't seem to be much variation. It's in the wired vs. wireless that you'll notice a difference.

Although wireless networks free us from the need to work with cabling and grant us mobility with our portable computers, wireless networks have three main drawbacks: cost, speed, and security. Cost is beginning to disappear as an issue—the price of wireless networking equipment has dropped dramatically as the technology has become more popular. In terms of speed, wireless networks can seem slow compared to their wired equivalents. Consider that mainstream, copper-based network solutions can give you speeds of 1000 Mbps or more for each system on a switched network, whereas a wireless network provides shared bandwidth around 300 Mbps at best.

Travel Assistance

See Chapter 10 for specifics on setting up and securing a Wi-Fi network.

Bluetooth

Bluetooth creates small wireless networks, called *wireless personal area networks (WPANs),* between PCs and peripheral devices such as smartphones and printers; input devices such as keyboards and mice; and consumer electronics such as cell phones, home stereos, televisions, home security systems, and so on. Bluetooth was *not* originally designed to be a full-function networking solution, although many vendors have used it for this purpose.

Bluetooth uses the FHSS spread-spectrum broadcasting method, switching among any of the 79 frequencies available in the 2.45 GHz range. Bluetooth hops from frequency to frequency some 1600 times per second, making it highly resistant to interference. The Bluetooth specification allows for transfers of data at rates from 723 Kbps to 1 Mbps, with a maximum range of 10 meters (about 33 feet).

Bluetooth devices interoperate in a *master/slave* scheme, in which one master device controls up to seven active slave devices. These roles are designated automatically and do not require any configuration. The personal area network (PAN) created by Bluetooth is sometimes called a *piconet*. More than seven Bluetooth slave devices (up to 255) can participate in a piconet at one time, but only seven of those devices can be active at one time. Inactive slave devices are referred to as *parked* devices.

Bluetooth devices use a four-stage process to find each other and create the PAN, as detailed in Table 2.6.

Bluetooth profiles—saved settings that devices use to communicate with other specific devices—make pairing with other devices efficient. These profiles

TABLE 2.6	Four Stages of Bluetooth
Stage	**Purpose**
Device discovery	The device broadcasts its MAC address and a code identifying the type of device.
Name discovery	The device identifies itself by a "friendly" name, such as *JonathaniPhone6*.
Association	The device joins the Bluetooth network.
Service discovery	The device announces the services that it can provide.

include the following: Generic Access Profile, which defines how Bluetooth units discover and establish a connection with each other; Service Discovery Profile, which enables the Bluetooth device's Service Discovery User Application to query other Bluetooth devices to determine what services they provide; LAN Access Profile, which defines how the Bluetooth device accesses a LAN and the Internet; and Synchronization Profile, used to synchronize data between Bluetooth PDAs and PCs.

Bluetooth devices have to support identical profiles to communicate; for example, your smartphone and PC both have to support the Bluetooth Synchronization Profile if you want them to sync up.

For security, Bluetooth offers proprietary 128-bit encryption and the ability to set per-user passwords to guard against unauthorized access to the Bluetooth network. Bluetooth also supports industry-standard encryption protocols such as Point-to-Point Tunneling Protocol (PPTP) and Secure Sockets Layer (SSL) through browser-based remote access. (PPTP and SSL are discussed in Chapters 7 and 9, respectively.) Access to Bluetooth networks can be controlled through MAC address filtering, and Bluetooth devices can be set to nondiscovery mode to hide them effectively from other Bluetooth devices. The Bluetooth specifications are shown in Table 2.7.

Exam Tip

Near field communication (NFC) devices have a distance limitation of 5 cm, compared to Bluetooth's 10 meters and infrared's 1 meter.

TABLE 2.7	Bluetooth Specifications
Standard	**Bluetooth**
Maximum throughput	1 Mbps (some devices boast 2 Mbps).
Maximum range	Typically 30 feet, but some high-powered Bluetooth devices have a maximum range of 300 feet.
Frequency	2.45 GHz.
Security	Proprietary 128-bit encryption, password-protected access, PPTP, and SSL (through browser-based remote access client).
Compatibility	Bluetooth.
Spread-spectrum method	FHSS.
Communication mode	Master/slave: a single master device with up to seven active slave devices.
Description	Bluetooth is designed to enable wireless communication between PCs and peripheral components, as well as consumer electronics. Bluetooth is not a full-fledged networking solution, and it is not intended to compete with or replace 802.11-based wireless networking technologies.

Objective 2.05 Structured Cabling

Connections from the outside world—whether network or telephone—come into a building at a location called a *demarc*, short for *demarcation point*. Demarc refers to the physical location of the connection and marks the dividing line of responsibility for the functioning of the network. You take care of the internal functioning; the person or company that supplies the upstream service to you must support connectivity and function on the far side of the demarc.

In a private home, the digital subscriber line (DSL) or cable modem supplied by your Internet service provider (ISP) is a *network interface unit (NIU)* that serves as a demarc between your home network and your ISP (see Figure 2.13). Most homes have a network interface box in addition that provides the connection for a telephone.

FIGURE 2.13   Typical home network interface box

In an office environment, the demarc is usually more complex, given that a typical building simply has to serve a much larger number of telephones and computers. Figure 2.14 shows the demarc for a midsized building, showing both Internet and telephone connections coming in from the outside.

One challenge to companies that supply ISP/telephone services is the need to diagnose faults in the system. Most of today's NIUs come with extra "smarts." These special (and very common) NIUs are known as *smart jacks*, and are mostly found with T1 lines. Smart jacks can convert signals, codes, and protocols, such as layer-2 frames, between the WAN and LAN. Smart jacks can buffer and regenerate signals to fix degraded signals. Smart jacks also have the very handy capability to set up a remote loopback, which is critical for testing and diagnostics from the central office, instead of having to travel to the customer site.

After the demarc, network and telephone cables connect to some type of box, owned by the customer, that acts as the primary distribution tool for the building. Any cabling that runs from the NIU to whatever box is being used by the customer is the *demarc extension*. For telephones, the cabling might connect to a special box called a *multiplexer* and, on the LAN side, almost certainly

FIGURE 2.14   Typical office demarc

to a powerful switch. This switch usually connects to a patch panel. This patch panel, in turn, leads to every telecommunications room in the building. The main patch panel is called a *vertical cross-connect.*

Cross-connects, MDF, and IDF

The combination of demarc, telephone cross-connects, and LAN cross-connects needs a place to live in a building. The room that stores all this equipment is known as a *main distribution frame (MDF)* to distinguish it from the multiple *intermediate distribution frame (IDF)* rooms (aka telecommunications rooms) that serve individual floors. Workstations connect to the patch panels at the

IDFs through cabling runs called *horizontal cabling*. The patch panel where the horizontal cabling connects is called a *horizontal cross-connect (HCC)*. The IDFs connect to the MDF with cables called *vertical cross-connect (VCC)* cables.

At the opposite end of the horizontal cabling from the telecommunications room is the work area. The work area is often simply an office or cubicle that potentially contains a PC and a telephone.

Typically, the MDF connects to the cable coming from outside the building. Then a separate IDF panel may be used to represent each floor in the building, with the workstations on a particular floor connecting to the panel associated with that floor.

Even a well-organized telecommunications room is a complex maze of equipment racks, switches, and patch panels. The most important issue to remember as you work is to keep your diagnostic process organized and documented. For example, if you're testing a series of cable runs along a patch panel, start at one end and don't skip connections. Place a sticker as you work to keep track of where you are on the panel.

Cables

Pulling cable is easily one of the most thankless and unpleasant jobs in the entire networking world. It may not look that hard from a distance, but the devil is in the details. First of all, pulling cable requires two people if you want to get the job done quickly; having three people is even better. Most pullers like to start from the telecommunications room and pull toward the drops. In an office area with a drop ceiling, pullers will often feed the cabling along the run by opening ceiling tiles and stringing the cable via hooks or cable trays that travel above the ceiling.

Professional cable pullers have an arsenal of interesting tools to help them move the cable horizontally, including telescoping poles, special nylon pull ropes, and even nifty little crossbows and pistols that can fire a pull rope long distances!

Cable trays are standard today, but a previous lack of codes or standards for handling cables led to a nightmare of disorganized cables in drop ceilings all over the world. Any cable puller will tell you that the hardest part of installing cables is the need to work around all the old cable installations in the ceiling.

Patch Panel

Ideally, once you install horizontal cabling, you should never move it. As you know, UTP horizontal cabling has a solid core, making it pretty stiff. Solid-core cables can handle some rearranging, but if you insert a wad of solid-core cables directly into your switches, every time you move a cable to a different port on the switch, or move the switch itself, you will jostle the cable. You don't have to move a solid-core cable many times before one of the solid copper wires breaks, and there goes a network connection!

Luckily for you, you can easily avoid this problem by using a patch panel. A patch panel is simply a box with a row of female ports in the front and per-manent connections in the back, to which you connect the horizontal cables. Figure 2.15 shows a line connecting the uplink port and a port labeled 2X. You may use only one of those two ports, not both at the same time.

Additionally, some hubs place a switch on one of the ports; you press this switch to make it either a regular port or an uplink port. Pressing the button electronically reverses the wires inside the hub.

Not only do patch panels prevent the horizontal cabling from being moved, but they are also your first line of defense in organizing the cables. All patch panels have space in the front for labels, and these labels are the network tech's best friend! Simply place a tiny label on the patch panel to identify each cable, and you will never have to experience that sinking feeling of standing in the telecommunications room of your nonfunctioning network, wondering which cable is which. If you want to be a purist, there is an official, and rather confus-ing, TIA/EIA naming convention called TIA/EIA 606, but a number of real-world network techs simply use their own internal codes. Figure 2.16 shows a typical patch panel.

The patch panel needs a *patch cable,* which is nothing but a short, stranded, straight-through cable, to connect between a port on the front of the patch panel and a port on a switch. When a computer connects to the network jack in the wall, the patch cable is used to map that system to the port on the switch. The concept of the patch panel allows ease of administration and flexibility in moving systems from one switch to another without visiting the workstation.

Proper patch panel cable management means documenting everything clearly and carefully. This way, any competent technician can follow behind you and troubleshoot connectivity problems.

FIGURE 2.15 Typical uplink port

FIGURE 2.16   A typical patch panel in a server room

Exam Tip

Cables are typically connected from the wall jack to the patch panel by a punch-down tool. A couple of standards deal with wiring patch panels: 66 block is used for wiring the telephone system, whereas 110 block is used to wire the patch panel for CAT 5/6 UTP cable.

Equipment Racks

The central component of every telecommunications room is one or more equipment racks. An equipment rack provides a safe, stable platform for all the different hardware components. All equipment racks are 19 inches wide, but they vary in height from two- to three-foot-high models that bolt onto a wall, to the more popular floor-to-ceiling model, free-standing racks.

You can mount almost any network hardware component into a rack. All manufacturers make rack-mounted switches that mount into a rack with a few screws. These switches are available with a wide assortment of ports and capabilities. There are even rack-mounted servers, complete with slide-out keyboards, and rack-mounted uninterruptible power supplies (UPSs) to power the equipment.

FIGURE 2.17   A rack-mounted UPS

All rack-mounted equipment uses a height measurement known simply as a unit (U), which is 1.75 inches. A device that fits in a 1.75-inch space is called a 1U, a device designed for a 3.5-inch space is a 2U, and a device that goes into a 7-inch space is called a 4U. Most rack-mounted devices are 1U, 2U, or 4U. The rack in Figure 2.17 is called a 42U rack to reflect the total number of U's it can hold.

The key when planning a rack system is to determine what sort of rack-mounted equipment you want to have and then get the rack or racks for your space. For example, if your rack will only have patch panels, switches, and routers, you can get away with a two-post rack. The pieces are small and easily supported.

If you're going to install big servers, on the other hand, you need to plan for a four-post rack or a server rail rack. A four-post rack supports all four corners of the server. The server rail rack enables you to slide the server out so you can open it up. This is very useful for swapping out dead drives for new ones in big file servers.

When planning how many racks you need in your rack system and where to place them, take proper air flow into consideration. You shouldn't cram servers and gear into every corner. Even with good air conditioning systems, bad air flow can cook components.

Finally, make sure to secure the telecommunications room. Rack security is a must for protecting valuable equipment. Get a lock!

Power Issues

A big concern for telecommunication rooms is power. All those boxes in the rack need good-quality power. Even the smallest rack should run off of a good uninterruptible power supply (UPS), a battery backup that plugs into the wall. Make sure you get one that can handle the amount of wattage used by all the equipment in the rack.

A UPS provides several benefits. First, it acts as an inverter. It stores power as direct current in its battery, then inverts that power to alternating current as the servers and other boxes in the rack system require. A good UPS also acts as a power-monitoring tool so it can report problems when any fluctuations in the electrical supply occur. All UPS boxes can provide security from power spikes and sags.

A UPS enables you to shut down in an orderly fashion. It does not provide enough power for you to continue working. The device that handles the latter service is called a generator.

Some mission-critical networks require specialized electrical hardware. Although the CompTIA Network+ exam objectives don't refer to these boxes by name—rack-mounted AC distribution boxes—they dance around some of the features. Notably, an AC distribution system can supply multiple dedicated AC circuits to handle any challenging setups. If you install such a box in your rack, make sure to add labels to both systems and circuits. Proper system labeling and circuit labeling can make life much easier in the event of problems later on.

Furthermore, an AC distribution system can supply multiple dedicated AC circuits to handle any challenging setups. If you install such a box in your rack, make sure to add labels to both systems and circuits. Proper system labeling and circuit labeling can make life much easier in the event of problems later on.

Many routers and other equipment will run directly on DC rather than AC. To accommodate both higher-end and standard equipment, therefore, you would run the higher-amperage circuits and then install one or more power converters to change from AC to DC.

Temperature Requirements

Besides power, another big concern for the telecommunications room is temperature, which should be maintained and monitored properly. If you lose the air conditioning, for example, and leave systems running, the equipment will overheat and shut down—sometimes with serious damage. To prevent this, all serious telecommunications rooms should have temperature monitors as part of their rack-monitoring system.

CHECKPOINT

✔**Objective 2.01: Coaxial Cabling** Coax cable is the classic example of bounded network media. Coax cable consists of an inner core and an overall metal screen, plus layers of insulation. The screen gives the cable a degree of protection against electromagnetic interference, but still, as with most copper-based media, it should be kept away from sources of interference. A wide variety of coax cable types exist, but specific types must be used for networking—not just any coax will do. Early Ethernet networks used baseband coax, the last of which sported a bayonet-style connector called a BNC.

✔**Objective 2.02: Twisted-Pair Cabling** The vast majority of network installations use unshielded twisted-pair (UTP) cable, a four-pair cable originally intended for telephone circuits but enhanced to carry data. Over time, various categories of UTP cable have been developed, each capable of operating at faster data rates than its predecessor. Two general types of UTP wiring can be used: patch cable uses stranded copper to make the wiring flexible, and premises cable (so-called *horizontal cable*) uses a solid core to give the wiring more strength to withstand rougher handling because it is installed in ducting and cable trays. Mixing the cable types—for example, using horizontal cable for patch leads—can lead to reliability problems.

Most UTP installations use RJ45 connectors and wall ports. RJ45 connectors have eight contacts to match the four pairs of wires in the UTP cable. The cable pairs are color-coded to make it easier to follow a standard wiring pattern when connecting media or fitting the cable to wall ports, such as T568A and T568B. Because UTP cable is not screened, it must be installed well away from other sources of electrical interference, and most installations are thoroughly tested to make sure they meet basic functional criteria. A screened version of UTP—called *STP*—is available, but it is much more expensive and rarely used unless local conditions demand a high level of screening.

✔**Objective 2.03: Optical Fiber** Optical fiber cabling is much more expensive to install than copper alternatives, but it offers several advantages, including greater maximum distance and improved security. Two main types of optical fiber are used: single-mode fiber (SMF) and multimode fiber (MMF), the latter being the most commonly used type for general networking. Optical fiber is specified according to the core (fiber) and cladding diameter (in microns), the most common size being 62.5/125.

Optical fiber has its own set of connectors because it's an optical system, not electrical. The most common connector types are ST, SC, LC, and MT-RJ. Optical fiber connectors should always be handled with care because they can be broken fairly easily.

✔**Objective 2.04: Wireless Media Types** Wireless networking solutions exist for both point-to-point building links and general intra-office connectivity. Today's office-based solutions use wireless networking standards such as 802.11n and 802.11ac, allowing different manufacturers to produce compatible equipment and increasing competition in the marketplace. Wireless networks operate in the office by means of one or more cells, each connecting users to the main network via an access point (AP).

✔**Objective 2.05: Structured Cabling** Successful implementation of a basic structured cabling network requires three essential ingredients: a telecommunications room, horizontal cabling, and a work area. The telecommunications room should have controls in place to regulate both the power and temperature.

REVIEW QUESTIONS

1. Which of the following connector types is associated with fiber-optic cable?
   A. RJ45
   B. BNC
   C. ST
   D. RG-58

2. Which of the following interconnections between devices requires a crossover cable?
   A. PC to switch
   B. Switch to router
   C. Switch to switch
   D. All of the above

3. Which of these standards uses multimode fiber cabling?
   A. 10GBaseSR
   B. 10GBaseLR
   C. 10GBaseLW
   D. 10GBaseER

4. Which of the following connector types is associated with UTP cable and is considered a Physical-layer device?

   A. RJ45

   B. BNC

   C. SC

   D. NBC

   E. USB 3.0

5. What name is given to the problem caused when signals from adjacent cables interfere with each other?

   A. Talkback

   B. Crossover

   C. Backchat

   D. Crosstalk

6. Which one of these cable types is used to manage a router or switch, rather than send Ethernet frames?

   A. Patch

   B. Straight-through

   C. Crossover

   D. Rollover

7. What are the names associated with cable used to connect to a patch panel and cable used to connect an MDF to an IDF?

   A. Horizontal and vertical cross-connect

   B. Rollover and loopback

   C. 586A and 586B

   D. Crossover and crossunder

8. What's the new wireless standard that only runs at the 5 GHz frequency range, with a maximum transfer rate of over 3 Gbps?

   A. 802.11n

   B. 802.11ac

   C. 802.11ad

   D. 802.11g

9. What device enables two or more Wi-Fi-enabled devices to connect to each other wirelessly and connect to a wired network?

   A. Router

   B. Switch

   C. MTRJ

   D. WAP

10. What feature of 802.11n enables devices to use multiple antennas to make multiple simultaneous connections and thus increase throughput?

   A. MIMO

   B. OFDM

   C. Transit beamforming

   D. CSMA/CD

REVIEW ANSWERS

1. **C** ST connectors are associated with fiber-optic cable.

2. **C** A crossover is needed to reverse the transmit and receive pins between two switches.

3. **A** 10GBaseSR uses multimode fiber-optic cabling.

4. **A** RJ45 connectors are associated with UTP cable and considered OSI Physical-layer devices.

5. **D** Crosstalk between adjacent cables causes interference.

6. **D** Rollover cables allow an administrator to configure and manage a router and switch. They never connect into a NIC, and therefore never carry actual network traffic.

7. **A** A patch cable that connects to the patch panel is called a horizontal cross-connect (HCC) cable. Cable that connects the MDF to the IDFs is called the vertical cross-connect (VCC) cable.

8. **B** 802.11ac is making its way into the wild, replacing 802.11n.

9. **D** A wireless access point (WAP) enables wireless nodes to connect to both wireless and wired networks.

10. **A** Multiple in/multiple out (MIMO) is the 802.11n standard for using multiple antennas simultaneously.

Network Topologies and Ethernet Standards

	NEWBIE	SOME EXPERIENCE	EXPERT
ETA	4 hours	2 hours	1 hour

A network *topology* provides a general description of how the devices on the network link to each other, either physically or logically. A *physical topology* describes precisely how devices connect, such as how the wires run from machine to machine. The devices could all connect to a single central box, for example, or in a daisy chain of one computer to another. A *logical topology,* in contrast, describes how the signals used on the network travel from one computer to another. In a logical topology, for example, all the computers might physically connect to a central box, but it's like there is a ring inside the box, so the signals flow as if the computers are all in a daisy chain. This chapter looks at both physical and logical topologies to help clarify these concepts.

Topologies do not define specifics about how to implement a network installation. They provide only a very high-level look at how network nodes connect. To move from a theoretical overview to a working solution, you must implement a specific network standard. This chapter also discusses the implementation of networks and network technologies, going into detail about Ethernet, the most widely used network standard.

Particular network topologies are generally associated with specific networking standards that provide the details that define how the network sends data between devices, the type of media used, the maximum network speed, and the number of devices (nodes) that can attach to the network. This chapter also looks at both the CSMA/CD and CSMA/CA access methods, used by wired and wireless networks, respectively. Questions regarding network topologies, standards, and access methods are well represented on the CompTIA Network+ exam.

Objective 3.01   Network Topologies

Bus, star, ring, mesh, and point-to-point topologies look and operate differently. Some are more common nowadays than others. Certain situations call for certain topologies, so without further adieu, let's take a look.

The Bus Topology

If you can imagine your laundry hanging on a long, straight clothesline, you have a pretty good idea of how a bus topology network is constructed. Everything hangs off one long run of cable, as shown in Figure 3.1.

FIGURE 3.1   A bus topology uses a main cable trunk.

The Star Topology

An early alternative topology to bus suggested connecting all the devices on a network into a single central box, effectively creating a star (see Figure 3.2). This network design became known as a *star topology*.

The key advantage of the star topology is that a break in a cable affects only the machine connected to that cable. In Figure 3.3, machine C cannot communicate with any other node, but machines A, B, D, E, and F communicate with each other just fine.

Early star topologies used a central device called a *hub*. All the devices on the network would connect to the hub, creating a physical star topology network, but electronically—logically—the network would function just like a bus network. This created a hybrid topology called a *star bus*.

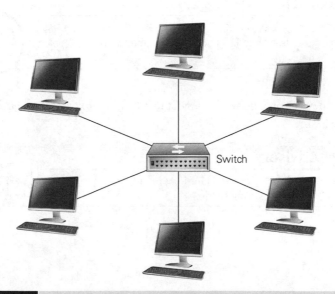

Switch

FIGURE 3.2   A modern star topology with a switch in the center

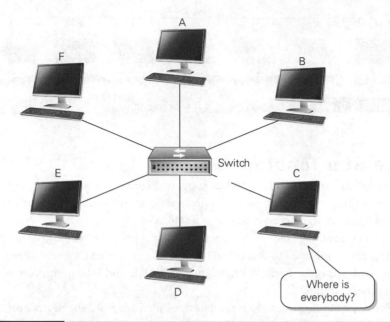

FIGURE 3.3   In a star topology, a broken cable affects only the machine connected to it.

Exam Tip

A hybrid topology is a topology that mixes the bus, star, and/or ring topologies (discussed later) together. For example, a star bus topology is a hybrid topology.

Today, devices on a network connect to a central box, called a *switch* (refer to Figure 3.2).

Travel Advisory

Switches are vastly superior to hubs. Chapter 4 covers the details about how switches and hubs differ.

The Ring Topology

In a true ring topology, all computer systems are connected together in a complete loop (see Figure 3.4).

The main selling point for ring networks was the deterministic method of communication. Devices on the ring played nicely and accessed the ring when it was their turn.

Ring and star-ring networks, where a central device forced the devices connected to it to communicate as if they were daisy-chained together, are long gone today.

The Mesh Topology

The mesh topology connects each node with multiple links, providing multiple paths between any two nodes. The mesh topology is rarely, if ever, seen in LANs because of cost: it requires so many separate links. A partial mesh, however, is used to connect networks together (see Figure 3.5). In essence, any series of interlinked networks where more than one possible data path exists between network locations can be considered to be using a mesh topology. Because mesh topologies support multiple paths between networks, the level of fault tolerance improves as the number of paths increases.

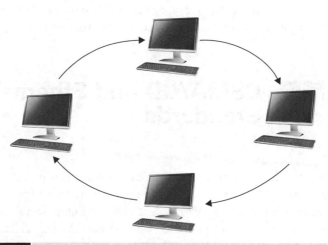

FIGURE 3.4   A ring topology network

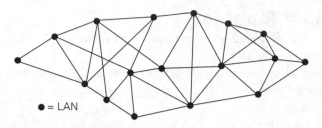

● = LAN

FIGURE 3.5   A mesh topology

Point-to-Point and Point-to-Multipoint Topologies

Two popular layouts for topologies are the point-to-point and point-to-multipoint topologies. In a *point-to-point* topology, two systems connect directly to one another. In the past, these systems would connect directly through the serial ports with a null modem cable, but these days you can connect them using a crossover cable or a wireless connection.

A *point-to-multipoint* topology uses a central device that connects all the devices together. This topology is popular with wireless networks. With a point-to-multipoint topology, when the central device sends data, it is received by all devices connected to the central device. These devices can be either clients or other central devices that extend the reach of the signal.

Objective 3.02 # CSMA/CD and Ethernet Standards

Ethernet, introduced by Xerox in 1973, remained a largely proprietary technology until 1979, when Xerox looked for partners to help promote Ethernet as an industry standard. Working with Digital Equipment Corporation (DEC) and Intel, the company published what became the Digital-Intel-Xerox (DIX) networking standard. The standard describes a bus topology network using coaxial cable that enables multiple computing systems and other devices to communicate with each other at 10 Mbps.

How Ethernet Works

Any network design must address a number of key elements: the type of media to use, how to send data across the wire, how to identify the sending and receiving computers, and how to determine which computer should use the shared cable next.

Chapter 2 discussed the physical cabling used in Ethernet. Ethernet networks can use coaxial cable, unshielded twisted-pair (UTP), shielded twisted-pair (STP), or fiber. Regardless of the physical cabling used, the data moves across the wire essentially the same way. Any network requires a method for determining which device uses the network media at a given time.

CSMA/CD

Older Ethernet networks that used half-duplex communications, where a node can only transmit or receive at one time (not simultaneously), used *carrier sense multiple access with collision detection (CSMA/CD)* to determine which computer should use the shared media at a given moment. *Carrier sense* means that each machine on the network examines the cable before sending a data frame (see Figure 3.6). If another machine is using the network, the node detects traffic and waits until the cable is free. If the node detects no traffic, the node sends its data frame.

Multiple access means that all machines have equal access to the wire. If the line is free, an Ethernet node does not have to get approval to use the wire—it just uses it. From the point of view of Ethernet, it does not matter what function the node is performing. The node could be a desktop system running Windows

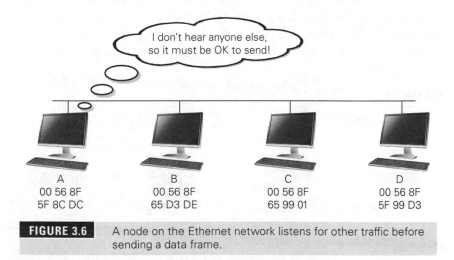

FIGURE 3.6 A node on the Ethernet network listens for other traffic before sending a data frame.

10, or a high-end file server running Windows Server 2012 R2 or a flavor of Linux. In Ethernet, all nodes are created equal. But what happens when two machines listen to the cable and simultaneously determine that it is free? They both try to send.

Exam Tip

CompTIA uses some seemingly sloppy language to describe CSMA in the objectives, calling it both CDMA (which is a completely different standard used for cell phones) and carrier detect/sense. You know what the technology means, so don't be thrown off if odd terminology appears on the exam.

Collisions

When two nodes use the cable simultaneously, a *collision* occurs, and both of the transmissions are lost (see Figure 3.7). Two nodes transmitting at the same time are like two people talking simultaneously: the listener hears the mixture of the two voices and can't understand either voice.

When a collision occurs, both nodes detect the collision by listening to their own transmissions. By comparing their own transmissions with the signal they receive, they can determine whether another node has transmitted at the same time, as shown in Figure 3.8. If the nodes detect a collision, both nodes immediately stop transmitting and wait for a short, random period of time before retrying.

Because CSMA/CD is easy to implement in hardware, Ethernet network interface cards (NICs) are relatively cheap. That simplicity comes at a price: an Ethernet node will waste some amount of its time dealing with collisions instead of sending data. As you add more devices to the network and/or increase the

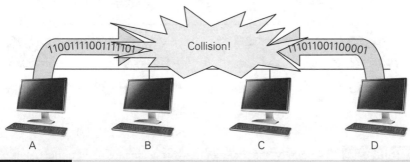

FIGURE 3.7   If two nodes transmit data at the same time, a data collision occurs.

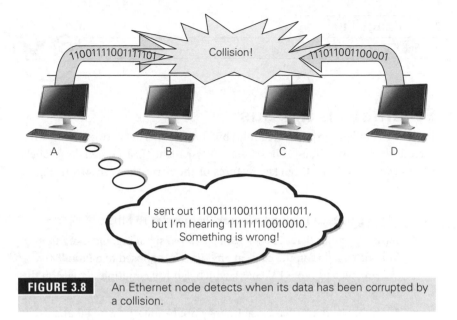

FIGURE 3.8 An Ethernet node detects when its data has been corrupted by a collision.

amount of traffic—for example, by installing new, data-intensive applications on the network—the number of collisions on the network will increase as the nodes generate more frames.

Every Ethernet network wastes some amount of its available bandwidth dealing with these collisions. The typical Ethernet network advertises that it runs at either 100 Mbps or 1000 Mbps, but the advertised speed assumes that no collisions ever take place!

Full-duplex communication, where devices can transmit and receive simultaneously, has replaced half-duplex on all but really old devices. Full-duplex started becoming the norm around the year 2000. When a NIC and the switch port the NIC is connected to are configured for full-duplex communication, CSMA/CD is actually disabled, and there is no listening before transmitting anymore. Collisions are, in fact, completely eliminated!

Ethernet Standards

In the early 1980s, the Institute of Electrical and Electronics Engineers (IEEE), an organization that defines industry-wide standards in the fields of electronics and computing, adopted the DIX Ethernet standard as a general standard for networking. The IEEE working group (or committee) responsible for general networking standards is known as the *802 committee,* and Ethernet became IEEE standard 802.3.

Exam Tip
IEEE 802.3 defines Ethernet standards.

Ethernet on the Bus

Two main standards exist for creating a bus-based Ethernet network, with wonderfully descriptive names: *10Base5* and *10Base2*. The IEEE coined these labels, and they each describe three key features of the network, as shown in Figure 3.9:

- **10**   Signifies an Ethernet network that runs at 10 Mbps.
- **Base**   Signifies that 10Base5 uses *baseband* signaling, meaning that just one signal is on the cable at any time, as opposed to a *broadband* system (such as cable TV coax), which can have multiple signals on the cable.
- **5**   Indicates that 10Base5 cables may not be longer than 500 meters, which is also an indication to the type of cable. The cable length that is 500 meters is called *Thicknet* cabling. (Note that the *2* in 10Base2 is the distance rounded up from 185 meters.)

Ethernet networks using the pure bus topology have long been replaced by networks running twisted-pair or fiber-optic cable.

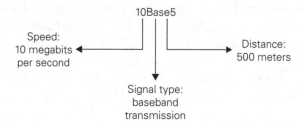

FIGURE 3.9   A term such as 10Base5 tells us three things about the network.

10BaseT and 100BaseT

The term *10BaseT* describes an Ethernet cabling system that uses a star bus topology. 10BaseT uses twisted-pair cabling rather than coax. Most of the other basic characteristics remain the same—for example, the network operates at the same speed (10 Mbps) and supports a maximum of 1024 nodes.

The name *10BaseT* doesn't quite follow the naming convention used for earlier Ethernet cabling systems. The *10* still refers to the speed: 10 Mbps. *Base* still refers to the signaling type: baseband. The *T*, however, doesn't refer to a distance limitation but to the type of cable used: twisted-pair. For the record, the maximum distance allowed between a node and a switch is 100 meters.

Once you have come to grips with 10BaseT, it is not a quantum leap to understand the key selling point of 100BaseT. *Fast Ethernet*, as 100BaseT is known, runs at 100 Mbps over twisted-pair cabling.

Most Ethernet NICs automatically switch between 10 Mbps, 100 Mbps, and 1000 Mbps operation to match the speed of the switch port they're plugged into, and all modern switches support a mix of devices running at either speed.

Exam Tip	
The distance limitation between a node and a switch is 100 meters due to the restrictions of UTP cabling.	

Before we leave this section, you should know that there are two types of 100 Mb (megabit) UTP Ethernet: 100BaseTX and 100BaseT4. 100BaseTX is, by far, the more popular version and runs over two pairs in a CAT 5 or better cable. 100BaseTX is so common that we just call it 100BaseT. 100BaseT4 was an earlier implementation that ran over CAT 3 cable, achieving the 100 Mbps speed by using all four pairs of wires.

Gigabit Ethernet

Modern developments have cranked Ethernet up to the heady speed of 1000 Mbps (1 Gbps) while retaining compatibility with the CSMA/CD standard, although you won't see Gigabit Ethernet using half-duplex or CSMA/CD.

Various others have now been ratified by the IEEE 802.3ab and the IEEE 802.3z Gigabit Ethernet Standardization projects, as follows:

- IEEE 802.3ab
  - **1000BaseT**   Gigabit Ethernet over four pairs of wires in CAT 5e or better UTP cabling.
- IEEE 802.3z
  - **1000BaseX**   Gigabit Ethernet over different cable types, which is broken down into 1000BaseSX, 1000BaseLX, and 1000BaseCX:
    - **1000BaseSX**   Gigabit Ethernet over multimode fiber-optic cabling. You can remember this by the *S*, meaning "short distance." Multimode fiber cabling is the type of cabling that is used over short distances (less than 2 km).
    - **1000BaseLX**   Gigabit Ethernet over single-mode fiber-optic cabling. You can remember this by the *L*, meaning "long distance." Single-mode fiber is the type of fiber used to cover large distances (greater than 2 km).
    - **1000BaseCX**   Gigabit Ethernet over coaxial cable, supporting distances of up to 25 meters.

10/100/1000BaseT Summary

Here are the key features that distinguish 10/100/1000BaseT cabling:

- Speed of 10, 100, or 1000 Mbps, according to the standard
- Baseband signal type
- Distance of 100 meters from node to hub or switch

Exam Tip

Be sure to focus on Fast Ethernet (100BaseT) and Gigabit Ethernet (1000BaseT) for the CompTIA Network+ exam. Also know that the standard known as 100BaseFX is 100 Mbps Ethernet over fiber-optic cabling.

---

10 Gigabit Ethernet (10 GbE)

For the highest bandwidth applications, such as interconnecting servers and connecting high-speed switches in corporate datacenters, the *10 Gigabit Ethernet* standards, also known as *10 GbE,* provides an amazingly fast Ethernet-based networking technology. Two major 10 GbE standards are 802.3ae for 10 GbE over fiber-optic cabling and 802.3an for 10 GbE over copper cabling.

In addition to speed, some 10 GbE variations are designed to interoperate with Synchronous Optical Network (SONET), making it an ideal choice for connecting local networks to preexisting long-distance fiber-optic links that already use SONET. (Refer to Table 3.1, and see Chapter 8 for more information on SONET.)

Exam Tip

The CompTIA Network+ objectives focus on the 1 Gbps and 10 Gbps standards (10 GbE), so spend some time memorizing what standard is used with what type of cable and distance. To help you with Table 3.1, the *S* at the end of the standard stands for "short distance," the *L* stands for "long distance," and the *E* stands for "extended distance." The *W* at the end of the standard implies "WAN," which means it is used with SONET (a WAN-based technology discussed in Chapter 8). The *R* at the end of the standard implies LAN-based signaling.

| **TABLE 3.1** | 10 Gbps Ethernet Standards |

Standard	Maximum Distance	Cabling	SONET Compatible
10GBaseSR	300 m	Multimode fiber	No
10GBaseSW	300 m	Multimode fiber	Yes
10GBaseLR	10 km	Single-mode fiber	No
10GBaseLW	10 km	Single-mode fiber	Yes
10GBaseER	40 km	Single-mode fiber	No
10GBaseEW	40 km	Single-mode fiber	Yes
10GBaseLX4 over single mode	300 m	Single-mode fiber	No
10GBaseLX4 over multimode	10 km	Multimode	No
10GBaseCX4	15 m	Infiniband copper cabling	No
10GBaseT	40/100 m	Category 6/6a UTP	No

Objective 3.03   ## CSMA/CA: The Wireless Equivalent to CSMA/CD

Wi-Fi networks are based on the IEEE 802.11 standards. Whether configured in a point-to-point or point-to-multipoint topology, Wi-Fi networks have some interesting obstacles to overcome so that communication happens properly. Half-duplex wired Ethernet networks, as you'll recall from earlier in this chapter, negotiate use of the bus through CSMA/CD. Devices listen, send if the bus is free, and re-send in the case of a collision.

Modern switched networks work way more efficiently, because full duplex, when implemented in both the computer's NIC and the switch port it connects to, completely eliminates collisions. *Full duplex* means that devices can send and receive at the same time, and as a result, they don't listen first.

Travel Assistance

I go into more detail on switches in Chapter 4.

CSMA/CD won't work for wireless networking for two reasons. First, a wireless device cannot listen and send at the same time, which is how collisions on half-duplex Ethernet networks are detected (even though the half-duplex wired clients can technically listen and send at the same time, the messages are garbled, and need to be retransmitted). Second, wireless clients may not know about the existence of another client due to signal strength. This is called the *hidden node* problem.

Exam Tip

You need to know the difference between full duplex and half duplex for the CompTIA Network+ exam. Old Ethernet devices ran in half duplex, as do Wi-Fi networks. Modern switched Ethernet, on the other hand, is full duplex.

Wireless networks need another way to deal with potential collisions. Wi-Fi networks use *carrier sense multiple access with collision avoidance (CSMA/CA)* rather than CSMA/CD. The CSMA/CA access method, as the name implies, proactively takes steps to avoid collisions, as does CSMA/CD.

CSMA/CA defines two methods for collision avoidance. First, if a wireless network node detects that the network is busy, that node waits a slightly lengthy *backoff* period before it tries to access the network again. Yes, so far, this is the same as CSMA/CD. However, CSMA/CA also requires that receiving nodes send an acknowledgment for every frame that they process. The ACK also includes a value that tells other wireless nodes to wait a certain duration before trying to access the network media. If the sending node doesn't receive an ACK, it retransmits the same data frame until it gets a confirmation that the frame reached its destination. Optionally, nodes can also send a request-to-send (RTS) message to the access point, and get a clear-to-send (CTS) message back that is heard by all nodes within range of the access point, including those nodes that weren't in range for the request-to-send message.

CHECKPOINT

✔**Objective 3.01: Network Topologies**   Bus, ring, star, hybrid, and mesh are different types of network topologies. Each looks and operates differently than the others.

✔**Objective 3.02: CSMA/CD and Ethernet Standards**   Ethernet addresses the type of media to use, how to send data across the wire, how to identify the sending and receiving computers, and how to determine which computer should use the shared cable next. Half-duplex Ethernet uses the CSMA/CD algorithm to mediate channel access.

✔**Objective 3.03: CSMA/CA: The Wireless Equivalent to CSMA/CD**   CSMA/CD can't work on wireless networks, so a different channel-access method is needed. CSMA/CA defines two required steps, and an optional step, that all wireless nodes use to mediate channel access.

REVIEW QUESTIONS

1. Which of the following physical topologies uses a switch?
   A. Bus
   B. Star
   C. Ring
   D. Point-to-point

2. What name is given to the access method used by wireless devices?
   A. Token passing
   B. Collision Domain Management (CDM)
   C. CSMA/CA
   D. CSMA/CD

3. What does a logical topology depend on?
   A. Physical layout
   B. How the nodes look
   C. How the signals move
   D. The Ethernet standard used

4. CSMA/CD applies to which of the following?
   A. Wired full-duplex networks
   B. Wireless full-duplex networks
   C. Wired half-duplex networks
   D. Wireless half-duplex networks

5. Which 10 Gbps Ethernet standard uses single-mode fiber-optic cabling, supports a distance of more than 2 km, and is not SONET-compatible?
   A. 10GBaseSR
   B. 10GBaseER
   C. 10GBaseLW
   D. 10GBaseEW

6. What network topology is most fault tolerant?
   A. Bus
   B. Ring
   C. Star
   D. Mesh

7. When full duplex is enabled on a link, which of the following is disabled?

    A. CSMA/CA

    B. CSMA/CD

    C. SSID/ESSID

    D. Point-to-point

    E. Point-to-multipoint

8. What term refers to a situation where two half-duplex nodes send messages at the same time?

    A. Collision

    B. Accident

    C. MAC

    D. Switch

9. Which of the following is a Gigabit standard that uses multimode fiber-optic cabling?

    A. 1000BaseT

    B. 1000BaseCX

    C. 1000BaseLX

    D. 1000BaseSX

10. What does the *base* in baseband refer to?

    A. One channel

    B. Multiple channels

    C. Speed

    D. Distance

REVIEW ANSWERS

1. **B** The physical star topology has a switch at the center.

2. **C** CSMA/CA is the access method used by wireless devices.

3. **C** A logical topology depends on how the signals move.

4. **C** CSMA/CD only applies to wired half-duplex networks. Furthermore, there is no such thing as a wireless full-duplex network.

5. **B** 10GBaseER is single-mode fiber over an extended range of up to 40 km.

6. **D** The mesh topology is the only one that allows multiple pathways between networks.

7. **B** Full-duplex Ethernet, where both ends of the link can simultaneously send and receive, has negated the need for CSMA/CD, and the algorithm is actually disabled on a full-duplex link.

8. **A** Collisions were handled with CSMA/CD on wired Ethernet networks, and are handled with CSMA/CA on wireless networks.

9. **D** 1000BaseSX is the Gigabit standard that uses multimode fiber-optic cabling, which is the type of fiber cabling used to cover short distances.

10. **A** Baseband, in Ethernet, uses just a single channel on the wire.

Network Hardware

	NEWBIE	SOME EXPERIENCE	EXPERT
ETA	4 hours	2 hours	1 hour

Network hardware enables networking devices—nodes—to cable together into a network. That's pretty straightforward and even redundant, at least in words. The CompTIA Network+ exam expects you to know the network hardware used in Ethernet and TCP/IP networks in some detail, even if some of the hardware is no longer in use. This chapter looks at network interfaces and the magic boxes that connect devices, both wired and wirelessly.

 ## Network Interfaces

A network interface enables a computing device to send and receive data across a network. All modern computing devices have a network interface, either wired to connect to an Ethernet network or wireless to connect to a wireless access point. The network interface traditionally has been called a *network interface card (NIC)*, because the interface came on a separate expansion card. However, for many years now, motherboards of both laptops and desktops have onboard (built-in) network interfaces (though most techs still call them NICs). Figure 4.1 shows a network interface on a motherboard.

Gigabit NIC

FIGURE 4.1 Gigabit Ethernet network interface

> **Travel Advisory**
>
> Don't say "NIC card" because the *C* in NIC stands for "card"!
> Saying NIC card would be like saying "ATM machine" or "PIN
> number," which are other common redundant terms.

NICs have several jobs. They provide a connection to the network media, of course, either through cables or wireless radio frequency waves. NICs also have a physical address (MAC address, explained in the next section) to enable communication with other devices on the network. Finally, NICs take data from the operating system and encapsulate that data into a frame suitable for traversing the Physical-layer network.

MAC Address

On every NIC, burned onto a ROM chip, is special firmware containing a unique identifier with a 48-bit value, called the *media access control address,* or *MAC address.*

No two NICs ever share the same MAC address—ever. Any company that makes NICs must contact the Institute of Electrical and Electronics Engineers (IEEE) and request a block of MAC addresses, which the company then burns into the ROMs on its NICs. Many NIC makers also print the MAC address on the surface of each NIC, as shown in Figure 4.2. MAC addresses are written with hexadecimal digits. Because each hex character represents 4 bits, it takes 12 hex characters to represent 48 bits.

The MAC address in Figure 4.2 is 004005–607D49, although in print, we represent the MAC address as 00–40–05–60–7D–49. The first six digits (in this example, 00–40–05) represent the number of the NIC manufacturer. Once the IEEE issues those six hex digits to a manufacturer—often referred to as the *organizationally unique identifier (OUI)*—no other manufacturer may use them. The last six digits (in this example, 60–7D–49) are the manufacturer's unique serial number for that NIC; this portion of the MAC is often referred to as the *device ID.*

Would you like to see the MAC address for your NIC? If you have a Windows system, type **ipconfig /all** from a command prompt to display the MAC address (see Figure 4.3). Note that in the ipconfig output, the MAC address is called the *physical address.*

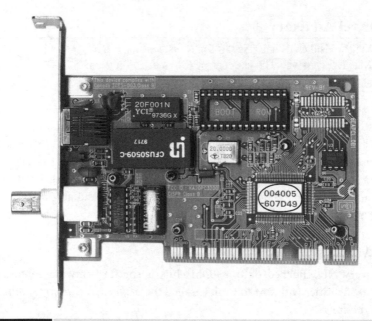

FIGURE 4.2 MAC address

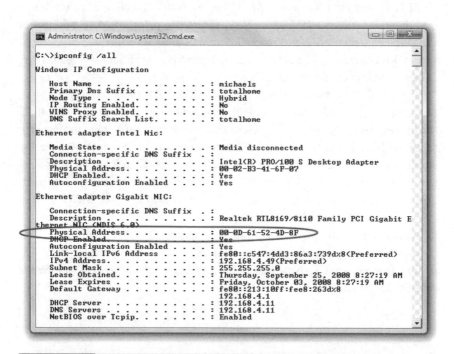

FIGURE 4.3 Output from ipconfig /all

Organizing the Data: Ethernet Frames

All network technologies break data transmitted between computers into smaller pieces called *frames,* as you'll recall from Chapter 1. Functioning at the Data Link layer (layer 2), NICs encapsulate data from the higher levels of the OSI model into frames to enable communication at the Physical layer.

Using frames makes the process of retransmitting lost data more efficient. In the real world, bad things can happen to good data. When errors occur during transmission, the sending system must retransmit the frames that failed to get to the receiving system in good shape. If a word processing document was transmitted as a single massive frame, and errors occurred, the sending system would have to retransmit the entire frame—in this case, the entire document. Breaking the file up into smaller frames enables the sending computer to retransmit only the damaged frames.

All networking technologies use frames, and Ethernet is no exception to that rule. A basic Ethernet frame contains five pieces of information: the MAC address of the frame's recipient, the MAC address of the sending system, the type of data encapsulated inside the frame (IP packet, for instance), the data itself, and a frame check sequence. Figure 4.4 shows these components.

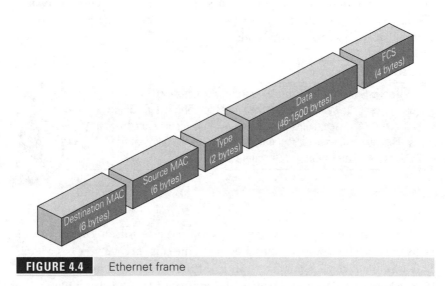

FIGURE 4.4　Ethernet frame

Preamble

All Ethernet frames begin with a *preamble,* a 64-bit series of alternating ones and zeroes that ends with 11. The preamble gives a receiving NIC time to realize a frame is coming, and to know exactly where the frame starts. Because the minimum size of an Ethernet frame is 64 bytes (including the data, which has to be a minimum of 46 bytes, plus the 18 bytes of the frame header and trailer, as listed in Figure 4.4), the preamble is not considered part of the actual frame.

Destination and Source MAC Addresses

The first and second fields of the frame identify the destination and sending NICs, respectively. In early Ethernet networks, every node on the network received every frame, because they were on a shared bus cable or connected via hubs. Nodes would use the destination MAC address to determine whether to process each frame. In today's switched Ethernet, the switch keeps a record of which node connects to which switch port, and forwards data to the precise destination node through its associated switch port. The only common traffic that goes to all switch ports (except the switch port that the message originated on) and is processed by all nodes is the broadcast traffic sent to the destination MAC of FF-FF-FF-FF-FF-FF, the *Ethernet/layer-2 broadcast address.* In addition, multicast traffic is processed by a select subset of the entire network. Nodes subscribe to a multicast group, and they subsequently process traffic sent to that group's special MAC address.

> **Travel Advisory**
>
> **Switches Sending Multiple Frames**   Switches send frames to all switch ports (except the switch port that the message originated on) in two non-broadcast circumstances: unknown unicasts (when the switch doesn't have an associated switch port for a destination MAC address) and multicasts (in some situations).

Type

An Ethernet frame may carry one of several "types" of data. The Type field helps the receiving computer interpret the frame contents at a very basic level. This way, the receiving computer can tell if the frame contains, for example, IPv4 data or IPv6 data. (See Chapter 5 for more details on IPv4 and IPv6.)

The Type field does *not* tell you if the frame carries higher-level data, such as an e-mail message or web page. You have to dig deeper into the data section of the frame to find that information.

Data

The data part of the frame contains whatever the frame carries, what's called the *payload*. This can be an IP packet or some other protocol such as Address Resolution Protocol (ARP). Regardless of the type of data in the payload, an Ethernet frame must have a payload of at least 46 bytes. If the payload is smaller than 46 bytes, the sending NIC will automatically add extra zeros, known as *padding*, to bring the payload up to the minimum.

Frame Check Sequence

The *frame check sequence (FCS)*—which Ethernet implements through an algorithm called *cyclic redundancy check (CRC)*—enables Ethernet nodes to recognize when bad things happen to good data. Machines on a network must be able to detect when data has been damaged in transit.

To detect errors, the computers on an Ethernet network attach a special code to each frame. When creating an Ethernet frame, the sending machine runs the data through a special mathematical formula, the CRC algorithm, and attaches the result, the frame check sequence, to the end of the frame (trailer). The receiving machine receives the frame, performs the same calculation, and compares its answer with the one included with the FCS field. If the answers match, the destination knows that the frame has integrity (no bits changed in transit) and then opens up the frame. If the answers do not match, the receiving machine simply drops the frame and lets higher level protocols, such as TCP, handle the retransmission.

Objective 4.02 Switched Ethernet

Although plain-vanilla 10BaseT Ethernet performed well enough for first-generation networks (which did little more than basic file and print sharing), by the early 1990s networks used more-demanding applications, which quickly saturated a 10BaseT network. Fortunately, those crazy kids over at the IEEE kept expanding the standard, giving the network tech in the trenches a new tool that provided additional bandwidth—the switch.

The Trouble with Hubs

A classic 10BaseT network with a hub can only have one message on the wire at any time. When two computers send at the same time, the hub dutifully repeats both signals. The nodes recognize the collision and, following the rules of CSMA/CD, attempt to resend. Add in enough computers, and the number of collisions increases, lowering the effective transmission speed for the whole network. A busy network becomes a slow network because all the computers share the same collision domain.

Switches to the Rescue

An Ethernet *switch* looks like a hub because all nodes plug into it (see Figure 4.5). But switches don't function like hubs inside. Switches come with extra smarts that enable them to take advantage of MAC addresses, effectively creating point-to-point connections between two conversing computers. This gives every switch port the full bandwidth of the actual switch.

To see a switch in action, check out Figure 4.6. When you first turn on a switch, it acts exactly as though it were a hub, flooding all incoming frames right back out to all the other ports (except the switch port that the frame originated on). As it receives all frames, however, the switch copies the source MAC addresses and quickly creates a logical table of the MAC addresses of each connected computer. The table is called a *source address table (SAT)*, because entries are added for the source of traffic when it sends frames into the switch.

> ### Exam Tip
>
> One classic difference between a hub and a switch is in the repeating of frames during normal use. Although it's true that switches initially forward all frames, they filter by MAC addresses as soon as they're learned. Hubs never learn and always forward all frames.

As soon as this table is created, the switch begins to do something amazing. When a computer sends a frame into the switch destined for another computer

FIGURE 4.5   Hub (top) and switch (bottom) comparison

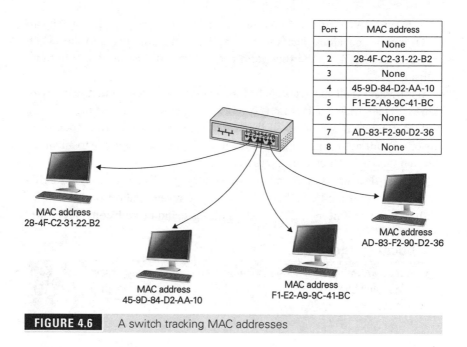

Port	MAC address
1	None
2	28-4F-C2-31-22-B2
3	None
4	45-9D-84-D2-AA-10
5	F1-E2-A9-9C-41-BC
6	None
7	AD-83-F2-90-D2-36
8	None

MAC address
28-4F-C2-31-22-B2

MAC address
AD-83-F2-90-D2-36

MAC address
45-9D-84-D2-AA-10

MAC address
F1-E2-A9-9C-41-BC

FIGURE 4.6   A switch tracking MAC addresses

on the same switch, the switch acts like a telephone operator, creating an on-the-fly connection between the two devices. While these two devices communicate, it's as though they are the only two computers on the network. Figure 4.7 shows this in action. Because the switch handles each conversation individually, each conversation runs at 1000 Mbps.

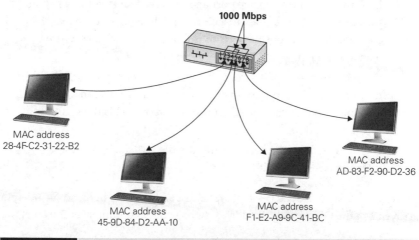

1000 Mbps

MAC address
28-4F-C2-31-22-B2

MAC address
AD-83-F2-90-D2-36

MAC address
45-9D-84-D2-AA-10

MAC address
F1-E2-A9-9C-41-BC

FIGURE 4.7   A switch making two separate connections

Each port on a switch is in its own collision domain, plus the switch can buffer incoming frames. That means that two nodes connected to the switch can send data at the same time, and the switch will handle it without any collision.

With legacy half-duplex switches, collisions can occur and the rules of CSMA/CD apply. These collisions can only happen between the switch and a node, not between two nodes. If the switch forwards a frame to a node from any other node at the same time that the node tries to send a frame to any node through the same switch port, that's a collision.

Network developers eventually figured out how to make switches and NICs run in full-duplex mode, so they could send and receive data at the same time. With full-duplex Ethernet, CSMA/CD is disabled and no collisions can occur.

Local Lingo

Layer-2 switch   Because a switch filters traffic on MAC addresses (and MAC addresses run at layer 2 of the OSI seven-layer model), they are called *layer-2 switches*.

Managed Switches

Managed switches have the extra programming and logic to handle switching, security, and many other functions. A managed switch, by definition, requires some configuration. You can connect to a managed switch to tell it what you want it to do. Exactly how you do this varies from switch to switch, but generally there are three ways:

- Directly plug into a console port and use a virtual terminal program such as PuTTY to connect to a command-line interface. It's very common to use a console port for initial configuration of a new managed switch.
- Get the switch on the network and then use Secure Shell (SSH) to connect to the same command-line interface. This can also be done with the insecure telnet protocol, but SSH is the secure recommendation.
- Get the switch on the network and use the switch's built-in web interface (see Figure 4.8).

Wait! It's a switch. Switches that we've discussed in the book so far operate at layer 2 of the OSI model. IP addresses don't show up until layer 3. Here's the

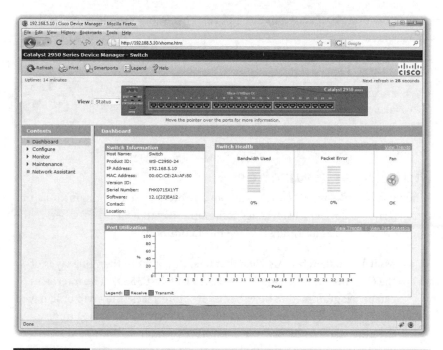

FIGURE 4.8   A web browser interface to a managed switch

scoop in a nutshell: a managed switch needs an IP address to enable configuration on layer 3. This means a new, out-of-the-box managed switch has all the same configuration issues a new router would have. It needs an IP address, subnet mask, default gateway, user name, and password. Armed with the IP address of the switch, configure your client or client software to connect to the managed switch. However, unlike a router, the IP address, subnet mask, default gateway, and other TCP/IP settings are for the switch itself and not individual ports.

Like any IP device, a managed switch needs good, basic maintenance. One example would be updating the firmware. Many managed switches support firmware updates over the Internet. As you might imagine, it would be scary to let unauthorized people have access to your switch management configuration. In the preceding examples, where you configure the switch over the network (in-band management), anyone who knows the IP addresses of your managed devices will be able to access them if they can get past the user name and password. To reduce exposure, it's common to dedicate one port on every managed device as a *management port*. You can do *interface configuration* only by directly connecting to that port. Then, you can plug that dedicated port into a switch that's totally separate from the rest of the network, which will prevent unauthorized access to those ports. This is an example of out-of-band management.

Exam Tip
A managed switch enables you to configure every port on the switch in a lot of different ways. For example, it's easy to set the speed and duplexing of a port to match the client.

Multilayer Switches

When you hear the word "switch" without any prefix, you can assume it's a traditional layer-2 device. However, it's common today to hear prefixes before the word "switch." Here's a rundown of the most common:

- **Multilayer switch**   A switch that operates at more than one layer of the OSI model (for example, the Cisco Catalyst 3560). The interfaces can be programmed to be either layer-2 interfaces (they will only have MAC addresses), acting like traditional switch ports that examine the Ethernet frames, or layer-3 interfaces (and have both MAC and IP addresses), acting exactly like router ports that examine the IP packets encapsulated in the Ethernet frames. Furthermore, there can be a switched virtual interface (SVI), which represents an IP address that is not tied to any physical port on the device, but can serve as the default gateway (more on that coming up later in this chapter) for PCs connected to that multilayer switch.

- **Layer-3 switch**   A router that does in hardware what a traditional router does in software, which is much quicker. A layer-3 switch, by definition, is a multilayer switch.

- **Layer-4 switch**   A switch that can load balance, by sending traffic to one of many servers that perform the same function and are replicated. This way, the load on servers is distributed, and the efficiency of the network goes up.

- **Layer-7 switch**   A switch that can read application information at layer 7 (HTTP, FTP, and so on), and make decisions based on that.

- **Layer 4–7 switch**   A switch that can load balance between multiple servers and examine Application-layer data.

- **Content switch (content filter network appliance)**   Same as a layer-7 switch.

Spanning Tree Protocol

Because you can connect switches together in any fashion, you can create redundant connections in a network. These are called *bridging loops* or *switching loops* (see Figure 4.9). An unknown unicast sent into Switch A from a PC will be flooded to both Switch 2 and Switch 3. If neither of those switches knows about the destination MAC address either, Switch 2 will forward its copy to Switch 3, and Switch 3 will forward its copy to Switch 2. Then, because the destination MAC address is still unknown, both Switch 2 and Switch 3 will send their frames back to Switch 1, and the process will repeat again (and again and again), until the traffic brings down the switch altogether!

Exam Tip
The CompTIA Network+ exam refers to bridging loops as switching loops, so we will use the term *switching loop* from this point forward. Be prepared for either term on the exam, though.

The Ethernet standards body adopted the *Spanning Tree Protocol (STP)* to eliminate the problem of accidental switching loops. Switches have STP enabled by default. This allows them to detect potential loops before they happen, communicate with other switches, and take preventative measures to make sure that frames are never looped around.

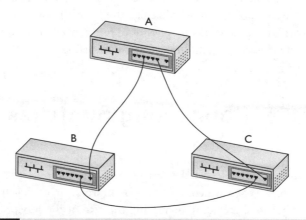

FIGURE 4.9   A switching loop

STP-enabled switches use a frame called a *Bridge Protocol Data Unit (BPDU)* to communicate with each other to determine things such as the distances between them and to keep track of changes and potential loops on the network.

Travel Advisory

Switches today all have STP enabled, and network designers create switching loops in their networks to provide fault tolerance. Ports set as blocking still listen to the BPDUs on the network. If a link fails, the blocking port can become a forwarding port, thus enabling traffic to flow properly.

Administrators can manually change STP settings for specific ports on managed switches. A switch port directly connected to a port on a busy server, for example, could be set as *portfast*—meaning it always forwards traffic. Likewise, an administrator could apply BPDU filtering to the port so it doesn't send or receive BPDU traffic. The original Spanning Tree Protocol, introduced as IEEE 802.1D, was replaced a long time ago (2001) by the Rapid Spanning Tree Protocol (RSTP), 802.1w. RSTP offers significantly faster convergence time following some kind of network change. STP could take up to 50 seconds to get back to a steady state, for example, whereas an RSTP network could return to convergence in 6 seconds.

As a possible replacement to any form of STP, Shortest Path Bridging (SPB) is a routing metric standard that provides true shortest-path forwarding within an Ethernet mesh topology. Standardized by the IEEE 802.1aq committee, SPB supports large layer-2 networks by providing fast convergence and improved usage of mesh networks with multiple, equal-cost paths.

Objective 4.03 Connecting Switches

Combining two or more switches is a common and important function on any network. When we connect two or more switches together, we get a number of benefits, including increasing the size of the broadcast domain (allowing more nodes to connect) and allowing a larger physical distance between nodes on a network. There are a couple of ways of doing this. The first is through an uplink port on one switch and a regular port on a second, using a straight-through cable between two switches. The second is to use a crossover cable between two regular switch ports.

Uplink Ports

Uplink ports enable you to connect two switches using a *straight-through cable*. They're always clearly marked on the switch, as shown in Figure 4.10. To connect two switches, insert one end of a cable to the uplink on one switch and the other end of the cable to any one of the regular ports on the other switch. To connect more than two switches, you must daisy-chain your switches by using one uplink port and one regular port. Figure 4.11 shows properly daisy-chained switches.

Working with uplink ports is sometimes tricky, so you need to take your time. Switch makers give their uplink ports many different names, such as crossover, MDI-X, and OUT. There are also tricks to using uplink ports. See the line connecting the uplink port and the port labeled 2X in Figure 4.10? You may use only one of those two ports, not both at the same time. Additionally, some switches place a button on one of the ports; you press this button to make it either a regular port or an uplink port (see Figure 4.12). Pressing the button electronically reverses the wires inside the switch.

FIGURE 4.10   Typical uplink port

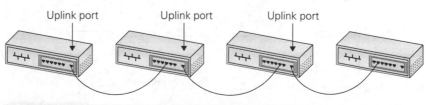

FIGURE 4.11   Daisy-chained switches

FIGURE 4.12   Pressing the Normal/Uplink button toggles the port between regular and uplink

---

Travel Advisory

A *media-dependent interface (MDI)* is a regular port on a switch. A *media-dependent interface crossover (MDI-X)* is an uplink port. Nowadays, newer switch ports have a feature called Auto MDI-X that is able to sense what cable is needed and then fix any mistakes a human might have made, by changing MDI to MDI-X, or vice versa. However, it's always best to use the "right" cable and not to rely on this Auto MDI-X feature. If you assume Auto MDI-X is present on a switch, and it's not, your reputation could be at stake!

Crossover Cables

Switches can also connect to each other via special twisted-pair cables called *crossover cables*. A standard cable cannot be used to connect two switches without using an uplink port because both switches will attempt to send data on the second pair of wires (3 and 6) and will listen for data on the first pair (1 and 2). A crossover cable reverses the sending and receiving pairs on one end of the cable. One end of the cable is wired according to the T568A standard, whereas the other end is wired according to the T568B standard (see Figure 4.13). With the sending and receiving pairs reversed, the switches can communicate; hence, the need for two wiring standards.

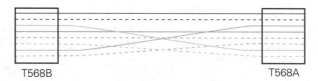

T568B   T568A

FIGURE 4.13   A crossover cable reverses the sending and receiving pairs.

A crossover cable connects to a regular port on each switch. Keep in mind that you can still daisy-chain, even when you use crossover cables.

In a pinch, you can use a crossover cable to connect two computers together through their NICs, with no switch between them at all. This is handy for quickie connections, such as for a nice little home network or when you absolutely, positively must chase down a friend in a computer game!

Be careful about confusing crossover cables with uplink ports. First, never connect two switches by their uplink ports with a straight-through cable. This creates two crossings, and you always need an odd amount of crossings for this to work. Take a straight-through cable and connect one end to the uplink port on one switch and the other end to any regular port on the other switch. Second, if you use a crossover cable, just plug each end into any handy regular port on each switch.

Travel Advisory

Crossing Crossovers If you mess up your crossover connections, you won't cause any damage, but the connection will not work. Think about it. If you take a straight-through cable and try to connect two PCs directly, it won't work. Both PCs will try to use the same send and receive wires. When you plug the two PCs into a switch, the switch electronically crosses the data wires, so one NIC sends and the other can receive. If you plug a second switch to the first switch using regular ports, you essentially cross the cross and create a straight connection again between the two PCs! That won't work. Luckily, nothing gets hurt—except your reputation if one of your colleagues notes your mistake!

Port Bonding

There are times when the data capacity of a connection between a switch and another device isn't enough to meet demand. Situations like these are encountered regularly in large data centers where tremendous amounts of data must be moved between racks of storage devices to vast numbers of users. Sometimes the solution is simple, such as changing from a low-capacity standard like 100-megabit Ethernet to Gigabit Ethernet.

But there are other ways to achieve high-speed links between devices without having to upgrade the infrastructure. One of those ways is to join two or more connections' ports logically in a switch so that the resulting bandwidth is treated as a single connection and the throughput is multiplied by the number of linked connectors. All of the cables from the joined ports must go to the same device— often another switch. That device must also support the logical joining of all of the involved ports. In CompTIA terms, this is called *port bonding*. The IEEE specification of port bonding is called *Link Aggregation Control Protocol (LACP)*.

Objective 4.04   Routers

Routers connect networks together. They filter and forward traffic relying on layer-3 addresses to get that traffic to the proper network. Because of the more sophisticated addressing schemes used by routers, they can support multiple routes between networks. The networks connected by the routers can be different types of networks (for example, Ethernet, wireless, and DOCSIS).

Local Lingo

DOCSIS   Cable companies use a network standard called DOCSIS (Data Over Cable Service Interface Specification) to enable communication via coax and cable modems. You'll learn more about this in Chapter 8.

Router technology holds the Internet together, providing multiple pathways between the hundreds of thousands of networks that make up the entire system (see Figure 4.14). Most routers, however, see much more humble service, linking networks or sites to form a wide area network (WAN).

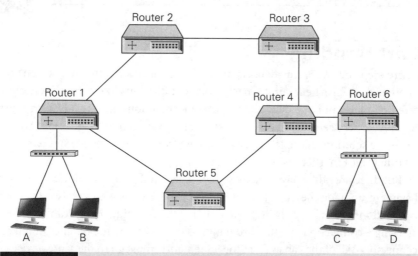

FIGURE 4.14   A network with multiple routers

Exam Tip

Routers operate at layer 3 of the OSI model, also known as the Network layer.

Routers rely on layer-3 addressing, also called *network addressing*. A network address tells the router two pieces of information: the specific machine to which a packet should be delivered, and the network on which that machine resides. The IP addresses used on the Internet are examples of network addresses (see Chapter 5 for a discussion of IP addressing).

Given the destination network address, a properly configured router can determine the best route to the destination machine. In Figure 4.14, Router 1 needs to deliver a packet from Machine A to Machine D. Assuming that all the links between the routers operate at the same speed, the most efficient route for the packet should be Router 1 to 5 to 4 to 6. That route requires four hops. A *hop* is the process of passing through a router en route to the final destination. Alternative routes exist, but the router ignores them because they require more hops. In the event of a break in the link between Routers 1 and 5, Router 1 should automatically calculate the next-best route (if one exists) and redirect traffic to the alternative route: Router 1 to 2 to 3 to 4 to 6 (see Figure 4.15).

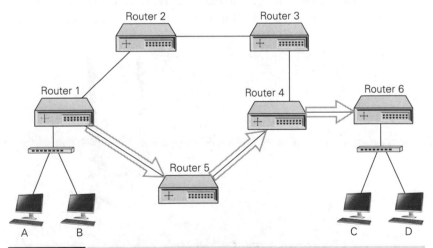

FIGURE 4.15 Properly configured routers choose the best route.

Travel Assistance

You'll find more discussion on routers and routing in Chapter 6.
For instance, there are times when more hops to a destination are
preferred over a path that has fewer hops. I can't do these topics
justice here, before giving you details about addressing in a TCP/IP
network, which you'll get in Chapter 5.

Objective 4.05 # Wireless Access Points

A wireless access point (WAP) enables nodes with Wi-Fi NICs to connect into a LAN using radio waves. WAPs support one or more 802.11 standards and nodes that use those standards. Many WAPs support multiple standards, thus enabling a variety of Wi-Fi devices to connect and network. The newest wireless standard, 802.11ac, for example, can support devices running all previous standards, including 802.11n, 802.11g, 802.11b, and 802.11a.

WAPs provide a connection between wired and wireless networks. Wired nodes can communicate seamlessly with wireless nodes, and vice versa.

WAPs designed for small office/home office (SOHO) environments generally come as part of a much larger bundle of hardware, usually called a "router," although routing is but one of the functions. The Linksys box in Figure 4.16,

FIGURE 4.16   Linksys WAP, router, and switch, all-in-one box

for example, is a combination WAP, router, and four-port switch, plus it offers excellent security features through its firmware.

CHECKPOINT

✔**Objective 4.01: Network Interfaces** A network interface card gets you on the network, but it must be the right fit for your computer system or whatever you're plugging it into. You must also make sure that it has the right connectors for the network media and that it supports the right network standard and speeds—for example, 100/1000 Mbps Ethernet. One very important task performed by a NIC is to give your computer system a unique address in the network; this is known as the *media access control (MAC)* address. This address is unique on every NIC produced, but the top 24 bits of the MAC always represent the NIC manufacturer.

✔**Objective 4.02: Switched Ethernet** Switches are layer-2 devices that filter traffic by sending the data only to the port that has the destination MAC address connected to it. This increases overall network performance and adds to the security of the network. Managed switches can be configured with many different settings and options. Multilayer switches can function at more than one layer of the OSI model, and function partially as routers at layer 3, load distributors at layer 4, and content filters at layer 7.

✔**Objective 4.03: Connecting Switches** You can combine multiple switches in two ways: via an uplink port or a crossover cable. To connect two switches, insert one end of a straight-through cable to the uplink and the other end of the cable to any one of the regular ports on the other switch. The CompTIA Network+ name for an uplink port is MDI-X. To connect using a crossover cable, plug the ends of the cable into regular ports on each switch.

✔**Objective 4.04: Routers** Routers, unlike switches, connect networks, not nodes of the same network. They also support multiple paths between networks and can link together dissimilar network types, such as Ethernet and DOCSIS. Routers are used for wide area networking, providing interconnectivity between networked sites. Routers never forward broadcast traffic.

✔**Objective 4.05: Wireless Access Points** Wireless access points are ubiquitous network devices that allow a wireless client to connect to a wired network. Today's WAPs also offer a number of capabilities such as routing and switching.

REVIEW QUESTIONS

1. What is the minimum size of an Ethernet frame?
   A. 8 bytes
   B. 64 bytes
   C. 128 bytes
   D. 256 bytes

2. Which part of the frame contains information used for checking the validity of the frame?
   A. FCS
   B. Pad
   C. Preamble
   D. Type

3. Which device enables you to connect two networks, and discards broadcast traffic?
   A. Bridge
   B. Hub
   C. Switch
   D. Router

4. At which layer of the OSI model do traditional switches work?
   A. Layer 1
   B. Layer 2
   C. Layer 3
   D. Layer 4

5. At which layer of the OSI model don't multilayer switches work?
   A. Layer 1
   B. Layer 2
   C. Layer 3
   D. Layer 4

6. Which protocol resolves switching loops?
   A. FTP
   B. STP
   C. Ethernet
   D. SAT

7. At which layer of the OSI model do routers work?

    A. Layer 1

    B. Layer 2

    C. Layer 3

    D. Layer 4

8. How are the connectors wired on a crossover cable?

    A. One end is T568A; the other end is T568B.

    B. Both ends are T568A.

    C. Both ends are T568B.

    D. One end is an RJ45; the other end is an RG-6.

9. What feature of switches prevents the problem of switching loops?

    A. STP

    B. TCP/IP

    C. IEEE 802.3

    D. UTP

10. What feature of switches keeps track of which MAC address goes to each port?

    A. FCS

    B. SAT

    C. STP

    D. UTP

REVIEW ANSWERS

1. **B**   The minimum size of an Ethernet frame is 64 bytes.

2. **A**   The frame check sequence (FCS) contains error-checking information.

3. **D**   Routers connect networks, and discard broadcast traffic.

4. **B**   Switches work at layer 2, the Data Link layer, because they manage traffic using MAC addresses.

5. **A**   Multilayer switches can operate at any layer above layer 1.

6. **B**   Spanning Tree Protocol (STP) prevents switching loops from forming.

7. **C**   Routers work at layer 3, connecting different networks together.

8. **A**   A properly wired crossover cable is T568A on one end and T568B on the other. All T568A or all T568B defines a straight-through cable. RJ45 is for UTP; RG-6 is for coaxial. You wouldn't find them on the same cable.

9. **A**   Spanning Tree Protocol (STP) prevents switching loops. STP also stands for shielded twisted-pair; knowing the context in which the acronym is being used is important.

10. **B**   A switch keeps track of which MAC address goes to each port with its source address table (SAT).

TCP/IP

	NEWBIE	SOME EXPERIENCE	EXPERT
ETA	6 hours	3 hours	2 hours

In 1973, the U.S. Defense Advanced Research Projects Agency (DARPA) first proposed TCP/IP as a standard for connecting various existing networks so that they could exchange information. One aim was to develop a common standard to replace the growing number of proprietary and incompatible networks that were emerging. The work undertaken as part of the DARPA project eventually led to the development of the TCP/IP protocol suite and the Internet as we know it today. In the early days of networking, many protocols competed for market share. Microsoft networks used NetBIOS/NetBEUI, for example, and NetWare networks used IPX/SPX. Today, everybody uses TCP/IP.

 The TCP/IP Protocol Suite

TCP/IP is made up of a number of protocols that work together to make it the most popular protocol in networking today. Each protocol in the *TCP/IP protocol suite* performs a specific role. This section identifies some of the popular ones.

Application Protocols

Application-level protocols are responsible for initiating some sort of request (on the client) or answering that request (on the server). When you surf the Internet, for example, you use an application (a web browser) that sends a request to a web server for a specific page. This communication happens across TCP/IP using an Application-layer protocol known as *Hypertext Transfer Protocol (HTTP)*.

Port Numbers

A TCP/IP client computer initiates contact with a server computer and uses specific values, called *port numbers,* to request a particular kind of service. Servers listen on ports that correspond to the services they offer. A web browser, for example, contacts a web server at the destination port number 80; the web server listens to port 80 so it knows that the client wants a web page.

The use of port numbers enables servers to provide more than one type of service. One of the servers in my office, for example, handles internal web pages for essential company policies. It also acts as a file server and a print server. Finally, it handles our lunchtime gaming needs by running as a *Counter-Strike* or *League of Legends* server. Clients request each of these different services using different port numbers.

Clearly defined port numbers exist for every popular (or *well-known*) TCP/IP application. A port number is a 16-bit value between 0 and 65535. Port numbers from 0 to 1023 are called *well-known port numbers* and are reserved for specific TCP/IP applications. (No TCP or UDP application can use the reserved port 0.)

Exam Tip

The CompTIA Network+ objectives view web-based e-mail as one of many web services. Web services also include applications that you access on the Internet, such as Google Docs and Google Sheets (online word processing and spreadsheet programs, respectively). The major contrast between web services and local services involves access. Web services offer access from any machine, as long as that machine is connected to the Internet. Local applications, such as accessing a folder on another system, usually require local access, but don't need any other connectivity.

Destination and Source Port Numbers   The client uses a *destination port number* to request a service. To communicate back and establish a session with the client, the server uses a port number specified by the client. The web client, in essence, says, "Hey, server! I'm requesting on port 80. You can reach me through my port 50002." In this example, port 50002 is the *source port number*. Port numbers that devices allocate on the fly for a source port number are also called *ephemeral ports*.

Registered and Dynamic Port Numbers   The port numbers from 1024 to 49151 are called *registered ports*. Less-common TCP/IP applications can register their ports with the Internet Assigned Numbers Authority (IANA). Unlike well-known ports, these port numbers can be used by anyone for their servers or for ephemeral numbers on clients. Most operating systems steer away (or are in the process of steering away) from using these port numbers for ephemeral ports, opting instead for the dynamic/private port numbers. Here's the full list of ports:

0–1023	Well-known port numbers
1024–49151	Registered ports
49152–65535	Dynamic or private ports

Sockets

Each computer on each side of a session must keep track of the status of the communication. In TCP/IP, the session information (a combination of the IP address and port number) stored in RAM is called a *socket* or *endpoint*. When discussing the information each computer stores about the connection between two computers' TCP/IP applications, we use the term *socket pairs* or *endpoints*. A *session* or *connection* refers to the connection in general, rather than anything specific to TCP/IP. Many people still use the term *session,* however. Here's a summary of the terms used:

- The term used for the connection information stored on a single computer is *socket* or *endpoint.*

- The term used for the connection information stored on two computers about the same connection is *socket pairs* or *endpoints.*

- The term used for the whole interconnection is *connection* or *session.* As two computers begin to communicate, they store the information about the session—the endpoints—so they know where to send and receive data. At any given point in time, your computer probably has a large number of communications going on. If you want to know who your computer is communicating with, you need to see this list of endpoints. Windows, Linux, and Mac OS X come with *netstat,* the universal "show me the endpoints" utility. The netstat utility works at the command line, so open one up and type **netstat –n** to see something like this:

```
C:\>netstat -n
Active Connections
Proto Local Address Foreign Address State
TCP 192.168.4.27:57913 209.29.33.25:80 ESTABLISHED
TCP 192.168.4.27:61707 192.168.4.10:21 ESTABLISHED
C:\>
```

Travel Advisory

Even though almost all operating systems use netstat, there are subtle differences in options and output among the different versions.

When you run netstat –n on a typical computer, you'll see many more than just two connections! The preceding example is simplified for the purposes of discussing the details. It shows two connections: My computer's IP address is 192.168.4.27. The top connection is a connection to a web server (port 80) at 209.29.33.25. The second connection is to a file transfer protocol (FTP) server (port 21) at 192.168.4.10.

Both connections require open ports on my computer. These show up under the Local Address column. Ephemeral port 57913 is open for the web browser; port 61707 is open for the FTP client.

List of Application Protocols

Here are some examples of popular Application-layer protocols and the port number(s) they use by default. And, yes, you need to memorize the port numbers for the CompTIA Network+ exam.

Application-Layer Protocol	Ports	Transport Protocol	Description
FTP	20 (rarely used today) and 21	TCP	*File Transfer Protocol* transfers files between clients and servers. It originally used two ports: 21 for control messages and 20 for the actual data. Only port 21 is in common use today. The server now opens a dynamic port for the data transfer, instead of using port 20, as was the case in the past. User names, passwords, and data are sent in clear text, posing a potentially serious security risk.
Telnet	23	TCP	*Telnet* enables a user to log in remotely and execute commands on a remote host. It is often used to log into UNIX/Linux hosts and managed network devices such as routers and switches. Telnet sends user names, passwords, and data in clear text, thus posing a potentially serious security risk.
SSH	22	TCP	*Secure Shell*, a secure replacement for Telnet, encrypts both login information and data sent over the connection.
DNS	53	UDP and TCP	*Domain Name System* maps computer names to IP addresses. UDP is used for DNS queries and replies. TCP is used for DNS zone transfers.

(Continued)

Application-Layer Protocol	Ports	Transport Protocol	Description
DHCP	67, 68	UDP	*Dynamic Host Configuration Protocol* is used to assign IP addresses automatically to clients on the network. Servers use port 67, and clients use port 68.
TFTP	69	UDP	*Trivial File Transfer Protocol* transfers files between servers and clients without requiring any user login. It is most commonly used for downloading operating systems and configuration files to systems with no local hard disk (for example, diskless workstations and routers). User names, passwords, and data are sent in clear text, thus posing a potentially serious security risk. But it's even worse than that, because unlike FTP, there is no authentication at all!
HTTP	80	TCP	Web servers, such as Apache and Microsoft's IIS, use *Hypertext Transfer Protocol* to accept connections from and to send data to web browsers, such as Google Chrome and Mozilla Firefox.
HTTPS	443	TCP	HTTPS is not really a protocol, but rather HTTP using SSL/TLS for authentication and encryption.
SMTP	25	TCP	*Simple Mail Transfer Protocol* sends e-mail messages between mail servers. Mail clients also use SMTP to send outgoing e-mail to a mail server.
POP3	110	TCP	E-mail clients (such as Microsoft Outlook) use *Post Office Protocol version 3* to retrieve e-mail from mail servers.
IMAP4	143	TCP	E-mail clients use *Internet Message Access Protocol version 4* to access e-mail messages while leaving the messages themselves stored on the server.

Application-Layer Protocol	Ports	Transport Protocol	Description
NetBIOS	137, 138, 139	TCP	Used to support functions such as Microsoft File and Print Sharing over TCP/IP networks.
SMB	445	TCP	When NetBIOS support is disabled, Microsoft File and Print Sharing uses port 445.
SNMP	161	UDP	*Simple Network Management Protocol* enables network management applications to monitor network devices remotely.
RDP	3389	TCP	Microsoft's *Remote Desktop Protocol* allows users to see the GUI of another computer as if they were sitting in front of it.
RTP	5004, 5005	UDP	*Real-time Transport Protocol* delivers audio and video, and compensates for jitter and UDP datagrams that arrive out of sequence. RTP requires much less overhead than if TCP was being used instead.
SIP	5060 (clear text), 5061 (encrypted)	TCP/UDP	*Session Initiation Protocol* handles the initiation, setup, and delivery of VoIP sessions. SIP is an alternative to H.323.
H.323	1720	TCP	Handles the initiation, setup, and delivery of VoIP sessions. H.323 is an alternative to SIP.
MGCP	2427, 2727	TCP	*Media Gateway Control Protocol* is designed from the ground up to be a complete VoIP or video presentation connection and session controller; in essence, it takes over all the work from VoIP the SIP protocol used to do and all the work from video presentation done by H.323.

Compound Application Protocols

Some common Application-layer protocols use multiple protocols to accomplish their tasks. HTTPS and VoIP provide good examples.

HTTP over Secure Sockets Layer (SSL) provides an encrypted connection between a web server and a web client. Most web browsers display a closed padlock to indicate a secure connection. HTTPS provides the basic fabric for e-commerce on the Internet. Although the protocol name still refers to SSL, current HTTPS implementations use *Transport Layer Security (TLS)*, an improved cryptographic protocol. HTTPS uses TCP port 443.

Exam Tip	
TLS is up to version 1.2 as of this writing.	

Voice over IP (VoIP) enables users to make phone calls over an IP network, such as the Internet. The user uses special VoIP boxes that support telephones that connect to the IP network instead of the user being required to use a PC. VoIP uses a number of different protocols, two of which you must know for the CompTIA Network+ exam. The *Session Initiation Protocol (SIP)* establishes and takes down the communication channel for VoIP. The *Real-time Transport Protocol (RTP)* delivers the voice across the connection after it has been established.

SIP uses either TCP or UDP ports 5060 and/or 5061. RTP has no fixed port number, though many implementations use UDP ports 5004 and 5005.

Transport Protocols

When an application sends out a request, the request needs to be specified as either a connection-oriented request or a connectionless request, as you'll recall from Chapter 1. Two protocols handle the Transport-layer traffic in TCP/IP networks: TCP and UDP.

TCP

The *Transmission Control Protocol (TCP)* enables connection-oriented communication in networks that use the TCP/IP protocol suite. Figure 5.1 shows two computers. One computer (Server) runs a web server and the other (Client) runs a web browser. When you enter a computer's address in the browser

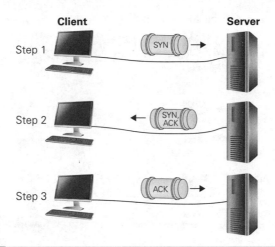

FIGURE 5.1   A connection-oriented session starting

running on Client, it sends a segment with the SYN (synchronize) flag acti-
vated to the web server. If Server gets that segment, it returns a segment with
SYN, ACK (synchronize, acknowledge) flags active. Client then sends Server a
single segment with an active ACK flag. This process is called the *TCP three-
way handshake.*

Client then immediately requests that Server begin sending the web page.
Once Server finishes sending the web page, it sends a FIN (final) segment. Client responds with an ACK (acknowledge) segment and then sends its own FIN
segment. The server then responds with an ACK; now both parties consider
the session closed. Each FIN is accompanied by an ACK to tie the segments to
previous ones, but these ACKs have nothing to do with this teardown process
(see Figure 5.2).

Most TCP/IP applications use TCP, because connection-oriented sessions
are designed to check for errors. If a receiving computer detects a missing segment, it just asks for a repeat as needed.

Figure 5.3 shows a simplified TCP header. Notice the source port and the
destination port, part of the TCP segment encapsulated in the IP packet.

Ports aren't the only items of interest in the TCP header. The header also
contains these fields:

- **Sequence number**   This value is used to assemble/disassemble data.
- **Acknowledgment Number**   This value indicates what data was
  successfully received, as well as the next expected sequence number.

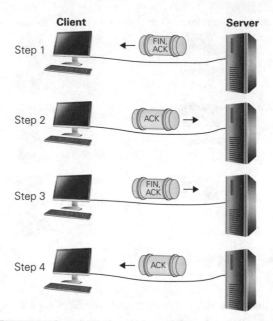

FIGURE 5.2 A connection-oriented session ending

FIGURE 5.3 Simplified TCP header

- **Flags** These individual bits give both sides detailed information about the state of the connection.
- **Checksum** The checksum functions like the FCS field in Ethernet frames. If the value doesn't match the computed value on the other side of the connection, the segment is discarded.

UDP

Even though *User Datagram Protocol (UDP)* runs a distant second to TCP in terms of the number of applications that use it, that doesn't mean UDP is not important. UDP is perfect for the types of sessions that don't require the overhead of all that connection-oriented stuff. Two of the most important networking protocols—DNS and DHCP—rely on UDP, as well as Voice over Internet Protocol (VoIP).

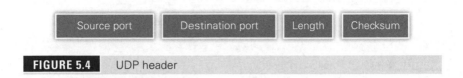

| Source port | Destination port | Length | Checksum |

FIGURE 5.4 UDP header

Exam Tip

Be sure that you know the difference between TCP and UDP when preparing for the CompTIA Network+ exam.

A UDP *datagram* doesn't possess any of the extras you see in TCP to make sure the data is received intact (see Figure 5.4). UDP works best when you have a lot of data that doesn't need to be perfect or when the systems are so close to each other that the chances of a problem occurring are too small to bother worrying about. A few dropped datagrams on a Voice over IP call, for example, won't make much difference in the communication between two people. So there's a good reason to use UDP: it's smoking fast compared to TCP.

Exam Tip

Protocol data units (PDUs) at layer 4 are called *segments* if TCP is used, and *datagrams* if UDP is used.

Internet Protocols

Internet-layer protocols handle addressing in a TCP/IP network. They help devices determine whether an intended recipient is local or remote.

Internet Protocol (IP)

The *Internet Protocol (IP)* is responsible for the addressing and routing of data to the remote system. *Addressing* means that IP is responsible for some sort of addressing scheme used to identify each system on the network (or Internet) and for determining how to use that address to route the data to the destination. The addressing scheme that IP uses is known as an *IP address*.

FIGURE 5.5   Simplified IP header

The IP address is a unique number assigned to your system that looks something like this: 192.168.1.10.

The full IP packet has 14 different fields. As you would expect, the destination and source IP addresses are part of the Network/Internet layer. Other fields include version, header length, and more. Dissecting the entire set of fields isn't important, but here are a few descriptions just to whet your appetite:

- **Version**   The version field defines the IP address type: 4 for IPv4, 6 for IPv6.
- **Header Length**   The total size of the IP portion of the packet in words (of size 32 bits) is displayed in the header length field.
- **Differentiated Services**   The DS field contains data used for prioritization by bandwidth-sensitive applications such as Voice over IP. (Network techs with long memories will note that this field used to be called the *Type of Service* field.)
- **Time to Live**   Routers on the Internet are not perfect and sometimes create loops. The Time to Live (TTL) field prevents an IP packet from indefinitely spinning through the Internet by using a counter that decrements by one every time a packet goes through a router. This number cannot start higher than 255. The packet is never forwarded again, once the TTL decrements to zero.
- **Protocol**   This field specifies what's encapsulated in the IP packet. In the vast majority of cases, the protocol field is either TCP, UDP, or ICMP (covered in the next section).

Figure 5.5 shows a highly simplified IP header.

An entire section is devoted to IP addressing later in this chapter, so I will leave the rest of our discussion on IP for that section.

Internet Control Message Protocol (ICMP)

Internet Control Message Protocol (ICMP) works at layer 3 to deliver informational and error messages. ICMP handles mundane issues such as disconnect messages (destination unreachable) that applications use to let the other side of a session know what's happening.

ICMP features are called automatically by applications as needed without you ever knowing. There is one very famous program that runs under ICMP, however: the venerable *ping* utility. Run ping from a command prompt to query if a host is reachable. Ping will show the *round trip time (RTT)* for the ICMP packet (in milliseconds). If ping can't find the host, the packet will time out, and ping will show you that information as well.

 **Objective 5.02** **IPv4 Addressing**

TCP/IP networks have long used the *Internet Protocol version 4 (IPv4)* protocol for addressing. (See "IPv6 Addressing" later in this chapter for a discussion about the protocol poised to replace IPv4.)

IPv4 addresses originally followed rigid blocks called *classes*. Today's IPv4 addresses don't use classes, but are doled out under a different set of rules. Let's look at classic IPv4 addressing first, and then turn to modern IPv4 usage.

> ### Local Lingo
>
> **IPv4** Most writers drop the version number when discussing IP addressing. The assumption is that if there's no version number listed, it must be IPv4.

When installing TCP/IP on a system, techs need to configure three settings:

- **IP address** A unique value that represents a node on a TCP/IP network.
- **Subnet mask** A value used to help devices distinguish the host's network.
- **Default gateway** The IP address of the router interface for the network. The router is responsible for sending data off the network if needed.

IP Addresses

The most common type of IP address consists of a 32-bit value. Here's an example:

11000000101010000000010000000010

Whoa! IP addresses are just strings of 32 binary digits? Yes, they are, but to make IP addresses easier for humans to use, the 32-bit binary value is broken down into four groups of eight, separated by periods (or *dots*), like this:

11000000.10101000.00000100.00000010

Each of these 8-bit values—called an *octet*—is, in turn, converted into a decimal number between 0 and 255.

If you took every possible combination of eight binary values and placed them in a spreadsheet, it would look something like the list in the left column. The right column shows the same list with a decimal value assigned to each.

Binary Value	Equivalent Decimal Value
00000000	0
00000001	1
00000010	2
00000011	3
00000100	4
00000101	5
00000110	6
00000111	7
00001000	8
(skip a bunch in the middle)	*(skip a bunch in the middle)*
11111000	248
11111001	249
11111010	250
11111011	251
11111100	252
11111101	253
11111110	254
11111111	255

Converted, the original value of 11000000.10101000.00000100.00000010 is displayed as 192.168.4.2 in IPv4's *dotted decimal notation* (also referred to as the *dotted octet numbering system*). Note that dotted decimal is simply a shorthand way for people to discuss and configure the binary IP addresses computers use. When you type an IP address into a computer, the computer ignores the periods and immediately converts the decimal numbers into binary. People need dotted decimal notation, but computers do not.

Exam Tip

Binary, Decimal, and Octal Numbering   We know binary numbering at heart is a single digit that represents on or off, a 1 or a 0. Another term for this numbering is *base two*. How do you represent a 1 in binary? Well, "1" of course. But what's the next number? How do you display a 2? Add another column, just like in the preceding table: 10 equals the number 2 in binary. Base ten, or decimal numbering, is what humans use for the most part. We count from 0 to 9 and then add a second column, 10. So 10 equals the number 10 in decimal. Base eight, or octal numbering, counts from 0 to 7 with a single digit and then adds a column. So how would you display the number 8? Right, 10 equals the number 8 in octal. The only reason to use octal in computing is that it's easy to display all eight numbers using only three binary characters. Conveniently, really ancient computers (think IBM mainframes here) were 12-, 24-, or 36-bit systems, meaning their programming very easily divided into chunks of three. Why did CompTIA decide to add octal numbering to the objectives? We may never know. We do know, however, that "octal" is very much not the same as "octet." The latter refers to the groups of 8 bits in an IP address.

People who work on TCP/IP networks must know how to convert dotted decimal to binary and back. You can convert easily using any operating system's calculator. Every OS has a calculator (UNIX/Linux systems have about 100 different ones to choose from) that has a scientific or programmer mode like the one shown in Figure 5.6.

FIGURE 5.6   Mac OS X Calculator in Programmer mode

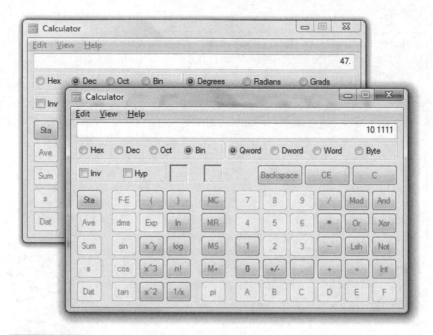

FIGURE 5.7   Converting decimal to binary with Windows 7's Calculator

To convert from decimal to binary, just go to decimal view, type in the value, and then switch to binary view to get the result. To convert to decimal, just go into binary view, enter the binary value, and switch to decimal view to get the result.

Figure 5.7 shows the result of Windows 7's Calculator converting the decimal value 47 into binary. Notice the result is 101111—the leading two zeroes do not appear. When you work with IP addresses, you must always have eight digits, so just add two more to the left to get 00101111.

Travel Advisory

Using a calculator utility to convert to and from binary/decimal is a critical skill for a network tech. Later on you'll do this again, but by hand!

Just as every MAC address must be unique on a network, every IP address must be unique as well. For logical addressing to work, no two computers on the same network may have the same IP address. On any network running TCP/IP, every device has both an IP address and a MAC address. Figure 5.8 illustrates a small network where each device has these two addresses.

Every GUI operating system comes with graphical and command-line utilities to display a system's IP address and MAC address. Figure 5.9 shows a Mac OS X system's Network utility. Note the MAC address (00:14:51:65:84:a1) and the IP address (192.168.4.57).

You can use the command-line utility *ipconfig* to display the IP and MAC addresses. Run **ipconfig /all** to see the results shown in Figure 5.10.

In UNIX/Linux/Mac OS X, you can run the very similar *ifconfig* command. Figure 5.11, for example, shows the result of running **ifconfig** ("eth0" is the NIC) in Ubuntu. Linux has actually deprecated ifconfig in favor of the more robust iproute2 utilities, but certain Linux distros still support ifconfig, and many people still use it.

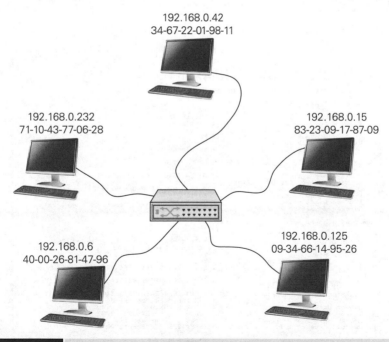

| **FIGURE 5.8** | A small network with both IP and MAC addresses |

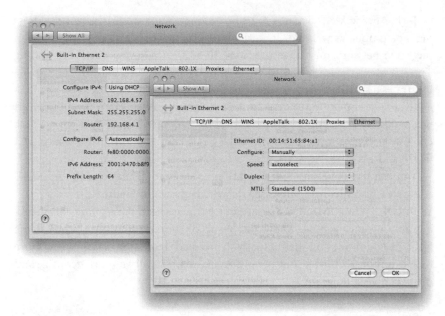

FIGURE 5.9 Mac OS X Network utility

```
Administrator: Command Prompt                                    _ □ X

Microsoft Windows [Version 6.0.6001]
Copyright (c) 2006 Microsoft Corporation.  All rights reserved.

C:\Users\scottj.TOTALHOME>ipconfig /all

Windows IP Configuration

    Host Name . . . . . . . . . . . . : scott-vista
    Primary Dns Suffix  . . . . . . . : totalhome
    Node Type . . . . . . . . . . . . : Hybrid
    IP Routing Enabled. . . . . . . . : No
    WINS Proxy Enabled. . . . . . . . : No
    DNS Suffix Search List. . . . . . : totalhome

Ethernet adapter Local Area Connection 2:

    Media State . . . . . . . . . . . : Media disconnected
    Connection-specific DNS Suffix  . :
    Description . . . . . . . . . . . : NUIDIA nForce Networking Controller #2
    Physical Address. . . . . . . . . : 00-15-F2-F4-AE-15
    DHCP Enabled. . . . . . . . . . . : Yes
    Autoconfiguration Enabled . . . . : Yes

Ethernet adapter Local Area Connection:

    Connection-specific DNS Suffix  . :
    Description . . . . . . . . . . . : NUIDIA nForce Networking Controller
    Physical Address. . . . . . . . . : 00-15-F2-F4-AE-14
    DHCP Enabled. . . . . . . . . . . : Yes
    Autoconfiguration Enabled . . . . : Yes
    IPv6 Address. . . . . . . . . . . : 2001:470:b8f9:1:1584:889a:269f:887(Deprec
ated)
    Temporary IPv6 Address. . . . . . : 2001:470:b8f9:1:4476:46b2:648c:ecdc(Depre
cated)
    Link-local IPv6 Address . . . . . : fe80::1584:889a:269f:887%8(Preferred)
    IPv4 Address. . . . . . . . . . . : 192.168.4.60(Preferred)
    Subnet Mask . . . . . . . . . . . : 255.255.255.0
    Lease Obtained. . . . . . . . . . : Monday, February 02, 2009 9:51:44 AM
    Lease Expires . . . . . . . . . . : Tuesday, February 10, 2009 9:51:13 AM
    Default Gateway . . . . . . . . . : fe80::223:4ff:fe8c:b720%8
                                        192.168.4.1
    DHCP Server . . . . . . . . . . . : 192.168.4.11
    DNS Servers . . . . . . . . . . . : 192.168.4.11
    NetBIOS over Tcpip. . . . . . . . : Enabled
```

FIGURE 5.10 The results from running ipconfig /all

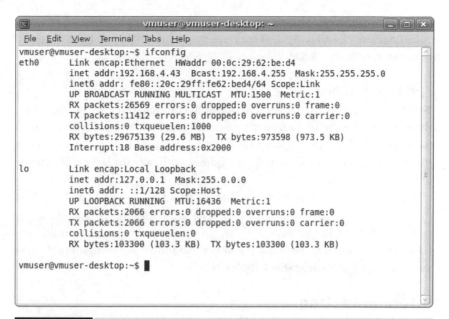

```
vmuser@vmuser-desktop: ~
File  Edit  View  Terminal  Tabs  Help
vmuser@vmuser-desktop:~$ ifconfig
eth0      Link encap:Ethernet  HWaddr 00:0c:29:62:be:d4
          inet addr:192.168.4.43  Bcast:192.168.4.255  Mask:255.255.255.0
          inet6 addr: fe80::20c:29ff:fe62:bed4/64 Scope:Link
          UP BROADCAST RUNNING MULTICAST  MTU:1500  Metric:1
          RX packets:26569 errors:0 dropped:0 overruns:0 frame:0
          TX packets:11412 errors:0 dropped:0 overruns:0 carrier:0
          collisions:0 txqueuelen:1000
          RX bytes:29675139 (29.6 MB)  TX bytes:973598 (973.5 KB)
          Interrupt:18 Base address:0x2000

lo        Link encap:Local Loopback
          inet addr:127.0.0.1  Mask:255.0.0.0
          inet6 addr: ::1/128 Scope:Host
          UP LOOPBACK RUNNING  MTU:16436  Metric:1
          RX packets:2066 errors:0 dropped:0 overruns:0 frame:0
          TX packets:2066 errors:0 dropped:0 overruns:0 carrier:0
          collisions:0 txqueuelen:0
          RX bytes:103300 (103.3 KB)  TX bytes:103300 (103.3 KB)

vmuser@vmuser-desktop:~$
```

FIGURE 5.11   Results from running ifconfig in Ubuntu

Exam Tip

Make sure you know that ipconfig and ifconfig provide a tremendous amount of information regarding a system's TCP/IP settings.

IP Addresses in Action

Both LANs and WANs use IP addresses. This can create problems in some circumstances, such as when a computer needs to send data both to computers in its own network and to computers in other networks. How can this be accomplished?

To make all this work, IP must do three things:

- Create some way to use IP addresses so that each LAN has its own identification.
- Interconnect all of the LANs using routers and give those routers some way to use the network identification to send packets to the right network.

- Give each computer on the network some way to recognize whether a packet is for the LAN or for a computer on the WAN so it knows how to handle the packet.

Network IDs

To differentiate LANs from one another, each computer on a single LAN must share a very similar IP address. Some parts of the IP address will match all the others on the LAN. Figure 5.12 shows a LAN where all of the computers share the first three numbers of the IP address, with only the last number being unique on each system.

In this example, every computer has an IP address of 202.120.10.*x*. That means the *network ID* is 202.120.10.0. The *x* part of the IP address is the *host ID*. Combine the network ID (after dropping the ending 0) with the host ID to get an individual system's IP address. No individual computer can have an IP address that matches the network ID.

Interconnecting

To organize all those individual LANs into a larger network, every TCP/IP LAN that wants to connect to another TCP/IP LAN must have a router connection.

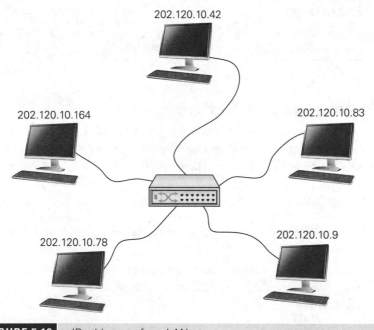

| FIGURE 5.12 | IP addresses for a LAN |

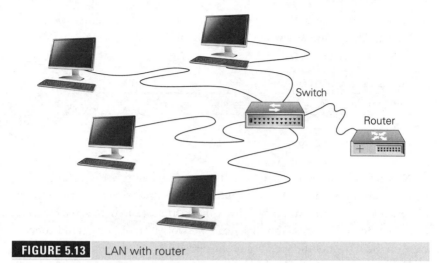

FIGURE 5.13   LAN with router

There is no exception to this critical rule. A router, therefore, needs separate IP addresses for its interfaces on all the LANs that it serves, as shown in Figure 5.13, so it can correctly route packets.

The router interface on a LAN is known as the *default gateway*. When configuring a client to access the network beyond the router, you use the IP address for the default gateway.

Routers use network IDs to determine network traffic. Figure 5.14 shows a diagram for a small, two-NIC router similar to the ones you see in many homes. Note that one port (202.120.10.1) connects to the LAN and the other port connects to the Internet service provider's network (14.23.54.223). Built into this

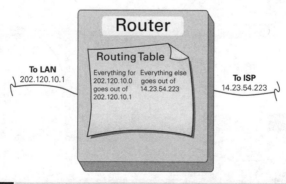

FIGURE 5.14   Router diagram

router is a *routing table,* the actual instructions that tell the router what to do with incoming packets and where to send them.

Travel Assistance

Routing tables are covered in more detail in Chapter 6.

Now let's add in the LAN and the Internet (see Figure 5.15). (The LAN, of course, connects via a switch to the router.) When discussing networks in terms of network IDs, by the way, especially with illustrations in books, the common practice is to draw circles around stylized networks. Here, you should concentrate on the IDs—not the specifics of the networks.

Network IDs are very flexible, as long as no two interconnected networks share the same network ID. If you wish, you could change the network ID of the 202.120.10.0 network to 202.155.5.0, or 202.21.8.0, just as long as you can guarantee no other LAN on the WAN shares the same network ID. On the Internet, powerful governing bodies carefully allocate network IDs to ensure no two LANs share the same network ID. I'll talk more about how this works later in the chapter.

So far you've only seen examples of network IDs where the last value is zero. This is common for small networks, but it creates a limitation. With a network ID of 202.120.10.0, for example, a network is limited to IP addresses from 202.120.10.1 to 202.120.10.254. (202.120.10.255 is a broadcast address used to talk to every computer on the LAN.) This provides only 254 IP addresses:

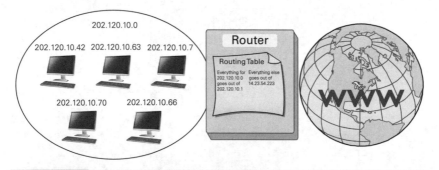

FIGURE 5.15   LAN, router, and the Internet

enough for a small network, but many organizations need many more IP addresses. No worries! You can simply use a network ID with more zeroes, such as 170.45.0.0, for a total of 65,534 theoretical hosts, or even 12.0.0.0, for around 16.7 million theoretical hosts. I say *theoretical* because, in reality, you'd never put more than 500–1000 hosts on a single network. These larger-sized networks allow you to break them up into multiple smaller networks (a concept known as *subnetting,* discussed later in this chapter) and still have a nice amount of hosts on each network.

Network IDs enable you to connect multiple LANs into a WAN. Routers then connect everything together, using routing tables to keep track of which packets go where. So that takes care of the second task: interconnecting the LANs using routers and giving those routers a way to send packets to the right network.

Now that you know how IP addressing works with LANs and WANs, let's turn to how IP enables each computer on a network to recognize if a packet is going to a computer on the LAN or to a computer on the WAN. The secret to this is something called the subnet mask.

Subnet Mask

Picture this scenario: Three friends sit at their computers—Computers A, B, and C—and want to communicate with each other. Figure 5.16 illustrates the situation. You can tell from the drawing that Computers A and B are in the same LAN, whereas Computer C is on a completely different LAN.

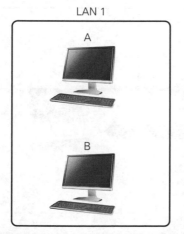

LAN 1   LAN 2

A

B

C

FIGURE 5.16   The three amigos, separated by walls or miles

The IP addressing scheme can handle this communication, so let's see how it works.

The process to get a packet to a local computer is very different from the process to get a packet to a faraway computer. If one computer wants to send a packet to a local computer, it must send a broadcast to get the other computer's MAC address. (It's easy to forget about the MAC address, but remember that the network uses Ethernet and *must* have the MAC address to get the frame that encapsulates the packet to the other computer.) If the packet is for some computer on a faraway network, the sending computer must send the packet to the default gateway (see Figure 5.17).

In the scenario illustrated in Figure 5.16, Computer A wants to send a packet to Computer B. Computer B is on the same LAN as Computer A, but that begs a question: how does Computer A know this? Every TCP/IP computer needs a tool to tell the sending computer whether the destination IP address is local or long distance. This tool is the subnet mask.

A *subnet mask* is nothing more than a string of ones followed by some number of zeroes, always totaling exactly 32 bits, typed into every TCP/IP host. Here's an example of a typical subnet mask:

11111111.11111111.11111111.00000000

Using a calculator, you can convert each octet into decimal:

255.255.255.0

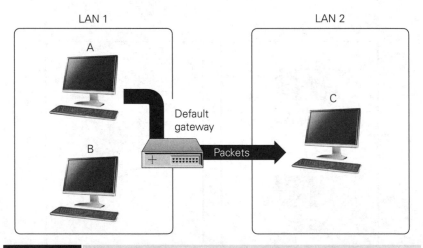

FIGURE 5.17   Sending a packet remotely

Exam Tip

At this point, you should memorize that 0 = 00000000 and 255 = 11111111. You'll find knowing this very helpful throughout the rest of the book.

When you line up an IP address with a corresponding subnet mask in binary, the portion of the IP address that aligns with the ones of the subnet mask is the network ID portion of the IP address. The portion that aligns with the zeroes is the host ID. With simple IP addresses, you can see this with dotted decimal, but you'll want to see this in binary for a true understanding of how the computers work.

The IP address 192.168.5.23 has a subnet mask of 255.255.255.0. Convert both numbers to binary and then compare the full IP address to the ones and zeroes of the subnet mask:

	Dotted Decimal	Binary
IP address	192.168.5.23	11000000.10101000.00000101.00010111
Subnet mask	255.255.255.0	11111111.11111111.11111111.00000000
Network ID	192.168.5.0	11000000.10101000.00000101.x
Host ID	$x.x.x.23$	$x.x.x.$00010111

Before a computer sends out any data, it first compares the destination IP address to its own IP address using the subnet mask. If the destination IP address matches the computer's IP wherever there's a one in the subnet mask, then the sending computer knows the destination is local. *The network IDs match.*

If even one bit of the destination IP address where the ones are on the subnet mask is different, then the sending computer knows it's a long-distance call. *The network IDs do not match.*

Travel Advisory

The explanation about comparing an IP address to a subnet mask simplifies the process, leaving out how the computer uses its routing table to accomplish the goal. We'll get to routing and routing tables in Chapter 6. For now, stick with the concept of the node using the subnet mask to determine the network ID.

Let's head over to Computer A and see how the subnet mask works. Computer A's IP address is 192.168.5.23. Convert that into binary:

11000000.10101000.00000101.00010111

Let's say Computer A wants to send a packet to Computer B. Computer A's subnet mask is 255.255.255.0. Computer B's IP address is 192.168.5.45. Convert this address to binary:

11000000.10101000.00000101.00101101

Computer A compares its IP address to Computer B's IP address using the subnet mask, as shown in Figure 5.18. For clarity, I've added a line to show you where the ones end and the zeroes begin in the subnet mask. Computers certainly don't need the line!

A-ha! Computer A's and Computer B's network IDs match! It's a local call. Knowing this, Computer A can now send out an ARP request, which is a broadcast, as shown in Figure 5.19, to determine Computer B's MAC address. The *Address Resolution Protocol (ARP)* is how nodes in a TCP/IP network discover the destination MAC address based on the destination IP address.

FIGURE 5.18   Comparing addresses

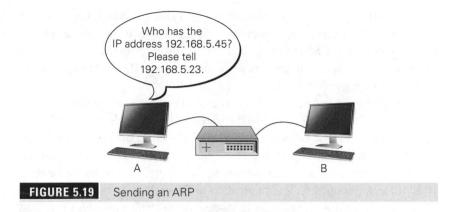

FIGURE 5.19 Sending an ARP

The addressing for the ARP frame looks like Figure 5.20. Note that Computer A's IP address and MAC address are included.

Computer B responds to the ARP by sending Computer A an ARP reply (see Figure 5.21). Once Computer A has Computer B's MAC address, it starts sending packets.

Ethernet Header   ARP frame

| To: Broadcast MAC | From: Source MAC | Source MAC | Source IP | What's your MAC | Target IP |

FIGURE 5.20 Simplified ARP frame

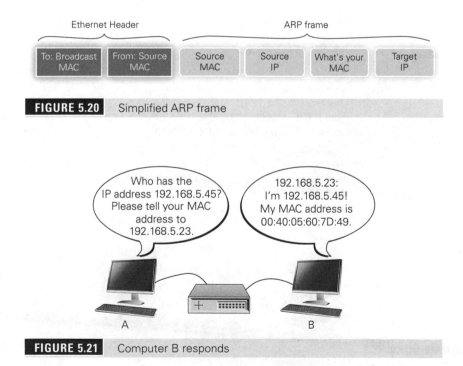

FIGURE 5.21 Computer B responds

But what happens when Computer A wants to send a packet to Computer C? First, Computer A compares Computer C's IP address to its own using the subnet mask (see Figure 5.22). It sees that the IP addresses do not match in the "ones" part of the subnet mask—meaning the network IDs don't match; therefore, this is a long-distance call.

Whenever a computer wants to send to an IP address on another LAN, it knows to send the packet to the default gateway. It still sends out an ARP, but this time to the default gateway (see Figure 5.23). Once Computer A gets the default gateway's MAC address, it then begins to send packets with the destination MAC address of the default gateway in the frame, but with the destination IP address of the actual remote destination in the packet.

Subnet masks are represented in dotted decimal like IP addresses—just remember that both are really 32-bit binary numbers. All of the following (shown in both binary and dotted decimal formats) can be subnet masks:

11111111111111111111111100000000 = 255.255.255.0
11111111111111110000000000000000 = 255.255.0.0
11111111000000000000000000000000 = 255.0.0.0

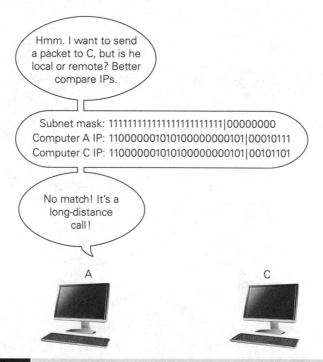

FIGURE 5.22   Comparing addresses again

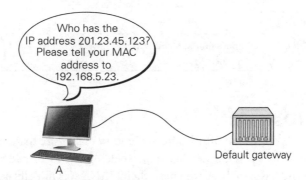

FIGURE 5.23 Sending an ARP to the gateway

Most network folks represent subnet masks using special shorthand: a forward slash (/) character followed by a number equal to the number of ones in the subnet mask. Here are a few examples:

11111111111111111111111100000000 = /24 (24 ones)
11111111111111110000000000000000 = /16 (16 ones)
11111111000000000000000000000000 = /8 (8 ones)

Local Lingo

Classless Inter-Domain Routing (CIDR) notation *CIDR notation* is the official term for this slash notation.

An IP address followed by a forward slash and number tells you the IP address and the subnet mask in one statement. For example, 201.23.45.123/24 is an IP address of 201.23.45.123 with a subnet mask of 255.255.255.0. Similarly, 184.222.4.36/16 is an IP address of 184.222.4.36 with a subnet mask of 255.255.0.0.

Fortunately, computers do all of this subnet filtering automatically. Network administrators need only to enter the correct IP address and subnet mask when they first set up their systems, and the rest happens without any human intervention.

Exam Tip

By definition, all computers on the same network have the same subnet mask and network ID.

Class IDs

To support the dispersion of IP addresses, and to make sure that no organizations used duplicate IP addresses on the Internet, IANA was formed to track and disperse IP addresses to those who need them. IANA was initially handled by a single person (the famous Jon Postel) until 1998, when the Internet Corporation for Assigned Names and Numbers (ICANN) was established to oversee IANA.

IANA has grown dramatically, and now oversees a number of Regional Internet Registries (RIRs) that parcel out IP addresses to large ISPs and major corporations. The RIR for North America is *American Registry for Internet Numbers (ARIN)*. The vast majority of end users get their IP addresses from their respective ISPs. IANA originally passed out IP addresses in contiguous chunks, which are outlined in the following table:

	First Decimal Value	Addresses	Hosts per Network ID
Class A	1–126	1.0.0.0–126.255.255.255	16,277,214
Class B	128–191	128.0.0.0–191.255.255.255	65,534
Class C	192–223	192.0.0.0–223.255.255.255	254
Class D	224–239	224.0.0.0–239.255.255.255	Multicast
Class E	240–255	240.0.0.0–255.255.255.255	Experimental

Travel Advisory

127.0.0.0 Careful readers might have picked up on the missing range of numbers in this list: 127.0.0.0–127.255.255.255. These numbers are used for *loopback testing* (that is, running diagnostics on a local computer). Any number in this range automatically maps to 127.0.0.1, also called the *loopback,* the *local machine,* or simply *home*.

A typical Class A range, for example, has a network ID that starts between 1 and 126; hosts on that network have only the first octet in common, with any numbers for the other three octets. Having three octets to use for hosts means you have an enormous number of possible hosts—over 16 million different number combinations. The subnet mask for Class A licenses is 255.0.0.0, which means you have 24 bits for host IDs.

Do you remember binary math? $2^{24} = 16,277,216$. Because the host can't use all zeroes or all ones (those are reserved for the network ID and broadcast IP, respectively), you subtract two from the final number to get the available host IDs.

Travel Assistance

The Internet Corporation for Assigned Names and Numbers (ICANN) manages IANA. See www.icann.org for more details.

A Class B range, with a subnet mask of 255.255.0.0, uses the first two octets to define the network ID. This leaves two octets to define host IDs, which means each Class B network ID can have up to 65,534 different hosts.

A Class C range uses the first three octets to define only the network ID. All hosts in network 192.168.35.0, for example, would have all three first numbers in common. Only the last octet defines the host IDs, which leaves only 254 possible unique addresses. The subnet mask for Class C licenses is 255.255.255.0.

Multicast class addresses are used for one-to-many communication, such as in streaming video conferencing. There are three types of ways to send a packet: a *broadcast,* which is where every computer on the LAN hears the message; a *unicast,* where one computer sends a message directly to another user; and a *multicast,* where a single computer sends a packet to a group of interested computers. Multicast is often used when routers talk to each other.

Experimental addresses are reserved and never used except for occasional experimental reasons. These were originally called reserved addresses.

Exam Tip

Make sure you memorize the IP class ranges! You should be able to look at any IP address and know its class range. Here's a trick to help: The first binary octet of a Class A address always begins with a 0 (0*xxxxxxx*); for Class B, it begins with a 10 (10*xxxxxx*); for Class C, it begins with 110 (110*xxxxx*); for Class D, it begins with 1110 (1110*xxxx*); and for Class E, it begins with 1111 (1111*xxxx*).

Private versus Public IP Addresses

Certain groups of IP addresses, known as *private IP addresses,* are available to be used as well. Those addresses can never be used on the Internet because Internet backbone routers will drop packets containing private addresses. Anyone can use these private IP addresses, but they're really designed to be used with Network Address Translation (NAT), which I'll discuss in the next chapter. For the moment, however, let's just look at the ranges of addresses that are designated as private IP addresses:

- 10.0.0.0 through 10.255.255.255 (one Class A network)
- 172.16.0.0 through 172.31.255.255 (16 Class B networks)
- 192.168.0.0 through 192.168.255.255 (256 Class C networks)

All other Class A, B, and C IP addresses are *public IP addresses,* meaning they are routable and usable on the Internet.

Exam Tip	
Make sure you can quickly tell the difference between a private and a public IP address for the CompTIA Network+ exam.	

Objective 5.03   CIDR and Subnetting

Classless Inter-Domain Routing (CIDR) was introduced in 1993 to solve the following three problems, as listed in RFC 1519, "Classless Inter-Domain Routing (CIDR): An Address Assignment and Aggregation Strategy":

1. *Exhaustion of the class B network address space. One fundamental cause of this problem is the lack of a network class of a size which is appropriate for mid-sized organization; class C, with a maximum of 254 host addresses, is too small, while class B, which allows up to 65534 addresses, is too large for most organizations.*

2. *Growth of routing tables in Internet routers beyond the ability of current software, hardware, and people to effectively manage.*

3. *Eventual exhaustion of the 32-bit IP address space.*

The first problem was solved with concepts known as *subnetting* and *variable-length subnet masking (VLSM)*. The second problem was solved with a concept known as *supernetting*, and the third problem was solved with a new protocol known as *IPv6*. Let's look at each of these in greater detail.

Subnetting

Subnetting is taking a single network ID and chopping it up into multiple smaller subnets. Subnetting is done by an organization—the organization is given a block of addresses and then breaks the single block of addresses into multiple subnets. Classless addressing (one component of CIDR) is done by an ISP or RIR. For example, an ISP is given a block of addresses, breaks the block into multiple subnets and different sizes (a concept known as VLSM, discussed later), and then passes out the smaller individual subnets to customers. Subnetting enables a much more efficient use of IP addresses compared to class licenses. It also enables you to separate a network for security (separating a bank of public access computers from your more private computers) and for bandwidth control (separating a heavily used LAN from one that's not so heavily used).

> ### Exam Tip
> You need to know how to subnet to pass the CompTIA Network+ exam.

The cornerstone to subnetting lies in the subnet mask. You take an existing /8, /16, or /24 subnet and extend the subnet mask by adding more ones by taking away the corresponding number of zeroes. For example, let's say you have an Internet café with about 50 computers, 40 of which are for public use and 10 of which are used in the back office for accounting and such (see Figure 5.24). Your network ID is 192.168.4.0/24. You want to prevent people using the public systems from accessing your private machines, so you decide to create subnets. You also have Wi-Fi and want to separate wireless clients (never more than 10) on their own subnet.

You need to keep two things in mind about subnetting. First, start with the given subnet mask and add more ones to the right until you have the number of subnets you need. Second, forget the dots. They no longer define the subnets.

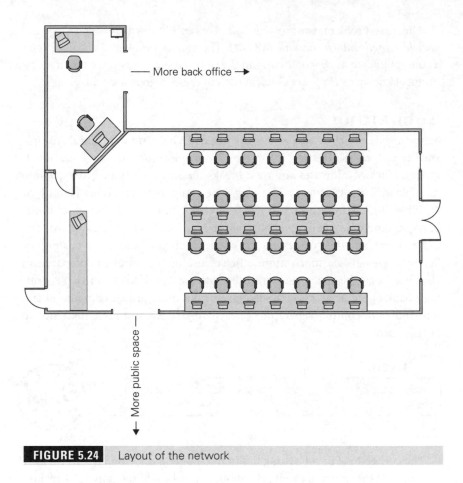

FIGURE 5.24   Layout of the network

Never try to subnet without first converting to binary. Too many techs are what I call "victims of the dots." They are so used to working only with class licenses that they forget there's more to subnets than just /8, /16, and /24 networks. There is no reason network IDs must end on the dots. The computers, at least, think it's perfectly fine to have subnets that end at points between the periods, such as /26, /27, or even /22. The trick here is to stop thinking about network IDs and subnet masks just in their dotted decimal format and instead return to thinking of them as binary numbers.

Let's begin subnetting the café's network of 192.168.4.0/24. Start by changing a zero to a one on the subnet mask so that the /24 becomes a /25 subnet:

11111111111111111111111110000000

Calculating Hosts

Before going even one step further, you need to answer this question: on a /24 network, how many hosts can you have? Well, if you used dotted decimal notation, you might say

192.168.4.1 to 192.168.4.254 = 254 hosts

But do this from the binary instead. In a /24 network, you have eight zeroes that can be the host ID:

00000001 to 11111110 = 254

There's a simple piece of math here: $2^x - 2$, where x represents the number of zeroes in the subnet mask:

$2^8 - 2 = 254$

If you remember this simple formula, you can always determine the number of hosts for a given subnet. This is critical! Memorize this!

If you have a /26 subnet mask on your network, what is the maximum number of hosts you can have on that network?

Because a subnet mask always has 32 bits, a /26 subnet means you have 6 zeroes left after the 26 ones. $2^6 - 2 = 62$ total hosts.

Excellent! Knowing how to determine the number of hosts for a particular subnet mask will help you tremendously in a moment.

Your First Subnet

Let's now make a subnet. All subnetting begins with a single network ID. In this scenario, you need to convert the 192.168.4.0/24 network ID for the café into three network IDs: one for the public computers, one for the private computers, and one for the wireless clients.

Travel Advisory
You cannot subnet without using binary!

The primary tool for subnetting is the existing subnet mask. Write it out in binary. Place a line at the end of the ones, as shown in Figure 5.25.

Subnet mask 11111111111111111111111|00000000

FIGURE 5.25 Step 1 in subnetting

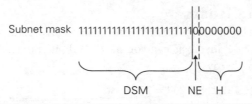

Subnet mask 1111111111111111111111110 0000000

DSM　　　NE　H

FIGURE 5.26　Organizing the subnet mask

Now draw a second line one digit to the right, as shown in Figure 5.26. You've now separated the subnet mask into three areas that I call (from left to right) the default subnet mask (DSM), the network ID extension (NE), and the hosts (H). These are not industry terms, so you won't see them on the Comp-TIA Network+ exam, but they're a handy Mike Trick that makes the process of subnetting a lot easier.

You now have a /25 subnet mask. At this point, most people first learning how to subnet start to freak out. They're challenged by the idea that a subnet mask of /25 isn't going to fit into one of the three pretty subnets of 255.0.0.0, 255.255.0.0, or 255.255.255.0. They think, "That can't be right! Subnet masks are made out of only 255s and 0s." That's not correct. A subnet mask is a string of ones followed by a string of zeroes. People only convert it into dotted decimal to enter things into computers. So convert /25 into dotted decimal. First write out 25 ones, followed by seven zeroes. (Remember, subnet masks are *always* 32 binary digits long.)

```
11111111111111111111111110000000
```

Insert the periods in between every eight digits:

```
11111111.11111111.11111111.10000000
```

Then convert the result into dotted decimal:

```
255.255.255.128
```

Get used to the idea of subnet masks that use more than 255s and 0s. Here are some examples of perfectly legitimate subnet masks. Try converting these to binary to see for yourself.

```
255.255.255.224
255.255.128.0
255.248.0.0
```

Calculating Subnets

When you subnet a network ID, you need to follow the rules and conventions dictated by the good folks who developed TCP/IP to ensure that your new subnets can interact properly with each other and with larger networks. All you need to remember for subnetting is this: start with a beginning subnet mask and extend the subnet extension until you have the number of subnets you need. The formula for determining how many subnets you create is 2^y, where y is the number of bits you turn from host bits (zeroes) to network bits (ones) in the subnet mask.

Figure 5.27 shows a starting subnet of 255.255.255.0. If you move the network ID extension over one, it's only a single digit: 2^1.

That single digit is only a zero or a one, which gives you two subnets. You have only one problem—the café needs three subnets, not just two! So let's take the original /24 and subnet it down to /26. Extending the network ID by two digits creates four new network IDs: $2^2 = 4$. To see each of these network IDs, first convert the original network ID—192.168.4.0—into binary. Then add the four different network ID extensions to the end, as shown in Figure 5.28.

Figure 5.29 shows a sampling of the IP addresses for each of the four new network IDs.

Starting subnet: 255.255.255.0

Subnet mask   11111111111111111111111100000000

Moving over one digit

FIGURE 5.27   Organizing the subnet mask

Original network ID: 192.168.4.0 /24
Translates to this in binary:
11000000.10101000.00000100.00000000

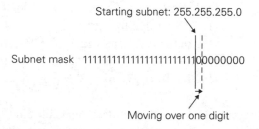

```
110000001010100000000100 00 000000
110000001010100000000100 01 000000
110000001010100000000100 10 000000
110000001010100000000100 11 000000
```

FIGURE 5.28   Creating the new network IDs

```
11000000101010000000100 00 000001
11000000101010000000100 00 000010
11000000101010000000100 00 000011
11000000101010000000100 00 000100

11000000101010000000100 01 000001
11000000101010000000100 01 000010
11000000101010000000100 01 000011
11000000101010000000100 01 000100

11000000101010000000100 10 000001
11000000101010000000100 10 000010
11000000101010000000100 10 000011
11000000101010000000100 10 000100

11000000101010000000100 11 000001
11000000101010000000100 11 000010
11000000101010000000100 11 000011
11000000101010000000100 11 000100
```

FIGURE 5.29   New network ID address ranges

Now convert these four network IDs back to dotted decimal:

Network ID	Host Range	Broadcast Address
192.168.4.0/26	(192.168.4.1–192.168.4.62)	192.168.4.63
192.168.4.64/26	(192.168.4.65–192.168.4.126)	192.168.4.127
192.168.4.128/26	(192.168.4.129–192.168.4.190)	192.168.4.191
192.168.4.192/26	(192.168.4.193–192.168.4.254)	192.168.4.255

The host ranges start with the first address available after the network ID. The first one is obvious, because the network ID ends with 0 in the fourth octet, so the first host would have a 1 in the fourth octet. The last number available in the host range is one number before the start of the next network ID, because the last available address on the subnet is the broadcast address.

Congratulations! You've just taken a single network ID, 192.168.4.0/24, and subnetted it into four new network IDs! Figure 5.30 shows how you can use these new network IDs in a network.

You may notice that the café only needs three subnets, but you created four—you have an extra subnet now. Because subnets are created by powers of two, you will often create more subnets than you need—welcome to subnetting.

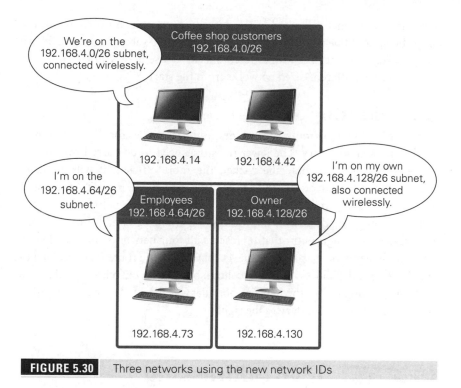

FIGURE 5.30 Three networks using the new network IDs

| Travel Advisory |

In terms of this example, the unused network ID sets the café up for scalability. If the café grows to need another subnet, it's already there for them to use without messing with the existing subnets.

VLSM

When you subnet a network, each subnet will always have the exact amount of hosts per subnet. This "one-size-fits-all" approach doesn't scale well. Think about two routers that are directly connected, when only two addresses are needed for that subnet. If your subnetting scheme allows for 30 hosts on each subnet, you're literally wasting 28 addresses! Variable-length subnet masking (VLSM) is basically subnetting a subnet, and allows an internetwork to have different subnet masks (which translates into different sizes) for different networks. In a nutshell, take one of your subnets, treat it like a major classful network, and subnet it further. In the preceding example, one or more of the /26 subnets could be turned into a /27, /28, /29, or /30 subnet. Now you'll have networks of different sizes with different masks. It also allows an ISP or RIR to give customers different-sized networks from the start.

Supernetting

Supernetting, done by routers, combines multiple entries for destination networks into a single entry. The fewer rows that need to be parsed by a router to determine how to route the packet, the more efficient it will perform. For example, instead of 192.168.4.0/24, 192.168.5.0/24, 192.168.6.0/24, and 192.168.7.0/24 in a router's routing table (where all these networks have the same next-hop IP address on the router), supernetting combines those four networks into a single entry that represents all four networks: 192.168.4.0/22. Each of the networks has a "1" in the 4s column, so the router is instructed to stop looking at the address after this column by the new /22 mask. You'll notice that supernetting moves the network boundary to the left, whereas subnetting moves the network boundary to the right.

Objective 5.04   **IPv6 Addressing**

The word is out (actually, it has been out for some time)—the Internet's running out of spare 32-bit IP addresses. What is the Internet to do? Simple—use bigger addresses. But is that possible while making everything backward-compatible with the existing address scheme? Sure it is; here's IP version 6.

It sounds easy, but it has taken many years to perfect a replacement for the 32-bit IP addressing scheme.

With a 128-bit address range, IPv6 supports a mind-blowing 340,282,366, 920,938,463,463,374,607,431,768,211,456 addresses, which equates to approximately 665,570,793,348,866,943,898,599 addresses per square meter of the surface of the planet Earth.

IPv6 is in use today on parts of the Internet, but it's not having much impact on the desktop (yet). The new addressing scheme was designed to slide in place of IPv4 relatively seamlessly, and parts of the Internet infrastructure are being upgraded all the time without us noticing. IPv6 will address two major issues that plague IPv4: a shortage of addresses and the increasing complexity of routing information.

IPv6 Addresses

An IPv6 address is a 128-bit address displayed in hexadecimal format and not the dotted decimal notation that is used by IPv4. The IPv6 address is divided into eight 16-bit groups that are separated by a colon (:). Many techs call these groups *hextets*, although that's not an official name. The following is an example of an IPv6 address:

```
65b3:b834:45a3:0000:0000:762e:0270:5224
```

An IPv6 address is not case-sensitive, and you do not need to place leading zeroes at the beginning of a hextet. For instance, in the preceding address, the seventh hextet could have been written as 270, without the leading 0 (0270), as follows:

```
65b3:b834:45a3:0000:0000:762e:270:5224
```

Furthermore, you can also replace consecutive hextets of all zeroes with double colons (::) when referencing an address that has a group of zeroes in the address. In the preceding address, the fourth and fifth hextets could have been omitted with the double colons as follows:

```
65b3:b834:45a3::762e:270:5224
```

Note that the double-colon notation can only be used for one contiguous set of hextets, but not more, because it would be ambiguous on how to fill in the rest of the address.

As another example, the loopback address in IPv6 is 0:0:0:0:0:0:0:1 and can be shortened to ::1, with the :: replacing all the consecutive hextets of all zeroes at the beginning of the address. Compressing zeroes, in this fashion, greatly improves the configuration and readability of IPv6 addresses.

IPv6 uses three types of addresses:

- **Unicast**   Used for one-to-one communication.
- **Multicast**   Used for one-to-many communication.
- **Anycast**   Applied to a group of systems (sharing the same unicast IP address) providing a service. Clients that send data to the anycast address have their communication routed to the nearest server that's a part of the anycast address.

To make life more complicated, you should be familiar with different types of unicast addresses for the CompTIA Network+ exam. Following is a quick breakdown of the two main types of unicast addresses:

- **Global unicast**   A public IPv6 address that is routable on the Internet. The address assigned to the host must be unique on the Internet. This address type is equivalent to a public IP address with IPv4. This address always starts with a hex character of 2 or 3.
- **Link-local unicast**   An address that's automatically assigned to the system and is used to communicate only with other nodes on the link (a term that means network/subnet/LAN in the world of IPv6). Link-local addresses always start with FE80. This address type is equivalent to an APIPA address (169.254.0.0/16) with IPv4. The big difference is that APIPA addresses are never desired in IPv4, because it means the inability to contact a DHCP server, and therefore a lack of routing capabilities. In IPv6, the link-local address is actually the actual address used for communicating with nodes on your same network.

Exam Tip

You should be familiar with two of the reserved addresses in IPv6: the loopback address, which is 0:0:0:0:0:0:0:1 (or ::1), and the address for a system with no address specified: 0:0:0:0:0:0:0:0 (or ::).

IPv6 Protocols

Not only has the address scheme changed with IPv6, but so have the protocols that exist in the IPv6 protocol suite. ICMPv6 provides a great example.

ICMPv6

The ICMPv6 protocol (not the sixth version of ICMP, but ICMP that is used for IPv6) is responsible for error and status information, as in IPv4, but it has been modified. ICMPv6 uses types and codes, just like its predecessor, ICMP (by itself, without the v6 suffix, it's assumed to be ICMP for IPv4).

For ICMPv6, types from 0 to 127 are used by error messages, whereas types 128 to 255 are for information messages. For example, the echo request message is type 128 with ICMPv6, and the echo reply message is type 129. Codes give further clarification of a type. For instance, for "Type 1 – Destination Unreachable," there are eight different codes numbered from 0 to 7, representing different situations for why the destination was unreachable, including no route to destination, communication with destination administratively prohibited, port unreachable, and more.

ICMPv6 has expanded on its features from the ICMPv4 days. You should be familiar with the following two features of the ICMPv6 protocol:

- **Multicast Listener Discovery (MLD)**   Replaces the multicast protocol in IPv4 known as Internet Group Management Protocol (IGMP) and is used for multicast communication.
- **Neighboring Discovery (ND)**   Replaces ARP from the IPv4 days by performing the same function, but it's also responsible for neighboring router discovery, automatic address assignment, and duplicate address detection, to name a few features.

DHCPv6

DHCP is alive and well in the IPv6 world but works very differently than IPv4's DHCP. At first glance, you'd think you wouldn't need DHCP anymore. IPv6 clients get their IP address and subnet mask from their gateway router's advertisements (so they also know the default gateway). Although this is true, IPv6 router advertisements do not pass out a number of other very important pieces of information that clients need, such as DNS server information, thus giving DHCP a very important place in IPv6.

EUI-64

When a computer running IPv6 first boots up, it gives itself a link-local address (mentioned earlier). The first 64 bits of a link-local address are always FE80::/10, followed by 54 zero bits. That means every address always begins with FE80:0000:0000:0000.

The second 64 bits of a link-local address, called the *interface identifier,* are generated in two ways. Windows clients since Windows Vista generate a random 64-bit number. Other operating systems, such as Mac OS X Lion (10.7) or later and Windows Server 2008 and beyond, also use random numbers. Cisco router interfaces, and very old operating systems, such as Windows XP and

Windows Server 2003, use the device's MAC address to create a 64-bit number called an *Extended Unique Identifier, 64-bit (EUI-64).* Linux distros default to EUI-64, but can easily be changed to randomized identifiers.

Tunnels

Almost all operating systems support IPv6, and almost all serious routers support IPv6, but very few of the small home routers support IPv6. Plus, not all routers on the Internet have their IPv6 support turned on.

In order for IPv6 to work, every router and every computer on the Internet needs to support IPv6, but the Internet is not yet there. The problem is that the routers and DNS servers between your IPv6-capable computer and the other IPv6-capable computers to which you would like to connect are not yet ready for IPv6. How do you get past this IPv6 gap?

To get on the IPv6 Internet, you need to leap over this gap, by implementing an IPv4-to-IPv6 tunnel. The folks who developed IPv6 have a number of ways for you to do this, using one of many IPv4-to-IPv6 tunneling standards. An IPv4-to-IPv6 tunnel works like any other tunnel, encapsulating one type of data into another. In this case, you are encapsulating your IPv6 traffic into an IPv4 tunnel to get to an IPv6-capable router.

6to4

The 6to4 standard is a tunneling protocol that enables IPv6 traffic to use the IPv4 Internet without having to set up explicit tunnels. 6to4 is generally used to connect two routers directly because it normally requires a public IPv4 address. 6to4 addresses always start with 2002::/16. If you have an IPv6-capable router, or if you have a computer directly connected to the Internet, you can set up a 6to4 tunnel. 6to4 uses public relay routers all around the world. Search the Web for "public 6to4 relays" to find one close to you. One IPv4 address, 192.88.99.1, is called the 6to4 anycast address and works everywhere.

Setting up a 6to4 tunnel can be more challenging than setting up the tunnels that use tunnel brokers. If you're feeling adventurous, just do a web search on "6to4 setup" and include the name of your operating system. You'll find hundreds of websites to show you how to set up a 6to4 tunnel.

Exam Tip

The exam objectives include a special type of tunnel called 4to6. A 4to6 tunnel allows IPv6-only hosts to communicate over an IPv4 infrastructure.

Teredo and Miredo

Teredo is a NAT-traversal IPv6 tunneling protocol (NAT is covered in Chapter 6). Teredo is built into Microsoft Windows and, as a result, sees some adoption. Teredo addresses start with 2001:0000:/32.

Miredo is an open-source implementation of Teredo for Linux and some other UNIX-based systems. (A version was briefly available for OS X, but that was a blip in terms of technology.)

Travel Assistance

Further information on IPv6 can be found at http://technet.microsoft .com/en-ca/network/bb530961.aspx.

 **Objective 5.05** ## DNS and DHCP

Two of the most important protocols on networks are DNS and DHCP. Although it's technically possible to get away without one or both of these valuable protocols, you'd be hard pressed to find a network that isn't utilizing these ubiquitous protocols to the fullest!

DNS

TCP/IP networks use *Domain Name System (DNS)* servers to translate IP addresses into names that humans can better handle and remember. DNS has a set of rules for names and rules for name resolution that enable computers to communicate over networks large and small.

DNS uses a hierarchical naming scheme. When a device wants to know the IP address for a device somewhere else in a network, it queries the local DNS server. The DNS server on a local network knows all the names and IP addresses for local computers. If the LAN connects to other LANs, the DNS server will know the IP address for a DNS server higher up the chain. That way, if a local computer needs to find the IP address for a remote computer, the DNS server doesn't have to know it. It simply forwards the DNS request up to the next higher DNS server. This continues until resolution occurs (see Figure 5.31).

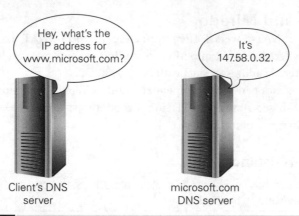

Client's DNS server

microsoft.com DNS server

FIGURE 5.31 A host's DNS server resolves a fully qualified domain name (FQDN) using a hierarchy of DNS servers.

Let's say you wanted to go to www.microsoft.com. Your machine would actually check its local cache first, to see if it has the corresponding IP address. If it doesn't, your client will query its DNS server. At this point, your DNS server checks a cache of previously resolved FQDNs to see if www.microsoft.com is there. In this case, www.microsoft.com is not in the cache.

Now your DNS server needs to get to work. The local DNS server may not know the address for www.microsoft.com, but it does know the addresses of the DNS root servers. The root servers, hundreds of machines logically represented as 13 servers, know all the addresses of the top-level domain (TLD) authoritative DNS servers, which are just below the DNS root servers in the hierarchy. These TLD servers handle what are known as the *top-level domain (TLD) names,* such as .com, .org, .net, .edu, .gov, .mil, and many more.

The root server that was queried sends your DNS server an IP address for the .com authoritative DNS server.

The .com authoritative DNS server also doesn't know the address of www.microsoft.com, but it knows the IP address of the microsoft.com authoritative DNS server, as well as all the other DNS servers that are authoritative for their respective domains. It sends that IP address to your DNS server. Your local DNS server makes a final query, this time to the Microsoft.com authoritative DNS server. The microsoft.com authoritative DNS server does in fact know the IP address of www.microsoft.com and can send that information back to the local DNS server, which is exactly what happens next.

Now that your DNS server has the IP address for www.microsoft.com, it stores a copy in its cache and sends the IP information to your PC. Your web browser then begins the HTTP request to get the web page.

A complete DNS name, including the hostname and all of its domains (in order), is called a *fully qualified domain name (FQDN),* and it's written with the root on the far right, followed by the names of the domains (in order) added to the left of the root, and the hostname on the far left.

A typical DNS name for a web server, such as www.google.com, has three components:

- **com**   Refers to the root domain
- **google** Refers to the google subdomain of the root domain
- **www**   Refers to the specific computer (or cluster of computers, in this case)

The www.google.com FQDN maps directly to an IP address. DNS servers at the .com level certainly know the IP address for the google.com authoritative DNS server; the google.com authoritative DNS server knows the IP address for the www host.

FQDNs also work at the local level, by the way, even in networks that don't connect to the Internet. My office LAN is totalhome, with no .com or anything. So to access my file server, my employees and I click the Windows button, type **\\fs7.totalhome** in the "Search programs and files" box, and the file server opens up. I'm using Internet FQDNs for the primary example of how DNS works because that's what most people are used to seeing.

Although this process might sound a bit complex, it works very well and provides a great deal of flexibility. Prior to the existence of DNS, every computer that wanted to use domain names had to have a local file—called a HOSTS file—that contained a table of IP addresses and their associated names. This file was stored on every system's hard disk. Because the HOSTS file changed on a daily basis, network techs had to keep downloading updates from the Internet! You can still use a HOSTS file today if you just have a small number of computers on a local network, but DNS is the way to go for bigger networks. A simple HOSTS file would look something like this:

```
109.54.94.197   jonathan.mikemeyersworld.com
138.125.163.17  mike.jonathansweissmansworld.com
127.0.0.1       localhost
```

Notice that the name localhost appears in the HOSTS file as an alias for the loopback address 127.0.0.1.

Exam Tip

Most DNS servers support a feature known as *Dynamic DNS (DDNS)*, which means that client systems can automatically register their own records in DNS upon booting up using DHCP (see the upcoming "DHCP" section). This is a popular feature with Windows DNS servers. You could add a special option to the DHCP server, which is generally called the *DNS suffix*. The DNS suffix helps clients access network resources more efficiently.

A DNS server maintains a database of information about the domain names it knows, separating them according to type, using different *records*. For example, an A record maps a hostname to its IPv4 address. An AAAA record does the same for a hostname in an IPv6 network.

Local Lingo

MX, CNAME, and PTR   Other, less common DNS record types are *MX (Mail eXchanger)*, used by SMTP servers to determine where to send mail; *CNAME (Canonical Name)*, which maps aliases to names; and *PTR (Pointer)*, which is used in reverse lookups (when trying to map an IP address to a name, like the traceroute/tracert utility does). As an example of CNAME, my computer's name is mikespc.totalhome, but people in my office can ping mike.totalhome and reach the same physical computer.

DHCP

With so many settings (IP address, subnet mask, default gateway, and DNS servers) to specify, the typical TCP/IP network administrator can spend days properly configuring each host manually. For troubleshooting purposes, you sometimes must put in all these settings manually, what we call *static configuration,* because the settings only change when you manually make the changes.

Fortunately, TCP/IP provides a protocol that takes much of the drudgery out of TCP/IP configuration: DHCP.

Travel Advisory

DHCPv6 is not the sixth version of DHCP, but rather DHCP for IPv6 (the naming convention is the same as ICMPv6). DHCP without any suffix is assumed to be DHCP for IPv4.

FIGURE 5.32 Computer sending out a DHCP Discover message

Dynamic Host Configuration Protocol (DHCP) servers distribute IP addresses and additional IP settings to machines on the network. Once a computer is configured to use DHCP, we call it a DHCP client. When a DHCP client boots up, it automatically sends out a special DHCP Discover broadcast datagram. This DHCP Discover message asks, "Are there any DHCP servers out there?" (see Figure 5.32). What follows is a series of back-and-forth messages.

The DHCP server responds to DHCP Discover requests with a DHCP Offer. The DHCP server is configured to pass out IP addresses from a range (called a *DHCP scope*) and a subnet mask (see Figure 5.33). It also passes out other

Server Settings (DHCP)		
DHCP Server:	◉ **Enable** ○ **Disable** ○ **DHCP Relay**	
DHCP Server:	[ ] . [ ] . [ ] . [ ]	
Starting IP Address:	192.168.1. [100]	
Maximum Number of DHCP Users:	[50]	
Client Lease Time:	[0]	minutes (0 means one day)
Static DNS 1:	[ ] . [ ] . [ ] . [ ]	
Static DNS 2:	[ ] . [ ] . [ ] . [ ]	
Static DNS 3:	[ ] . [ ] . [ ] . [ ]	
WINS:	[ ] . [ ] . [ ] . [ ]	

FIGURE 5.33 DHCP server main screen

information, known generically as options that cover an outrageously large number of choices, such as your default gateway, DNS server, Network Time server, and so on.

> ## Exam Tip
>
> DHCP servers can be set up to reserve addresses for specific machines through what's called, appropriately, *DHCP* reservations. You use these for machines inside your network, for example, so if you had to change their IP addresses for some reason, you could do it from a central location. The other option is to use static IPs, which is the way to go for servers and router interfaces. You might wonder why static addressing beats DHCP reservations for servers, but it's quite simple. If you're using DHCP reservations, and the DHCP server goes down, when the leases of your other servers/routers expire, they won't be able to renew their addresses. Now you've got much bigger problems!

The DHCP client sends out a DHCP Request, requesting the address that was offered in the previous step. The DHCP server then sends a DHCP Acknowledge and lists the client's MAC address as well as the IP information given to the DHCP client in a database (see Figure 5.34).

The result of the acceptance from the DHCP client of the DHCP server's data is called a *DHCP lease,* which is set for a fixed amount of time, generally five to eight days. Halfway through the lease time, the DHCP client tries to renew the lease, with a DHCP Request (skipping the DHCP Discover and DHCP Offer steps done initially), requesting to extend the lease of the address

FIGURE 5.34   DHCP Request and DHCP Acknowledge

it currently has. The DHCP server then sends back a DHCP Acknowledge, and the client starts a new lease with the same parameters as the previous lease.

Living with DHCP

DHCP is very convenient and, as such, very popular. It's so popular that you'll very rarely see a client computer on any network using static addressing (remember, though, that static addressing is proper for servers and routers).

You should know how to deal with the problems that arise with DHCP. The single biggest issue is when a DHCP client tries to get a DHCP address and fails. You'll know when this happens because the operating system will post some form of error telling you there's a problem, as shown in Figure 5.35, and the DHCP client will have a rather strange address in the 169.254.0.0/16 subnet.

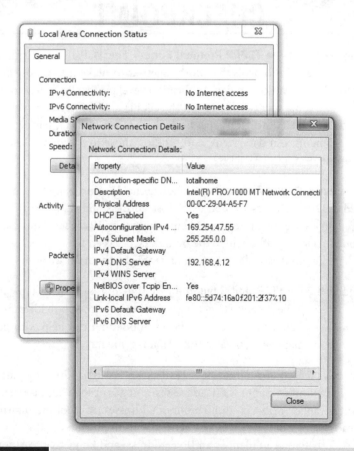

DHCP error in Windows 7

This special IP address is generated by a technology known as Zero-Configuration Networking (zeroconf), or as Microsoft calls it, *Automatic Private IP Addressing (APIPA)*. All DHCP clients are designed to generate an APIPA address automatically if they do not receive a response to a DHCP Discover message after a certain amount of retries. The client only generates the last two octets of an APIPA address. This at least allows the dynamic clients on a single network to continue to communicate with each other because they are on the same network. However, these clients will never be able to communicate with nodes on any other network because there is never a default gateway configured for the 169.254.0.0/16 network.

CHECKPOINT

✔**Objective 5.01: The TCP/IP Protocol Suite** The TCP/IP suite is made up of a number of protocols that work together to make it the most popular protocol in networking today. Application-level protocols use port numbers to initiate some sort of request (on the client) and answer that request (on the server). TCP and UDP operate at the Transport layer, packaging data into segments and datagrams, and sending those to the network layer for encapsulation into IP packets.

✔**Objective 5.02: IPv4 Addressing** The original IP addressing scheme (IPv4) used a 32-bit address to identify a host address and its network address based on a series of addressing schemes known as *IP classes*. The associated subnet mask identifies where the boundary between the network and host address lies and also allows us to change this boundary if we wish.

✔**Objective 5.03: CIDR and Subnetting** CIDR did away with typical class IDs. Altering the default subnet mask enables you to subdivide a network ID into smaller sections, called *subnets*. Subnetting can help with general network management and also traffic management.

✔**Objective 5.04: IPv6 Addressing** IPv6 uses a 128-bit addressing scheme to provide a limitless supply of IP addresses, and it is needed because the 32-bit address range of IPv4 is running out of addresses. Parts of the Internet are already using IPv6, but it is not generally in use at the desktop level yet. Be sure that you can identify an IPv6 address, and know that the loopback address is 0:0:0:0:0:0:0:1 or (::1) and that an unspecified address shows as 0:0:0:0:0:0:0:0 (or ::).

✔**Objective 5.05: DNS and DHCP**   Although it's easier for humans to refer to computer systems using computer names or fully qualified domain names (such as www.totalsem.com), communication between two systems can take place only if the target machine's IP address is known. TCP/IP environments use a database system called DNS (Domain Name System) to resolve IP addresses from fully qualified domain names, such as www. totalsem.com. DNS uses a hierarchical structure, with separate servers (or groups of servers) managing the resolution of various parts of a domain name. Use DHCP for automatic setup of hosts on a network, so you don't have to manually configure the IP address, subnet mask, default gateway, and more.

REVIEW QUESTIONS

1. Which of the following does not represent an IPv6 address?

   A. 2001:0db8:3c4d:0015:0000:0000:abcd:ef12

   B. 0:0:0:0:0:0:0:1

   C. 255.255.0.0

   D. ::1

2. Which of the following is a valid Class B host address?

   A. 147.28.0.0

   B. 192.168.14.50

   C. 12.12.12.12

   D. 128.14.255.0

3. What is the minimum number of data bits required for subnet addressing to allow a total of five subnets to be created?

   A. 1

   B. 2

   C. 3

   D. 4

4. What port number does SSH use?

   A. 443

   B. 22

   C. 80

   D. 43

5. Which of the following protocols provides TCP/IP name resolution?
   A. DHCP
   B. SNMP
   C. Telnet
   D. DNS

6. Which protocol provides automatic host IP address assignment?
   A. DHCP
   B. DNS
   C. NetBIOS
   D. BOOTR

7. Which layer-4 protocol is used for connectionless communication?
   A. DNS
   B. DHCP
   C. TCP
   D. UDP

8. What port number is used to connect to a DNS server?
   A. 20
   B. 23
   C. 53
   D. 67

9. A user calls and says his IP address is 169.154.50.12. What kind of address does he have?
   A. APIPA
   B. DHCP
   C. DNS
   D. Loopback

10. Which of the following is a valid Class A address?
    A. 10.256.128.12
    B. 120.255.128.12
    C. 169.154.128.12
    D. 192.168.1.12

REVIEW ANSWERS

1. **C**   255.255.0.0 is an IPv4 Class B subnet mask address. All other choices are valid IPv6 addresses.

2. **D**   128.14.255.0 is a valid Class B address. Although answer A is a Class B address, it is an invalid host address of all zeroes (*x.x*.0.0).

3. **C**   Three bits allow a total of six subnets to be created, giving scope for the five that need to be created. Two bits (answer B) would allow only for two subnets.

4. **B**   SSH uses port 22.

5. **D**   DNS provides name resolution. DHCP dynamically dishes out IP addresses and other important information to clients. SNMP is for network management, and Telnet provides terminal emulation functionality.

6. **A**   DHCP, Dynamic Host Configuration Protocol, provides automatic host IP address assignment.

7. **D**   UDP is the layer-4 protocol used for connectionless communication.

8. **C**   DNS servers listen on port 53.

9. **A**   The poor guy's computer can't reach a DHCP server, which means it has an APIPA address.

10. **B**   Both answers A and B start in the right address range (first octet between 1 and 126), but the second octet in answer A contains an invalid number, because 255 is the highest number in an IPv4 octet.

Routing

CHAPTER
6

ETA

NEWBIE	SOME EXPERIENCE	EXPERT
4 hours	2 hours	1 hour

Routers interconnect networks to enable communication and resource sharing among those networks. Routers connect through physical means, such as cables or wireless radio frequency waves. Various routing protocols enable routers to exchange information and thus govern the flow of data. We touched on routers in Chapter 4 and then briefly again in Chapter 5. This chapter explores routers in more detail and looks at the process and protocols for routing.

Classically, routers are dedicated boxes that contain at least two connections, although many routers contain many more connections. In a business setting, for example, you might see a Cisco 2600 Series device, one of the most popular routers ever made. These routers are a bit on the older side, but Cisco builds their routers to last. With occasional software upgrades, a typical router will last for many years. The 2611 router shown in Figure 6.1 has two connections (the other connections are used for maintenance and configuration). The two "working" connections are circled. One port leads to one network; the other leads to another network. The router reads the IP addresses of the packets to determine where to send the packets. (I'll elaborate on how that works in a moment.)

Most techs today get their first exposure to routers with the ubiquitous home routers that enable PCs to connect to a fiber modem, cable modem (shown in Figure 6.2), or a DSL modem. The typical home router, however, serves multiple functions, often combining a router, a switch, and other features—such as a firewall (for protecting your network from intruders), a DHCP server, a DNS server, a wireless access point, and much more—into a single box.

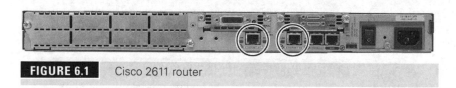

FIGURE 6.1 Cisco 2611 router

FIGURE 6.2 Business end of a typical home router

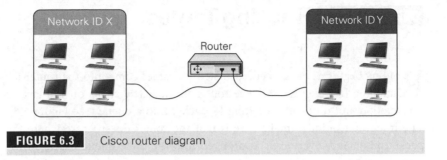

FIGURE 6.3   Cisco router diagram

Figure 6.3 shows the electronic diagram for a two-port Cisco router, whereas Figure 6.4 shows the diagram for a Linksys home router.

Note that both boxes connect two networks. The big difference is that the LAN side of the Linksys home router connects immediately to the built-in switch. That's convenient! You don't have to buy a separate switch to connect multiple computers to the cable or DSL modem. Many users, and even some new techs, look at that router, though, and say, "It has five ports so it'll connect to five different networks," when in reality it can connect only two networks. The extra physical ports belong to the built-in switch.

All routers—big and small, plain or bundled with a switch—examine packets and then send the packets to the proper destination. Let's take a look at that process in more detail now.

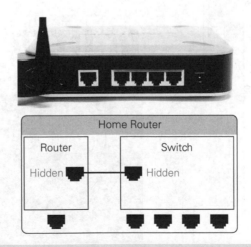

FIGURE 6.4   Linksys home router diagram

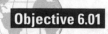 **Objective 6.01** ## Routing Tables

R outing begins as packets encapsulated in frames come into the router for handling (see Figure 6.5). The router immediately strips off the layer-2 information and drops the resulting IP packet into a queue (see Figure 6.6). The important point to make here is that the router doesn't care where the packet originated. Everything is dropped into the same queue based on the time it arrived.

The router inspects each packet's destination IP address and then sends the IP packet out the correct port. To perform this inspection, each router comes with a *routing table* that tells the router exactly where to send the packets. Figure 6.7 shows the simple routing table for a typical home router. This router has only two ports internally: one that connects to whichever type of service provider you use to bring the Internet into your home (fiber, cable, DSL)— labeled as "WAN" in the Interface column of the table—and another one that connects to a built-in four-port switch, which is labeled "LAN" in the table. Figure 6.8 is a diagram for the router. Let's inspect this router's routing table; this table is the key to understanding and controlling the process of forwarding packets to their proper destination.

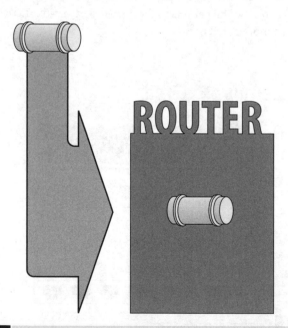

| **FIGURE 6.5** | Incoming packets |

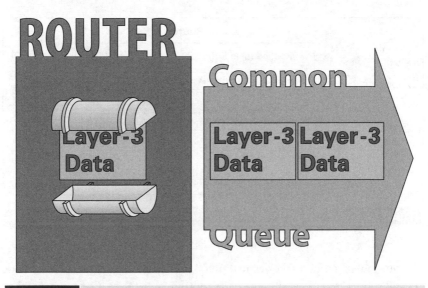

FIGURE 6.6 All incoming packets stripped of layer-2 data and dropped into a common queue

Each row in this little router's simple routing table defines a single route. Each column identifies specific criteria. Reading Figure 6.7 from left to right shows the following:

- **Destination LAN IP** A defined network ID. Every network ID directly connected to one of the router's ports is always listed here.
- **Subnet Mask** To identify the network ID from an IP address, you need a subnet mask (described in Chapter 5).

Routing Table Entry List

Destination LAN IP	Subnet Mask	Gateway	Interface
10.12.14.0	255.255.255.0	0.0.0.0	LAN
76.30.4.0	255.255.254.0	0.0.0.0	WAN
0.0.0.0	0.0.0.0	76.30.4.1	WAN

Refresh

Close

FIGURE 6.7 Routing table from a home router

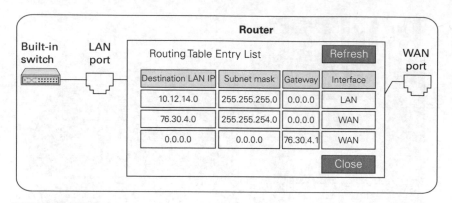

FIGURE 6.8   Electronic diagram of the router

Your router compares the destination LAN IP in the packet with the network ID and subnet mask in each route of its routing table to see if a packet matches that route. For example, if you had a packet with the destination 10.12.14.26 coming into the router, the router would use its routing table to determine that the packet matches the first route shown in Figure 6.7. The other two columns in the routing table then tell the router what to do with the packet:

- **Gateway**   The IP address for the *next hop* router; in other words, where the packet should go. If the outgoing packet is for a network ID that's not directly connected to the router, the Gateway column tells the router the IP address of a router to which to send this packet. That router then handles the packet, and your router is done (you count on well-configured routers to make sure your packet will get to where it needs to go!). If the network ID is directly connected, then you don't need a gateway. Based on what's needed, this is set to 0.0.0.0, or to the IP address of the directly connected port.

- **Interface**   This tells the router which of its ports to use. On this router, it uses the terms "LAN" and "WAN." Other routing tables use the port's IP address or some other type of abbreviation. Cisco routers, for example, use f0/0, f0/1, and so on.

The router compares the destination IP address on a packet to every listing in the routing table and then sends the packet out. It reads every line and then decides what to do. The most important trick to reading a routing table is to remember that a zero (0) means "anything." For example, in Figure 6.7, the first route's destination LAN IP is 10.12.14.0. You can compare that to the subnet mask (255.255.255.0) to confirm that this is a /24 network. This tells you that

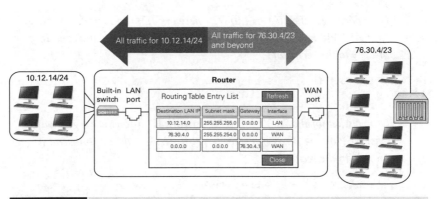

FIGURE 6.9 The network based on the routing table in Figure 6.7

any value (between 1 and 254) is acceptable for the last value in the 10.12.14/24 network ID.

Routing tables tell you a lot about the network connections. From just this single routing table, for example, the diagram in Figure 6.9 can be drawn.

So how do I know the 76.30.4.1 port connects to another network? The third line of the routing table shows the default route for this router, and almost every router has one. This line says

> *(Any destination address) (with any subnet mask) (forward it to 76.30.4.1) (using my WAN port)*

Travel Advisory

Exceptions to Default Routes There are two places where you'll find routers that do not have default routes: private (as in not on the Internet) internetworks, where every router knows about every single network, and the monstrous "Tier One" backbone, where you'll find the routers that make the main connections of the Internet. Every other router has a default route.

```
Destination LAN IP      Subnet Mask        Gateway         Interface
0.0.0.0                 0.0.0.0            76.30.4.1       WAN
```

The default route is very important because this tells the router exactly what to do with every incoming packet *unless* another line in the routing table gives another route. Excellent! We can interpret the other two lines of the routing table in Figure 6.7 in the same fashion:

(Any packet for the 10.12.14.0) (/24 network ID) (don't use a gateway)
(just ARP on the LAN interface to get the MAC address and send it
directly to the recipient)

```
Destination LAN IP      Subnet Mask      Gateway        Interface
10.12.14.0              255.255.255.0    0.0.0.0        LAN
```

(Any packet for the 76.30.4.0) (/24 network ID) (don't use a gateway)
(just ARP on the WAN interface to get the MAC address and send it
directly to the recipient)

```
Destination LAN IP      Subnet Mask      Gateway        Interface
76.30.4.0               255.255.254.0    0.0.0.0        WAN
```

I'll let you in on a little secret. Routers aren't the only devices that use routing tables. In fact, every node (computer, printer, TCP/IP-capable vending machine, whatever) on the network also has a routing table.

At first, this may seem silly—doesn't every computer only have a single Ethernet connection and, therefore, all data traffic has to go out that port? First of all, many computers have more than one NIC. (These are called *multihomed computers*.) But even if your computer has only a single NIC, how does it know what to do with an IP address such as 127.0.0.1? Second, every packet sent out of your computer uses the routing table to figure out where the packet should go, whether directly to a node on your network or to your gateway. Third, the routing table tells the PC whether the communication is unicast, multicast, or broadcast.

Here's an example of a routing table in Windows. This machine connects to the home router described earlier, so you'll recognize the IP addresses it uses. The results screen of the route print command is very long, even on a basic system, so I've deleted a few parts of the output for the sake of brevity.

```
C:\>route print
===========================================================================
Interface List
13 ...00 11 d8 30 16 c0......NVIDIA nForce Networking Controller
 1...........................Software Loopback Interface 1
57...00 00 00 00 00 00 00 e0 Microsoft ISATAP Adapter #15
56...00 00 00 00 00 00 00 e0 Teredo Tunneling Pseudo-Interface
===========================================================================
IPv4 Route Table
===========================================================================
```

```
Active Routes:
Network Destination        Netmask          Gateway      Interface  Metric
          0.0.0.0          0.0.0.0       10.12.14.1    10.12.14.201      25
        127.0.0.0        255.0.0.0          On-link       127.0.0.1     306
        127.0.0.1  255.255.255.255          On-link       127.0.0.1     306
  127.255.255.255  255.255.255.255          On-link       127.0.0.1     306
       10.12.14.0    255.255.255.0          On-link    10.12.14.201     281
     10.12.14.201  255.255.255.255          On-link    10.12.14.201     281
     10.12.14.255  255.255.255.255          On-link    10.12.14.201     281
        224.0.0.0        240.0.0.0          On-link       127.0.0.1     306
        224.0.0.0        240.0.0.0          On-link    10.12.14.201     281
  255.255.255.255  255.255.255.255          On-link       127.0.0.1     306
  255.255.255.255  255.255.255.255          On-link    10.12.14.201     281
===========================================================================
Persistent Routes:
None
```

Unlike the routing table for the typical home router, this one seems a bit more complicated. My PC has only a single NIC, though, so it's not quite as complicated as it might seem at first glance. Let's take a look at the details. First, note that my computer has an IP address of 10.12.14.201/24 and that 10.12.14.1 is its default gateway.

Travel Advisory

Viewing Routing Tables in Linux and OS X   Every modern operating system gives you tools to view a computer's routing table. Most techs use the command line or terminal window interface—often called simply *terminal*—because it's fast. To see your routing table in Windows, Linux, or Mac OS X, for example, type this command at a terminal:

`netstat -r`

In Windows, try this command as an alternative:

`route print`

You should note two differences in the columns from what you saw in the previous routing table. First, the interface has an actual IP address—10.12.14.201, plus the loopback of 127.0.0.1—instead of the word "LAN." Second—and this is part of the magic of routing—is something called the metric.

A *metric* is a relative value that defines the "cost" of using this route. The power of routing is that a packet can take more than one route to get to the same place. If a route were to suddenly cut off, then you have an alternative. Figure 6.10 shows a networked router with two routes to the same place. The router has a route to network X with a metric of 1 using router X, and a second route to network X using router Y with a metric of 10.

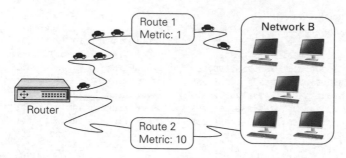

FIGURE 6.10   Two routes to the same network

Travel Advisory

When a router has more than one route to the same network, it's up to the person in charge of that router to assign a different metric for each route. With dynamic routing protocols (discussed in detail later in the chapter in the "Dynamic Routing" section), the routers determine the proper metric for each route.

Lowest cost routes always win. In this case, the router will always use the route with the metric of 1, unless that route suddenly stopped working. In that case, the router would automatically switch to the route with the 10 metric (see Figure 6.11). This is the cornerstone of how the Internet works! The entire Internet is nothing more than a whole bunch of big, powerful routers connected to lots of other big, powerful routers. Connections go up and down all the time,

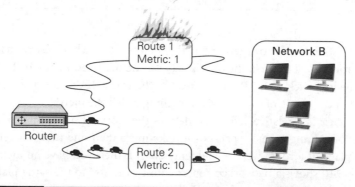

FIGURE 6.11   When a route no longer works, the router automatically switches.

and routers (with multiple routes) constantly talk to each other, detecting when a connection goes down and automatically switching to alternate routes.

I'll go through this routing table one line at a time. Remember, every address is compared to every line in the routing table before it goes out, so it's no big deal if the default route is at the beginning or the end.

The bottom lines define the flooded broadcast address. If you send out an IP broadcast (255.255.255.255), your NIC knows to send it out to the local network. Because the metric for the NIC interface (281) is lower than the metric for the loopback interface (306), it will be the one that's used because both have the same flooded broadcast address.

```
Network Destination    Netmask          Gateway      Interface     Metric
255.255.255.255        255.255.255.255  On-link      127.0.0.1     306
255.255.255.255        255.255.255.255  On-link      10.12.14.201  281
```

The next two lines up are for the multicast address range. Again, there are two entries, one for the NIC and one for the loopback interface.

```
Network Destination    Netmask          Gateway      Interface     Metric
224.0.0.0              240.0.0.0        On-link      127.0.0.1     306
224.0.0.0              240.0.0.0        On-link      10.12.14.201  281
```

The next line up is the directed broadcast address, which is specific to a particular subnet, unlike the flooded broadcast, which applies to any network:

```
Network Destination    Netmask          Gateway      Interface     Metric
10.12.14.255           255.255.255.255  On-link      10.12.14.201  1
```

Okay, on to the next line up. Anything addressed to this machine should go right back to it through the loopback interface (127.0.0.1).

```
Network Destination    Netmask          Gateway      Interface     Metric
10.12.14.201           255.255.255.255  On-Link      127.0.0.1     1
```

The next line up defines the local connection: Any packet for the 10.12.14.0/24 network just requires an ARP on the LAN interface to get the MAC address, and then the packet can be sent directly to the recipient. (There's a cost of 1 to use this route.)

```
Network Destination    Netmask          Gateway      Interface     Metric
10.12.14.0             255.255.255.0    On-link      10.12.14.201  1
```

The next three lines up tell your system how to handle the loopback address. The second line is straightforward, but examine the first and third lines carefully. Earlier you learned that 127.0.0.1 is the loopback address, but according to the first route, any 127.0.0.0/8 address is the loopback. The third line, the loopback broadcast address, is placed in the routing table to satisfy a loopback addressing requirement. Bottom line: no matter how you use a loopback address, as long as you start the address with 127, it will always go to 127.0.0.1.

```
Network Destination   Netmask            Gateway     Interface    Metric
127.0.0.0             255.0.0.0          On-link     127.0.0.1    306
127.0.0.1             255.255.255.255    On-link     127.0.0.1    306
127.255.255.255       255.255.255.255    On-link     127.0.0.1    306
```

The very top line defines the default route:

> *(Any destination address) (with any subnet mask) (forward it to my default gateway) (using my NIC, which is what* On-link *refers to) (Metric of 25 to use this route)*

Anything that's not local goes to the router, and from there out to the destination (with the help of other routers). It's the only row where the gateway column is not "On-link," which means it's the only row that matches traffic for a remote subnet, requiring you to ARP for the MAC address of the default gateway.

```
Network Destination   Netmask      Gateway       Interface      Metric
0.0.0.0               0.0.0.0      10.12.14.1    10.12.14.201   25
```

Freedom from Layer 2

Routers enable you to connect different types of network technologies. You now know that routers strip off all the layer-2 data from the incoming packets, but thus far you've only seen routers that connect to different Ethernet networks—and that's just fine with routers. But routers can connect to almost anything that stores IP packets. Not to take away from some very exciting upcoming chapters, but Ethernet is not the only networking technology out there. Once you want to start making long-distance connections, Ethernet disappears, and technologies with names such as Data Over Cable Service Interface Specification (DOCSIS used with cable modems), Point-to-Point Protocol over Ethernet (PPPoE commonly used with DSL modems), Frame Relay, and Asynchronous Transfer Mode (ATM) take over. These technologies are not Ethernet, and they all work very differently than Ethernet. The only common feature of these technologies is they all carry IP packets inside their layer-2 encapsulations.

Most industry-level routers enable you to add interfaces. You buy the router and then snap in different types of interfaces depending on your needs. Note the Cisco router in Figure 6.12. Like most Cisco routers, it comes with removable modules.

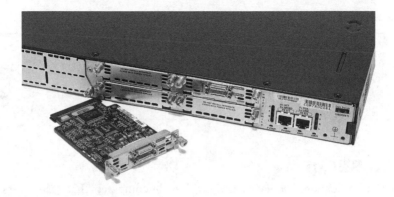

Modular Cisco router

If you're connecting Ethernet to ATM, you buy an Ethernet module and an ATM module. If you're connecting Ethernet to a DOCSIS (cable modem) network, you buy an Ethernet module and a DOCSIS module.

 **Objective 6.02** **Network Address Translation and High Availability**

R outers running some form of *Network Address Translation (NAT)* allow an ISP to give one single public IP address to a home or company, private IP addresses (discussed last chapter) to be used on the LAN, and those computers using the private IP addresses to communicate over the Internet. NAT extended the useful life of IPv4 addressing on the Internet for many years. It is extremely common and heavily in use, so learning how it works is important. Note that routers offer NAT as a feature *in addition to* the core capability of routing. NAT is not routing, but a separate technology. With that said, you are ready to dive into how NAT works to conserve IP addresses.

> **Travel Advisory**
>
> **Intent** Developers created NAT specifically to extend the life of IPv4, to be used in conjunction with private IP addresses (discussed last chapter). NAT was never designed as a security implementation. Relying on it for security, by the thought of using private inside IP addresses, is a big mistake.

The Setup

Here's the situation: You have a LAN with eight computers that need access to the Internet. With classic TCP/IP and routing, several things have to happen. First, you need to get a block of legitimate, unique, expensive IP addresses from an Internet service provider (ISP). You could call up an ISP and purchase a network ID (say, 1.2.3.136/29). Second, you assign an IP address to each computer and to the LAN connection on the router. Third, you assign the IP address for the ISP's router to the WAN connection on the local router, such as 1.2.4.1. After everything is configured, the network looks like Figure 6.13. All of the clients on the network have the same default gateway (1.2.3.137). This router,

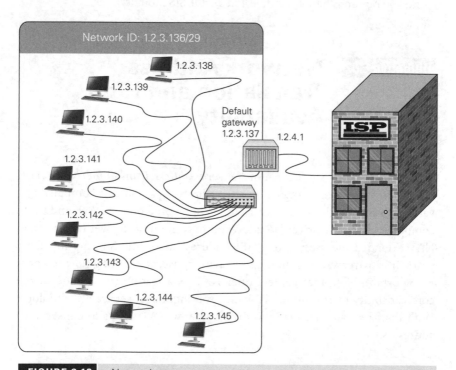

FIGURE 6.13 Network setup

called a *gateway router* (or simply a *gateway)*, acts as the default gateway for a number of client computers.

This style of network mirrors how computers in LANs throughout the world connected to the Internet for the first 20 years, but the major problems of cost and decreasing number of available IP addresses necessitated NAT.

NAT has solved both of these issues for many years.

Port Address Translation

Most internal networks today don't have one machine, of course. Instead, they use blocks of private IP addresses for the hosts inside the network. They connect to the Internet through one or more public IP addresses.

The most common form of NAT that handles this one-to-many connection— called *Port Address Translation (PAT)*—uses port numbers to map traffic from specific machines in the network. Let's use a simple example to make the process clear. John has a network at his office that uses the private IP addressing space of 192.168.1.0/24. All the computers in the private network connect to the Internet through a single NAT router with the global IP address of 208.190.121.12/24 (see Figure 6.14).

When an internal machine initiates a session with an external machine, such as a web browser accessing a website, the source and destination IP addresses and port numbers for the TCP segment or UDP datagram are recorded in the PAT table, and the private IP address is swapped for the public IP address

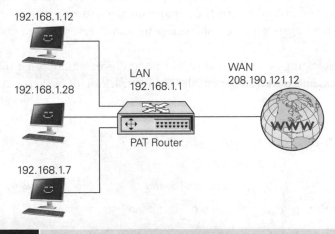

FIGURE 6.14   Sample network setup

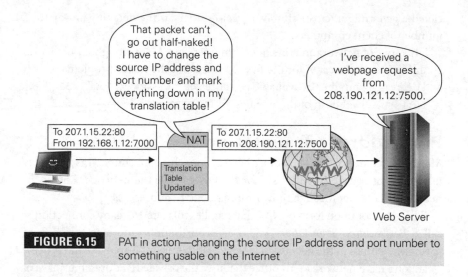

of the outside router interface on each outgoing packet. Plus, the port number used by the internal computer for the session is also translated into a unique port number, and the router records this as well (see Figure 6.15).

Table 6.1 shows a sample of the translation table inside the PAT router. Note that more than one computer translation has been recorded.

When the receiving system sends the packet back, it reverses the IP addresses and ports. The NAT router compares the incoming destination port and source IP address to the entry in the *NAT table* to determine which destination IP address and destination port to put back on the packet. It then sends the packet to the correct computer on the network. This works even when two computers on the inside access the same server on the outside, like in Table 6.1.

This mapping of an internal IP address and port number to a translated IP address and port number enables perfect tracking of packets out and in.

TABLE 6.1   Sample NAT Table

Source	Translated Source	Destination
192.168.1.12:7000	208.190.121.12:7500	17.5.85.11:80
192.168.1.246:10314	208.190.121.12:15000	17.5.85.11:80

PAT can handle many internal computers with a single public IP address because the TCP/IP port number space is big, as you'll recall from Chapter 5, with values ranging from 0 to 65535. Some of those port numbers are used for common protocols, but many thousands are available for PAT to work its magic.

Local Lingo

dynamic NAT With dynamic NAT, many computers can share a pool of public routable IP addresses that number fewer than the computers. The NAT might have 10 public routable IP addresses, for example, to serve 40 computers on the LAN. LAN traffic uses the internal, private IP addresses. When a computer requests information beyond the network, the NAT doles out a routable IP address from its pool for that communication. Dynamic NAT is also called *pooled NAT*. This works well enough—unless you're the unlucky 11th person to try to access the Internet from behind the company NAT—but has the obvious limitation of still needing many true, expensive, routable IP addresses.

PAT takes care of all the problems facing a network exposed to the Internet. You don't have to use legitimate Internet IP addresses on the LAN, and the IP addresses of the computers behind the routers are invisible and protected from the outside world.

Because the router is revising the packets and recording the IP address and port information already, why not enable it to handle ports more aggressively? Enter port forwarding, stage left.

Port Forwarding

The obvious drawback to relying exclusively on PAT for network address translation is that it only works for outgoing communication, not incoming communication. For traffic originating *outside* the network to access an *internal* machine, such as a web server hosted inside your network, you need to use other technologies.

Static NAT (SNAT) maps a single routable (that is, not private) IP address to a single machine, enabling you to access that machine from outside the network. The NAT keeps track of the IP address or addresses and applies them permanently on a one-to-one basis with computers on the network. You could run a web server on an internal host, for example, that has a private IP address but could still be accessed over the Internet. Because outside traffic won't know the internal IP address, you've added a layer of security from attacks on that IP address.

Exam Tip

Despite the many uses in the industry of the acronym SNAT, the CompTIA Network+ exam uses SNAT for *Static NAT* exclusively.

With *port forwarding*, you can designate a specific local address for various network services. Computers outside the network can request a service using the public IP address of the router and the port number of the desired service. The port-forwarding router would examine the packet, look at the list of services mapped to local addresses, and then send that packet along to the proper recipient.

You can use port forwarding to hide a service hosted inside your network by changing the default port number for that service. To hide an internal web server, for example, you could change the request port number to something other than port 80, the default for HTTP traffic. The router in Figure 6.16, for example, is configured to forward all port 8080 traffic to the internal web server at port 80.

To access that internal website from outside your local network, you would have to change the URL in the web browser by specifying the port request number. Figure 6.17 shows a browser that has :8080 appended to the URL, which tells the browser to make the HTTP request to port 8080 rather than port 80.

Configuring NAT

Configuring NAT on home routers is a no-brainer because these boxes invariably have NAT turned on automatically. Figure 6.18 shows the screen on my home router for NAT. Note the radio buttons labeled "Gateway" and "Router."

By default, the router is set to Gateway, which is Linksys-speak for "NAT is turned on." If I wanted to turn off NAT, I would set the radio button to Router.

Figure 6.19 shows a router configuration screen on a Cisco router. Commercial routers enable you to do a lot more with NAT.

High Availability

A *virtual IP* is a single IP address shared by multiple systems. If that sounds a lot like what Network Address Translation (NAT) does, well, you're right. The public IP address on NATed networks is a common implementation of a virtual IP, but virtual IPs are not limited to NAT.

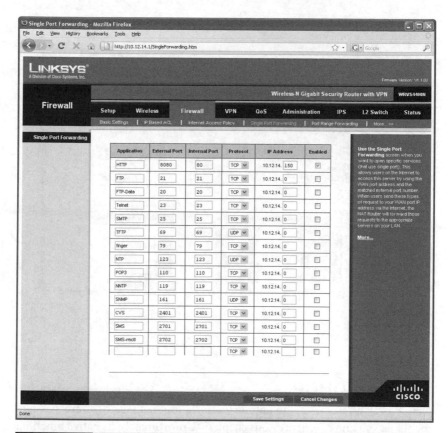

FIGURE 6.16 Setting up port forwarding on a home router

The way servers can fail over without dropping off the network is for all the servers in the cluster to accept traffic from a single, common IP—this common address is considered a virtual IP.

VRRP and HSRP

Building with high availability in mind extends to more than just servers; default gateway routers are another critical node that can be protected by adding redundant backups. The two protocols used to provide this redundancy are the open standard Virtual Router Redundancy Protocol (VRRP) and the Cisco proprietary Host Standby Router Protocol (HSRP). The nice thing about VRRP and HSRP is that, conceptually, they both perform the same function. They take multiple routers and gang them together into a single virtual router with a single virtual IP that clients use as a default gateway.

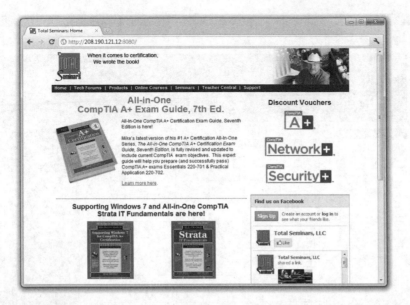

FIGURE 6.17   Changing the URL to access a website using a nondefault port number

Routing DHCP

DHCP is an awesome tool to automate, track, and manage IP address assignments, as you know from previous chapters. Unfortunately, its native functions are limited to a single subnet, because routers don't forward broadcasts. So if you have LANs in a network, connected via routers, you need some method for getting IP addresses and other TCP/IP information to hosts. That's where *DHCP relay* comes into play.

When DHCP relay is enabled and configured within a router, the router will pass DHCP requests and responses across the router interfaces, by taking DHCP broadcasts and turning them into unicasts, sourced by the router itself. Now a single DHCP server can serve addresses to multiple networks.

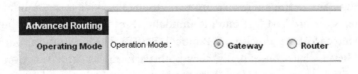

FIGURE 6.18   NAT setup on home router

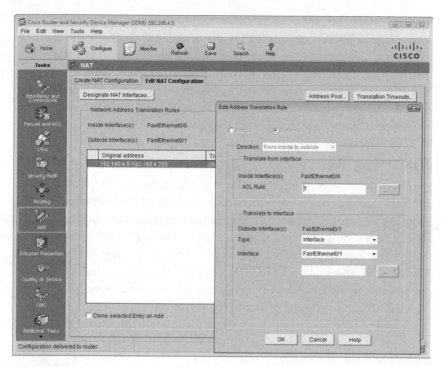

FIGURE 6.19 Configuring NAT on a commercial-grade router

Cisco implements DHCP relay through a configuration command called *IP helper* (the command is technically **ip helper-address**). IP helper enables DHCP relay support (DHCP uses ports 67 for the server and 68 for the client). It also enables relaying for TFTP (port 69), Time Protocol (port 68), TACACS (port 49), DNS (port 53), NetBIOS (port 137), and NetBIOS Datagram (port 138).

Objective 6.03 **Dynamic Routing**

Based on what you've read up to this point, it would seem that routes in your routing tables come from two sources: either they are manually entered or they are detected at setup by the router. In either case, a route seems to be a static beast, just sitting there and never changing. And based on what you've seen so far, that is absolutely true. Routers have *static routes*. But most routers also have the capability to update their routes *dynamically,* assuming they're provided with the extra smarts in the form of *dynamic routing* protocols.

Routing protocols have been around for a long time, and, like any technology, there have been a number of different choices and variants over those years. CompTIA Network+ competencies break these many types of routing protocols into three distinct groups: distance vector, link state, and hybrid. Let's start with a deeper discussion of metrics and then sort out the various dynamic routing protocols.

Routing Metrics

Earlier in the chapter, you learned that routing tables contain a factor called a *metric,* which is a relative value that routers use when they have more than one route to get to another network. Unlike the gateway routers in our homes, a more serious router will often have multiple connections to get to a particular network.

Dynamic routing protocols enable routers to update routing tables by communicating with other routers. If a router suddenly loses a connection, it checks alternative routes to the same network. It's the role of the metric setting for the router to decide which route to use. It always chooses the route with the lowest metric.

There is no uniform rule to set the metric value in a routing table. The various types of dynamic protocols use different criteria. Here are the most common criteria for determining a metric:

- **Bandwidth**   Some connections handle more data than others. An old dial-up connection moves, at best, 64 Kbps. A cable modem easily handles many millions of bits per second.
- **Latency**   Hundreds of issues occur that slow down network connections between routers. These issues are known collectively as *latency.* A great example is a satellite connection. The distance between the satellite and the antenna causes a delay that has nothing to do with the speed of the connection.

Different dynamic routing protocols use one or more routing metrics to calculate their own routing metrics. As you learn about these protocols, you will see how each of these calculates its own metrics differently.

Travel Advisory

Maximum Transmission Unit (MTU) was never used as an actual metric, although it is sent in routing table updates by certain routing protocols.

Distance Vector

Distance vector routing protocols use one of several algorithms to determine the best route to other routers based on the distance (*cost*) and direction (*vector*).

The simplest total cost sums the hops (the hop count) between a router and a network. A *hop* is defined as each time a packet goes through a router. So if you had a router one hop away from a network, the cost for that route would be 1; if it were two hops away, the cost would be 2.

All network connections are not equal. A router might have a pair of one-hop routes to a network—one using a fast connection and the other using a slow connection. The slow single-hop route, for example, might have a metric of 10 rather than the default of 1 to reflect the fact that it's slow. The total cost for this one-hop route is 10, even though it's only one hop. (Don't assume a one-hop route always has a cost of 1.)

Routers using a distance vector routing protocol transfer their entire routing table to other routers in the WAN. Each distance vector routing protocol has a maximum number of hops that a router will send its routing table to keep traffic down.

Assume you have four routers connected as shown in Figure 6.20. All of the routers have static routes set up between each other with the metrics shown. You add two new networks: one that connects to Router A and the other to Router D. For simplicity, call them Network ID X and Network ID Y. A computer on one network wants to send packets to a computer on the other network, but the routers in between Routers A and D don't yet know the two new network IDs. That's when distance vector routing protocols work their magic.

Because all the routers use a distance vector routing protocol, the problem gets solved quickly. At a certain defined time interval (usually 30 seconds or more), the routers begin sending each other their routing tables (each router sends its entire routing table, but for simplicity, just concentrate on the two network IDs in question). On the first iteration, Router A sends its route to

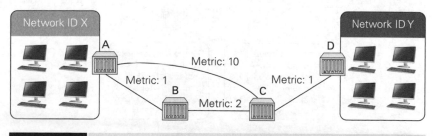

FIGURE 6.20   Getting a packet from Network ID X to Network ID Y

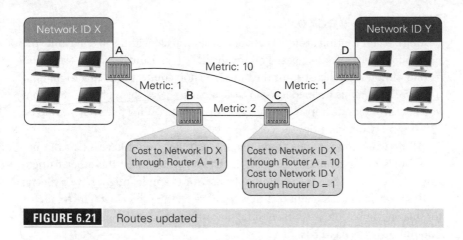

FIGURE 6.21 Routes updated

Network ID X to Routers B and C. Router D sends its route to Network ID Y to Router C (see Figure 6.21).

This is great—Routers B and C now know how to get to Network ID X, and Router C can get to Network ID Y. There's still no complete path, however, between Network ID X and Network ID Y. That's going to take another interval. After another set amount of time, the routers again send their now-updated routing tables to each other, as shown in Figure 6.22.

Router A knows a path now to Network ID Y, and Router D knows a path to Network ID X. As a side effect, Router B and Router C have two routes

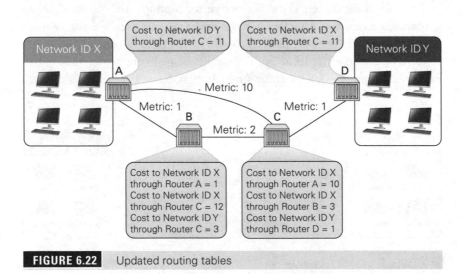

FIGURE 6.22 Updated routing tables

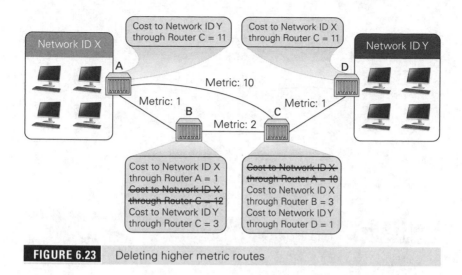

FIGURE 6.23 Deleting higher metric routes

to Network ID X. Router B can get to Network ID X through Router A and through Router C. Similarly, Router C can get to Network ID X through Router A and through Router B. What to do? In cases where the router discovers multiple routes to the same network ID, the distance vector routing protocol deletes all but the route with the lowest metric (see Figure 6.23).

On the next iteration, Routers A and D get updated information about the lower total-cost hops to connect to Network IDs X and Y (see Figure 6.24).

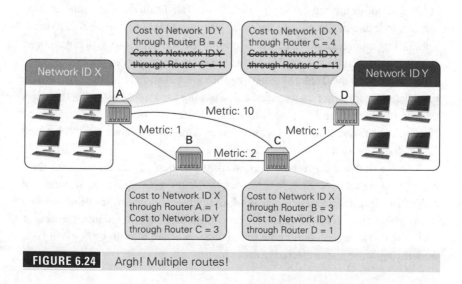

FIGURE 6.24 Argh! Multiple routes!

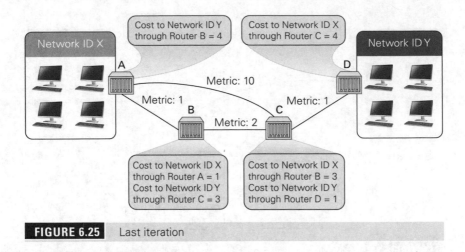

FIGURE 6.25   Last iteration

Just as Routers B and C only kept the routes with the lowest costs, Routers A and D keep only the lowest-cost routes to the networks (see Figure 6.25).

Now Routers A and D have a lower-cost route to Network IDs X and Y. They've removed the higher-cost routes and begin sending data.

At this point, if routers were human they'd realize that each router has all the information about the network and stop sending each other routing tables. Routers using distance vector routing protocols, however, aren't that smart. The routers continue to send their complete routing tables to each other, but because the information is the same, the routing tables don't change.

At this point, the routers are in *convergence* (also called *steady state*), meaning the updating of the routing tables for all the routers has completed. Assuming nothing changes in terms of connections, the routing tables will not change. In this example, it takes three iterations to reach convergence.

So what happens if the route between Routers B and C breaks? The routers have deleted the higher-cost routes, only keeping the lower-cost route that goes between Routers B and C. Does this mean Router A can no longer connect to Network ID Y and Router D can no longer connect to Network ID X? Yikes! Yes, it does—at least for a while.

Routers that use distance vector routing protocols continue to send their entire routing table to each other at regular intervals, but in the situation of a downed link, they will actually send a triggered update to let other routers know about the situation. After the next regular interval updates, Routers A and D will once again know how to reach each other, although they will connect through the once-rejected slower connection.

Distance vector routing protocols work fine in a scenario such as the previous one that has only four routers. Even if you lose a router, a few minutes later the network returns to convergence. But imagine if you had tens of thousands of routers (the Internet). Convergence could take a very long time indeed. As a result, a pure distance vector routing protocol works fine for a network with a small number of routers (fewer than 10), but it isn't good for large networks.

Routers can use one of three distance vector routing protocols: RIPv1, RIPv2, or Cisco's proprietary Enhanced Interior Gateway Routing Protocol (EIGRP), which is not covered on the Network+ Exam.

> **Travel Advisory**
>
> Cisco recently changed from its original classification of EIGRP as a hybrid protocol, and now is calling it what it should have been called all along: an *advanced* distance vector routing protocol.

RIPv1

The granddaddy of all distance vector routing protocols is the *Routing Information Protocol (RIP)*. The first version of RIP—called *RIPv1*—dates from the 1980s, although its predecessors go back all the way to the beginnings of the Internet in the 1960s. RIP had several limitations that made it unsuitable for the growing number of network connections. It had a maximum hop count of only 15. RIPv1 sent out an update every 30 seconds. In addition, RIPv1 routers had no authentication, leaving them open to hackers sending false routing table information. RIP needed an update.

RIPv2

RIPv2, adopted in 1994, is the current version of RIP. It works the same way as RIPv1, but fixes many of the problems. VLSM support has been added, and authentication is built into the protocol. The maximum hop count of 15 continues to apply to RIPv2, but the easy configuration makes it suitable for internetworks using only a few routers. Most routers support RIPv2 (see Figure 6.26).

Dynamic Routing

RIP:	◉ Enabled ○ Disabled
RIP Send Packet Version:	RIPv2
RIP Recv Packet Version:	RIPv2

FIGURE 6.26   Setting RIP in a home router

Link State

The limitations of RIP motivated the demand for a faster protocol that took up less bandwidth on a WAN. The basic idea was to come up with a dynamic routing protocol that was more efficient than routers that simply sent out their entire routing table at regular intervals. Why not instead simply announce and forward individual route changes as they appeared? That is the basic idea of a *link state* dynamic routing protocol.

Distance vector routing protocols require routers to accept full routing tables from adjacent routers at predetermined intervals, and learn the topology of the internetwork in that fashion. It's like the old game of telephone we used to play. Link state routing protocols allow routers to construct their own topology map of the internetwork, after hearing about the state of the links from the actual routers connected to each link themselves (hence the term *link state*), and make their own decisions on how to get to destination networks. There are only two link state dynamic routing protocols: OSPF and IS-IS.

OSPF

Open Shortest Path First (OSPF) is the most commonly used IGP. Most companies (as opposed to ISPs) use OSPF on their internal networks. Even a company, while still using BGP on its edge routers, will use OSPF internally, because OSPF was designed from the ground up to work within a single AS. OSPF converges dramatically faster and is much more efficient than RIP. Odds are good that if you are using dynamic routing protocols to connect your own routers, you're using OSPF.

OSPF offers a number of improvements over RIP. When you first launch OSPF-capable routers, they send out *Hello packets,* looking for other OSPF routers (see Figure 6.27). After two adjacent routers form a neighborship through the Hello packets, they exchange information about routers and networks through Link State Advertisement (LSA) packets. LSAs are sourced by each router, and are flooded from router to router through each OSPF area.

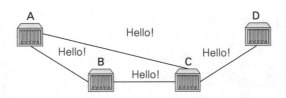

FIGURE 6.27   Hello!

Once all the routers communicate, they individually decide their own optimal routes, and convergence happens almost immediately. If a route goes down, OSPF routers quickly recompute a new route with stored LSAs.

Travel Advisory

OSPF corrects link failures and creates convergence almost immediately. This helps prevent routing loops, a condition where two routers send packets back and forth to each other, with each thinking the other router is the direction in which the packet needs to go. OSPFv3 has many improvements over its predecessor (OSPFv2), including IPv6 support.

IS-IS

If you want to use a link state dynamic routing protocol and you don't want to use OSPF, your only other option is *Intermediate System to Intermediate System (IS-IS)*. IS-IS is extremely similar to OSPF. It uses the concept of areas and send-only updates to routing tables. IS-IS was developed at roughly the same time as OSPF and had the one major advantage of working with IPv6 from the start. IS-IS is a link state dynamic routing protocol that has great usage in the niche market of ISP backbones.

BGP

The explosive growth of the Internet in the 1980s required a fundamental reorganization in the structure of the Internet itself, and one big part of this reorganization was the call to make the "big" routers use a standardized dynamic routing protocol. Implementing this was much harder than you might think because the entities that govern how the Internet works do so in a highly decentralized fashion. Even the organized groups, such as the Internet Society (ISOC), the Internet Assigned Numbers Authority (IANA), and the Internet Engineering Task Force (IETF), are made up of many individuals, companies, and government organizations from across the globe.

What came out of the reorganization eventually was a multitiered structure. At the top of the structure sits many Autonomous Systems. An *Autonomous System (AS)* is one or more networks, controlled by a single organization (such as an ISP) whose routers are governed by a single dynamic routing policy, and often a single protocol within that AS. Figure 6.28 illustrates the central structure of the Internet.

An Autonomous System, in addition to IP addresses, uses a special globally unique Autonomous System Number (ASN) assigned by IANA. Originally

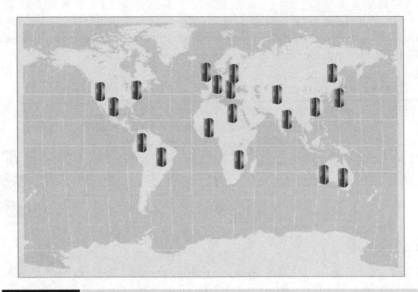

FIGURE 6.28   The Internet

16 bit, the current ASNs are 32 bits, displayed as two 16-bit numbers separated by a dot. So, 1.33457 would be a typical ASN. Just as you would assign an IP address to a router, you would configure the router to use the ASN assigned by the IANA (see Figure 6.29).

Autonomous Systems communicate with each other using a protocol called generically an *exterior gateway protocol (EGP)*. The network or networks within an AS communicate with protocols as well; these are called generically *interior gateway protocols (IGPs)*.

Neither EGP nor IGP is a dynamic routing protocol; rather, these are categories that represent routing protocols exchanged between routers of the same AS (IGP—further subdivided into distance vector vs. link state) or between different ASes (EGP).

```
Router2811(config)#router bgp ?
  <1-65535>  Autonomous system number

Router2811(config)#router bgp 1902
```

FIGURE 6.29   Configuring a Cisco router to use an ASN

The easy way to keep these terms separate is to appreciate that although many protocols are used *within* Autonomous Systems, such as RIP, the Internet has settled on one protocol for communication between each AS: the *Border Gateway Protocol (BGP-4)*. BGP is the glue of the Internet, connecting all the Autonomous Systems. Other dynamic routing protocols, such as RIP, are, by definition, IGPs.

BGP routers advertise information passed to them from different Autonomous Systems' *edge routers*—that's what the AS-to-AS routers are called. BGP forwards these advertisements that include the ASN and other items.

BGP also knows how to handle a number of situations unique to the Internet. If a router advertises a new route that isn't reliable, most BGP routers will ignore it. BGP also supports policies for limiting which and how other routers may access an ISP.

BGP implements and supports route aggregation, a way to simplify routing tables into manageable levels. Rather than trying to keep track of every other router on the Internet, the backbone routers track the location of routers that connect to subsets of locations.

BGP is an amazing and powerful routing protocol, but unless you're working deep in the router room of an AS, odds are good you'll never see it in action. Those who need to connect a few routers together usually turn to a family of dynamic routing protocols that work very differently than distance vector routing protocols.

Exam Tip

iBGP and eBGP   You can use BGP within an AS to connect networks; therefore, you can and do run into situations where BGP is both the interior and exterior protocol for an AS. To distinguish between the two uses of the protocol, network folks refer to the BGP on the interior as the internal BGP (iBGP); the exterior connection then becomes the exterior BGP (eBGP). The CompTIA Network+ exam objectives list BGP as a hybrid routing protocol, because it can be used as an IGP as well as an EGP. It's actually not a distance vector or link state protocol, but rather a path vector protocol. *Path vector* means that the exact path to destination networks is stored, instead of just the next-hop router, which is just what both distance vector and link state routing protocols store.

Dynamic Routing Makes the Internet

Without dynamic routing, the complex, self-healing Internet we all enjoy today couldn't exist. So many routes come and go so often that manually updating

TABLE 6.2		Dynamic Routing Protocols	
Protocol	**Type**	**IGP or EGP?**	**Notes**
RIPv1	Distance vector	IGP	Old, should never be used.
RIPv2	Distance vector	IGP	Old, should never be used. Supports VLSM and noncontiguous subnets.
OSPF	Link state	IGP	Fast, popular; uses Area IDs.
IS-IS	Link state	IGP	ISP alternative to OSPF.
BGP-4	Path vector	IGP and EGP (hybrid)	Used on the Internet as an EGP. Can also be used within an Autonomous System as an IGP.

static routes would be impossible. Review Table 6.2 to familiarize yourself with the differences among the different types of dynamic routing protocols.

Route Redistribution

The routers cannot use different routing protocols to communicate with each other, but many routers can speak multiple routing protocols simultaneously. When a router takes routes it has learned by one method—say, RIP or a statically set route—and announces those routes over another protocol such as OSPF, this is called *route redistribution*. This feature can come in handy when you have a mix of equipment and protocols in your network, such as occurs when you switch vendors or merge with another organization.

Administrative Distance

Routers that use multiple routing protocols can have multiple paths to the same destination with different routing protocols (such as EIGRP and OSPF, for example). *Administrative distance* is a number assigned to a routing protocol to allow routers to prefer one protocol over the other, if a destination network can be reached with multiple routing protocols. Finally, we have a way to compare apples to oranges!

CHECKPOINT

✔**Objective 6.01: Routing Tables** Routers use routing tables to determine where to send incoming packets. After stripping off the incoming frame information, a router examines the IP packet's destination address and begins comparing that address to the many routes in its routing table to determine the proper interface to use to send the packet to its destination. The router will encapsulate the packet into the appropriate frame and then send it along. You can use command-line tools to view routing tables in an OS, most commonly by running **netstat –r**.

✔**Objective 6.02: Network Address Translation and High Availability** Routers running some form of *Network Address Translation (NAT)* hide the IP addresses of computers on the LAN, but still enable those computers to communicate with the broader Internet. The most common form of NAT, called Port Address Translation (PAT), uses one or more public IP addresses to enable devices on the inside of a LAN to use a block of private IP addresses. The PAT router uses port numbers to map traffic to and from specific machines in the network. VRRP and HSRP are protocols that allow multiple routers to "share" a default gateway IP address. DHCP relay agents can take DHCP broadcasts and turn them into unicast messages, allowing DHCP servers on a single subnet to give out IP addresses to clients on different LANs.

✔**Objective 6.03: Dynamic Routing** Dynamic routing protocols enable routers to update routing tables by interacting with other routers rather than through human intervention. CompTIA expects techs to know about three categories: distance vector, link state, and hybrid. Routers using a distance vector protocol, such as RIP or EIGRP, send their routing tables to other routers at regular intervals. Routers using a link state protocol, such as OSPF or IS-IS, only send updates to routes, making them faster and more efficient, especially as you scale up the size of the internetwork. BGP is a distance vector routing protocol that can be both an IGP and an EGP. For that reason, CompTIA calls it a hybrid routing protocol.

REVIEW QUESTIONS

1. How many lines of a routing table does the router read when comparing the IP address and subnet mask of an incoming packet?
   - **A.** The router reads only the first two lines to determine the proper route.
   - **B.** The router reads the lines from the top until it reaches the proper route.
   - **C.** The router reads the lines from the bottom until it reaches the proper route.
   - **D.** The router reads all the lines and then determines the proper route.

2. What is the purpose of the default route in a routing table?
   - **A.** The default route tells the router where to send every packet.
   - **B.** The default route is used by routers solely for updating routing tables.
   - **C.** The default route tells the router where to send every packet if not explicitly listed on another line in the routing table.
   - **D.** The default route is used to configure the router.

3. How many IP addresses should a router have?
   - **A.** One
   - **B.** One or more
   - **C.** Two
   - **D.** Two or more

4. Which version of NAT maps a single routable IP address to a single network node?
   - **A.** Static NAT
   - **B.** Dynamic NAT
   - **C.** Pooled NAT
   - **D.** Secure NAT

5. What technology enables you to designate a specific local address for various network services?
   - **A.** Dynamic NAT
   - **B.** Port Address Translation
   - **C.** Port forwarding
   - **D.** Port filtering

6. How is the distance between routers measured?

   A. In meters

   B. In hops

   C. In routes

   D. In segments

7. Link state routing protocols include which of the following? (Select two.)

   A. RIP

   B. OSPF

   C. BGP

   D. IS-IS

8. What do routers do when there is more than one path to a destination network?

   A. Use the route with the lowest metric.

   B. Use the route with the highest metric.

   C. Randomly pick a route on a packet-by-packet basis.

   D. Use all routes in a round-robin fashion.

9. Why are link state protocols more efficient than distance vector routing protocols?

   A. Entire routing tables are updated on a stricter schedule.

   B. They forward only changes to individual routes instead of forwarding entire routing tables.

   C. Packets can be sent along multiple routes at the same time.

   D. Link state can send larger packets.

10. Which of the following is a hybrid dynamic routing protocol because it can be used as both an IGP and an EGP?

   A. RIP

   B. OSPF

   C. BGP

   D. EIGRP

REVIEW ANSWERS

1. **D**   The router reads all the lines and then determines the proper route.

2. **C**   The default route tells the router where to send every packet unless another line in the routing table gives another route.

3. **D**   By definition, a router should have two or more IP addresses to connect different networks with its routing function.

4. **A**   Static NAT maps a single routable (that is, not private) IP address to a single machine.

5. **C**   Port forwarding enables you to designate a specific local address for various network services.

6. **B**   The distance between routers is measured in hops.

7. **B D**   Link state routing protocols include OSPF and IS-IS.

8. **A**   The lowest metric is always the most preferred by routers.

9. **B**   Link state protocols forward only changes to individual routes, whereas distance vector protocols forward entire routing tables.

10. **C**   BGP can be used as both an IGP and an EGP.

Virtualization

	NEWBIE	SOME EXPERIENCE	EXPERT
ETA	4 hours	2 hours	1 hour

Modern networks are often hugely complex and intricate, with many different devices filling many different roles. Hungry for greater flexibility and lower hardware costs, the IT industry now uses software to do many jobs traditionally handled by hardware. In this chapter, you will learn about *virtualization*, specialized programs that act like physical devices. First, you will learn about virtual LANs, which use a single switch to create multiple broadcast domains. After that, you will read about virtual computing, or using one physical computer to run multiple virtual systems. Next, you will learn about the place virtualization has in today's networking world. Continuing in our exploration, this chapter will examine virtual private networks, SAN/NAS, and cloud computing concepts as well.

Objective 7.01   Virtual LANs

It's rare these days to see a serious network that doesn't have remote incoming connections, public servers, and wireless networks, as well as the basic string of connected switches. Although it's possible, even easy, to leave all these different aspects of your network on a single broadcast domain, doing so potentially produces a tremendous amount of broadcast traffic and creates a security nightmare. What if you could segment the network using the switches you already own? A *virtual local area network (VLAN)* enables you to do just that.

To create a VLAN, you take a single physical broadcast domain and chop it up into multiple virtual broadcast domains. Switches, for over a decade, have supported VLANs. Imagine a single switch with a number of computers connected to it. Up to this point, a single switch has always been a single broadcast domain, but that's about to change. You've decided to take this single switch and turn it into two VLANs. VLANs are spoken as "VLAN" plus a number, as in VLAN1 or VLAN275. In this example, I'll configure the ports on my single switch to be in one of two VLANs—VLAN1 or VLAN2 (see Figure 7.1). I promise to show you how to configure ports for different VLANs shortly, but I have a couple other concepts to cover first.

A single switch configured into two VLANs is the simplest form of VLANs possible. More serious networks usually have more than one switch. Let's say you added a switch to a simple network. You'd like to keep VLAN1 and VLAN2, but use both switches. You can configure the new switch to use VLAN1 and VLAN2, but you've got to enable data to flow between the two switches, regardless of VLAN. That's where trunking comes into play.

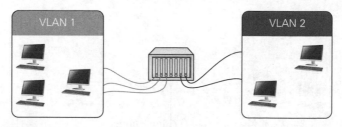

FIGURE 7.1 Switch with two VLANs

Trunking

Trunking is the process of transferring VLAN traffic between two or more switches. Imagine two switches, each configured with a VLAN1 and a VLAN2, as shown in Figure 7.2.

You want all the computers connected to VLAN1 on one switch to talk to all of the computers connected to VLAN1 on the other switch. Of course, you also want to do this with VLAN2. To do this, you configure a port on each switch as a *trunk port,* which is a port on a switch configured to carry all traffic, regardless of VLAN number, between all switches in a LAN (see Figure 7.3).

Today, every Ethernet switch prefers the IEEE 802.1Q trunk standard that enables you to connect switches from different manufacturers.

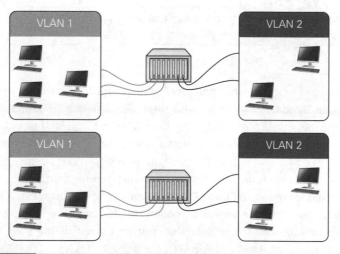

FIGURE 7.2 Two switches, each with VLAN 1 and VLAN 2

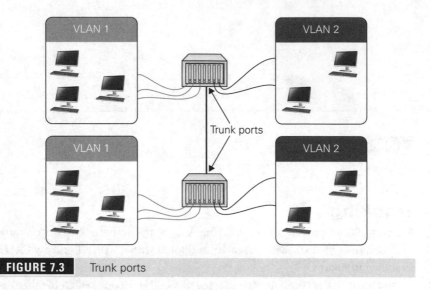

| **FIGURE 7.3** | Trunk ports |

Configuring a VLAN-Capable Switch

If you want to configure a VLAN-capable switch, you need a method to perform that configuration. One method uses a serial (console) port, while another
method is to access the switch with a web browser interface, like the one shown
in Figure 7.4.

> **Local Lingo**
>
> **unmanaged switch**   A simple switch without any configuration
> capability is called an *unmanaged switch*.

A managed switch can be configured with an IP address, similar to the pre-
set, private IP addresses you see on routers. This switch IP address isn't for
any of the individual ports (they only have MAC addresses), but rather is for
the whole switch. That means no matter where you physically connect to the
switch, the IP address to get to the configuration screen is the same.

Every switch manufacturer has its own interface for configuring VLANs,
but the interface shown in Figure 7.5 is a classic example. This is Cisco Network
Assistant, a very popular tool that enables you to configure multiple devices
through the same interface. Note that you first must define your VLANs,
although every port starts with VLAN1, the default VLAN.

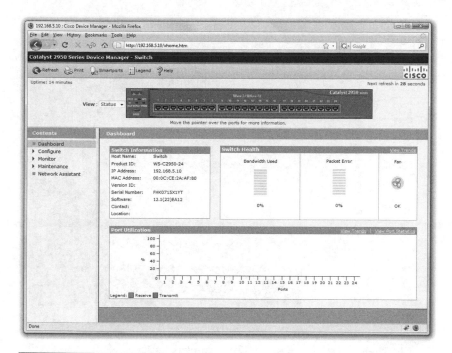

FIGURE 7.4   Catalyst 2950 Series Device Manager

After you create the VLANs, you assign ports to them. Assigning each port to a VLAN means that whatever frames go into that port will be tagged with membership information for that VLAN. Figure 7.6 shows a port being assigned to a particular VLAN.

Travel Advisory

If you've just plugged into a VLAN, but can't seem to access the other computers on your VLAN, make sure you've plugged your computer into a port assigned to the correct VLAN. If there are no more available ports, you'll have to configure the port you're plugged into to be on the right VLAN.

Tagging

All of the preceding information about VLANs begs the question, when you have a busy network with multiple switches and multiple VLANs, how does a frame from a workstation in VLAN100 make it to a destination workstation

FIGURE 7.5 Defining VLANs in Cisco Network Assistant

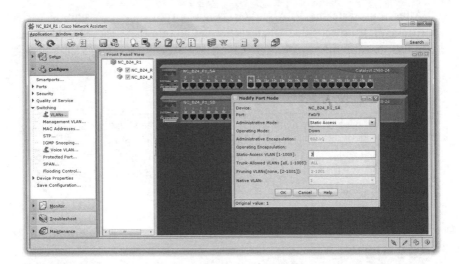

FIGURE 7.6 Assigning a port to a VLAN

in the same VLAN? What about if the workstations are several switches apart? The key tool that makes this happen is called *tagging.*

Workstations plug into access ports—regular ports that have been configured as part of a VLAN—that do the work of tagging traffic with the appropriate VLAN when frames enter the switch, and removing the tag, when frames leave the switch. Note that access ports are ports, just like trunk ports, but configured for the opposite purpose. Access ports connect to workstations, while trunk ports connect to trunk ports on other switches.

When the data enters the access port, the switch tags the frames with the appropriate VLAN (see Figure 7.7). If the destination workstation is connected to the same switch, the frames flow to that workstation's access port. The tag is stripped off each frame, and traffic flows as you would expect. If the destination workstation connects to a different switch, the initial switch sends the frames out its trunk port. What happens next is determined by how the trunk port is configured.

The VLAN designation for a trunk port is its native VLAN. If the trunk port has a native VLAN that differs from the tag placed on the frame as it entered the access port, the switch leaves the tag on the frame and sends the tagged frame along to the next switch. If the trunk port's native VLAN is the same as the access port's VLAN, then the switch drops the tag and sends the untagged frame out of the trunk port.

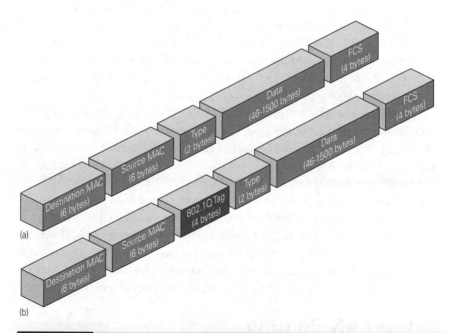

FIGURE 7.7   (a) Untagged Ethernet frame and (b) tagged Ethernet frame

Native VLANs exist to provide compatibility with older or simpler non-VLAN tagging switches, but there is a catch. The native VLAN opens your network to a nasty vulnerability called a *double-tagging attack,* which lets the attacker access VLANs they should not be able to access. For this reason, in modern networks the native VLAN is set to an unused VLAN, and the trunk port is configured to tag its native VLAN traffic as well.

> **Exam Tip**
>
> Let's keep our ports straight! A *switch port* is a physical port on a switch that an Ethernet cable plugs into. An *access port* is a switch port that connects to a NIC in a PC. A *trunk port* is a switch port that connects to another switch port (which is also a trunk port) on a different switch.

VLAN Trunking Protocol

A busy network with many VLAN switches can require periods of intensive work to update. Imagine the work required to redo all the VLAN switches if you changed the VLAN configuration by adding or removing a VLAN. You'd have to access every switch individually, change the port configuration to alter the VLAN assignment, and so on. The potential for errors is staggering.

If you misconfigure the port or assign the wrong VLAN to a set of ports, that would manifest as users who previously could access the proper resources no longer being able to access them. Worse, you could have users loose in places they should not be authorized to access. Manually tracking down and trouble-shooting these kinds of errors takes way too much time.

Cisco uses a proprietary protocol called *VLAN Trunking Protocol (VTP)* to automate the updating of multiple VLAN switches. With VTP, you put each switch into one of three states: server, client, or transparent. When you make changes to the VLAN configuration of the server switch, all the connected client switches and other server switches update their configurations within minutes. Likewise, updates sent from VTP clients can change the VLAN database on VLAN servers. The only difference between VTP clients and VTP servers is that VLAN information can be added, modified, or deleted manually on VTP servers.

When you set a VLAN switch to transparent, you tell it not to update but to hold on to its manual settings. You would use a transparent mode VLAN switch in circumstances where the overall VLAN configuration assignments did not apply.

InterVLAN Routing

Once you've configured a switch to support multiple VLANs, each VLAN is its own broadcast domain, just as if the two VLANs were on two completely

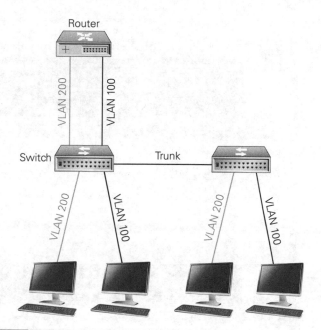

| **FIGURE 7.8** | One router connecting multiple VLANs |

separate switches and networks. There is no way for data to get from one VLAN to another unless you use a router. The process of making a router work between two VLANs is called *interVLAN routing*. Figure 7.8 shows one possible way to connect two VLANs with a single router. Note that the router has one port connected to VLAN 100 and another connected to VLAN 200. Devices on VLAN 100 may now communicate with devices on VLAN 200.

Adding a physical router like this isn't a very elegant way to connect VLANs. This forces almost all traffic to go through the router, and it's not a very flexible solution if you want to add more VLANs in the future. This is where a multilayer switch comes into play. Figure 7.9 shows an older but very popular multilayer switch, the Cisco 3550.

The Cisco 3550 not only supports VLANs, but also enables you to create switched virtual interfaces (SVIs), which are IP addresses assigned to VLANs that serve as default gateways for devices plugged into the switch, as well as

| **FIGURE 7.9** | Cisco 3550 |

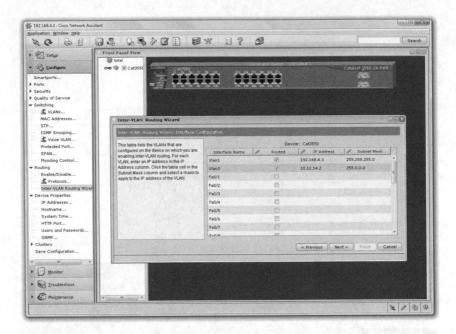

FIGURE 7.10   Setting up interVLAN routing

physical routed ports (a simple command can change a default layer-2 switch port into a layer-3 router port—*no switchport*), to interconnect these VLANs. Figure 7.10 shows the configuration screen for the 3550's interVLAN routing between two VLANs.

Being a switch that also has the capability to create SVIs and physical routed ports, the Cisco 3550 works at both layers 2 and 3 at the same time, and is also referred to as a *multilayer switch* as well as a *layer-3 switch*.

Objective 7.02   Virtual Computing

In the simplest terms, *virtualization* is the process of using special software—a class of programs called *hypervisors* or *virtual machine managers*—to create a complete environment in which a guest operating system can function as though it were installed on its own computer. That guest environment is called a *virtual machine (VM)*. Figure 7.11 shows one such example: a system running Windows 7 using a program called VMware Workstation to host a virtual machine running Ubuntu Linux.

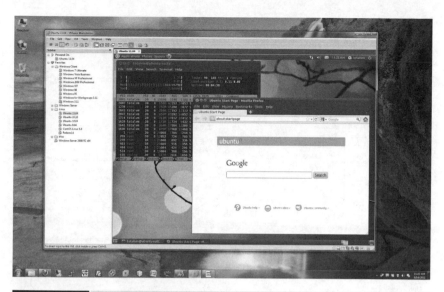

FIGURE 7.11   VMware running Linux

Meet the Hypervisor

A normal operating system uses programming called a *supervisor* to handle very low-level interactions among hardware and software, such as task scheduling, allotment of time and resources, and so on.

Because virtualization enables one machine—called the *host*—to run multiple operating systems simultaneously, full virtualization requires an extra layer of sophisticated programming to manage the vastly more complex interactions. That's where the terms *hypervisor* and *virtual machine manager (VMM)* came from.

A hypervisor has to handle every input and output that the operating system would request of normal hardware. With a good hypervisor like VMware Workstation, you can easily add and remove virtual hard drives, virtual network cards, virtual RAM, and so on. Figure 7.12 shows the hardware configuration screen from VMware Workstation.

Virtualization even goes so far as to provide a virtualized BIOS and system setup utility for every virtual machine. Figure 7.13 shows VMware Workstation displaying the system setup utility, just like you'd see it on a regular computer.

Travel Advisory

The host machine allocates real RAM and CPU time to every running virtual machine. A host can only handle a finite number of simultaneous virtual machines before experiencing degraded performance.

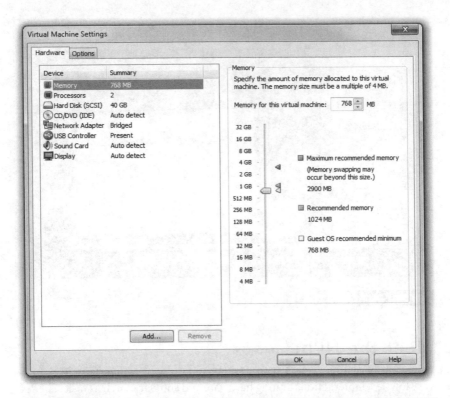

FIGURE 7.12   Configuring virtual hardware in VMware Workstation

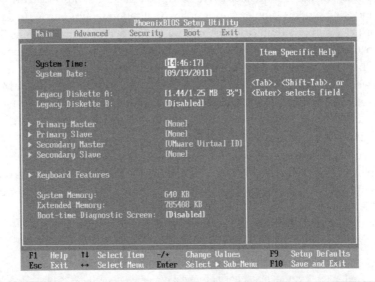

FIGURE 7.13   System setup utility in VMware Workstation

Why Do We Virtualize?

Virtualization has taken the networking world by storm, but for those who have never seen virtualization, the big question has got to be, why? Let's talk about the benefits of virtualization. While you read this section, keep in mind two important things:

- A single hypervisor on a single system will happily run as many virtual machines as its RAM, CPU, and drive space allow (RAM is almost always the main limiting factor).
- A virtual machine that's shut down is little more than a file (or a few files) sitting on a hard drive.

Power Savings

Before virtualization, each server OS needed to be on a unique physical system. With virtualization, you can place multiple virtual servers on a single physical system, thus reducing electrical power use substantially. Rather than one machine running Windows Server 2012 R2 and acting as a DNS server, and a second machine running Linux as a DHCP server, for example, the same computer can handle both operating systems simultaneously. Expand this electricity savings over an enterprise network or on a data server farm, and the savings—both in terms of dollars spent and electricity used—is tremendous.

Hardware Consolidation

Similar to power savings, why buy a high-end server box, complete with multiple processors, RAID arrays, redundant power supplies, and so on, and only run a single server? With virtualization, you can easily beef up the RAM and run a number of servers on a single box.

System Recovery

Possibly the most popular reason for virtualizing is to keep uptime percentage as high as possible. Let's say you have a web server installed on a single system. If that system goes down—due to hacking or malware—you need to restore the system from a backup, which may or may not be easily at hand. With virtualization, you merely need to shut down the virtual machine and reload a previously saved copy of it.

FIGURE 7.14 Saving a snapshot

Local Lingo

uptime Uptime refers to the amount of time a computer has been consecutively online.

Think of virtual machines like you would a word processing document. Virtual machines don't have a "File | Save" equivalent, but they do have something called a *snapshot* that enables you to save an extra copy of the virtual machine as it is exactly at the moment the snapshot is taken. Figure 7.14 shows VMware Workstation saving a snapshot.

System Duplication

Closely tied to system recovery, system duplication takes advantage of the fact that VMs are simply files, and like any file, they can be copied. Let's say you want to teach 20 students about Ubuntu Linux. Depending on the hypervisor you choose, you can simply install a hypervisor on 20 machines and copy a single virtual machine to all the computers. Equally, if you have a virtualized web server and need to add another web server (assuming your physical box has the hardware to support it), why not just make a copy of the server and fire it up as well?

Research

Here's a great example that happens in my own company: I sell my popular Total Tester test banks—practice questions for you to test your skills on a broad number of certification topics. As with any distributed program, I tend to get a few support calls. Running a problem through the same OS, even down to the service pack, helps me solve the problem. In the pre-virtualization days, I commonly had seven to ten PCs, multi-booting them, with each keeping copies of a particular Windows version. Today, a single hypervisor enables me to support a huge number of Windows versions on a single machine (see Figure 7.15).

Clearly there are a number of good reasons to virtualize some of the computers in a network. Let's look at implementation now.

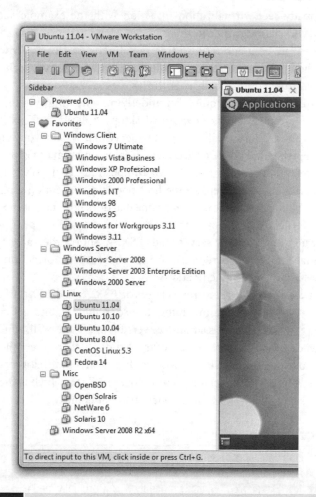

FIGURE 7.15   Lots of VMs used for research

Objective 7.03 Virtualization in Modern Networks

Virtualization manifests in many ways in modern networks. Hypervisors serve many roles in businesses, and you can choose from one of many varieties when you want to implement virtualization. This section examines modern virtualization.

Hypervisors

You've already seen virtualization in action with the example shown using VMware Workstation earlier in this chapter. Many networks use a few virtual machines to augment and refine a traditional network closet. VMware Workstation is how I first performed virtualization on PCs, but the technology and power have grown dramatically over the last few years.

VMware Workstation requires an underlying operating system, so it functions essentially like a very powerful desktop application. Hypervisors that operate in this fashion are called Type 2 hypervisors. What if you could remove the OS altogether and create a bare-metal implementation of virtualization?

VMware introduced ESX in 2002 to accomplish this goal. ESX is a hypervisor that's powerful enough to replace the host operating system on a physical box, turning the physical machine into a machine that does nothing but support virtual machines. Hypervisors that operate in this fashion are called Type 1 hypervisors.

Power up the server; the server loads ESX. In short order, a very rudimentary interface appears where you can input essential information, such as a master password and a static IP address.

VMware came out with a free version of ESX, called ESXi, in 2008. This strategic move allowed administrators to use, publicize, and get comfortable with ESXi at no cost. There is a non-free version of ESXi as well, which is highly recommended for production networks. Although there are still some ESX machines out there, as of 2010, VMware discontinued development on ESX, and strongly urged its customers to move over to ESXi, which is the only platform now supported by VMware vSphere (explained next).

Local Lingo
ESX   For all you abbreviation lovers, I have some good news and some bad news about "ESX." Officially, it means nothing. Unofficially, it stands for "Elastic Sky," which is probably why it officially means nothing.

Don't let ESXi's small size fool you. It's small because it only has one job: to host virtual machines. ESXi is an extremely powerful operating system/hypervisor.

Powerful hypervisors like ESXi are not administered directly at the box. Instead, you use tools such as VMware's vSphere Client, so you can create, configure, and maintain virtual machines on the hypervisor server from the comfort of a client computer running this program. Once the VM is up and running, you can close the vSphere Client, but the VM will continue to run happily on the server. So you now really have two different ways to virtualize: using hypervisors such as VMware's Workstation to manage virtual desktops and using powerful hypervisors such as ESXi to manage virtual servers.

Thus far, this chapter sounds like an advertisement for VMware. VMware really brought virtualization to the PC world and still holds a strong presence, but there are a number of alternatives to VMware products. Let's see what else is available.

Type 2 Hypervisors

When it comes to the more basic hypervisors, you have a huge number of choices. The one you use is going to be based on features and prices.

VMware Workstation

The granddaddy and front leader for virtualization, VMware Workstation, comes in both Windows and Linux versions. VMware Workstation runs on virtually any operating system you'll ever need (pun intended!). It's incredibly stable and proven. Too bad it's not free.

One of the more interesting features of VMware Workstation is VMTools. VMTools adds useful features such as copy/cut and paste between the host and guest operating systems.

VMware Player

Compared to VMware Workstation, VMware Player is free, but doesn't include a lot of bells and whistles in the non-free VMware Workstation.

Parallels Desktop for Mac, Server for Mac, Workstation

Parallels Desktop for Mac, Server for Mac, and Workstation (discontinued in 2013 for Windows and Linux) are the most popular virtualization managers for Mac OS X, although VMware Fusion is a close second. Parallels supports all popular operating systems (except Workstation since 2013), and even has a fair degree of 3D graphics support; more so than even the mighty VMware. Figure 7.16 shows Windows running on a Mac through Parallels Desktop.

FIGURE 7.16   Parallels Desktop for Mac running a copy of Windows

KVM

Of course, the open-source world has its players, too. Kernel-based Virtual Machine (KVM) is one of many available Linux-based hypervisors. KVM originally supported x86 processors, but now supports multiple processor types, including IA-64.

Type 1/Bare-Metal Hypervisors

Although you have lots of choices when it comes to virtual machine managers, your choices for real embedded hypervisors are limited to the two biggies: VMware's ESXi and Microsoft's Hyper-V. There are others, such as Oracle's VM Server, but nothing has the market share of ESXi or Hyper-V.

ESXi

I've already discussed a few aspects of ESXi, so in this section I'll delve into the features that make ESXi so popular. When it comes to real server virtualization, VMware truly leads the pack with a host of innovations (some of which are add-on products) that make ESXi almost unstoppable. Here are a few examples:

- **Interface with large storage** ESXi virtual machines easily integrate with network-attached storage (NAS) and storage area networks (SANs) to handle massive data storage.
- **Transparent fault tolerance** ESXi can monitor and automatically recover failed VMs with little or no input.
- **Transparent server transfer** You can move a *running* VM from one machine to another. How cool is that?
- **High virtual CPUs** Most hypervisors support a limited number of virtual CPUs, usually two at most. ESXi can support up to 32 CPUs, depending on the vSphere product version you purchase to support it.

Hyper-V

Although Hyper-V can't stand toe-to-toe with ESXi, it has a few aces up its sleeve that give it some appeal. First, it's free. This is important in that ESXi, with only a few extra add-ons, can cost thousands of dollars. Second, it comes as a stand-alone product or as part of Windows Server 2012 R2; it even comes with Windows 8/8.1/10 as Client Hyper-V, making it easy for those who like to play to access it. Third, its simplicity makes it easier to learn for those new to using hypervisors. Watch Hyper-V. If Microsoft does one thing well, it's taking market share away from arguably better, more powerful competitors, while slowly making its product better.

Virtual Switches

Imagine for a moment that you have three virtual machines running as virtual desktops. You want all these machines to have access to the Internet. Therefore, you need to give them all legitimate IP addresses. The physical server, however, only has a single NIC. There are two ways in which virtualization gives individual VMs valid IP addresses. The oldest and simplest way is to bridge the NICs. Each virtual NIC is given a bridged connection to the real NIC (see Figure 7.17). This bridge works at layer 2 of the OSI model, so each virtual NIC has a legitimate, unique MAC address, to which a unique IP address is bound.

A subset of this type of bridging is to give every VM its own physical NIC (see Figure 7.18). In this case, you're still bridging, but every virtual NIC goes straight to a dedicated physical NIC.

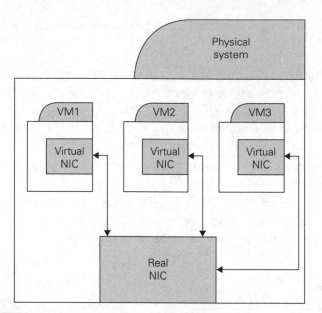

FIGURE 7.17 Bridged NICs

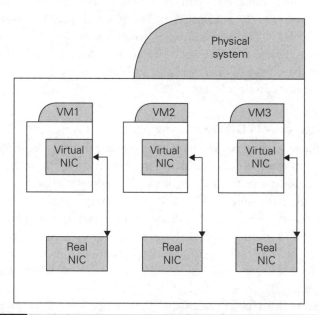

FIGURE 7.18 Dedicated bridged NICs

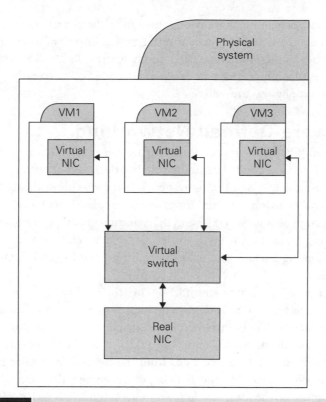

FIGURE 7.19　Virtual switch

Your second option is to create a *virtual switch,* which is special software that enables VMs to communicate with each other without going outside of the host system. Hypervisors allow you to connect all of your virtual machines to the same virtual switch. Depending on your hypervisor, this switch can do everything you'd expect from a typical managed layer-2 switch, including VLANs (see Figure 7.19).

If you really want to go crazy on virtual switches (and have lots of money), Cisco will sell you an appliance such as the Cisco Nexus 1000V that offloads all of the virtual switching from the hypervisor and adds higher-layer features such as firewalls/ACLs, DHCP servers, and many other features.

Virtual Routers and Firewalls

Similar to how virtual machines enable us to easily reallocate computing resources when demand changes, virtual routers let us dynamically reconfigure networks. This lets the network keep up when VMs are moved from host to host to meet demand or improve resource use. The virtual routers can have more resources allocated to them as traffic grows, instead of us having to buy bigger, better physical routers. When it comes to firewalls, the same rules apply: virtual firewalls can protect servers where it would be hard, costly, or impossible to insert physical firewalls.

Software-Defined Networking

Traditionally, hardware routers and switches were designed with two closely integrated parts: a control plane that makes decisions about how to move traffic, and a data plane that is responsible for executing those decisions. The control plane on a router, for example, is what actually transmits the routing protocols such as OSPF and BGP, discussed in Chapter 6, and builds the routing tables that it gives to the data plane. The router's data plane reads incoming packets and uses the routing table to send them to their destination.

Software-defined networking (SDN) cuts the control plane of individual devices out of the picture and lets an all-knowing program called a *network controller* dictate how both physical and virtual network components move traffic through the network (Figure 7.20). SDN requires components with data planes designed to take instructions from the network controller instead of their own control plane. Although it's important enough that SDN allows for a master controller, the really revolutionary idea behind SDN is that the network controller is programmable: we can write code that controls how the entire network will behave.

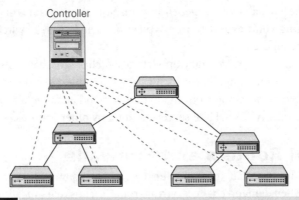

Controller

FIGURE 7.20   SDN in action

Objective 7.04 Virtual Private Networks

Several standards use encrypted tunnels between a computer or a remote network and a private network through the Internet (see Figure 7.21), resulting in what is called a *virtual private network (VPN)*.

An encrypted tunnel requires *endpoints*—the ends of the tunnel where the data is encrypted and decrypted. Either some software running on a computer or, in some cases, a dedicated box must act as an endpoint for a VPN (see Figure 7.22).

Exam Tip

CompTIA calls devices that handle encrypted tunnels *encryption devices*.

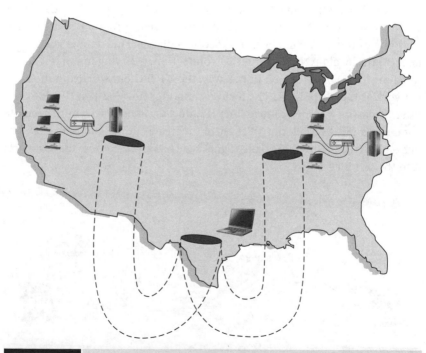

FIGURE 7.21 VPN connecting computers across the United States

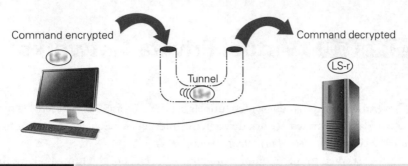

Command encrypted   Command decrypted

Tunnel

FIGURE 7.22   Typical tunnel

The key with the VPN is that all the computers should be on the same network—and that means they must all have the same network ID. For example, you would want the laptop that you are using in an airport lounge to have the same network ID as all the computers in your LAN back at the office. But there's no simple way to do this. If it's a single client trying to access a network, that client is going to take on the IP address from its local DHCP server. In the case of your laptop in the airport, your network ID and IP address come from the DHCP server in the airport, not the DHCP server back at the office.

To make the VPN work, you need a VPN client program protocol that uses one of the many tunneling protocols available. This remote client connects to the local LAN via its Internet connection, querying for an IP address from the local DHCP server. In this way, the VPN client will be on the same network as the office LAN. The remote computer now has two IP addresses. First, it has its Internet connection's IP address, obtained from the remote computer's ISP. Second, the VPN client creates a tunnel endpoint that acts like a NIC (see Figure 7.23). This virtual NIC has an IP address that connects it to the office LAN.

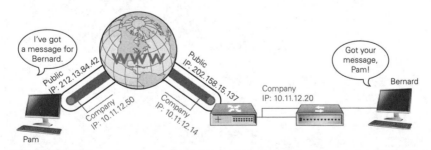

FIGURE 7.23   Endpoints must have their own IP addresses.

There are many ways to make this work, and those implementations function at different layers of the OSI model. PPTP and L2TP, for example, work at the Data Link layer. Many VPNs use IPsec at the Network layer to handle encryption needs. SSL/TLS VPNs don't really fit into the OSI model well at all, with some features in the Session layer and others in the Presentation layer.

PPTP VPNs

So how do you make IP addresses appear out of thin air? Microsoft got the ball rolling with the *Point-to-Point Tunneling Protocol (PPTP),* an advanced version of the older Point-to-Point-Protocol (PPP) that handles this right out of the box. The only trick is the endpoints. In Microsoft's view, a VPN is intended for individual clients to connect to a private network, so Microsoft places the PPTP endpoints on the client and the server. The server endpoint is a special remote-access server program, originally only available on Windows Server, called *Routing and Remote Access Service (RRAS)*(see Figure 7.24).

On the Windows client side, you run Create a New Connection. This creates a virtual NIC that, like any other NIC, does a DHCP query and gets an IP address from the DHCP server on the private network (see Figure 7.25).

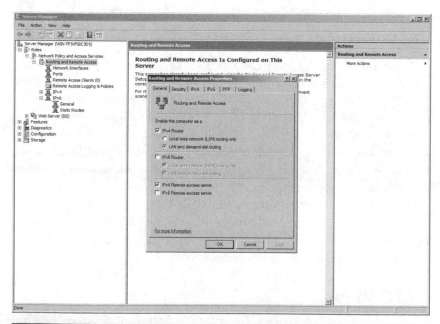

FIGURE 7.24 RRAS in action

FIGURE 7.25 VPN connection in Windows

Exam Tip

A system connected to a VPN looks as though it's on the local network, but performs much slower than if the system was connected directly back at the office because it's not local at all.

When your computer connects to the RRAS server on the private network, PPTP creates a secure tunnel through the Internet back to the private LAN. Your client takes on an IP address of that network as if your computer is directly connected to the LAN back at the office, even down to the default gateway. If you open your web browser, your client will go across the Internet to the local LAN and then use the LAN's default gateway to get to the Internet! Using a web browser will be much slower when you are on a VPN. Every operating system comes with some type of built-in VPN client that supports PPTP (among others). Figure 7.26 shows Network, the Mac OS X VPN connection tool.

This type of VPN connection, where a single computer logs into a remote network and becomes, for all intents and purposes, a member of that network, is commonly called a *client-to-site* connection.

L2TP VPNs

Layer 2 Tunneling Protocol (L2TP), based on Microsoft's PPTP and Cisco's Layer 2 Forwarding (L2F), took all the good features of PPTP and L2F

FIGURE 7.26   VPN on a Macintosh OS X system

and added support to run on almost any type of connection possible, from telephones to Ethernet to ultra-high-speed optical connections. The endpoint on the local LAN was moved from a server program to a VPN-capable router, called a *VPN concentrator,* such as the Cisco 2811 Integrated Services Router shown in Figure 7.27.

Exam Tip

Cisco made hardware that supported PPP traffic using a proprietary protocol called *Layer 2 Forwarding (L2F).* L2F did not come with encryption capabilities, so it was replaced by L2TP a long time ago.

FIGURE 7.27   Cisco 2811 Integrated Services Router

Cisco provides free client software to connect a single faraway PC to a Cisco VPN. This creates a typical client-to-site connection. Network people often directly connect two Cisco VPN concentrators to connect two separate LANs permanently. It's slow, but inexpensive, compared to a dedicated high-speed connection between two faraway LANs. This kind of connection enables two separate LANs to function as a single network, sharing files and services as if in the same building. This is called a *site-to-site* VPN connection. L2TP differs from PPTP in that it has no authentication or encryption. L2TP generally uses Internet Protocol Security (IPsec) for all security needs. Technically, you should call an L2TP VPN an "L2TP/IPsec" VPN. L2TP works perfectly well in the single-client-connecting-to-a-LAN world, too. Every operating system's VPN client fully supports L2TP/IPsec VPNs.

Travel Advisory

The years have seen plenty of crossover between Microsoft and Cisco. Microsoft RRAS supports L2TP, and Cisco routers support PPTP.

SSL VPNs

Cisco has made a big push for companies to adopt VPN hardware that enables VPNs using Secure Sockets Layer (SSL). These types of VPN offer an advantage over Data Link–based or Network-based VPNs because they don't require any special client software. Clients connect to the VPN server using a standard web browser, with the traffic secured using SSL. The two most common types of SSL VPNs are SSL portal VPNs and SSL tunnel VPNs.

With SSL portal VPNs, a client accesses the VPN and is presented with a secure web page. The client gains access to anything linked on that page, be it e-mail, data, links to other pages, and so on.

With tunnel VPNs, in contrast, the client web browser runs some kind of active control, such as Java or Flash, and gains much greater access to the VPN-connected network. SSL tunnel VPNs create a more typical host-to-site connection than SSL portal VPNs, but the user must have sufficient permissions to run the active browser controls.

Travel Advisory

With a program like Cisco's AnyConnect SSL VPN Client, the client computer can act as if it was literally on the company network, and does not have to use a browser.

IPsec

The most common VPN today offers pure (no L2TP) IPsec solutions. These VPN technologies use IPsec tunneling for VPNs. IPsec VPNs are really the only viable option today for site-to-site VPNs, and are also used for client-to-site VPNs. IPsec works at layer 3 of the OSI model (which is why it is called IPsec). The major component to IPsec is Encapsulating Security Payload (ESP), which deals with both encryption and authentication.

GRE

Another VPN alternative is the Generic Routing Encapsulation (GRE) protocol. You can use GRE to make a point-to-point tunnel connection that carries all sorts of traffic over layer 3, including multicast and IPv6 traffic. GRE doesn't have any security, though, and will be combined with another VPN technology, so that different types of traffic can be sent over a secure tunnel.

Travel Advisory

OpenVPN and the Secure Shell (SSH) protocol can also be used for VPNs.

 **Objective 7.05** # SAN/NAS

Storage tends to be either highly under- or over-utilized on individual hosts. One of the ways to overcome these two issues is to take the storage from all the hosts and consolidate the data in a single, separate system. In this section, you'll learn about two popular methods: SAN and NAS.

SAN

You might remember from CompTIA A+ that hard drive storage is broken up into tiny sectors, but you might not know that these sectors are also known as *blocks*. You might also remember that to access the hard drive, you have to plug it into an interface such as SATA or maybe even SCSI, which your operating system uses to read and write to blocks on the disk. A *storage area network (SAN)* is a server that can take a pool of hard disks and present them over the network as any number of logical disks. The interface it presents to a client computer pretends to be a hard disk and enables the client's operating system to read and write blocks over a network.

Think of a drive accessed through the SAN as a virtual disk; much as the hypervisor convinces the operating system it runs on its own hardware, the SAN convinces the OS it is interacting with a physical hard drive. Just like with a traditional hard disk, we have to format a virtual disk before we can use it. But unlike a traditional hard disk, the virtual disk the SAN presents to us could be mapped to a number of physical drives in a number of physical locations, or even to other forms of storage.

One of the benefits of using a SAN is that, by just reading and writing at the block level, it avoids the performance costs of implementing its own file system. The SAN leaves it up to the client computers to implement their own file systems—these clients often use specialized shared file system software designed for high volume, performance, reliability, and the ability to support multiple clients using one drive.

When it comes to the infrastructure to support a SAN, there are two main choices: Fibre Channel (FC) and Internet Small Computer System Interface (iSCSI).

Fibre Channel

Fibre Channel is, for the most part, its own ecosystem designed for high-performance storage. It has its own cables, protocols, and switches, all increasing the cost associated with its use. Although more recent developments such as Fibre Channel over Ethernet (FCoE) make Fibre Channel a little more flexible within a local wired network, long-distance FC is still clumsy without expensive cabling and hardware.

iSCSI

iSCSI is built on top of TCP/IP, enabling devices that use the SCSI protocol to communicate across existing networks using cheap, readily available hardware. Because the existing networks and their hardware weren't built as a disk interface, performance can suffer. Part of this performance cost is time spent processing frame headers. We can ease some of the cost of moving large amounts of data around the network at a standard frame size by using jumbo frames. Jumbo frames are usually 9000 bytes long—though technically anything over 1500 qualifies—and they reduce the total number of frames moving through the network.

NAS

Network-attached storage (NAS) is essentially a dedicated file server that has its own file system and typically uses hardware and software designed for serving and storing files. Whereas a SAN shares a fast, low-level interface that the OS can treat just like it was a disk, the NAS—because it has its own internal file system—has to perform file system work for all its clients. Although the simplicity and low price of a NAS make it attractive for some uses, these performance issues limit its utility for use in high-performance virtualization clusters.

Objective 7.06 **Cloud Computing**

The cloud is the vast array of on-demand computing resources sold by Amazon, Microsoft, and many other companies over the open Internet. Different models are able to suit the needs of different types of computing. Let's take a look at them.

Infrastructure as a Service

Large-scale global Infrastructure as a Service (IaaS) providers use virtualization to minimize idle hardware, protect against data loss and downtime, and respond to spikes in demand. IaaS providers such as Amazon Web Services (AWS) can launch new virtual servers using the operating system of choice, on demand, for pennies an hour. The beauty of IaaS is that you no longer need to purchase expensive, heavy hardware. You are using Amazon's powerful infrastructure as a service (see Figure 7.28).

A huge number of websites are really more easily understood if you use the term *web applications*. If you want to access Mike Meyers' videos, you go to

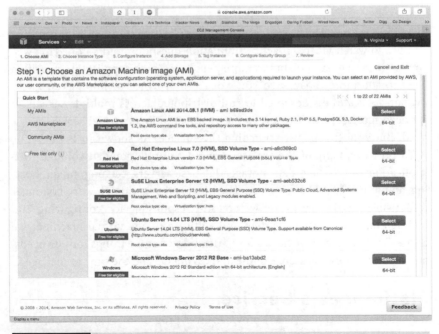

FIGURE 7.28 Creating an instance on AWS EC2

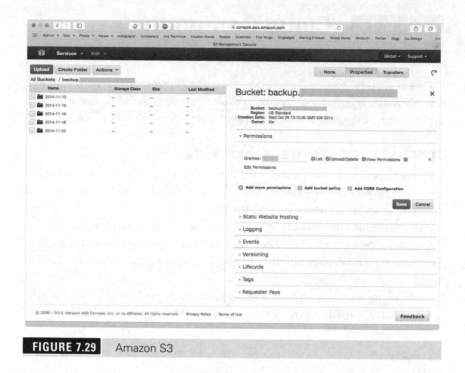

FIGURE 7.29   Amazon S3

hub.totalsem.com. This website is really an application (written in-house) that you use to watch videos, practice simulation questions, and so on. This web application is a great tool, but as more people access the application, we often need to add more capacity so you won't yell at us for a slow server. Luckily, our application is designed to run distributed across multiple servers. If we need more servers, we just add as many additional virtual servers as we need. But even this is just scratching the surface. As shown in Figure 7.29, AWS provides many of the services needed to drive popular, complex web applications—unlimited data storage, database servers, caching, media hosting, and more—all billed by usage. The hitch is that, although we're no longer responsible for the hardware, we are still responsible for configuring and maintaining the operating system and software of any virtual machines we create. This can mean we have a lot of flexibility to tune things for our needs, but it also requires knowledge of the underlying OS and the time to manage it.

Platform as a Service

A Platform as a Service (PaaS) provider gives programmers all the tools they need to deploy, administer, and maintain a web application. They have some form of infrastructure, which could be provided by an IaaS, but on top of that infrastructure the PaaS provider builds a platform: a complete deployment and management system to handle every aspect of a web application.

The important point of PaaS is that the infrastructure underneath the PaaS is largely invisible to the developer. The PaaS provider is aware of their infrastructure, but the developer cannot control it directly and doesn't need to think about its complexity. As far as the programmer is concerned, the PaaS is just a place to deploy and run their application.

Heroku, one of the earliest PaaS providers, creates a simple interface on top of the IaaS offerings of AWS, further reducing the complexity of developing and scaling web applications. Heroku's management console, shown in Figure 7.30, enables developers to increase or decrease the capacity of an application with a single slider, or easily set up add-ons that add a database, monitor your logs, track performance, and more. It could take days for a tech or developer unfamiliar with the software and services to install, configure, and integrate a set of these services with a running application; PaaS providers help cut this down to minutes or hours.

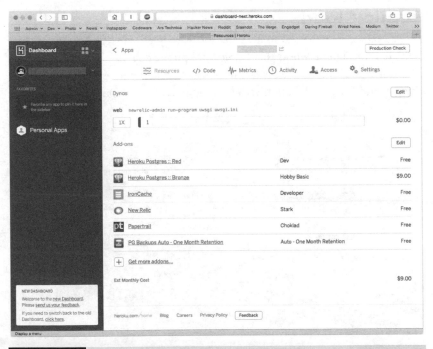

FIGURE 7.30   Heroku's management console

Software as a Service

The best examples of SaaS are the web applications we just discussed. Some web applications, such as Total Seminars Training Hub, charge for access. Other Web applications, such as Google Maps, are offered for free. Users of these web applications don't own this software; you don't get an installation DVD, nor is it something you can download once and keep using. If you want to use a web application, you must get on the Internet and access the site. Although this may seem like a disadvantage at first, the Software as a Service (SaaS) model provides access to necessary applications wherever you have an Internet connection, often without having to carry data with you or regularly update software. At the enterprise level, the subscription model of many SaaS providers makes it easier to budget and keep hundreds or thousands of computers up to date (see Figure 7.31).

In exchange for the flexibility of using public, third-party SaaS, you often have to trade strict control of your data. Security might not be crucial when someone uses Google Drive to draft a blog post, but many companies are concerned about sensitive intellectual property or business secrets traveling through untrusted networks and being stored on servers they don't control.

Public Cloud

Public cloud is a term used to describe software, platforms, and infrastructure delivered through networks that the general public can use. The public doesn't own this cloud—the hardware is often owned by companies such as Amazon, Google, and Microsoft—but there's nothing to stop a company such as Netflix

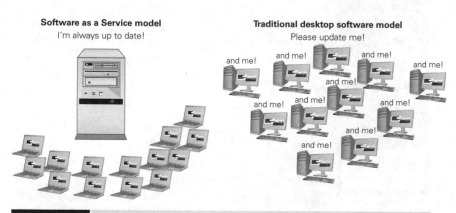

Software as a Service model
I'm always up to date!

Traditional desktop software model
Please update me!

and me! and me! and me! and me! and me! and me! and me! and me! and me! and me!

FIGURE 7.31   SaaS versus every desktop for itself

from building its web application atop the IaaS offerings of all three of these companies at once.

The public cloud sees examples of all the XaaS varieties (Public IaaS, Public PaaS, and Public SaaS).

Private Cloud

If a business wants some of the flexibility of the cloud, needs complete owner-ship of its data, and can afford both, it can build an internal cloud the busi-ness actually owns—a *private cloud*. A security-minded company with enough resources could build an internal IaaS network in an onsite data center. Depart-ments within the company could create and destroy virtual machines as needed, and develop SaaS to meet collaboration, planning, or task and time manage-ment needs, all without sending the data over the open Internet. A company with these needs but without the space or knowledge to build and maintain a private cloud can also contract a third party to maintain or host it.

There are private versions of each of the cloud concepts (Private IaaS, Pri-vate PaaS, and Private SaaS).

Community Cloud

Whereas a community center is usually a public gathering place for those in the community it serves, a *community cloud* is more like a private cloud paid for and used by more than one organization. Community clouds aren't run by a city or state for the use of citizens; the "community" in this case is a group of organizations with similar goals or needs. For example, if you're a military con-tractor working on classified projects, wouldn't it be nice to share the burden of defending your cloud against sophisticated attackers sponsored by foreign states with other military and intelligence contractors?

Just like with the public and private cloud, there are community cloud ver-sions of all the XaaS varieties (Community IaaS, Community PaaS, and Com-munity SaaS).

Hybrid Cloud

A *hybrid cloud* is a combination of public, private, and community clouds, allowing communication between them. Using a hybrid cloud model can mean not having to maintain a private cloud powerful enough to meet peak demand—for example, an application can grow into a public cloud instead of grind to a halt, a technique called *cloud bursting*. Integration among services is a great feature of a hybrid cloud. Like the other three clouds, the hybrid cloud sees examples of all the XaaS varieties (Hybrid IaaS, Hybrid PaaS, and Hybrid SaaS).

CHECKPOINT

✔**Objective 7.01: Virtual LANs**   A virtual local area network (VLAN) enables you to segment a network using VLAN-capable switches. To create a VLAN, you take a single physical broadcast domain and chop it up into multiple virtual broadcast domains. VLANs help manage busy networks by reducing traffic. With interVLAN routing, you can connect the virtual networks just as if you had a physical router between them.

✔**Objective 7.02: Virtual Computing**   Virtualization uses special software called hypervisors or virtual machine managers to create a complete environment in which a guest operating system can function as though it were installed on its own computer. That guest environment is called a virtual machine (VM). Going virtual offers many benefits, such as power savings, hardware consolidation, easier system recovery and duplication, and risk-free testing and research environments.

✔**Objective 7.03: Virtualization in Modern Networks**   Virtualization manifests in many ways in modern networks. Hypervisors serve many roles in businesses, and you can choose from one of many varieties when you want to implement virtualization. In addition, virtual switches, virtual routers, and virtual firewalls provide solutions to very specific issues.

✔**Objective 7.04: Virtual Private Networks**   Protocols such as IPsec, SSL, GRE, PPTP, and L2TP are used to create VPNs, encrypted tunnels between a computer or remote network and a private network.

✔**Objective 7.05: SAN/NAS**   Storage area networks, which are basically virtual disks, are made possible through Fibre Channel (FC) and Internet Small Computer System Interface (iSCSI) technologies for data transfer and retrieval. Network-attached storage, an alternative to SAN, uses a file system and is optimized to work with files.

✔**Objective 7.06: Cloud Computing**   Infrastructure as a Service, Platform as a Service, and Software as a Service are three models that virtualize aspects of computing today. They can be applied in four different types of clouds: public, private, community, and hybrid.

REVIEW QUESTIONS

1. What is one benefit of a VLAN?
   A. It enables remote users to connect to a local network via the Internet.
   B. It reduces broadcast traffic on a LAN.
   C. It can create a WAN from multiple disjointed LANs.
   D. It provides encryption services on networks that have no default encryption protocol.

2. The number of running virtual machines on a single host is limited by what factor?
   A. Physical RAM
   B. Virtual RAM
   C. Physical NICs
   D. Virtual NICs

3. When a virtual machine is not running, where is it stored?
   A. Firmware
   B. RAM drive
   C. Optical disc
   D. Files

4. Fibre Channel and iSCSI are used in conjunction with which technology?
   A. NAS
   B. SAN
   C. TCP/IP
   D. NTFS

5. Which of the following pairs represents the most modern and common VPN protocols?
   A. PPTP and L2TP
   B. IPsec and SSL
   C. PPTP and IPsec
   D. SSH and SSL

6. Which of the following virtualization programs works well with Mac OS X? (Select the best answer.)
   A. ESXi
   B. KVM
   C. Parallels
   D. Virtual PC

7. The boss flies into your office yelling that the virtualized web server has been hacked and now displays only purple dinosaurs. Which of the following would be the fastest way to fix the problem?
   A. Restore from backup.
   B. Run System Restore.
   C. Reinstall Windows.
   D. Load an earlier snapshot.

8. Which of these models comes with a preconfigured environment for developers?
   A. SaaS
   B. IaaS
   C. PaaS
   D. NaaS

9. Which technology allows programmers to write code to control routers and switches?
   A. SAN
   B. DNS
   C. SDN
   D. NAS

10. The hypervisor market is dominated by which company?
    A. VMware
    B. Apple
    C. Microsoft
    D. Cisco

REVIEW ANSWERS

1. **B**   VLANs reduce broadcast traffic by breaking up broadcast domains.

2. **A**   Physical RAM imposes limits on the number of VMs you can run at the same time.

3. **D**   VMs are just files, usually stored on a hard drive.

4. **B**   Fibre Channel and iSCSI deal with files at the block level in a storage area network.

5. **B**   IPsec and SSL are the most modern and common VPN protocols.

6. **C**   Parallels is the dominant virtualization program for OS X.

7. **D**   The beauty of VMs is that you can load an earlier snapshot in a matter of moments.

8. **C**   Platform as a Service is similar to Infrastructure as a Service, but it comes preconfigured.

9. **C**   Software-defined networking separates the control plane from the data plane.

10. **A**   VMware hypervisors dominate the hypervisor market.

Wide Area Networking

	NEWBIE	SOME EXPERIENCE	EXPERT
ETA	4 hours	2 hours	1 hour

Computers connect to other computers locally in a local area network (LAN)—you've read about LAN connections throughout this book—and remotely through a number of different methods. This chapter takes both a historical and a modern look at ways to interconnect a local computer or network with distant computers, what's called *remote connectivity*.

Remote connections have been around for a long time. Before the Internet, network users and developers created ways to take a single system or network and connect it to another faraway system or network. These were private interconnections of private networks. These connections were very expensive and, compared to today's options, pretty slow.

As the Internet developed, most of the same technologies used to make the earlier private remote connections became the way the Internet itself interconnects. Before the Internet was popular, many organizations used dedicated lines, called *T1 lines* (discussed in more detail later in this chapter), to connect far-flung offices. Some people still use T1 lines privately, but more often you'll see them used as an Internet connection to a company's local ISP. Private interconnections are only used today by organizations that need massive bandwidth or high security.

This chapter shows you all the ways you can make remote connections. You'll see every type of remote connection currently in popular use, from good-old telephone lines to advanced fiber-optic carriers, and even satellites. Each discussion includes details of speed, distance, and *transmission media* (the wires or wireless signals used). There are so many ways to make remote connections that this chapter is broken into three parts. The first part, "Telephony and Beyond," gives you a tour of the technologies that originally existed for long-distance voice connections that now also support data. The next part, "The Last Mile," goes into how we as individual users connect to those long-distance technologies and demonstrates how wireless technologies come into play in remote connectivity. Last, "Using Remote Access" shows you the many different ways to use these connections to connect to another, faraway computer.

Objective 8.01 Telephony and Beyond

Describing the Tier 1 Internet service providers (ISPs) of the Internet is always an interesting topic. Those of us in the instruction business invariably start this description by drawing a picture of the United States and then adding lines connecting big cities, as shown in Figure 8.1.

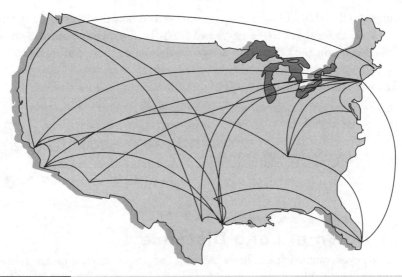

FIGURE 8.1   The Tier 1 Internet

But what are these lines and where did they come from? If the Internet is just a big TCP/IP network, wouldn't these lines be Ethernet connections? Maybe copper, maybe fiber, but surely they're Ethernet? Well, traditionally they're not (with one exception; see the following Travel Advisory). The vast majority of the long-distance connections that make up the Internet use a unique type of signal called SONET. SONET was originally designed to handle special heavy-duty circuits with names such as T1. Never heard of SONET or T1? Don't worry—you're about to learn quite a bit.

Travel Advisory

Even as you read this, more and more of the Internet interconnections are moving toward Gigabit and 10 Gigabit Ethernet, and 100 Gigabit is just around the corner. Cable and telephone technologies, however, continue to dominate.

Most of the connections that make up the high-speed backbone of the Internet use technologies designed at least 20 years ago to support telephone calls. We're not talking about your cool cell phone–type calls here, but rather the old-school, wire-runs-up-to-the-house, telephone-connected-to-a-phone-jack connections. (See "Public Switched Telephone Network" later in this chapter for more on this subject.) If you want to understand how the Internet connects, you have to go way back to the 1970s and 1980s, before the Internet really took off, and learn how the U.S. telephone system developed to support networks.

> **Travel Advisory**
>
> This section is just the lightest of overviews to get you through the CompTIA Network+ exam. The full history of long-distance communication is an incredible story, full of good guys, bad guys, crazy technology, and huge fortunes won and lost.

The Dawn of Long Distance

Have you ever watched one of those old-time movies in which someone makes a phone call by picking up the phone and saying, "Operator, get me Mohawk 4, 3-8-2-5!"? Suddenly, the scene changes to some person sitting at a switchboard like the one shown in Figure 8.2.

That was the telephone operator. The telephone operator made a physical link between your phone and the other phone, making your connection. The switchboard acted as a *circuit switch*, as plugging in the two wires created a physical circuit between the two phones. This worked pretty well in the first

FIGURE 8.2   Old-time telephone operator (photo courtesy of the Richardson Historical and Genealogical Society)

FIGURE 8.3 Another problem of early long-distance telephone systems

few years of telephones, but it quickly became a problem as more and more phone lines began to fill the skies overhead (see Figure 8.3).

These first generations of long-distance telephone systems (think 1930s here) used analog signals, because that was how your telephone worked. If you graphed out a voice signal, it looked something like Figure 8.4. This type of transmission had issues, however, because analog signals over long distances, even if you amplified them, lost sound quality very quickly.

The first problem to take care of was the number of telephone wires. Individual wires were slowly replaced with special boxes called multiplexers.

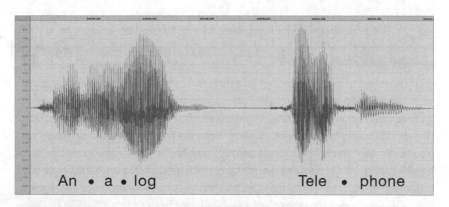

FIGURE 8.4 Another problem of early long-distance telephone systems

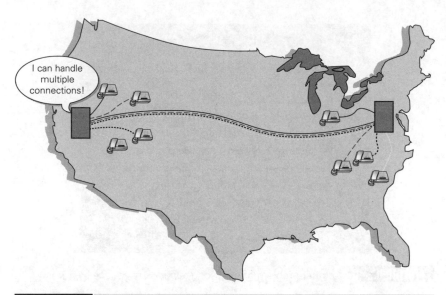

| FIGURE 8.5 | Multiplexers combine multiple circuits. |

A *multiplexer* took a circuit and combined it with a few hundred other circuits into a single complex circuit on one wire. A *demultiplexer* (devices were both multiplexers and demultiplexers) on the other end of the connection split the individual connections back out (see Figure 8.5).

Exam Tip

The various multiplexing and demultiplexing technologies and protocols, both analog and digital, are collectively referred to on the CompTIA Network+ exam as examples of *modulation* techniques. Modulation more technically means converting a digital signal to analog or pushing an analog signal to a higher frequency. Pay attention to the wording of any exam questions on modulation.

Over time, the entire United States was divided into hundreds, eventually thousands, of *local exchanges,* which were defined groupings of individual phone circuits served by a single multiplexer (calls within the exchange were handled first by human operators, who were replaced, eventually, with dial tones and special switches that interpreted your pulses or tones for a number). One or more exchanges were (and still are) housed in a physical building called a *central office* (see Figure 8.6), where individual voice circuits all came

FIGURE 8.6 A central office building

together. Local calls were still manually connected (although dial-up began to appear in earnest by the 1950s, after which many operators lost their jobs), but any connection between exchanges was carried over these special multiplexed trunk lines. Figure 8.7 shows a very stylized example of how this worked.

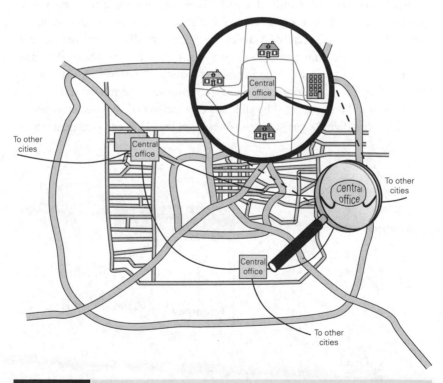

FIGURE 8.7 Interconnected central offices

How did they put a bunch of voice calls on a single piece of cable, yet still somehow keep them separate? To understand the trick, you need to appreciate a little bit about frequency. A typical telephone only detects a fairly limited frequency range—from around 350 Hz to around 4,000 Hz. This range covers enough of the human speech range to make a decent phone call. As the individual calls came into the multiplexer, it added a certain frequency multiplier to each call, keeping every separate call in its own unique frequency range (see Figure 8.8). This process is called *frequency division multiplexing (FDM)*.

This analog network still required a physical connection from one phone to the other, even if those phones were on opposite sides of the country. Long distance used a series of trunk lines, and at each intersection of those lines an operator had to connect the calls. When you physically connect two phones together on one circuit, you are using something called *circuit switching*. As you might imagine, circuit switching isn't that great for long distance, but it's your only option when you use analog.

This analog system worked pretty well from the 1930s through the 1950s, but telephones became so common and demand so heavy that the United States needed a new system to handle the load. The folks developing this new system realized that they had to dump analog and replace it with a digital system— sowing the seeds for the remote connections that eventually became the Internet.

Digital data transmits much easier over long distances than analog data does because you can use a device called a repeater (which doesn't work for analog signals). An amplifier, used for analog signals, just increases the voltage and includes all the pops and hisses created by all kinds of interference. A repeater, however, takes the entire digital signal and re-creates it out the other end (see Figure 8.9).

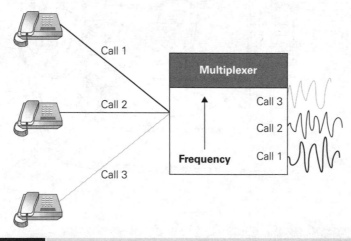

FIGURE 8.8 Multiplexed FDM

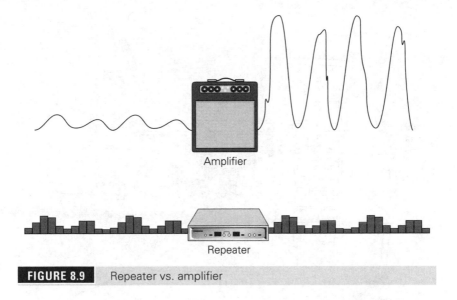

Amplifier

Repeater

FIGURE 8.9   Repeater vs. amplifier

The downside to adopting a digital system was that the entire telephone system was analog: every telephone, every switch, every multiplexer. The task of converting the entire analog voice system to digital was a massive undertaking. Luckily, much of the U.S. phone system at that time was a monopoly run by a company called AT&T. A single company could make all of its own decisions and its own standards—one of the few times in history where a monopoly was probably a good thing. The AT&T folks had a choice here: completely revamp the entire U.S. phone system, including replacing every single telephone in the United States, or just make the trunk lines digital and let the central offices convert from analog to digital. They chose the latter.

Even today, a classic telephone line in your home or small office uses analog signals—the rest of the entire telephone system is digital. The telecommunications industry calls the connection from a central office to individual users the *last mile*. The telephone company's decision to keep the last mile analog has had serious repercussions that still challenge us even in the 21st century (see Figure 8.10).

Travel Assistance

Attempts were made to convert the entire telephone system, including your telephones, to digital, but these technologies never took off (except in a few niches). See "ISDN" later in this chapter.

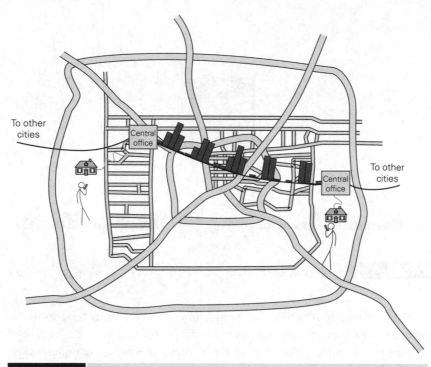

FIGURE 8.10   Analog and digital

Digital Telephony

When you learned about networks in the first few chapters of this book, you learned about cabling, frame types, speeds, switching, and so on. All of these are important for computer networks. Well, let's do it again (in a much simpler format) to see the cabling, frame types, speed, and switching used in telephone systems. Don't worry—unlike computer networks, in which a certain type of cable might run different types of frames at different speeds, most of the remote connections used in the telephony world tend to have one type of cable that only runs one type of frame at one speed.

Let's begin with the most basic data chunk you get in the telephone world: DS0.

It All Starts with DS0

When AT&T decided to go digital, it knew all phone calls had to be broken into a digital sample. AT&T decided (some people say "guessed" or "compromised") that if it took an analog signal of a human voice and converted it into eight-bit chunks 8,000 times a second, it would be good enough to re-create the sound

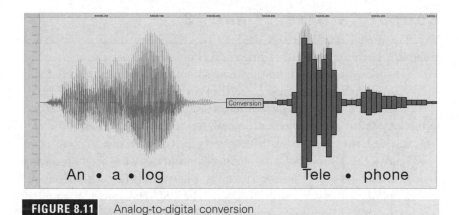

An • a • log   Tele • phone

FIGURE 8.11   Analog-to-digital conversion

later. Figure 8.11 shows an example of the analog human voice seen earlier being converted into a digital sample.

> ### Local Lingo
>
> **modem**   A modulator takes a digital signal and converts it into an analog signal. A demodulator takes an analog signal and converts it into a digital signal. The typical modulator/demodulator device in computers is a *modem*.

Converting analog sound into eight-bit chunks 8,000 times a second creates a data stream (called a *digital signal)* of 8 × 8,000 = 64 kilobits per second (Kbps). This digital signal rate, known as *DS0,* makes up the simplest data stream (and the slowest rate) of the digital part of the telephone system. Each analog voice call gets converted into a DS0 signal at the telephone company's central office. From there the calls are multiplexed into larger circuits.

Now that we have our voice calls converted to digital data, we need to get them to the right telephone. First, we need network technologies to handle the cabling, frames, and speed. Second, we need to come up with a method to switch the digital voice calls across a network. To handle the former, we need to define the types of interconnections, with names such as T1 and OC3. To handle the latter, we no longer connect via multiplexed circuit switching, as we did back with analog, but rather are now using packet switching. I'll show you what I mean as I discuss the digital lines in use today.

Copper Carriers: T1 and T3

The first digital trunk carriers used by the telephone industry are called *T-carriers*. There are a number of different versions of T-carriers, and the CompTIA Network+ exam expects you to know something about them. Let's begin with the most common and most basic, the venerable T-carrier level 1 (T1).

T1 has several meanings. First, it refers to a high-speed digital networking technology called a *T1 connection*. Second, the term *T1 line* refers to the specific, shielded, two-pair cabling that connects the two ends of a T1 connection (see Figure 8.12). Two wires are for sending data and two wires are for receiving data. At either end of a T1 line, you'll find an unassuming box called a *channel service unit/digital service unit (CSU/DSU)*. The CSU/DSU provides an interface between the T1 line and some other device, often a router. A T1 connection is point-to-point—you cannot have more than two CSU/DSUs on a single T1 line. The cable ends with a modular jack called an RJ48C, which looks a lot like the RJ45 connector you're used to seeing with Ethernet cables. T1 uses a special signaling method called a *digital signal 1 (DS1)*.

> ### Exam Tip
>
> You can connect two CSU/DSU boxes together directly by using a *T1* crossover cable. Like the UTP crossover cables you've seen previously in the book, the T1 crossover cable simply reverses the send/receive pairs on one end of the cable. You'll only see this in use to connect older routers together. The CSU/DSU connections provide convenient link points.

DS1 uses a relatively primitive frame—the frame doesn't need to be complex because with point-to-point no addressing is necessary. Each DS1 frame has

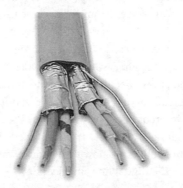

FIGURE 8.12   T1 line

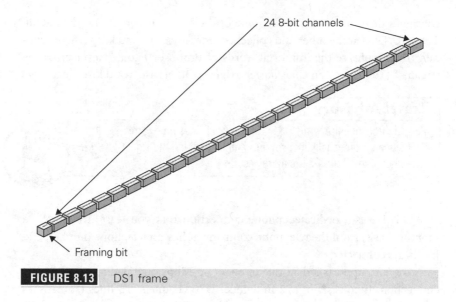

24 8-bit channels

Framing bit

FIGURE 8.13 DS1 frame

25 pieces: a framing bit and 24 channels. Each DS1 channel holds a single eight-bit DS0 data sample. The framing bit and data channels combine to make 193 bits per DS1 frame. These frames are transmitted 8,000 times/sec, making for a total throughput of 1.544 Mbps (see Figure 8.13). DS1 defines, therefore, a data transfer speed of 1.544 Mbps, split into twenty-five 64 Kbps DS0 channels. The process of having frames that carry a portion of every channel in every frame sent on a regular interval is called *time division multiplexing (TDM)*.

Exam Tip

Each 64 Kbps channel in a DS1 signal is a DS0.

With Ethernet, the whole frame encapsulates a single set of data, such as an IP packet that, in turn, encapsulates a single type of TCP segment or UDP datagram. It generally takes multiple frames to get the data to the recipient, where the frames are removed, the IP packet is removed, and the segment or datagram gets put together to make the data transfer complete.

The cool thing about the DS1 frame, though, is that you don't have to use the whole frame for a single set of data. With the right CSU/DSU at either end, you can specify which channels go with a specific thread of data. The frame continues down the line even if some of the channels contain no data at all. The CSU/DSU at the other end collects the data streams and keeps them separate. To paraphrase the immortal words of Professor Egon, "Never cross the streams." (You have seen *Ghostbusters,* right?) Otherwise, you'd lose data.

Travel Advisory

People rarely use the term "DS1." Because T1 lines only carry DS1 signals, you usually just say T1 when describing the signal, even though the term DS1 is more accurate.

A T1 line is a dedicated phone connection that you lease, usually on a monthly basis, from the telephone company. It has no telephone number, and it's always connected.

A *T3 line* supports a data rate of about 45 Mbps on a dedicated telephone connection. It consists of 672 individual DS0 channels. T3 lines (sometimes referred to as *DS3 lines)* are mainly used by regional telephone companies and ISPs connecting to the Internet.

Similar to the North American T1 line, E-carrier level 1 (*E1*) is the European format for digital transmission. An E1 line carries signals at 2.048 Mbps (32 channels at 64 Kbps), compared to the T1's 1.544 Mbps (24 channels at 64 Kbps). E1 and T1 lines can interconnect for international use. There are also E3 lines, which carry 16 E1 lines, with a bandwidth of about 34 Mbps.

Exam Tip

E1 and SONET use a derivative of the *High-Level Data Link Control (HDLC)* protocol as the control channel.

A CSU/DSU, as mentioned earlier, connects a leased T1 or T3 line from the telephone company to a customer's equipment. A CSU/DSU has (at least) two connectors: one that goes to the T1/T3 line running out of your demarc and another connection that goes to your router. It performs line encoding and conditioning functions and often has a loopback function for testing. Many newer routers have CSU/DSUs built into them. Figure 8.14 shows the front of a Juniper Networks router with two T1 interfaces.

Many routers feature two interfaces on one router, with the dual links providing redundancy if one link goes down. The CSU part of a CSU/DSU

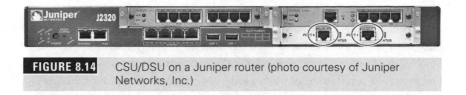

FIGURE 8.14 CSU/DSU on a Juniper router (photo courtesy of Juniper Networks, Inc.)

protects the T1 or T3 line and the user equipment from lightning strikes and other types of electrical interference. It also stores statistics and has capabilities for loopback testing. The DSU part supplies timing to each user port, taking the incoming user's data signals and converting the input signal into the specified line code and then framing the format for transmission over the provided line.

Make sure you know the four T-carriers shown in Table 8.1.

Fiber Carriers: SONET/SDH and OC

T-carriers were a great start into the digital world, but in the mid-1980s, fiber-optic cabling became the primary tool for long-distance communication all over the world. By then, AT&T's monopoly was gone, replaced by a number of competing carriers. Competition was strong and everyone was making their own fiber transmission standards. In an incredible moment of corporate cooperation, in 1987, all of the primary fiber-optic carriers decided to drop their own standards and move to a new international standard called *Synchronous Optical Network (SONET)* in the United States and *Synchronous Digital Hierarchy (SDH)* in Europe.

All of these carriers adopting the same standard created a world of simple interconnections between competing voice and data carriers. This adoption defined the moment that truly made the Internet a universal network. Before SONET, interconnections happened, but they were outlandishly expensive, preventing the Internet from reaching many areas of the world.

SONET remains the primary standard for long-distance, high-speed, fiber-optic transmission systems. SONET, like Ethernet, defines interface standards

TABLE 8.1	T-carriers	
Carrier	**Channels**	**Speed**
T1	24	1.544 Mbps
T3	672	44.736 Mbps
E1	32	2.048 Mbps
E3	512	34.368 Mbps

at the Physical and Data Link layers of the OSI seven-layer model. The physical aspect of SONET is partially covered by the Optical Carrier standards, but it also defines a ring-based topology that most SONET adopters now use. SONET does not require a ring, but a SONET ring has fault tolerance in case of line loss. As a result, most of the big long-distance optical pipes for the world's telecommunications networks are SONET rings.

Exam Tip

SONET is one of the most important standards for making all WAN interconnections—and it's also the least likely standard you'll ever see because it's hidden away from all but the biggest networks.

The real beauty of SONET lies in its multiplexing capabilities. A single SONET ring can combine multiple DS1, DS3, and even European E1 signals and package them into single, huge SONET frames for transmission. Clearly, SONET needs high-capacity fiber optics to handle such large data rates. That's where the Optical Carrier standards come into play!

The *Optical Carrier (OC)* standards denote the optical data-carrying capacity (in bps) of fiber-optic cables in networks conforming to the SONET standard. The OC standard describes an escalating series of speeds, designed to meet the needs of medium-to-large corporations. SONET establishes OC speeds from 51.8 Mbps (OC-1) to 39.8 Gbps (OC-768).

Still want more throughput? Many fiber devices now use a very clever feature called *Wavelength Division Multiplexing (WDM)* or its newer and more popular version, *Dense WDM (DWDM)*. DWDM enables an individual single-mode fiber to carry multiple signals by giving each signal a different wavelength. The result varies, but a single DWDM fiber can support around 150 signals, enabling, for example, a 51.8 Mbps OC-1 line to run at 51.8 Mbps × 150 signals, which is 7.77 *gigabytes per second!* DWDM has become very popular for long-distance lines because it's usually less expensive to replace older SONET/OC-*x* equipment with DWDM than it is to add more fiber lines.

Exam Tip

DWDM isn't just upgrading SONET lines; DWDM works just as well on long-distance fiber Ethernet.

A related technology, coarse wavelength division multiplexing (CWDM), also relies on multiple wavelengths of light to carry a fast signal over long

TABLE 8.2	Common Optical Carriers	
SONET Optical Level	**Line Speed**	**Signal Method**
OC-1	51.85 Mbps	STS-1
OC-3	155.52 Mbps	STS-3
OC-12	622.08 Mbps	STS-12
OC-24	1.244 Gbps	STS-24
OC-48	2.488 Gbps	STS-48
OC-192	9.955 Gbps	STS-192
OC-256	13.22 Gbps	STS-256
OC-768	39.82 Gbps	STS-768

distances. It's simpler than DWDM, which limits its practivcal distances to a mere 60 km. You'll see it used in higher-end LANs with 10GBase-LX4 networks, for example, where its lower cost (compared to direct competitors) offers benefits.

SONET uses the *Synchronous Transport Signal (STS)* signal method. The STS consists of two parts: the *STS payload* (which carries data) and the *STS overhead* (which carries the signaling and protocol information). When folks talk about STS, they add a number to the end of "STS" to designate the speed of the signal. For example, STS-1 runs a 51.85 Mbps signal on an OC-1 line. STS-3 runs at 155.52 Mbps on OC-3 lines, and so on. Table 8.2 describes the most common optical carriers.

Packet Switching

All of these impressive connections that start with *T*s and *O*s are powerful, but they are not in and of themselves a complete WAN solution. These WAN connections with their unique packets (DS0, STS, and so on) make up the entire mesh of long-range connections called the Internet, carrying both packetized voice data and TCP/IP data packets. All of these connections are point-to-point, so you need to add another level of devices to enable you to connect multiple T1s, T3s, or OC connections together to make that mesh. That's where packet switching comes into play.

> ### Exam Tip
>
> The first generation of packet-switching technology was called *X.25*. It enabled remote devices to communicate with each other across high-speed digital links without the expense of individual leased lines. CompTIA also refers to X.25 as the *CCITT Packet Switching Protocol*.

Packets, as you know, need some form of addressing scheme to get from one location to another. The telephone industry came up with its own types of packets that run on T-carrier and OC lines to get data from one central office to another. These packet-switching protocols are functionally identical to routable network protocols such as TCP/IP.

> **Local Lingo**
>
> **packet switches** Machines that store and forward packets using any type of packet-switching protocol are called *packet switches.*

Frame Relay

Frame Relay is an extremely efficient packet-switching standard, designed for and used primarily with T-carrier lines. It works especially well for the off-again/on-again traffic typical of most LAN applications. Frame Relay switches packets quickly, but without any guarantee of data integrity at all. You can't even count on it to deliver all the frames, because it will discard frames whenever there is network congestion. At first this might sound problematic—what happens if you have a data problem? In practice, however, a Frame Relay network delivers data quite reliably because T-carrier digital lines that use Frame Relay have very low error rates. It's up to the higher-level protocols to error-check as needed. Frame Relay was extremely popular in its day, but newer technologies such as ATM and especially MPLS are beginning to replace it. If you decide to go with a T1 line in the United States, you'll probably get a T1 line running Frame Relay, although many companies use the newer ATM standard as their packet-switching solution with T-carrier lines.

ATM

Don't think automatic teller machine here! *Asynchronous Transfer Mode (ATM)* is a network technology originally designed for high-speed LANs in the early 1990s. ATM only saw limited success in the LAN world but became extremely popular in the WAN world. In fact, until the recent advent of Multiprotocol Label Switching (see "MPLS" next), most of the SONET rings that moved voice and data all over the world used ATM for packet switching. ATM integrated voice, video, and data on one connection, using short and fixed-length packets called *cells* to transfer information. Every cell sent with the same source and destination traveled over the same route.

ATM existed because data and audio/video transmissions have different transfer requirements. Data tolerates a delay in transfer, but not signal loss (if it takes a moment for a web page to appear, you don't care). Audio and video transmissions, on the other hand, tolerate signal loss but not delay (delay makes phone calls sound choppy and clipped). Because ATM transferred information in cells of one set size (53 bytes long), it handled both types of transfers well. ATM transfer speeds ranged from 155.52 to 622.08 Mbps and beyond. If your location was big enough to order an OC line from your ISP, odds were good that OC line connected to an ATM switch.

> **Travel Advisory**
>
> Referring to ATM in the past tense might seem a bit premature. Plenty of ISPs still use ATM, but it's definitely on the way out due to MPLS.

MPLS

Frame Relay and ATM were both fantastic packet-switching technologies, but they were designed to support any type of traffic that might come over the network. Today, TCP/IP, the predominant data technology, has a number of issues that neither Frame Relay nor ATM addresses. For example, ATM uses a very small frame, only 53 bytes, which adds quite a bit of overhead to 1,500-byte Ethernet frames. To address this and other issues, many ISPs (and large ISP clients) use an improved technology called *Multiprotocol Label Switching (MPLS)* as a replacement for Frame Relay and ATM switching.

MPLS adds an MPLS label that sits between the layer-2 header and the layer-3 information. Layer 3 is always IP, so MPLS labels sit between layer 2 and the IP headers. Figure 8.15 shows the structure of an MPLS header.

The MPLS header consists of four parts:

- **Label**   A unique identifier, used by MPLS-capable routers to determine how to move data.
- **Cost of Service (CoS)**   A relative value used to determine the importance of the labeled packet. (This is also often labeled Exp, for *experimental*.)

| Label | CoS | S | TTL |

FIGURE 8.15   MPLS header

- **S**   In certain situations, a single packet may have multiple MPLS labels. This single bit value is set to 1 for the initial label.
- **Time to Live (TTL)**   The TTL determines the number of hops the label can make before it's eliminated.

Figure 8.16 shows the location of the MPLS header. The original idea for MPLS was to give individual ISPs a way to move traffic through their morass of different interconnections and switches more quickly and efficiently by providing network-wide *Quality of Service (QoS)*. QoS is a means of sorting IP packets to provide priority based on header information. MPLS-capable routers avoid running IP packets through their full routing tables and instead use the header information to route packets quickly. Where "regular" routers use QoS on an individual basis, MPLS routers use their existing dynamic routing protocols to send each other messages about their overhead, enabling QoS to span an entire group of routers (see Figure 8.17). This creates an *MPLS-topology* network.

Layer-2 header	Label	CoS	S	TTL	Layer-3 header

FIGURE 8.16   MPLS header inserted in a frame

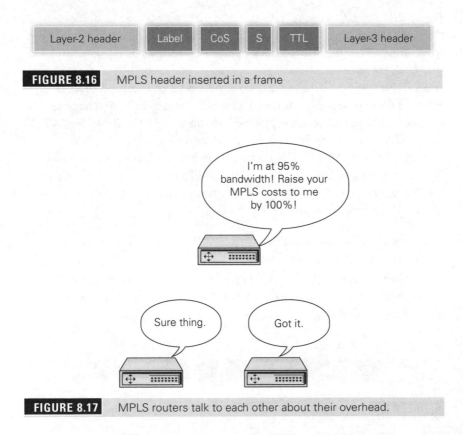

FIGURE 8.17   MPLS routers talk to each other about their overhead.

Let's see how the MPLS-labeled packets, combined with MPLS-capable routers, create improved throughput. To show you how this happens, I need to introduce a few MPLS terms:

- **Forwarding Equivalence Class (FEC)**   FEC is a group of devices (usually computers) that tend to send packets to the same place, such as a single broadcast domain of computers connected to a router.
- **Label switching router (LSR)**   An LSR looks for and forwards packets based on their MPLS label. These are the "MPLS routers" mentioned previously.
- **Label edge router (LER)**   An LER is an MPLS router that has the job of adding MPLS labels to incoming packets that do not yet have a label.
- **Label Distribution Protocol (LDP)**   LSRs and LERs use LDP to communicate dynamic information about their state. Figure 8.17 shows an example of LDP in action.

Figure 8.18 shows a highly simplified MPLS network. Note the position of the LERs and LSRs.

When an MPLS network comes online, administrators will configure initial routing information, primarily setting metrics to routes (see Figure 8.19).

LERs have the real power in determining routes. Because LERs are the entrances and exits for an MPLS network, they talk to each other to determine the best possible routes. As data moves from one FEC, the LERs add an MPLS label to every packet. LSRs strip away incoming labels and add their own. This progresses until the packets exit out the opposing LER (see Figure 8.20).

Although MPLS was originally used just to move data quickly between LERs, MPLS's label-stacking ability makes it a perfect candidate for end-user VPNs. Instead of having to set up your own VPN, an ISP using MPLS can

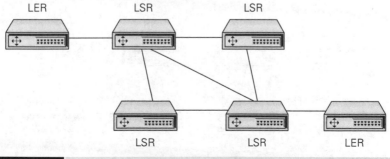

FIGURE 8.18   Sample MPLS-topology network

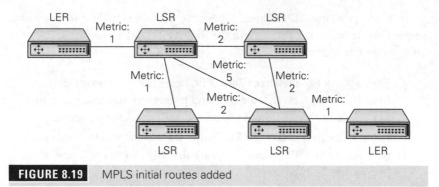

FIGURE 8.19 MPLS initial routes added

set up and lease you a fully functional connection to your network. The ISP makes the VPN for you; you just insert an RJ45 plug into the switch in your office and it works. This feature of MPLS is called a *permanent virtual circuit (PVC)* and is a popular product sold by ISPs to connect two customer locations.

Real-world WAN

There are two reasons to use a telephony WAN connection: to get your LAN on the Internet and to make a private connection between two or more of your private LANs. How you go about getting one of these lines changes a bit depending on which you want to do. Let's start with connecting to the Internet.

Traditionally, getting a WAN Internet connection was a two-step process: you talked to the telephone company to get the line physically installed and then talked to an ISP to provide you with Internet access. Today, almost every telephone company is also an ISP, so this process is usually simple. Just go online and do a web search of ISPs in your area and give them a call. You'll get a price quote, and, if you sign up, the ISP will do the installation.

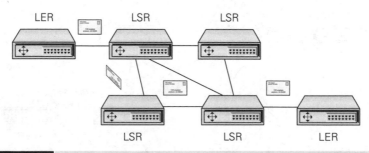

FIGURE 8.20 Data routing through an MPLS network

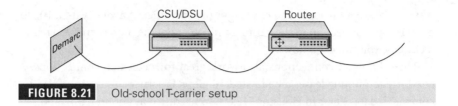

FIGURE 8.21   Old-school T-carrier setup

You can use a few tricks to reduce the price, however. If you're in an office building, odds are good that a T1 or better line is already installed and that an ISP is already serving people in your building. Talk to the building supervisor. If there isn't a T1 or better line, you have to pay for a new line. If an interconnect is nearby, this option might be inexpensive. If you want the telephone company to run an OC line to your house, however, brace for a quote of thousands of dollars just to get the line.

The telephone company runs your T-carrier (or better) line to a demarc. This demarc is important because this is where the phone company's responsibility ends! Everything on "your" side of the demarc is your responsibility. From there, you or your ISP installs a CSU/DSU (for T-carriers), and that device connects to your router.

Depending on who does this for you, you may encounter a tremendous amount of variance here. The classic example (sticking with T-carrier) consists of a demarc, CSU/DSU, and router setup, as shown in Figure 8.21.

T-carriers have been around so long that many of these parts are combined. You'll often see a single box that combines the CSU/DSU and the router in one handy device, such as the Juniper router shown earlier in Figure 8.14.

WAN telephony carriers are incredibly dependable—far more dependable than inexpensive alternatives (such as cable modems)—and that's one of the main reasons people still use them. But you should definitely know how to test your end of the connection if you ever suspect a problem. The single most important test is called the *Bit Error Rate Test (BERT)*. A BERT test verifies the T-carrier connection from end to end. Every CSU/DSU has a different way to BERT test. Just make sure you know how to perform the test on yours!

Alternative to Telephony WAN

Over the last few years, many ISPs started replacing their T1, T3, and OC-*x* equipment with good-old Ethernet. Well, not "good-old" Ethernet—rather, superfast 10 Gbps Ethernet, 40 Gbps Ethernet, or 100 Gbps Ethernet running on single-mode fiber and connected to DWDM-capable switches. As a result, in many areas—especially metropolitan areas—you can get metro-Ethernet (that is, Ethernet throughout a city) right to your office. Anyone want a 10, 40, or 100 Gbps connection to their router? If you've got the money and you're in a lucky city, you can get it now.

These Ethernet connections also work great for dedicated connections. A good friend of mine leases a dedicated 10 Gbps Ethernet connection from his company's data center in Houston, Texas, to his office in London, England.

Objective 8.02 The Last Mile

Speed is the key to the Internet, but historically there has always been one big challenge: getting data from central offices to individual users. Although this wasn't a problem for larger companies that could afford their own WAN connections, what about individuals and small companies that couldn't or wouldn't pay hundreds of dollars a month for a T1? This area, the infamous last mile, was a serious challenge early on for both Internet connections and private connections because the only common medium was standard telephone lines. A number of last-mile solutions have appeared over the years, and the CompTIA Network+ exam tests you on the most popular ones—and a few obscure ones as well. Here's the list:

- Dial-up
- DSL
- Broadband cable
- Satellite
- Cellular WAN
- Fiber

Dial-up

Many different types of telephone lines are available, but all the choices break down into two groups: dedicated and dial-up. *Dedicated lines* are always off the hook (that is, they never hang up on each other). They are always on.

A dedicated line (such as a T1) does not have a phone number. In essence, the telephone company creates a permanent, hard-wired connection between the two locations, rendering a phone number superfluous. *Dial-up lines,* by contrast, have phone numbers; they must dial each other up to make a connection.

When they're finished communicating, they hang up. Two technologies make up the overwhelming majority of dial-up connections: PSTN and ISDN.

Public Switched Telephone Network

The oldest, slowest, and most common original phone connection is the *public switched telephone network (PSTN)*. PSTN is also known as *plain old telephone service (POTS)*. PSTN is just a regular phone line, the same line that used to run into everybody's home RJ11 telephone jacks from the central office of the *Local Exchange Carrier (LEC)*. The LEC is the telephone company (telco) that provides local connections and usually the one that owns your local central office.

Because PSTN was designed long before computers were common, it was designed to work with only one type of data: sound. Here's how it works. The telephone's microphone takes the sound of your voice and translates it into an electrical analog waveform. The telephone then sends that signal through the PSTN line to the phone on the other end of the connection. That phone translates the signal into sound on the other end using its speaker. Note the word *analog*. The telephone microphone converts the sounds into electrical waveforms that cycle 2,400 times a second. An individual cycle is known as a *baud*. The number of bauds per second is called the *baud rate*. Pretty much all phone companies' PSTN lines have a baud rate of 2,400. PSTN connections use a connector called RJ11. It's the classic connector you see on all telephones (see Figure 8.22).

When you connect your modem to a phone jack, the line then runs to your *network interface unit (NIU)*, or demarc. The term "network interface unit" is more commonly used to describe the small box on the side of a home that accepts the incoming lines from the telephone company and then splits them to the different wall outlets. "Demarc" more commonly describes large

FIGURE 8.22 RJ11 connectors (top and side views)

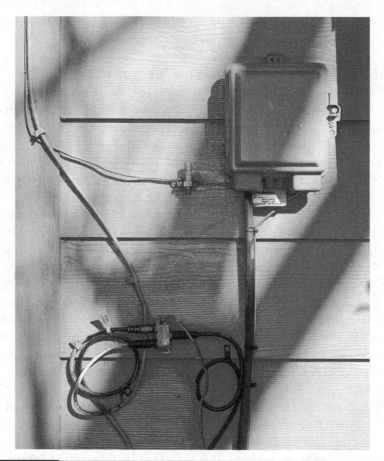

FIGURE 8.23   Typical home demarc

connections used in businesses. The terms are interchangeable and always describe the interface between the lines the telephone company is responsible for and the lines for which you are responsible (see Figure 8.23).

Computers, as you know, don't speak analog—only digital/binary (0 or 1) will do. In addition, the people who invented the way PCs communicate decided to divide any digital signal going in and out of your computer into eight bits at a time. To connect over phone lines, PCs need two devices: one that converts this eight-bit-wide (parallel) digital signal from the computer into serial (one-bit-wide) digital data and then another device to convert (modulate) the data into analog waveforms that can travel across PSTN lines. You already know that the device that converts the digital data to analog and back is called a *modulator-demodulator (modem)*. The modem also contains a device

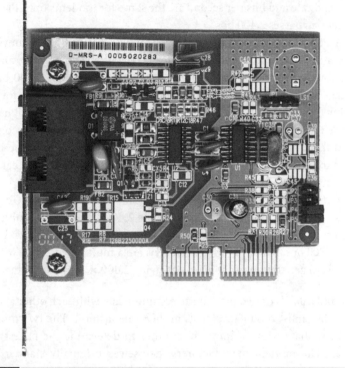

FIGURE 8.24 Internal modem

called a *Universal Asynchronous Receiver/Transmitter (UART)*. The UART takes the eight-bit-wide digital data and converts it into one-bit-wide digital data and hands it to the modem for conversion to analog. The process is reversed for incoming data. Even though internal modems are actually both a UART and a modem, we just say the word "modem" (see Figure 8.24).

Exam Tip

Internal modems are both a UART and a modem. External modems use a serial or USB port. The serial or USB port contains the UART, so the external modem truly is just a modem.

Baud vs. Bits per Second Modems use phone lines to transmit data at various speeds. These speeds cause a world of confusion and problems for computer people. This is where a little bit of knowledge becomes dangerous. Standard modems you can buy for your home computer normally transmit data at speeds up to 56 Kbps. That's 56 kilobits per second, *not* 56 kilobaud! Many people confuse the terms *baud* and *bits per second*. This confusion arises because the baud rate and bits per second are the same for modems until the data transfer rate surpasses 2,400 bps.

A PSTN phone line takes analog samples of sound 2,400 times a second. This standard sampling size was determined a long time ago as an acceptable rate for sending voice traffic over phone lines. Although 2,400-baud analog signals are fine for voice communication, they are a big problem for computers trying to send data because computers only work with digital signals. The job of the modem is to take the digital signals it receives from the computer and send them out over the phone line in an analog form, using the baud cycles from the phone system. A 2,400 bps modem—often erroneously called a 2,400-baud modem—uses 1 analog baud to send one bit of data.

As technology progressed, modems became faster and faster. To get past the 2,400-baud limit, modems modulated the 2,400-baud signal multiple times in each cycle. A 4,800 bps modem modulated two bits per baud, thereby transmitting 4,800 bps. All PSTN modem speeds are a multiple of 2,400, with the latest (and last) generation of modems achieving $2,400 \times 24 = 57,600$ bps (56 Kbps).

V Standards For two modems to communicate with each other at their fastest rate, they must modulate signals in the same fashion. The two modems must also negotiate with, or *query*, each other to determine the fastest speed they share. The modem manufacturers themselves originally standardized these processes as a set of proprietary protocols. The downside to these protocols was that unless you had two modems from the same manufacturer, modems often would not work together. In response, the International Telegraph and Telephone Consultative Committee (*CCITT*), a European standards body, established standards for modems. These standards, known generically as the *V standards*, define the speeds at which modems can modulate. The most common of these speed standards are as follows:

- **V.22**   1,200 bps
- **V.22bis**   2,400 bps
- **V.32**   9,600 bps
- **V.32bis**   14,400 bps

- **V.34**   28,000 bps
- **V.90**   57,600 bps
- **V.92**   57,600 bps

Local Lingo

ITU-T   The CCITT was renamed the International Telecommunication Union Telecommunication Standardization Sector (ITU-T) way back in 1993.

The current modem standard now on the market is the *V.92 standard*. V.92 has the same download speed as the V.90, but upstream rates increase to as much as 48 Kbps.

Point-to-Point Protocol

Modems use a protocol called *Point-to-Point Protocol (PPP)* for making a secure connection to an ISP. PPP enables two devices to connect directly, authenticate with username and password, and negotiate a network protocol. That protocol today, of course, is TCP/IP.

One of the creative ways people way back in the day (in the mid-1990s) sped up Internet connections was by using more than one modem at the same time. This link aggregation could join a couple of 56 Kbps modems, for example, and run a protocol such as multilink PPP to achieve blazing speeds at a fraction of the cost of ISDN (mentioned next).

ISDN

PSTN lines traditionally just aren't that good. Although the digital equipment that connects to a PSTN supports a full 64 Kbps DS0 channel, the combination of the lines themselves and the conversion from analog to digital means that most PSTN lines rarely go faster than 33 Kbps—and, yes, that includes the 56 Kbps connections.

The phone companies were motivated to come up with a way to generate higher capacities. Their answer was fairly straightforward: make the last mile digital. Because everything but the last mile was already digital, by adding special equipment at the central office and the user's location, phone companies felt they could achieve a true, steady, dependable throughput of 64 Kbps per line over the same copper wires already used by PSTN lines. This process of sending telephone transmission across fully digital lines end-to-end is called *Integrated Services Digital Network (ISDN)* service.

Exam Tip
ISDN also supports voice but requires special ISDN telephones.

ISDN service consists of two types of channels: *Bearer channels (B channels)* carry data and voice information using standard DS0 channels (64 Kbps), whereas *Delta channels (D channels)* carry setup and configuration information at 16 Kbps. Most ISDN providers let the customer choose either one or two B channels. The more common setup is two B channels and one D channel, called a *Basic Rate Interface (BRI)* setup. A BRI setup uses only one physical line, but each B channel sends 64 Kbps, thus doubling the throughput total to 128 Kbps.

Another type of ISDN is called *Primary Rate Interface (PRI)*. ISDN PRI is actually just a full T1 line, carrying 23 B channels.

The physical connections for ISDN bear some similarity to PSTN modems. An ISDN wall socket is usually something that looks like a standard RJ45 network jack. This line runs to your demarc. In home installations, many telephone companies install a second demarc separate from your PSTN demarc. The most common interface for your computer is a device called a *terminal adapter (TA)*. TAs look like regular modems and, like modems, come in external and internal variants. You can even get TAs that also function as hubs, enabling your system to support a direct LAN connection (see Figure 8.25).

FIGURE 8.25	A TeleWell ISDN terminal adapter

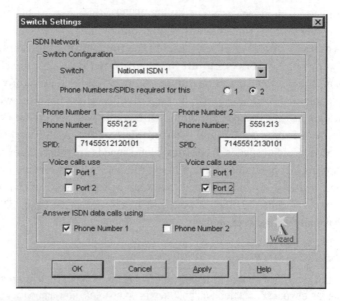

FIGURE 8.26 ISDN settings in an old version of Windows

Exam Tip

Remember, a B channel is a DS0 channel.

You generally need to be within approximately 18,000 feet of a central office to use ISDN. When you install an ISDN TA, you must configure the other ISDN telephone number you want to call, as well as a special number called the *Service Profile ID (SPID)*. Your ISP provides the telephone number, and the telephone company gives you the SPID. (In many cases, the telephone company is also the ISP.) Figure 8.26 shows a typical installation screen for an internal ISDN TA in an old version of Windows. Note that each channel has a phone number in this case.

DSL

Many telephone companies offer a *digital subscriber line (DSL)* connection, an almost fully digital, dedicated (no phone number) connection. DSL represented the next great leap forward past ISDN for telephone lines. A physical

DSL connection manifests as just another PSTN connection, using the same telephone lines and RJ11 jacks as any regular phone line.

DSL comes in a number of versions, but the three most important to know for the CompTIA Network+ exam are *Symmetric DSL (SDSL)*, *Asymmetric DSL (ADSL)*, and the newer *Very High Bitrate DSL (VDSL)*. SDSL lines provide the same upload and download speeds, making them excellent for those who send as much data as they receive, although SDSL is relatively expensive (VDSL is a new form of SDSL—see "VDSL" later in this section). ADSL uses different upload and download speeds. ADSL download speeds are much faster than the upload speeds. Most small office and home office (SOHO) users are primarily concerned with fast *downloads* for things such as web pages and can tolerate slower upload speeds. ADSL is always much less expensive than SDSL, and VDSL is usually the most expensive.

Travel Advisory

To use DSL, you must be within 18,000 feet of a central office. The closer you are, the faster your connection will be. Several companies offer a service called *Extended DSL (XDSL)* that can go much farther away from the central office, but that's not a standard. Depending on the implementation, Extended DSL is a rebranded T1 or partial T1 line or something completely proprietary to the telecommunications company offering the service. Buyer beware!

SDSL

SDSL provides equal upload and download speed and, in theory, provides speeds up to 15 Mbps, although the vast majority of ISPs provide packages ranging from 192 Kbps to 9 Mbps.

ADSL

ADSL provides theoretical maximum download speeds up to 15 Mbps and upload speeds up to 1 Mbps. All ADSL suppliers "throttle" their ADSL speeds, however, and provide different levels of service. Real-world ADSL download speeds vary from 384 Kbps to 15 Mbps, and upload speeds go from as low as 128 Kbps to around 768 Kbps.

VDSL

VDSL is the latest version of DSL to appear. Although not as many people use it as regular DSL (at least in the United States), its ability to provide speeds of 100+ Mbps in both directions makes it an attractive option. VDSL achieves these speeds by adding very advanced methods to encode the data. Don't get too excited about these great speed increases. They are very distance dependent: you won't get 100 Mbps unless you're around 300 meters from the DSLAM (see "DSL Features"). VDSL is designed to run on copper phone lines, but many VDSL suppliers use fiber-optic cabling to increase distances. In the United States, these fiber VDSL services are fiber-to-the-home solutions. The two most popular carriers are AT&T's U-verse and Verizon's Fiber Optic Service (FiOS).

> ### Exam Tip
>
> The CompTIA Network+ objectives offer *Variable* Digital Subscriber Line as the words that match the VDSL initials. No such DSL variant exists. VDSL stands for *Very High Bitrate* DSL. You'll probably only see the initials on the exam, so no worries on that score.

DSL Features

One nice aspect of DSL is that you don't have to run new phone lines. The same DSL lines you use for data can simultaneously transmit your voice calls.

All versions of DSL have the same central office–to–end user distance restrictions as ISDN—around 18,000 feet from your demarc to the central office. At the central office, your DSL provider has a device called a *DSL Access Multiplexer (DSLAM)* that connects multiple customers to the Internet.

> ### Travel Advisory
>
> No DSL provider guarantees any particular transmission speed and will only provide service as a "best efforts" contract—a nice way to say that DSL lines are notorious for substantial variations in throughput.

Installing DSL

DSL operates using your preexisting telephone lines (assuming they are up to specification). This is wonderful but also presents a technical challenge. For DSL and your run-of-the-mill POTS line to coexist, you need to filter out the DSL signal on the POTS line. A DSL line has three information channels: a high-speed downstream channel, a medium-speed duplex channel, and a POTS channel. Segregating the two DSL channels from the POTS channel guarantees that your POTS line will continue to operate even if the DSL fails. You accomplish this by inserting a filter on each POTS line, or a splitter mechanism that enables all three channels to flow to the DSL modem but sends only the POTS channel down the POTS line. The DSL company should provide you with a few POTS filters for your telephones. If you need more, most computer/electronics stores stock DSL POTS filters.

The most common DSL installation consists of a *DSL modem* connected to a telephone wall jack and to a standard NIC in your computer (see Figure 8.27). A DSL modem is not an actual modem—it's more like an ISDN terminal adapter—but the term stuck, and even the manufacturers of the devices now call them DSL modems.

Many offices use DSL. In my office, we use a special DSL line (we use a digital phone system, so the DSL must be separate) that runs directly into our equipment room (see Figure 8.28).

This DSL line runs into our DSL modem via a standard phone line with RJ11 connectors. The DSL modem connects to our gateway router with a CAT 5e patch cable, which, in turn, connects to the company's switch. Figure 8.29 shows an ADSL modem and a router, giving you an idea of the configuration in our office.

Home users often connect the DSL modem directly to their PC's NIC. Either way, you have nothing to do in terms of installing DSL equipment on an individual system—just make sure you have a NIC. The person who installs your DSL will test the DSL line, install the DSL modem, connect it to your system, and verify that it all works. With DSL, be aware that you might run into an issue with something called *Point-to-Point Protocol over Ethernet (PPPoE).*

The first generation of DSL providers used a *bridged connection;* once the DSL line was running, it was as if you had snapped an Ethernet cable into your NIC. You were on the network. Those were good days for DSL. You just plugged your DSL modem into your NIC and, assuming your IP settings were whatever the DSL folks told you to use, you were running.

The DSL providers didn't like that too much. There was no control—no way to monitor who was using the DSL modem. As a result, the DSL folks started to use PPPoE, a protocol that was originally designed to encapsulate PPP frames into Ethernet frames. The DSL people adopted it to make stronger controls over your DSL connection. In particular, you could no longer simply connect; you now had to log on with an account and a password to make the DSL connection. PPPoE is now predominant on DSL. If you get a DSL line, your operating system has software to enable you to log onto your DSL network. Most SOHO routers come with built-in PPPoE support, enabling you to enter your username and password into the router itself (see Figure 8.30).

Broadband Cable

The first big competition for ADSL came from the cable companies. Cable modems have the impressive benefit of phenomenal top speeds. These speeds

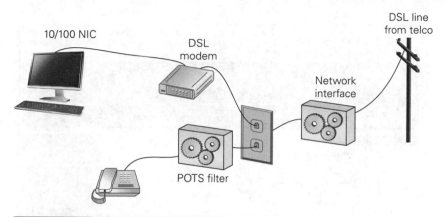

FIGURE 8.27 A DSL modem connection between a PC and telco

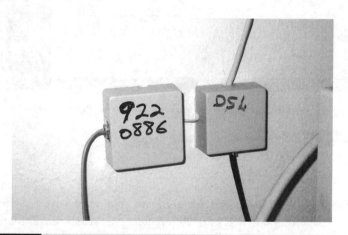

FIGURE 8.28 DSL line into equipment room

FIGURE 8.29 DSL connection

vary from cable company to cable company, but most advertise speeds in the (are you sitting down?) *5 to 100 megabits per second* range. Many cable modems provide a throughput speed of 5 to 30 Mbps for downloading and 2 Mbps to 10 Mbps for uploading—there is tremendous variance among different providers.

A cable modem installation consists of a cable modem connected to a cable. The cable modem gets its own cable connection, separate from the one that goes to the television. It's the same cable line, just split from the main line as if you were adding a second cable outlet for another television. As with ADSL, cable modems connect to PCs using a standard NIC (see Figure 8.31).

Cable modems connect using coax cable to a head end, similar to a telephone company's central office. Head ends, in turn, connect to the cable company's network. This network uses a unique protocol called *Data Over Cable Service Interface Specification (DOCSIS)*. Most recently, the specification was revised (DOCSIS 3.0) to increase transmission speeds significantly (this time

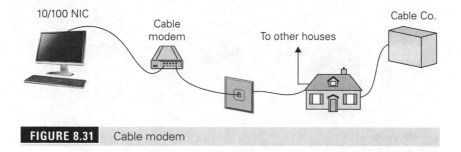

10/100 NIC

Cable modem

To other houses

Cable Co.

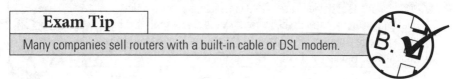

FIGURE 8.31   Cable modem

both upstream and downstream) and introduce support for Internet Protocol version 6 (IPv6).

> ### Exam Tip
> Many companies sell routers with a built-in cable or DSL modem.

You'll have a hard time telling a cable modem from a DSL modem. The only difference—other than the fact that one will have "cable modem" printed on it and the other will say "DSL modem"—is that the cable modem has a coax BNC connector and an RJ45 port, whereas the DSL modem has an RJ11 port and an RJ45 port.

Cable modems have proven themselves to be reliable and fast and have surpassed DSL as the broadband connection of choice in homes. Cable companies are also aggressively marketing to business customers with high-speed packages, making cable a viable option for businesses.

Satellite

Living in the countryside may have its charms, but you'll have a hard time getting high-speed Internet out on the farm. For those too far away to get anything else, satellite may be your only option. Satellite access comes in two types: one-way and two-way. *One-way* means that you download via satellite but you must use a PSTN/dial-up modem connection for uploads. *Two-way* means the satellite service handles both the uploading and downloading.

Satellite isn't as fast as DSL or cable modems, but it's still faster than PSTN. Both one-way and two-way satellite connections provide around 500 Kbps download and 50 Kbps upload.

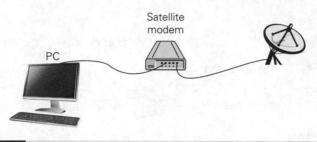

| FIGURE 8.32 | Satellite connection |

Travel Advisory

Companies that design satellite communications equipment haven't given up on their technology. At the time of this writing, at least one company, HughesNet, offered speeds up to 2 Mbps download. You can surf with that kind of speed!

Satellite requires a small satellite antenna, identical to the ones used for satellite television. This antenna connects to a satellite modem, which, in turn, connects to your PC or your network (see Figure 8.32).

Exam Tip

Neither cable modems nor satellites use PPP, PPPoE, or anything else that begins with three Ps.

Cellular WAN

Anyone with a smartphone these days appreciates the convenience of using wireless cellular technology on the road. Who doesn't love firing up an Android phone or iPhone and cruising the Internet from anywhere? As cell phone technology converges with Internet access technologies, competent techs need to understand what's happening behind the scenes. That means tackling an alphabet soup of standards.

Regardless of the standard, the voice and data you use on your smartphone (unless you have 802.11 wireless turned on) moves through a cellular wireless network of towers that now covers the world (see Figure 8.33). All of these

FIGURE 8.33   Cellular tower

technologies are really nothing more than signaling standards that use basically the same cellular infrastructure in different ways to improve speed, latency, configuration, and dependability over the years.

Mobile data services started in the mid-1980s and, as you might imagine, have gone through a dizzying number of standards and protocols, all of which have been revised, improved, abandoned, and reworked. Instead of trying to advertise these fairly complex and intimidating technologies, the industry instead came up with the marketing term *generations,* abbreviated as a number followed by the letter *G*: 2G, 3G, and 4G.

Salesmen and TV commercials use these terms to try to push mobile cellular services. These terms aren't generally used within the industry, and certainly not at a deeply technical level. As I go through the standards you'll see on the exam and encounter in real life, I'll mention both the technical name and the generation where applicable. I'll cover six common terms here:

- GSM
- EDGE
- CDMA
- HSPA+

- WiMAX
- LTE

GSM/EDGE

The *Global System for Mobile (GSM)*, the first group of networking technologies widely applied to mobile devices, relied on a type of time division multiplexing called *time division multiple access (TDMA)*. TDMA enabled multiple users to share the same channel more or less at the same time, with the switching from one user to another happening so quickly no one would notice.

GSM introduced the handy SIM card that is now so ubiquitous in smartphones. The SIM card identifies the phone, enabling access to the cellular networks, and stores some other information (contents differ according to many factors, none relevant for this discussion).

The original GSM standard was considered a 2G technology. The standard continued to improve over the years, getting new names and better data speeds. One of the last of these (and one you might see on the exam) was *Enhanced Data rates for GSM Evolution (EDGE)*, which offered data speeds up to 384 Kbps.

CDMA

Code division multiple access (CDMA) came out not long after GSM, but used a spread-spectrum form of transmission that was totally incompatible with GSM's TDMA. Rather than enabling multiple users to share a single channel by splitting the channel into time slices, spread-spectrum transmission changes the frequencies used by each user.

The original CDMA was considered superior to the original GSM, and U.S. carriers adopted CDMA en masse, which created some problems. The rest of the world went GSM, for example. Plus, CDMA lacked some key features, such as SIM cards.

The original CDMA was considered a 2G technology.

HSPA+

In the late 1990s, the ITU forwarded a new standard called International Mobile Telecommunications-2000 (IMT-2000) to address a number of shortcomings in mobile technology. IMT-2000 defined higher speeds, support for full-time Internet connections, and a number of other critical functions. The standard pushed support for multimedia messaging system (MMS, so you can send cat pictures in your text messages) and IP-based telephony.

Both GSM and CDMA went through a number of improvements in the late 1990s to the mid-2000s to address IMT-2000, all of which were marketed under probably the most confusing marketing term ever used: *3G*. Ideally, 3G meant a technology that supported IMT-2000, although the industry was very lax in how companies used this term. (This time period is so confusing that many technologies at the time were given decimal generations to clarify the situation. One example is GSM EDGE being called 2.9G due to its lack of full IMT-2000 support.)

The CompTIA Network+ exam only addresses one truly 3G technology: *Evolved High-Speed Packet Access (HSPA+)*. HSPA+ was the final 3G data standard, providing theoretical speeds up to 168 Mbps, although in reality most HSPA+ implementations rarely passed 10 Mbps.

WiMAX

Networks based on the IEEE 802.16 wireless standard called *WiMAX* seemed poised to take the crown as the wireless service that replaced DSL and cable to provide high-speed Internet to the masses. With early speeds running upwards of 30 Mbps and subsequent developments pushing the speeds above 1 Gbps, plus data ranges of 50+ kilometers, the world seemed to have true 4G awesome service.

Several major players in the telecom industry, such as Clear and Sprint, backed the technology and rolled out devices in the mid-to-late 2000s, but by 2011, most had stopped offering the service. Although some WiMAX networks around the world continue to operate (as of this writing), the end seems pretty near.

WiMAX provided the idea of wireless *metropolitan area networks (MANs)*, where cities could simply roll out fast Internet access to citizens at a fraction of the cost of physical connections. Despite good technology and a cool name, WiMAX ran into competition and lost.

LTE

Devices and networks using *Long Term Evolution (LTE)* technology rolled out worldwide in the early 2010s and now dominate wireless services. As early as 2013, for example, LTE already had around 20 percent market share in the United States and higher in parts of Asia. The numbers have only grown since then. Marketed as, and now generally accepted as, a true 4G technology, LTE networks feature speeds (in theory) of up to 300 Mbps download and 75 Mbps upload.

Where WiMAX seemed to stumble was in seamless integration with other cell phone technologies. LTE offers voice and data and coexists just fine with slower technologies.

FIGURE 8.34 Hotspot

With excellent speed and the broad coverage of cell towers, LTE can readily replace wired network technology. To connect a computer to the Internet when out in the country, for example, you don't need a physical connection, such as DSL, cable, or fiber to an ISP. You can instead connect to a wireless hotspot—a device that connects via cellular and enables other devices to access the Internet—and be on your merry way (see Figure 8.34). Conversely, you could get an LTE NIC and just plug that into a convenient USB port (see Figure 8.35).

Fiber

DSL was the first popular last-mile WAN option, but over the years cable modems have taken the lead. In an attempt to regain market share, telephone providers are now rolling out fiber-to-the-home/fiber-to-the-premises options that are giving the cable companies a scare. In the United States, two companies, AT&T (U-verse) and Verizon (FiOS), are offering very attractive ISP, television, and phone services at speeds that will eventually increase above 100 Mbps. These services are quickly gaining in popularity and giving cable companies a run for their money.

To make rollouts affordable, most fiber-to-the-home technologies employ a version of *passive optical network (PON)* architecture that uses a single fiber to the neighborhood switch and then individual fiber runs to each final destination.

FIGURE 8.35   Mobile wireless NIC

PON uses WDM to enable multiple signals to travel on the same fiber and then passively splits the signal at the switch to send traffic to its proper recipient.

Objective 8.03 Using Remote Access

Because most businesses are no longer limited to a simple little shop like you would find in a Dickens novel, many people need to be able to access files and resources over a great distance. Enter remote access. *Remote access* uses WAN and LAN connections to enable a computer user to log onto a network from the other side of a city, a state, or even the globe. As people travel, information has to remain accessible. Remote access enables users to connect to a server at the business location and log into the network as if they were in the same building as the company. The only problem with remote access is that there are so many ways to do it! I've listed the six most common forms of remote access here:

- **Dial-up to the Internet**   Using a dial-up connection to connect to your ISP
- **Private dial-up**   Using a dial-up connection to connect to your private network

- **Virtual private network**   Using an Internet connection to connect to a private network (discussed in Chapter 9)
- **Dedicated connection**   Using a non-dial-up connection to another private network or the Internet
- **Remote terminal**   Using a terminal emulation program to connect to another computer
- **VoIP**   Voice over IP

In this section, I discuss the issues related to configuring these six types of connections. After seeing how to configure these types of remote connections, I move into observing some security issues common to every type of remote connection.

Local Lingo

extranet   You'll see the term *extranet* more in books than in the day-to-day workings of networks and network techs. So what is an extranet? Whenever you allow authorized remote users to access some part of your private network, you have created an extranet.

Dial-up to the Internet

Dial-up is the oldest and least expensive method to connect to the Internet and is still somewhat common. Even with broadband and wireless so prevalent, every self-respecting network tech (or maybe just old network techs like me) keeps a dial-up account as a backup. You buy a dial-up account from an ISP (many wireless and broadband ISPs give free dial-up—just ask). All operating systems come with dial-up support programs, but you'll need to provide the following:

- A modem (most operating systems check for a modem before setting up a dial-up connection)
- The telephone number to dial (provided to you by the ISP)
- Username and password (provided to you by the ISP)
- Type of connection (dial-up always uses PPP)
- IP information (provided to you by the ISP—usually just DHCP)

Every operating system comes with the software to help you set up a dial-up connection. In Windows Vista or Windows 7, for example, select the "Set

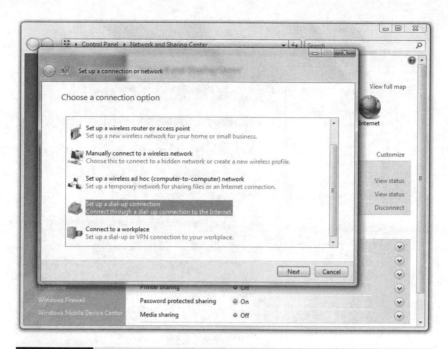

FIGURE 8.36 Dial-up on Windows 7

up a dial-up connection" option in the Network and Sharing Center (see Figure 8.36). Whatever the name, this tool is what you use to create dial-up connections.

Private Dial-up

A private dial-up connection connects a remote system to a private network via a dial-up connection. Private dial-up does not use the Internet! Private dial-up requires two systems. One system acts as a *remote access server (RAS)*. The other system, the client, runs a connection tool (usually the same tool you just read about in the previous section).

In Windows, a RAS is a server running Remote Access Service (RAS), dedicated to handling users who are not directly connected to a LAN but who need to access file and print services on the LAN from a remote location. For example, when a user dials into a network from home using an analog modem connection, she is dialing into a RAS. Once the user authenticates, she can access shared drives and printers as if her computer were physically connected to the office LAN.

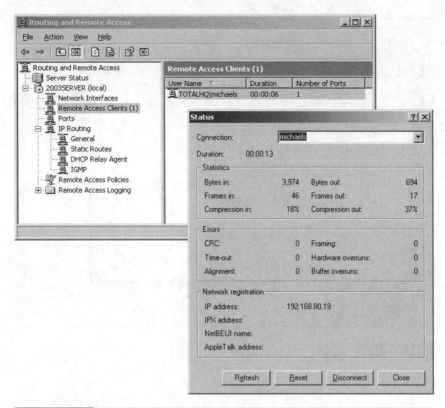

FIGURE 8.37   Windows RAS in action

You must set up a server in your LAN as a RAS server. That RAS server, which must have at least one modem, accepts incoming calls and handles password authentication. RAS servers use all the standard authentication methods (PAP, CHAP, EAP, 802.1X, and so on, which Chapter 9 covers in detail) and have separate sets of permissions for dial-in users and local users. You must also configure the RAS to set the rights and permissions for all of the dial-in users. Configuring a RAS system is outside the scope of this book, however, because each one is different (see Figure 8.37).

Creating the client side of a private dial-up connection is identical to setting up a dial-up connection to the Internet. The only difference is that instead of having an ISP tell you what IP settings, account name, and password to use, the person who sets up the RAS server tells you this information (see Figure 8.38).

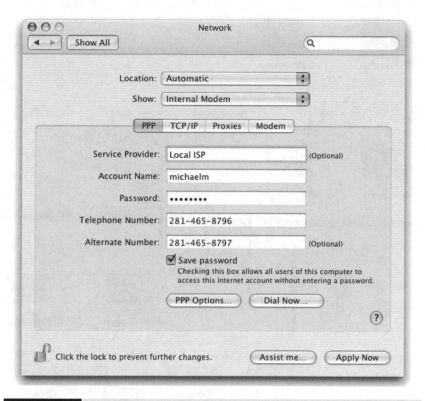

FIGURE 8.38 Dial-up on Macintosh OS X

Local Lingo

RAS *Remote access server* refers to both the hardware component (servers built to handle the unique stresses of a large number of clients calling in) and the software service component of a remote access solution. You might call it a catchall phrase. When you run Microsoft's Remote Access Service on a server, you turn that server into a remote access server.

Most techs call RAS "razz," rather than using the initials "R-A-S." This creates a seemingly redundant phrase used to describe a system running RAS: "RAS server." This helps distinguish servers from clients and makes geeks happier.

Dedicated Connection

Dedicated connections are remote connections that are never disconnected. Dedicated connections can be broken into two groups: dedicated private

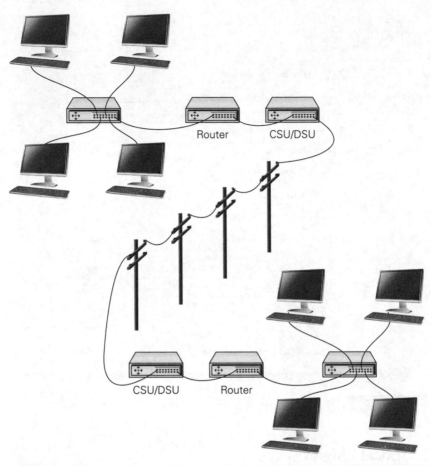

FIGURE 8.39 Dedicated private connection

connections between two locations and dedicated connections to the Internet. Dedicated private connections manifest themselves as two locations interconnected by a (usually high-speed) connection such as a T1 line (see Figure 8.39).

Each end of the T1 line goes into a router (after going through a CSU/DSU, of course). Note that this connection does not use the Internet in any way—it is not a VPN connection. Private dedicated connections of this type are expensive and are only used by organizations that need the high bandwidth and high security these connections provide. These connections are invisible to the individual computers on each network. There is no special remote connection configuration of the individual systems, although you may have to configure DHCP, DNS, and WINS servers to ensure that the network runs optimally.

DSL and Cable

Dedicated connections to the Internet are common today. Cable modems and DSL have made dedicated connections to the Internet inexpensive and very popular. In most cases, you don't have to configure anything in these dedicated connections. Many cable and DSL providers give you a CD-ROM that installs different items, such as testing software, PPPoE login support, and little extras such as e-mail clients and software firewalls. Personally, I prefer not to use these (they add a lot of stuff you don't need) and instead use the operating system's tools or a hardware router. Figure 8.40 shows the DSL wizard built into Windows 7. This program enables you to connect by entering your PPPoE information for your ADSL connection. Once started, these programs usually stay running in the system tray until your next reboot.

Cable Issues

Dedicated cable connections add a little complexity to the installation options because most cable networks bring television and often voice communication into the same line. This complicates things in one simple way: *splitters.*

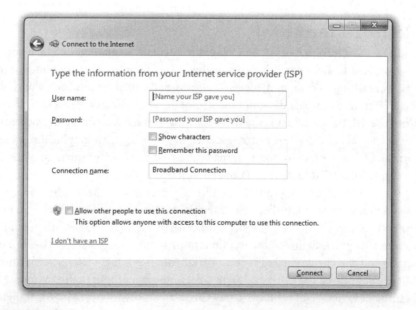

FIGURE 8.40   PPPoE connection

If you have a cable connection coming to your house and you have a television set in two rooms, how do you get cable in both rooms? Easy, right? Just grab a two-way splitter from RadioShack and run an extra pair of cables, one to each room. The problem comes from the fact that every time you split a cable signal, the signal degrades by half. This is called, logically, a *split cable* problem.

The quality of a signal can be measured in *decibels (dB)*, a unit that describes a ratio between an ideal point—a reference point—and the current state of the signal. When discussing signal strength, a solid signal is 0 dB. When that signal degrades, it's described as a *dB loss* and a negative number. An increase in signal is *gain* and gets a positive number. Decibels are *logarithmic units.* In case you've forgotten the high school math, this means that going up or down the scale in a simple number translates into a huge number in a percentage scale.

For example, when you split a cable signal into two, you get half the signal strength into each new cable. That's described as a –3 dB signal. Split it again and you've got a –6 dB signal. Although 6 isn't a big number in standard units, it's horribly huge in networking. You might have a 20 Mbps cable connection into your house, but split it twice and you're left with a 5 Mbps connection. Ouch!

The standard procedure with cable connections is to split them once: one cable goes to the cable modem and the other to the television. You can then split the television cable into as many connections as you need or can tolerate as far as reception quality.

Remote Terminal

You can use a terminal emulation program to create a *remote terminal,* a connection on a faraway computer that enables you to control that computer as if you were sitting in front of it, logged in. Terminal emulation has been a part of TCP/IP from its earliest days, in the form of good-old Telnet. Because it dates from pre-GUI days, Telnet is a text-based utility; all modern operating systems are graphical, so there was a strong desire to come up with graphical remote terminal tools. Citrix Corporation made the first popular terminal emulation products—the *WinFrame/MetaFrame* products (see Figure 8.41).

Remote terminal programs all require a server and a client. The *server* is the computer to be controlled. The *client* is the computer from which you do the controlling. Citrix created a standard called *Independent Computing Architecture (ICA)* that defined how terminal information was passed between the server and the client. Citrix made a breakthrough product—so powerful that Microsoft licensed the Citrix code and created its own product called Windows Terminal Services. Not wanting to pay Citrix any more money, Microsoft then

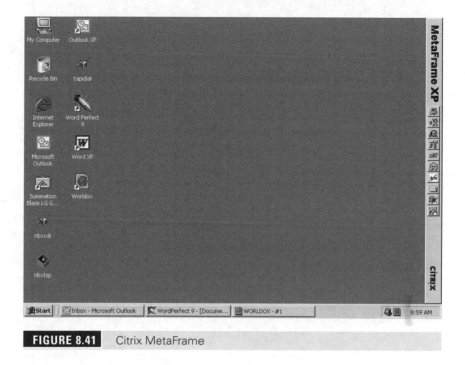

FIGURE 8.41   Citrix MetaFrame

created its own standard called *Remote Desktop Protocol (RDP)* and unveiled a new remote terminal called *Remote Desktop Connection (RDC)*. Figure 8.42 shows Windows Remote Desktop Connection running on a Windows 7 system, connecting to a Windows 2008 Server.

> **Exam Tip**
>
> All RDP applications run on port 3389 by default.

Unfortunately, Terminal Services only works in the Windows environment; however, a number of third parties make absolutely amazing terminal emulation programs that run on any operating system. The best of these, *VNC* (which stands for Virtual Network Computing), doesn't let you share folders or printers because it is only a terminal emulator (see Figure 8.43), but it runs on every operating system, is solid as a rock, and even runs from a web browser. It works nicely in Secure Shell (SSH) tunnels for great security, plus it comes by default with every copy of Mac OS X and almost every Linux distribution. Why bother

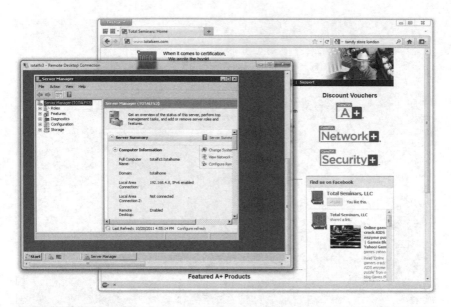

FIGURE 8.42   RDC in action

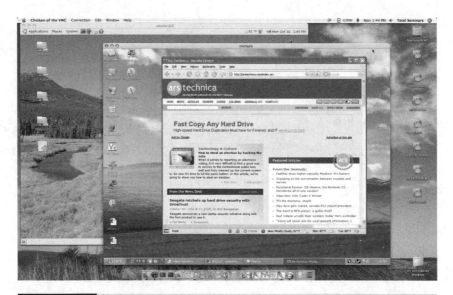

FIGURE 8.43   VNC in action

sharing if you can literally be at the screen? Oh, and did I mention that VNC is completely free?

VoIP

Voice over IP (VoIP) uses an IP network to transfer voice calls. VoIP works so well because it uses an existing network you're already paying for (your Internet connection) to replace another network you're also paying for (PSTN lines). The technology needed for VoIP isn't very challenging, but making a VoIP system that's standardized so everyone can use it (and still contact those who choose to use PSTN) requires international standards, making it quite a bit harder. VoIP is still a very fractured world, but it's getting closer to universally adopted standards—one day everyone will be able to contact everyone else, no matter what brand of VoIP they use. To do this, you need to know three important standards: RTP, SIP, and H.323.

RTP The *Real-time Transport Protocol (RTP)*, the heavily adopted bedrock of VoIP standards, defines the type of packets used on the Internet to move voice or data from a server to clients. The vast majority of VoIP solutions available today use RTP.

Exam Tip

The CompTIA Network+ objectives inexplicably drop the word "Transport" from this protocol and call it the *Real Time Protocol*. There's no such thing. It's the *Real-time Transport Protocol*.

SIP and H.323 *Session Initiation Protocol (SIP)* and *H.323* handle the initiation, setup, and delivery of VoIP sessions. VoIP requires a lot of special features that are not very common in many other Internet protocols. The biggest one is multicasting. You don't ever really use multicasting unless you want to show a number of people a video or want to make a conference call. SIP and H.323 both have methods for handling multicasting.

Exam Tip

SIP and H.323 both run on top of RTP. Most VoIP solutions are either SIP/RTP or H.323/RTP.

Skype

Almost every VoIP solution available today uses SIP or H.323 running on top of RTP, with one huge exception: the very famous and incredibly popular Skype. Skype was unveiled in 2003 by Niklas Zennström, a Swedish computer guy famous for inventing the Kazaa peer-to-peer file-sharing system. Skype is completely different from and completely incompatible with any other type of VoIP solution: Skype doesn't use servers, but instead uses a peer-to-peer topology that is identical to the old Kazaa network. Skype calls are also encrypted using a proprietary encryption method. No one has a standard method for VoIP encryption at this time, although many smart people are working hard on the issue.

Streaming Media with RTSP

VoIP isn't the only thing that takes advantage of protocols such as RTP. Streaming video is now mainstream, and many streaming video servers (Windows Media Player, QuickTime, and many others) use a popular protocol called *Real Time Streaming Protocol (RTSP)*. Like SIP and H.323, RTSP runs on top of RTP. RTSP has a number of features that are perfect for video streaming, such as the ability to run, pause, and stop videos. RTSP runs on TCP port 554.

CHECKPOINT

✔**Objective 8.01: Telephony and Beyond**   The Internet backbone uses technologies designed more than 20 years ago to support telephone calls. There are two reasons to use a telephony WAN connection: to get your LAN on the Internet and to make a private connection between two or more of your private LANs. T1, T3, E1, and E3 are all popular methods of high-speed communication. SONET is the primary standard for long-distance, high-speed, fiber-optic transmission in the United States. WANs use packet-switching technologies such as ATM and Frame Relay to transmit data over multiple connection types.

✔**Objective 8.02: The Last Mile**   The last mile represents the challenge of increasing connection speeds between the user and the central office. Many technologies exist to facilitate this connection, including Dial-up, DSL, Broadband cable, Satellite, Cellular WAN, and Fiber.

✔**Objective 8.03: Using Remote Access**   Remote access allows users to log onto networks remotely, making files and network resources available to users across the city, state, or globe. There are six common forms of remote access. You can make a dial-up connection to the Internet. You can connect to another computer using a private dial-up connection. Virtual private networks enable you to tunnel from a local computer to a remote network. Dedicated connections use non-dial-up methods to connect to a private network or the Internet. A remote terminal uses a terminal emulation program to connect to another computer. VoIP (voice over IP) uses an IP network to make voice calls.

REVIEW QUESTIONS

1. Which standard supports a throughput of up to 39.8 Gbps?
   A. ISDN
   B. VDSL
   C. SONET
   D. MPLS

2. If you purchase a T1 line in the United States, which technologies will be used to switch packets? (Select two.)
   A. OC
   B. Frame Relay
   C. ATM
   D. BERT

3. Which description identifies the problem with "the last mile"?
   A. The connection from a central office to a user's home is analog, whereas the rest of the network is digital.
   B. Users must live within a mile of a central office in order to guarantee Quality of Service (QoS).
   C. SONET connections are limited to a maximum distance of one mile, and connecting central offices via multiplexers is expensive and difficult to maintain.
   D. Copper wires that carry analog telephone signals are limited to a maximum distance of one mile.

4. Which terms describe a common telephone connection? (Select two.)
   A. ISDN
   B. POTS
   C. Fractional T1
   D. PSTN

5. What marks where the telephone company's responsibility ends and yours begins?
   A. Multiplexer
   B. Demarc
   C. Primary Rate Interface
   D. Bridges connection

6. The CCITT established which set of standards?
   A. Optical Carrier (OC)
   B. DSL (ADSL, SDSL, VDSL)
   C. Data Over Cable Service Interface Specification (DOCSIS)
   D. V standards

7. Which is the fastest ISDN connection?
   A. BERT
   B. BRI
   C. PRI
   D. ATM

8. Sinjay is 200 meters from his ISP's DSLAM. Which DSL version will provide him with, theoretically, up to 100 Mbps of both download and upload speed?
   A. DS3
   B. ADSL
   C. SDSL
   D. VDSL

9. Which protocol is used by cable companies?
   A. MPLS
   B. DOCSIS
   C. PSTN
   D. SIP

10. What is the benefit to using a satellite connection?

　　A. It offers speeds faster than both DSL and cable.

　　B. The upload and download speeds are always equal.

　　C. It is often available in remote locations where DSL and cable are not.

　　D. It offers better security than both DSL and cable.

REVIEW ANSWERS

1. **C**　SONET supports throughput up to 39.8 Gbps as defined in the OC-768 standard.

2. **B** **C**　Frame Relay and ATM are packet-switching technologies used on T1 lines.

3. **A**　The last mile describes the analog run from the central office to a user's location.

4. **B** **D**　POTS and PSTN are interchangeable terms for common telephone networks.

5. **B**　The telephone company's responsibility ends at the demarc. All wires and equipment on the other side are the responsibility of the customer.

6. **D**　The CCITT developed the V standards for modems.

7. **C**　A Primary Rate Interface combines 23 B channels for a total throughput of about 1.5 Mbps.

8. **D**　Because he is within 300 meters of his ISP's DSLAM, VDSL is a viable option, and it supports 100 Mbps in both directions.

9. **B**　Cable companies use Data Over Cable Service Interface Specification (DOCSIS).

10. **C**　Satellite connections are often the only option for users in remote locations.

Network Security

CHAPTER 9

ETA	NEWBIE	SOME EXPERIENCE	EXPERT
	5 hours	3 hours	1 hour

The very nature of networking makes networks vulnerable to many threats. By definition, a network must allow multiple users to access serving systems, but at the same time, you must protect the network from harm.

The news may be full of tales about *hackers* and other malicious people with nothing better to do than lurk around the Internet and trash the peace-loving systems of good folks like us, but in reality, hackers are only one of many serious network threats. The average network faces many more threats from the folks who are authorized to use it than from those who are not authorized.

> ### Local Lingo
>
> **hacker** In some circles, the term *hacker* describes someone who loves the challenge of overcoming obstacles and perceived limitations—and that's a positive thing! At least for this chapter, I define a hacker as an unauthorized person who intentionally tries to access resources on your network. That's the way the term is generally used today.

In addition, don't think all network threats are people. Let's not forget natural disasters such as floods and hurricanes. Even third parties can unintentionally wreak havoc—what will you do if your building suddenly lacks electricity? A *network threat* can be any number of factors or elements that share one essential feature: the potential to damage network data, machines, or users.

To protect your network, you need to implement proper *network access control (NAC),* which means control over information, people, access, machines, and everything in between.

This chapter starts off with risk-related concepts, and then moves on to common network vulnerabilities and threats. Then, we'll look at network-hardening techniques and physical security controls. We'll conclude the chapter with a look at firewalls, network access control models, and basic forensics concepts.

 **Objective 9.01** Risk-Related Concepts

An *asset* is something that holds value to a company. Data and information, of course, come to mind. A *data breach* is any form of attack where secured data is taken or destroyed. The many credit card hacks we've seen over the last few years are great examples of data breaches.

However, there are other types of assets. Physical assets could include hardware, furniture, buildings, and more. Employees? Of course, they, too, are assets to a company! Certain assets, though, are not as tangible as the previously mentioned ones. How about a company's reputation? That's certainly an asset that companies can't afford to lose!

A *vulnerability* is a weakness, physical or logical, that allows an asset to be exploited. Vulnerabilities need to be addressed. The entities that are doing the exploitation of assets are called *threats*. Risk represents the probability that an asset will be exploited through a threat or threat agent.

First Responders

The cornerstone of incident response is the incident response team—usually one or more trained, preassigned first responders with procedures in place for what to do. Depending on the type of event, the team may be responsible for the following:

- Deciding whether the event qualifies as an incident the team should address, ignore, or escalate
- Evaluating the scope and cause of the issue
- Preventing further disruption
- Resolving the cause
- Restoring order to affected systems
- Identifying ways to prevent a recurrence

Most incidents are handled at this level. However, if an incident is so vast that the incident response team cannot stop, contain, or remediate it, disaster recovery comes into play.

Disaster Recovery

Disaster recovery is a critical part of contingency planning that deals directly with providing methods of recovering your primary infrastructure from a disaster. A *disaster* is an event, such as a hurricane or flood, that disables or destroys substantial amounts of infrastructure.

Any company prepared for a disaster has one or more backup copies of essential data. The backed-up files comprise an archive of important data that the disaster recovery team can retrieve in case of some disaster.

Disaster recovery handles everything from restoring hardware to backups, but only at the primary business location. Anything that requires moving part of the organization's business offsite until recovery is complete is a part of business continuity.

Business Continuity

When the disaster disables, wipes out, covers in mud, or in some other way prevents the primary infrastructure from operating, the organization should have a plan of action to keep the business going at remote sites. The planning and processes necessary to make this happen are known as *business continuity (BC)*. Organizations plan for this with business continuity planning (BCP). Good BCP will deal with many issues, but one of the more important ones—and one that must be planned well in advance of a major disaster—is the concept of backup sites.

Battery Backups/UPS

Every network should have an uninterruptible power supply (UPS) as a backup for each server or rack of servers. The batteries in UPSs go out, so be certain to check them periodically and replace as necessary.

End User Awareness and Training

End users are probably the primary source of security problems for any organization. We must increase *end user awareness and training* so they know what to look for and how to act to avoid or reduce attacks. Training users is a critical piece of managing risk. Although a formal course is preferred, it's up to the IT department to do what it can to make sure users have an understanding of the following:

- **Security policies** Users need to read, understand, and, when necessary, sign all pertinent security policies.
- **Passwords** Make sure users understand basic password skills, such as sufficient length and complexity, refreshing passwords regularly, and password control.
- **System and workplace security** Make sure users understand how to keep their workstations secure through screen locking and not storing written passwords in plain sight.
- **Social engineering** Users need to recognize typical social-engineering tactics and know how to counter them.
- **Malware** Train users to recognize and deal with malware attacks.

Adherence to Standards and Policies

Given the importance of company policies and standards such as HIPPA and Sarbanes-Oxley, it's also imperative for an organization to adhere to standards and policies strictly. For company policies, this can often be a challenge. As technologies change, organizations must review and update policies to reflect those changes.

Single Point of Failure

System failures happen; that's not something we can completely prevent. The secret to dealing with failures is to avoid a single point of failure: one system that, if it fails, will bring down an entire process, workflow, or, worse yet, an entire organization. It's easy to say, "Oh, we will just make two of everything!" (This would create *redundancy* where needed.) But you can't simply make two of everything. That would create far too much unnecessary hardware and administration. Sure, redundancy is fairly easy to do, but the trick is to determine where the redundancy is needed to avoid single points of failure without too much complexity, cost, or administration. We do this process by identifying two things: critical assets and critical nodes.

Critical Assets

Every organization has assets that are critical to the operation of the organization. A bakery may have one PLC-controlled oven, a sales group might have a single database, or a web server rack might only be connected to the Internet through one ISP. The process of determining critical assets is tricky and is usually a senior management process.

Critical Nodes

Unlike critical assets, critical nodes are very much unique to IT equipment: servers, routers, workstations, printers, and so forth. Identifying critical nodes is usually much clearer than identifying critical assets because of the IT nature of critical nodes and the fact that the IT department is always going to be painfully aware of what nodes are critical. Here are a few examples of critical nodes:

- A file server that contains critical project files
- A single web server
- A single printer (assuming printed output is critical to the organization)
- An edge router

Vulnerability Testing

Given the huge number of vulnerabilities out there, it's impossible for even the most highly skilled technician to find them by manually inspecting an infrastructure. The best way to know your infrastructure's vulnerabilities is to run some form of program—a vulnerability scanner—that will inspect a huge number of potential vulnerabilities and create a report for you to then act upon.

There is no single vulnerability scanner that works for every aspect of your infrastructure. Instead, a good network tech will have a number of utilities that work for their type of network infrastructure. Here are a few of the more popular vulnerability scanners and where they are used.

Microsoft Baseline Security Analyzer (MBSA) is designed to test individual systems. It's getting a little old, but still does a great job of testing one Microsoft Windows system for vulnerabilities.

Nmap is a port scanner. Port scanners query individual nodes, looking for open or vulnerable ports and creating a report. Actually, it might be unfair to say that Nmap is *only* a port scanner because it adds a number of other tools. Written by Gordon Lyon, Nmap is very popular, free, and well maintained.

Figure 9.1 shows sample output from Zenmap, the GUI frontend for Nmap.

When you need to perform more serious vulnerability testing, it's common to turn to more aggressive and powerful comprehensive testers. There are plenty out there, but two dominate the field: Nessus and OpenVAS. Nessus, from Tenable Network Security, is arguably the first truly comprehensive vulnerability testing tool and has been around for almost two decades (see Figure 9.2). Nessus is an excellent, well-known tool. Once free to everyone, Nessus is still free for home users, but commercial users must purchase a subscription.

OpenVAS is an open source fork of Nessus that is also extremely popular and, in the opinion of many security types, superior to Nessus.

You need to be careful not to use the term *vulnerability scanning* to mean "just running some program to find weaknesses." Vulnerability scanning is only a small part of a more strategic program called *vulnerability management*. Vulnerability management is an ongoing process of identifying vulnerabilities and dealing with them. The tools we use are a small but important part of the overall process.

Penetration Testing

Once you've run your vulnerability tools and hardened your infrastructure, it's time to see if your network can stand up to an actual attack. The problem with this is that you don't want *real* bad guys making these attacks. You want to be attacked by a "white hat" hacker, who will find the existing vulnerabilities and,

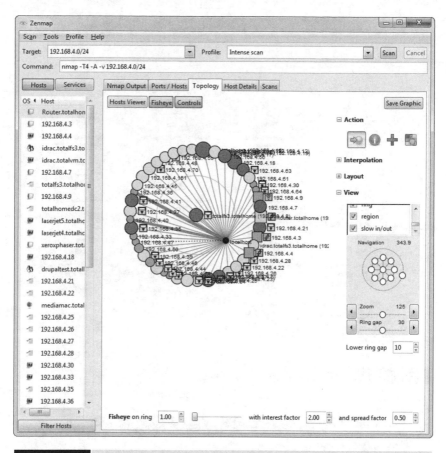

FIGURE 9.1   Zenmap output

instead of hurting your infrastructure, report findings so that you can further harden your network. This is called *penetration testing* (or *pentesting* for short).

Unlike vulnerability testing, a good pentest requires a skilled operator who understands the target and knows potential vulnerabilities. To that end, there are a number of tools that make this job easier. Two examples are Aircrack-ng and Metasploit. Aircrack-ng is an open source tool for pentesting pretty much every aspect of wireless networks. It's powerful, relatively easy to use, and completely free. Metasploit, another unique open source tool, enables the pentester to use a massive library of attacks as well as tweak those attacks for unique penetrations. Metasploit is the go-to tool for vulnerability testing. You simply won't find a professional in this arena who does not use Metasploit. Metasploit is run out of a text-only terminal, but for those who prefer GUIs, there is a GUI frontend called Armitage as well as a browser-based version (see Figure 9.3).

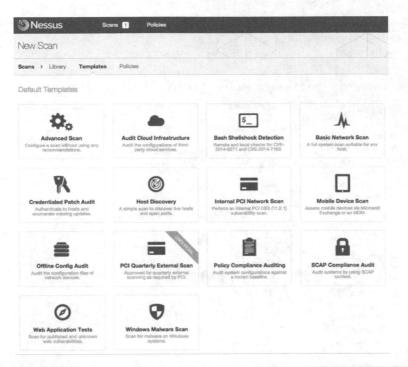

FIGURE 9.2   Nessus screen

FIGURE 9.3   Metasploit output

Also, a number of highly customized Linux-based tools incorporate many tools into a single bootable drive. One of the most famous operating systems, containing an insane amount of tools and utilities, is Kali Linux. It's hard to find a good security person who doesn't have a bootable Kali Linux USB drive.

Objective 9.02 Common Network Vulnerabilities and Threats

As mentioned earlier, a vulnerability is a weakness, physical or logical, that allows an asset to be exploited.

Some vulnerabilities are obvious, such as connecting to the Internet without an edge firewall or not using any form of account control for user files. Other vulnerabilities are unknown or missed, and that makes the study of vulnerabilities very important for a network tech.

Attacks/Threats

A network threat is any form of *potential* attack against your network. Don't think only about Internet attacks here! Sure, hacker-style threats are real, but there are so many others. A threat can be a person sneaking into your offices and stealing passwords, or an ignorant employee deleting files they should not have access to in the first place.

Denial of Service

A denial of service (DoS) attack is a targeted attack on a server (or servers) that provides some form of service on the Internet (such as a website), with the goal of making that site unable to process any incoming server requests. DoS attacks come in many different forms. The simplest example is a *physical attack,* where a person physically attacks the servers. Bad guys could go to where the servers are located and shut them down or disconnect their Internet connections—in some cases permanently. Physical DoS attacks are good to know for the exam, but they aren't very common unless the service is very small and served in only a single location.

Far more menacing, and far more common than a simple DoS attack, are distributed denial of service (DDoS) attacks. A DDoS attack uses hundreds, thousands, or even millions of computers under the control of a single operator to launch a coordinated strike. DDoS operators don't own these computers, but instead use malware (discussed later) to take control of computers. A single computer under the control of an operator is called a *zombie*. A group of computers under the control of one operator is called a *botnet*.

The goal of a botnet operator conducting a DDoS attack is to send as many amplified requests as possible, but botnets are only one way to do this. Another tactic used in DDoS attacks is to send requests with the target server's IP address to otherwise normally operating servers, such as DNS or NTP servers. This is called *reflection* or a *reflective DDoS*. These servers then send massive numbers of amplified responses to the target. Such a huge increase in the number of packets—a traffic spike—will bring the target down.

The smurf attack was an early form of DoS. The attacker flooded a network with ping packets sent to the broadcast address. The return address of the pings was spoofed to that of the intended victim. When all the computers on the network responded to the initial ping, they sent their response to the intended victim. The attacker then amplified the effect of the attack by the number of responding machines on the network. Due to modern network management procedures and controls built into modern operating systems, the danger of the smurf attack has been largely mitigated.

A *friendly* or *unintentional DoS* is just as it sounds: a system is brought down unintentionally. The most common form of friendly DoS occurs on a super-busy server: an organization's infrastructure isn't strong enough to keep up with legitimate demand. This is very common on the Web when a popular site makes a reference to a small site or someone mentions the small site on a radio or TV program, resulting in a massive increase in traffic to the small site. This "hug of death" goes by many names, such as Slashdotting and the Reddit effect.

A *permanent DoS (PDoS)* is an attack that damages the targeted machine—router, server, and so on—and renders that machine inoperable. The attacker gains control over the management interface of a router, for example, and makes malicious changes to brick that router. The router needs to be repaired or, worst case, replaced. PDoS attacks are sometimes referred to as *phlashing* attacks.

ARP Cache Poisoning

ARP cache poisoning attacks target the ARP caches on hosts and switches. The process and protocol used in resolving an IP address to an Ethernet MAC address is called *Address Resolution Protocol (ARP)*.

Every node on a TCP/IP network has an *ARP cache* that stores a list of known IP addresses and their associated MAC addresses. On a Windows system you can see the ARP cache using the arp –a command. Here's part of the result of typing **arp –a** on my system:

```
C:\Users\Mike>arp -a
Interface: 202.13.212.205 --- 0xc
   Internet Address        Physical Address        Type
   202.13.212.1            d0-d0-fd-39-f5-5e        dynamic
   202.13.212.100          30-05-5c-0d-ed-c5        dynamic
   202.13.212.101          00-02-d1-08-df-8d        dynamic
   202.13.212.208          00-22-6b-a0-a2-9b        dynamic
```

If a device wants to send an IP packet to another device, it must encapsulate the IP packet into an Ethernet frame. If the sending device doesn't know the destination device's MAC address, it sends a special broadcast called an *ARP request*. In turn, the device with that IP address responds with a unicast packet to the requesting device. An attacker can simply send an unsolicited ARP and associate his MAC address with the gateway's IP address. Now all packets destined for other networks will pass through the attacker first!

Packet/Protocol Abuse

No matter how hard the Internet's designers try, it seems there is always a way to take advantage of a protocol by using it in ways it was never meant to be used. Any time you do things with a protocol that it wasn't meant to do and that abuse ends up creating a threat, this is *protocol abuse*. A classic example involves the Network Time Protocol (NTP).

The Internet keeps time by using NTP servers. Without NTP providing accurate time for everything that happens on the Internet, anything that's time sensitive would be in big trouble.

Here's what happened. No computer's clock is perfect, so NTP is designed for each NTP server to have a number of peers. *Peers* are other NTP servers that one NTP server can compare its own time against to make sure its clock is accurate. Occasionally a person running an NTP server might want to query the server to determine what peers it uses. The command used on just about every NTP server to submit queries is called ntpdc. The ntpdc command puts the NTP server into interactive mode so that you can then make queries to the NTP server. One of these queries is called monlist. The monlist query asks the NTP server about the traffic going on between itself and peers. If you query a public NTP server with monlist, it makes a lot of output:

```
$ ntpdc -c monlist fake.timeserver5.org
```

remote address	port local address	count	m	ver	rstr	avgint	lstint
time.apple.com	123 192.168.4.78	13	4	4	1d0	319	399
ntp.notreal.com	123 46.3.129.78	1324	4	4	1	0	0
123.212.32.44	123 32.42.77.82	0	0	0	0	0	0

```
<a few hundred more lines here>

ntpdc>
```

A bad guy can hit multiple NTP servers with the same little command—with a spoofed source IP address—and generate a ton of responses from the NTP server to that source IP. Enough of these requests will bring the spoofed source computer—now called the target or victim—to its knees (denial of service).

If that's not sinister enough, hackers can also use evil programs that inject unwanted information into packets in an attempt to break another system. We call these *malformed packets*. Programs such as Metasploit give you the capability to custom form (or should we say malform?) packets and send them to anyone. You can use this to exploit a server that isn't designed to handle such attacks. What will happen if you send a DHCP request packet into which you have placed totally incorrect information in an Option field? The guy doing this to your DHCP server is hoping that when your DHCP reads the request, it will break the server somehow: giving root access, shutting down the DHCP server, whatever. This is an exploit created by packet abuse.

Spoofing

Spoofing is the process of pretending to be someone or something you are not by placing false information into your packets. Any data sent on a network can be spoofed. Here are a few quick examples of commonly spoofed data:

- Source MAC address and IP address, to make you think a packet came from somewhere else
- E-mail address, to make you think an e-mail came from somewhere else
- Web address, to make you think you are on a web page you are not on
- User name, to make you think a certain user is contacting you when in reality it's someone completely different

Generally, spoofing isn't so much a threat as it is a tool to make threats. If you spoof my e-mail address, for example, that by itself isn't a threat. If you use my e-mail address to pretend to be me, however, and to ask my employees to send in their user names and passwords for network login? That's clearly a threat.

Brute Force

Having a password that's too short leaves you at risk to attackers trying brute force attacks, a method where a threat agent guesses every permutation of some part of data. Most of the time the term *brute force* refers to an attempt to crack a password, but the term applies to other attacks. You can brute force a search for open ports, network IDs, user names, and so on. Pretty much any attempt to guess the contents of some kind of data field that isn't obvious (or is hidden) is a considered a brute force attack.

Man in the Middle

In a man-in-the-middle attack, an attacker taps into communications between two systems, covertly intercepting traffic thought to be only between those systems, reading or in some cases even changing the data and then sending the data on. A classic man-in-the-middle attack would be a person using special software on a wireless network to make all the clients think his laptop is a WAP. He could then listen in on that wireless network, gathering up all the conversations and gaining access to passwords, shared keys, or other sensitive information. Man-in-the-middle attacks are commonly perpetrated using ARP poisoning (mentioned earlier).

Session Hijacking

Session hijacking tries to intercept a valid computer session to get authentication information. Unlike man-in-the-middle attacks, session hijacking only tries to grab authentication information, not necessarily listening in like a man-in-the-middle attack.

Social Engineering

A considerable percentage of attacks against your network fall under the heading of social engineering—the process of using or manipulating people inside the networking environment to gain access to that network from the outside. The term *social engineering* covers the many ways humans can use other humans to gain unauthorized information. This unauthorized information may be a network login, a credit card number, company customer data—almost anything you might imagine that one person or organization may not want a person outside of that organization to access.

Social engineering attacks aren't considered hacking—at least in the classic sense of the word—although the goals are the same. Social engineering is where people attack an organization through the people in the organization or physically access the organization to get the information they need.

The most classic form of social engineering is the telephone scam in which someone calls a person and tries to get him or her to reveal his or her user name/password combination. In the same vein, someone may physically enter your building under the guise of having a legitimate reason for being there, such as a cleaning person, repair technician, or messenger. The attacker then snoops around desks, looking for whatever he or she has come to find (one of many good reasons not to put passwords on your desk or monitor). The attacker might talk with people inside the organization, gathering names, office numbers, or department names—little things in and of themselves, but powerful tools when combined later with other social engineering attacks.

VLAN Hopping

An older form of attack that still comes up from time to time is called VLAN hopping. The idea behind VLAN hopping is to take a system that's connected to one VLAN and, by abusing VLAN commands to the switch, convince the switch to change your switch port connection to a trunk link, or to place two VLAN tags in a frame. VLAN hopping is almost never seen anymore because modern switches are all hardened against this attack.

Compromised System

A system hit by malware will eventually show the effects, although in any number of ways. The most common symptoms of malware on a *compromised system* are general sluggishness and random crashes. In some cases, web browsers might default to unpleasant or unwanted websites. Frequently, compromised systems increase network outflow a lot.

If you get enough compromised systems in your network, especially if those systems form part of a botnet or DDoS attack force, your network will suffer. The amount of traffic specifically doing the bidding of the malware on the systems can hog network bandwidth, making the network sluggish.

Insider Threats/Malicious Employees

The greatest hackers in the world will all agree that being inside an organization, either physically or by access permissions, makes evildoing much easier. Malicious employees are a huge threat because of their ability to directly destroy data, inject malware, and initiate attacks.

Zero-Day Attacks

The way (software or methods) an exploit takes advantage of a vulnerability is called an *attack surface*. The timeframe in which a bad guy can apply an attack surface against a vulnerability before patches are applied to prevent the exploit is called an *attack window*. New attacks using vulnerabilities that haven't yet been identified (or fixed) are called *zero-day attacks*.

Unnecessary Running Services/ Open Ports

A typical system running any OS is going to have a large number of important programs called *services* running in the background. Services such as wireless network clients, DHCP clients, and web servers do the behind-the-scenes grunt work that users don't need to see. In a typical system, not all these services are necessary.

From a security standpoint, there are two reasons it's important not to run any unnecessary services. First, most OSs use services to listen on open TCP or UDP ports, potentially leaving systems open to attack. Second, bad guys often use services as a tool for the use and propagation of malware. In fact, one of the first techniques that malicious users try is to probe hosts to identify any open ports.

Unpatched/Legacy Systems

Unpatched systems—including operating systems and firmware—and legacy systems present a glaring security threat. You need to deal with such problems on live systems on your network. When it comes to unpatched OSs, well, patch or isolate them!

Unpatched firmware presents a little more of a challenge. Most firmware never needs to be or gets patched, but once in a while you'll run into devices that have a discovered flaw or security hole. These you'll need to patch.

Unencrypted Channels

The open nature of the Internet has made it fairly common for us to use *secure protocols* or channels such as VPNs, SSL/TLS, and SSH. It never ceases to amaze me, however, how often people use unencrypted channels—especially in the most unlikely places. It was only a few years ago I stumbled upon a tech using Telnet to do remote logins into a very critical router for an ISP.

In general, look for the following unsecure protocols and unencrypted channels:

- Using Telnet instead of SSH for remote terminal connections.
- Using HTTP instead of HTTPS on websites.
- Using unsecure remote desktops such as VNC.
- Using any unsecure protocol in the clear. Run them through a VPN!

Cleartext Credentials

Older protocols offer a modicum of security—you often need a valid user name and password, for example, when connecting to a File Transfer Protocol (FTP) server. The problem with such protocols (FTP, Telnet, POP3) is that user names and passwords are sent from the user to the server in cleartext. Credentials can be captured and, because they're not encrypted, cleartext credentials can be readily discovered.

There are many other places where cleartext turns up, such as in third-party applications and improperly configured applications that would normally have encrypted credentials.

The problem with third-party applications using cleartext credentials is that there's no way for you to know whether they do so or not. Luckily, we live in a world filled with people who run packet sniffers on just about everything. These vulnerabilities are often discovered fairly quickly and reported. Most likely, you'll get an automatic patch.

The last place where cleartext credentials can still come through is poor configuration of applications that would otherwise be well protected. Almost any remote control program has some form of "no security" level setting. This might be as obvious as a "turn off security" option, or it could be a setting.

Unsecure Protocols

In the early days of dial-up, we used the *Serial Line Internet Protocol (SLIP)* to connect a modem to an Internet service provider (ISP). SLIP was a totally unsecure protocol and therefore we migrated to Point-to-Point Protocol (PPP) as soon as we could.

Travel Assistance

PPP and other user authentication controls are discussed later in this chapter.

Simple Network Management Protocol (SNMP) is a useful tool for network administrators, but the first version, SNMPv1, sent all data, including the passwords, unencrypted over the network. SNMPv2 had good encryption but was rather challenging to use. SNMPv3 is the standard version used today and combines solid, fairly easy-to-use authentication and encryption.

FTP is not very secure because data transfers are not encrypted by default, so you don't want to use straight FTP for sensitive data. However, you can add user names and passwords to prevent all but the most serious hackers from accessing your FTP server. I avoid using the anonymous login because unscrupulous people could use the server for exchanging illegal software.

Another thing to check when deciding on an FTP server setup is the number of clients you want to support. Most anonymous FTP sites limit the number of users who may download at any one time to around 500. This protects you from a sudden influx of users flooding your server and eating up all your Internet bandwidth.

Trivial File Transfer Protocol (TFTP) is a poor man's FTP. The biggest security weakness is that TFTP has no login authentication process! Anyone with the IP address can access the TFTP server. TFTP uses port 69.

TEMPEST/RF Emanation

Radio waves can penetrate walls, to a certain extent, and accidental spill, called *RF emanation,* can lead to a security vulnerability. Avoid this by placing some form of filtering between your systems and the place where the bad guys are going to be using their super-high-tech Bourne Identity spy tools to pick up on the emanations. To combat these emanations, the U.S. National Security Agency (NSA) developed a series of standards called TEMPEST. TEMPEST defines how to shield systems and manifests in a number of different products, such as coverings for individual systems, wall coverings, and special window coatings. Unless you work for a U.S. government agency, the chances of you seeing TEMPEST technologies is pretty small.

Wireless Threats

Wireless communication has its own set of specific threats, starting with the concept of *jamming*, which is when a device blocks wireless signals. Let's look at others.

Rogue Access Point

A *rogue access point* (or rogue AP) is simply an unauthorized access point. Rogue access points have tortured every wireless network since the day Linksys came out with the first cheap wireless router back in the early 2000s.

Most rogue APs aren't evil: just a user wanting to connect to the network who installs a WAP in a handy location into the wired network. Evil rogue APs are far more nefarious, acting as a backdoor to a network or a man-in-the-middle attack, grabbing user names and passwords, among other items.

Evil Twin

The most infamous form of rogue AP is called an *evil twin*. An evil twin is a rogue AP that intentionally mimics an existing SSID in order to get people to connect to it instead of the proper WAP. Evil twins work best in unsecured networks such as those you see in airports and hotels.

War Driving/War Chalking

We need to take a moment to discuss one of those weird CompTIA Network+ topics that covers very old issues that don't really exist anymore: war driving and war chalking. A long time ago—as late as around 2005—there weren't very many wireless networks around. Nerdy types would conduct *war driving*: looking for wireless networks by using omnidirectional antennas connected to laptops using wireless sniffing programs (this was well before every OS came with a client that located SSIDs). When a network was found, the war driver would place a special chalk mark on a nearby curb or sidewalk to tell other war drivers the location of the SSID.

Bluejacking/Bluesnarfing

Bluejacking was the process of sending unsolicited messages to another Bluetooth device. These messages would pop up on your screen. Bluejacking wasn't considered anything more than irritating, but Bluesnarfing was another matter. *Bluesnarfing* used weaknesses in the Bluetooth standard to steal information from other Bluetooth devices.

WEP/WPA/WAP2/WPS Attacks

WEP is subject to many types of *WEP attacks*. Hackers can easily crack WEP, for two reasons: the size of the encryption key and the way the key is updated. First, the WEP keys were never really 64- and 128-bit. WEP uses a flawed encryption cipher called *RC4*. RC4 is a stream cipher that uses a little code to start the encryption process, stored in the key in the form of what's called an *initialization vector (IV)*. The IV with WEP is 24 bits, which means the encryption part of a WEP key is only 40-bit or 104-bit. It also means that the IV itself, being so small, is very crackable.

The second problem with WEP is that the encryption key is both static (never changes from session to session) and shared (the same key is used by all network nodes). This means it's not that hard to crack, assuming you can capture enough WEP-encrypted packets to figure out the code. WEP is simply a disaster.

WEP also fails to provide a mechanism for performing user authentication. That is, network nodes that use WEP encryption are identified by their MAC address, and no other credentials are offered or required. With just a laptop and some open source software, a hacker can very easily sniff out and duplicate MAC addresses, thus opening you up to a possible spoofing attack. WEP that it is outdated and should never be used. The only security WEP provides today is to prevent casual people from connecting to your WAP. Its encryption is so easily cracked that you might as well be transmitting plaintext. WEP is like a "No Trespassing" sign on a post, but without the fence.

Travel Advisory

WPA, like WEP, is now considered an obsolete unsecure protocol that should never be used.

WPA and WPA2 attacks can happen, especially with wireless networks using WPA-Personal or WPA2-Personal passphrases. The attacks take place by using sophisticated methods that make a number of assumptions about the passphrase, and the fact that certain passphrases are used quite often. The most important thing to do to prevent these attacks from succeeding is to use long passphrases (16 or more characters), thus making the network hard to crack. Otherwise, you need authentication. If you want authentication, you move into what most wireless folks will call an enterprise setup. For example, when you use a RADIUS server for authentication with WPA2 to create an amazingly secure wireless network, it gets a fancy name: WPA2-Enterprise.

To make configuration easier, the wireless industry created a special standard called Wi-Fi Protected Setup (WPS). WPS works in two modes: push button method or PIN method. (There were other modes, but they never were popular.) With the push button method, you press a button on one device (all WPS-compatible devices have a physical or virtual push button) and then press the WPS button on the other device. That's it. The two devices automatically configure themselves on an encrypted connection.

The PIN method was for connecting a PC to a WPS device (usually a WAP). You press the button on the WAP, locate the SSID on your device, and then enter an eight-digit PIN as the WPA-Personal shared key (more on WPA shortly). All WPS WAPs have the PIN printed on the device.

WPS is very easy to use, but is susceptible to different forms of *WPS attacks*. By design, the WPS PIN numbers are short. WPS attacks, therefore, concentrate on hacking the PIN number. By hacking the PIN, a bad actor can easily take control of the WAP, giving him or her access to the entire infrastructure. WPS has not been fixed, and since 2011 the wireless industry has told everyone to disable WPS on their WAPs.

Objective 9.03   Network Hardening Techniques

Once you've recognized threats and vulnerabilities, it's time to start applying security hardware, software, and processes to your network to prevent bad things from happening. This is called hardening your network. Let's now look at various hardening techniques.

Anti-malware Software

Anti-malware software, such as a classic antivirus program, protects your machine in two ways. It can be both sword and shield, working in an active seek-and-destroy mode and in a passive sentry mode. When ordered to seek and destroy, the program scans the computer's boot sector and files for viruses and, if it finds any, presents you with the available options for removing or disabling them. Anti-malware programs can also operate as virus shields that passively monitor a computer's activity, checking for viruses only when certain events occur, such as a program executing or a file being downloaded.

Anti-malware software comes in multiple forms today. First is the classic host-based anti-malware that is installed on individual systems. Host-based anti-malware works beautifully, but is hard to administer when you have a number of systems. An alternative used in larger networks is network-based anti-malware. In this case, a single anti-malware server runs on a number of systems (in some cases, each host has a small client). These network-based programs are much easier to update and administer. Last is cloud/server-based anti-malware. These servers store the software on a remote location (in the cloud or on a local server), but it's up to each host to access the software and run it. This has the advantage of storing nothing on the host system and making updating easier, but suffers from lack of administration, because it's still up to the user on each host to run the anti-malware program.

Switch Port Security

Implementing Dynamic ARP Inspection (DAI) and DHCP snooping enhances *switch port security,* a key network hardening technique.

Dynamic ARP Inspection

Dynamic ARP Inspection (DAI) helps prevent ARP poisoning. DAI learns about your network's systems and their correct MAC and IP addresses and then updates a database of trusted systems. DAI can then watch for false or suspicious ARP traffic and simply ignore it.

DHCP Snooping

DHCP snooping, although not exactly an ARP feature, goes hand in hand with DAI because they are almost always configured at the same time (and they use the same database). *DHCP snooping* prevents an attacker from pretending to be a DHCP server and, in turn, giving out fake gateway information (the attacker's IP address instead of the real gateway address) to downstream clients—thus thwarting man-in-the-middle attacks.

MAC Address Filtering

Most WAPs support MAC address filtering, a method that enables you to limit access to your network based on the physical addresses of wireless NICs. MAC address filtering creates a type of "accepted users" list, called *whitelisting,* to limit access to your wireless network. A table stored in the WAP lists the MAC addresses that are permitted to participate in the wireless network. Any network frames that don't contain the MAC address of a node listed in the table are rejected.

MAC address filtering can also deny specific MAC addresses from logging onto the network, a process called *blacklisting.* This works great in close quarters, such as apartments or office buildings, where your wireless network signal goes beyond your perimeter. You can check the WAP and see the MAC addresses of every node that connects to your network. Check that list against the list of your computers, and you can readily spot any unwanted interloper. Putting an offending MAC address in the "deny" column effectively blocks that system from piggybacking onto your wireless connection.

Although address filtering works, a hacker can very easily *spoof* a MAC address—make the NIC report an address other than its own—and access the network, thwarting blacklisting. Whitelisting is, in most cases, too much of an administrative overhead. Imagine a network engineer needing to collect MAC addresses of all devices of all users! Worse, a hacker doesn't have to connect to your network to grab your network traffic out of thin air! If you have data so important that a hacker would want to get at it, you should seriously consider using a wired network or separating the sensitive data from your wireless network in some fashion.

VLAN Assignments

To provide a properly segmented network, the various departments and components in the campus area network (CAN) need to be placed into unique *virtual local area networks (VLANs)*. As you'll recall from an earlier chapter, VLANs provide much better control over the network, with security and optimized performance.

Some of the VLANs are based on department. For example, the *quality assurance (QA)* lab doesn't need access to all the same resources as the accounting folks, and vice versa. The *testing lab* tests software and firmware and has very different needs than other departments.

We could take the network segmentation a step further and also create unique VLANs for network services. The wireless network will get its own VLAN, for example, plus we could split it into multiple VLANs to provide support for *separate private/public networks*. That way, visitors will get access to what they need, but not to important internal systems.

Security Policies

A *security policy* is a written document that defines how an organization will protect its IT infrastructure. There are hundreds of different security policies.

Acceptable Use Policy

The acceptable use policy defines what is and what is not acceptable to do on an organization's computers. It's arguably the most famous of all security policies because this is one document that pretty much everyone who works for any organization is required to read, and in many cases sign, before they can start work. The following are some provisions contained in a typical acceptable use policy:

- **Ownership**   Equipment and any proprietary information stored on the organization's computers are the property of the organization.
- **Network Access**   Users will access only information they are authorized to access.
- **Privacy/Consent to Monitoring**   Anything users do on the organization's computers is not private. The organization will monitor what is being done on computers at any time.
- **Illegal Use**   No one may use an organization's computers for anything that breaks a law. (This is usually broken down into many subheadings, such as introducing malware, hacking, scanning, spamming, and so forth.)

Network Policies

CompTIA uses the term "network policies" in a rather strange way, because there really aren't network policies. In all probability CompTIA means "network access policies." Companies need a policy that defines who can do what on the company's network. The network access policy defines who may access the network, how they may access the network, and what they can access. Network access policies may be embedded into policies such as VPN policy, password policy, encryption policy, and many others, but they need to be in place.

Policies are the cornerstone of an organization's IT security. Policies help define what equipment they use, how they organize data, and what actions people take to ensure the security of an organization. Policies tell an organization how to handle almost any situation that might arise (such as disaster recovery, which is covered later in this chapter).

Adherence to Policies

Given the importance of policies, it's also imperative for an organization to adhere to its policies strictly. This can often be a challenge. As technologies change, organizations must review and update policies to reflect those changes.

Disable Unneeded Network Services

In a typical system, not all running services are necessary, so you should *disable unneeded network services*. From a security standpoint, there are two reasons it's important not to run any unnecessary services. First, most operating systems use services to listen on open TCP or UDP ports, potentially leaving the systems open to attack. Second, bad guys often use services as a tool for the use and propagation of malware. It's up to you to research services running on a particular machine to determine whether or not they're needed. Stopping unnecessary services closes TCP/UDP ports.

Use Secure Protocols

It's important to use protocols that were built with security in mind from the ground up!

SSH

A secure replacement for Telnet called Secure Shell (SSH) involves SSH servers that use public key infrastructure (PKI) in the form of an RSA key. The first time a client tries to log into an SSH server, the server sends its public key to the client. After the client receives this key, it creates a session ID, encrypts it using the public key, and sends it back to the server. The server decrypts this session key ID and uses it in all data transfers going forward. Only the client and the server know this session ID.

SNMPv3

SNMPv3 added additional security with support for encryption and robust authentication; plus it provided features to make administering a large number of devices easier.

SSL/TLS

Secure Sockets Layer (SSL) requires a server with a certificate. When a client requests access to an SSL-secured server, the server sends to the client a copy of the certificate. The SSL client checks this certificate (all web browsers come with an exhaustive list of CA root certificates preloaded), and if the certificate checks out, the server is authenticated and the client negotiates a symmetric-key cipher for use in the session. The session is now in a very secure encrypted tunnel between the SSL server and the SSL client. Transport Layer Security (TLS) protocol was designed as an upgrade to SSL. TLS is very similar to SSL, working in almost the same way. TLS is more robust and flexible and works with just about any TCP application. SSL is limited to HTML, FTP, SMTP, and a few older TCP applications. TLS has no such restrictions and is used in securing Voice over IP (VoIP) and virtual private networks (VPNs), but it is still most heavily used in securing web pages. Every web browser today uses TLS for HTTPS-secured. Another way to think of it is HTTPS uses SSL/TLS for the actual authentication and encryption process.

SFTP

Secure FTP (SFTP), also called *SSH FTP*, was designed as a replacement for FTP after many of the inadequacies of Secure Copy (SCP), such as the inability to see the files on the other computer, were discovered. Although SFTP and FTP have similar names and perform the same job of transferring files, the way in which they do that job differs greatly.

The introduction of SSH made it easy to secure most TCP applications just by running them in an SSH tunnel. But FTP was a different case. FTP, at least active FTP, uses two ports, 20 and 21, for creating two-session communication. This makes FTP a challenge to run in its original form over SSH because SSH can only handle one session per tunnel. To fix this, a group of programmers from the OpenBSD organization developed a series of secure programs known collectively as OpenSSH. SFTP was one of those programs. SFTP looks like FTP, with servers and clients, but relies on an SSH tunnel.

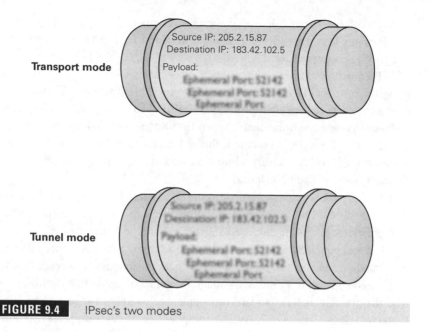

Transport mode

Source IP: 205.2.15.87
Destination IP: 183.42.102.5

Payload:

Ephemeral Port: 52142
Ephemeral Port: 52142
Ephemeral Port:

Tunnel mode

Source IP: 205.2.15.87
Destination IP: 183.42.102.5

Payload:

Ephemeral Port: 52142
Ephemeral Port: 52142
Ephemeral Port:

FIGURE 9.4   IPsec's two modes

IPsec

Internet Protocol Security (IPsec) is an authentication and encryption protocol suite that works at the Internet/Network layer and should become the dominant authentication and encryption protocol suite as IPv6 continues to roll out and replace IPv4.

IPsec works in two different modes: Transport mode and Tunnel mode (see Figure 9.4). In Transport mode, only the actual payload of the IP packet is encrypted: the destination and source IP addresses and other IP header information are still readable. In Tunnel mode, the entire IP packet is encrypted and then placed into an IPsec endpoint, where it is encapsulated inside another IP packet. The mode you use depends on the application. IPv6 will use the IPsec Transport mode by default.

The IPsec protocol suite uses many open source protocols to provide both tight authentication and robust encryption.

Wireless Security

Wired Equivalent Privacy (WEP) uses a 64- or 128-bit encryption algorithm to scramble data frames. But even with the strongest encryption enabled, WEP isn't a particularly robust security solution. In fact, WEP can be cracked in under a minute with just a regular laptop and open source software.

WPA offers security enhancements such as dynamic encryption key generation (keys are issued on a per-user and per-session basis) and an encryption key integrity-checking feature.

WPA works by using an extra layer of security, called the Temporal Key Integrity Protocol (TKIP), around the WEP encryption scheme. It's not, therefore, a complete replacement protocol for WEP. TKIP added a 128-bit encryption key that seemed unbreakable when first introduced. Within four years of introduction, however, researchers showed methods by which hackers could waltz through WPA security almost as quickly as through WEP security. Another solution had to be found.

The IEEE 802.11i standard amended the 802.11 standard to add much-needed security features. The 802.1X authentication measure using Extensible Authentication Protocol (EAP), discussed shortly, was a good first step. 802.11i also replaced the aging RC4 encryption with the much more robust Advanced Encryption Standard (AES), a 128-bit block cipher that's much tougher to crack than the TKIP used with WPA. Eventually, enough devices were made that could support AES that the full 802.11i standard was implemented under the sales term Wi-Fi Protected Access 2 (WPA2). A "WPA2-compliant-device" is really just a marketing term for a device that fully supports the 802.11i standard. WPA2 is the current top security standard used on 802.11 networks. WPA2 is not hack proof, but it definitely offers a much tougher encryption standard that stops the casual hacker cold.

The most common way to set up WPA or WPA2 encryption is to use a simple version called WPA (or WPA2) Personal Shared Key, also called PSK or Personal. Basically, with these Personal versions, you create a secret key that must be added to any device that is going to be on that SSID. There is no authentication with WPA-PSK or WPA2-PSK.

WPA2-Enterprise is a bit more involved. 802.11i uses the IEEE 802.1X standard (discussed later) to enable you to set up a network with some seriously secure authentication using a RADIUS server and passwords encrypted with Extensible Authentication Protocol (EAP).

User Authentication

Dial-up, using telephone lines for the most part, predates the Internet, but the nerds of their day didn't want just anybody dialing into their computers. To prevent unauthorized access, they developed some excellent authentication methods that TCP/IP adopted for itself. A number of authentication methods were used back in these early days, but, for the most part, TCP/IP authentication started with PPP, discussed earlier.

PPP came with two methods of user authentication, which is the process of authenticating a user name and password. The original way—called Password

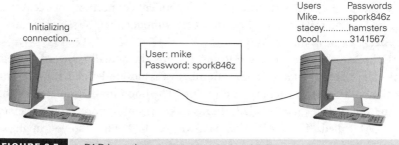

FIGURE 9.5   PAP in action

Authentication Protocol (PAP)—simply transmits the user name and password over the connection in plaintext. Unfortunately, that means anyone who can tap the connection can learn the user name and password (see Figure 9.5).

Fortunately, PPP also includes the safer Challenge Handshake Authentication Protocol (CHAP) to provide a more secure authentication routine. CHAP relies on hashes based on a shared secret, usually a password that both ends of the connection know. When the initiator of the connection makes the initial connection request, the authenticator creates some form of challenge message.

The initiator then makes a hash using the password and sends that to the authenticator. The authenticator, in turn, compares that value to its own hash calculation based on the password. If they match, the initiator is authenticated (see Figure 9.6).

Once the connection is up and running, CHAP keeps working by periodically repeating the entire authentication process. This prevents man-in-the-middle

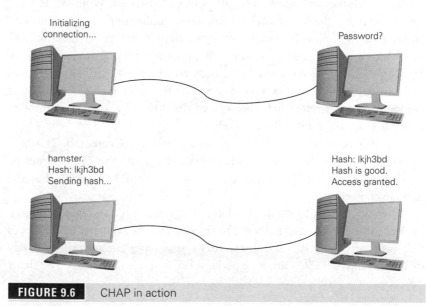

FIGURE 9.6   CHAP in action

attacks, where a third party inserts an independent connection, intercepts traffic, reads or alters it, and then forwards it on without either the sender or recipient being aware of the intrusion.

CHAP works nicely because it never sends the actual password over the link. The CHAP standard leaves a number of issues undefined, however, like "If the hash doesn't match, what do I do?" The boom in dial-up connections to the Internet in the 1990s led Microsoft to invent a more detailed version of CHAP called MS-CHAP. (CompTIA drops the hyphen, so you might see it as MSCHAP on the exam.) The current version of MS-CHAP is called MS-CHAPv2.

Travel Advisory

MS-CHAPv2 is still the most common authentication method for the few of us using dial-up connections. Believe it or not, dial-up is still being used, and even the latest operating systems support it.

Kerberos is an authentication protocol that has no connection to PPP. Twenty years ago, some Internet folks began to appreciate that TCP/IP was not secure and thus designed Kerberos. Kerberos is an authentication protocol for TCP/IP networks with many clients all connected to a single authenticating server—no point-to-point here! Kerberos works nicely in a network, so nicely that Microsoft adopted it as the authentication protocol for all Windows networks using a domain controller.

Kerberos is the cornerstone of the all-powerful Microsoft Windows domain. Be careful here—the use of domains I'm about to describe has nothing to do with DNS. A Windows domain is a group of computers that defers all authentication to a *domain controller,* a special computer running some version of Windows Server. The Windows domain controller stores a list of all user names and passwords. When you log on at a computer that is a member of a Windows domain, your user name and password go directly to the domain controller, which uses Kerberos for authentication.

The cornerstone of Kerberos is the Key Distribution Center (KDC), which has two processes: the Authentication Server (AS) and the Ticket-Granting Service (TGS). In Windows Server environments, the KDC is installed on the domain controller.

When your client logs onto the domain, it sends a request that includes a hash of the user name and password to the AS. The AS compares the results of that hash to its own hash (as it also stores the user name and password). If they match, it sends a Ticket-Granting Ticket (TGT) and a timestamp. The ticket has a default lifespan in Windows of ten hours. The client is now authenticated but not yet authorized.

Exam Tip

The ability to log in only one time and use the same token to access any resource (that you're allowed to access) on an entire network is called *single sign-on*.

But you can't stop with user names and passwords. What if someone gets a hold of your user name and password? To defeat those types of bad guys, some systems require a second form of authentication. These second forms of authentication include items you carry, such as a smart card. They might also be something that uniquely identifies you, such as your retinal patterns or fingerprints. We call these *biometrics*. Whatever the case, when you use passwords and one or more other forms of authentication, we call this *multifactor authentication* (or sometimes *two-factor authentication,* if just two factors are being used).

Hashes

In computer security, a hash (or more accurately, a *cryptographic hash function*) is a mathematical function that you run on a string of binary digits of any length that results in a value of some fixed length (often called a *checksum* or a *message digest*). A cryptographic hash function is a one-way function. *One-way* means the hash is practically irreversible. You should not be able to re-create the data, even if you know the hashing algorithm and the checksum. A cryptographic hash function should also have a unique message digest for any two different input streams.

Cryptographic hash functions have a huge number of uses, but a common one is for verifying file integrity. If I'm downloading a file from a reputable source, there are two main threats to its integrity: accidental damage caused by networking/storage issues, and tampering by an attack that has compromised the site or my connection.

When the download provider hashes the contents of the file and publishes the resulting message digest, I can hash the copy I downloaded and compare the digests to verify the file on my system is most likely identical. This provides the best protection from accidental damage; an attacker capable of altering the file I download might also be able to alter the message digest published on the site. I can increase my confidence in its integrity by verifying the digest with more than one reputable source.

These days, Secure Hash Algorithm (SHA) is the primary family of cryptographic hash functions. It includes SHA-1, SHA-2 (which includes the popular SHA-256 and SHA-512 variants), and the soon-to-be-finalized SHA-3. One thing to keep in mind about cryptographic functions is that we err on the side of caution. Once someone demonstrates a practical attack against an algorithm, recommendations shift quickly to newer functions with improved security. Still, existing uses of the old functions can linger for a long time.

As the result of a number of attacks published in 2009, 2012, and 2013, two widely used hash functions, SHA-1 and Message-Digest Algorithm version 5 (best known as MD5), have both ended up on this list of hash functions that are no longer recommended as safe.

EAP

One of the great challenges to authentication is getting the two ends of the authentication process to handle the many different types of authentication options. Even though PPP pretty much owned the user name/password authentication business, proprietary forms of authentication using smartcards/tokens, certificates, and so on, began to show up on the market, threatening to drop practical authentication into a huge mess of competing standards.

Extensible Authentication Protocol (EAP) was developed to create a single standard to allow two devices to authenticate. Despite the name, EAP is not a protocol in the classic sense, but rather it is a PPP wrapper that EAP-compliant applications can use to accept one of many types of authentication. Although EAP is a general-purpose authentication wrapper, its only substantial use is in wireless networks.

A RADIUS server stores user names and passwords, enabling you to set a user's rights once in the network. Here's how it works. The client wireless computer, called a *supplicant,* contacts the WAP, called a *Network Access Server (NAS),* and requests permission to access the network. The NAS collects the supplicant's user name and password and then contacts the RADIUS server to see if the supplicant appears in the RADIUS server's security database. If the supplicant appears and the user name and password are correct, the RADIUS server sends a packet back to the supplicant, through the WAP, with an Access-Accept code and an Authenticator section that proves the packet actually came from the RADIUS server. Then the remote user gets access to the network resources. The RADIUS server can even be configured to communicate with an Active Directory Domain Controller, instead of the administrator configuring it from scratch. That's some serious security!

EAP defines a framework for authentication but does not specify how the authentication happens. Developers have, therefore, come up with many ways to handle the specifics, such as EAP-TLS, EAP-TTLS, and PEAP, to name just a few. The CompTIA Network+ exam objectives mention implementing TLS/TTLS as network hardening. That happens in conjunction with EAP.

TACACS+

Routers and switches need administration. In a simple network, you can access the administration screen for each router and switch by entering a user name and password for each device. When a network becomes complex, with many routers and switches, logging into each device separately starts to become administratively messy. The answer is to make a single server store the credentials for all the devices in the network. To make this secure, you need to follow the *authentication, authorization, and accounting (AAA)* principles.

Terminal Access Controller Access Control System Plus (TACACS+) is a protocol developed by Cisco to support AAA in a network with many routers and switches. TACACS+ is very similar to RADIUS in function, but uses TCP port 49 by default and separates authorization, authentication, and accounting into different parts. TACACS+ uses PAP, CHAP, and MD5 hashes, but can also use something called Kerberos as part of the authentication scheme.

802.1X

The IEEE 802.1X standard allows EAP to be encapsulated inside of Ethernet frames instead of PPP. 802.11i (WPA2) uses the IEEE 802.1X standard to enable you to set up a network with some seriously secure authentication using a RADIUS server and passwords encrypted with Extensible Authentication Protocol (EAP).

 **Objective 9.04** **Physical Security Controls**

There's an old saying: "The finest swordsman in all of France has nothing to fear from the second finest swordsman in all of France." It means that they do the same things and know the same techniques. The only difference between the two is that one is a little better than the other. There's a more modern extension of the old saying that says, "On the other hand, the finest swordsman in all of France can be defeated by a kid with a rocket launcher!" Which is to say that the inexperienced, when properly equipped, can and will often do something totally unexpected.

Proper security must address threats from the second finest swordsman as well as the kid. We can leave no stone unturned when it comes to hardening the network, and this begins with physical security. Physical threats manifest themselves in many forms, including property theft, data loss due to natural damage such as fire or natural disaster, data loss due to physical access, and property destruction resulting from accident or sabotage. Let's look at ways to protect ourselves in the physical sense.

Security Guards

A locked front door can be opened by an authorized person, and an unauthorized person can attempt to enter through that already opened door. This is called *tailgating*. Although it is possible to prevent tailgating with policies, it is only human nature to "hold the door" for that person coming in behind you. Tailgating is especially easy to do when dealing with large organizations in which people don't know everyone else. If the tailgater dresses like everyone else and maybe has a badge that looks right, he or she probably won't be challenged. Add an armload of gear, and who could blame you for helping that person by holding the door?

There are a couple of techniques available to foil a tailgater. The first is a security guard. Guards are great. They get to know everyone's faces. They are there to protect assets and can lend a helping hand to the overloaded, but authorized, person who needs in. They are multipurpose in that they can secure building access, secure individual room and office access, and perform facility patrols. The guard station can serve as central control of security systems such as video surveillance and key control. Like all humans, security guards are subject to attacks such as social engineering, but for flexibility, common sense, and a way to take the edge off of high security, you can't beat a professional security guard or two.

Mantraps

For areas where an entry guard is not practical, there is another way to prevent tailgating called a *mantrap*, which is an entryway with two successive locked doors and a small space between them providing one-way entry or exit. After a person enters the first door, the second door cannot be unlocked until the first door is closed and secured. Access to the second door may be a simple key or may require approval by someone else who watches the trap space on video. Unauthorized persons remain trapped until they are approved for entry, let out the first door, or held for the appropriate authorities.

Network Closets

Locking the door to the network closet or equipment room that holds servers, switches, routers, and other network gear goes a long way in protecting the network. Key control is critical here and includes assigning keys to appropriate staff, tracking key assignments, and collecting the keys when they are no longer needed by individuals who move on. This type of access must be guarded against circumvention by ensuring policies are followed regarding who may have or use the keys. The administrator who assigns keys should never give one to an unauthorized person without completing the appropriate procedures and paperwork.

Video Monitoring

Video monitoring entails using remotely monitored visual systems and covers everything from identifying a delivery person knocking on the door at the loading dock, to looking over the shoulder of someone working on the keyboard of a server. IP cameras and closed-circuit televisions (CCTVs) are specific implementations of video monitoring. CCTV is a self-contained, closed system in which video cameras feed their signal to specific, dedicated monitors and storage devices. CCTV cameras can be monitored in real time by security staff, but the monitoring location is limited to wherever the video monitors are placed. If real-time monitoring is not required or viewing is delayed, stored video can be reviewed later as needed.

Door Access Controls

With physical door access controls, access is generally governed by something that is in the possession of someone who has authorization to enter a locked place. That something may be a key, a badge, a key fob with a chip, or some other physical token.

Proximity Readers

Twenty-five years ago, I worked in a campus facility with a lot of interconnected buildings. Initial access to buildings was through a security guard, and then we traveled between the buildings with connecting tunnels. Each end of the tunnels had a set of sliding glass doors that kind of worked like the doors on the starship *Enterprise*. We were assigned badges with built-in radio frequency ID (RFID) chips. As we neared a door, the RFID chip was queried by circuitry in the door frame called a proximity reader and checked against a database for authorization. Then the door slid open electromechanically.

Biometrics

The best way to prevent loss of access control is to build physical security around a key that cannot be shared or lost. Biometric access calls for using a unique physical characteristic of a person to permit access to a controlled IT resource. Doorways can be triggered to unlock using fingerprint readers, facial recognition cameras, voice analyzers, retinal blood vessel scanners, or other, more exotic characteristics. Although not perfect, biometrics represent a giant leap in secure access.

Keypad/Cipher Lock

To move from the physical possession problem of entry access, physical security can be governed by something that is known only to authorized persons. A code or password that is assigned to a specific individual for a particular asset can be entered on an alphanumeric keypad that controls an electric or electromechanical door lock. There is a similar door lock mechanism called a cipher lock. A *cipher lock* is a door unlocking system that uses a door handle, a latch, and a sequence of mechanical push buttons. When the buttons are pressed in the correct order, the door unlocks and the door handle works. Turning the handle opens the latch or, if you pressed the wrong order of buttons, clears the unlocking mechanism so you can try again. Care must be taken by staff who are assigned a code to protect that code.

 **Objective 9.05** **Firewalls**

Firewalls are devices or software that protect an internal network from unauthorized access by acting as a filter. That's right; all a firewall does is filter traffic that flows through. Firewalls are essential tools in the fight against malicious programs on the Internet.

The most basic job of the firewall is to look at each packet and decide based on a set of rules whether to block or allow the traffic. This traffic can be either inbound traffic, packets coming from outside the network, or outbound traffic, packets leaving the network.

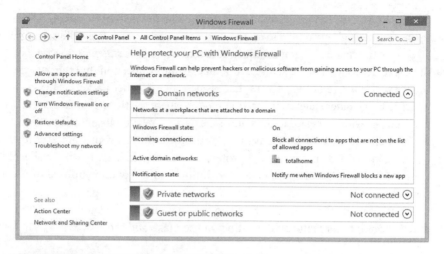

FIGURE 9.7   Windows Firewall in Windows 8.1

Types of Firewalls

The network-based firewall is often implemented in some sort of hardware appliance or is built into the router that is installed between the LAN and the wilds of the Internet. Most network techs' first encounter with a network-based firewall is the small office/home office (SOHO) firewall built into most consumer-grade routers. These firewalls form the first line of defense, providing protection for the whole network. Although they do a great job of protecting whole networks, they can't provide any help if the malicious traffic is originating from inside the network itself. That is why we have host-based firewalls.

A host-based firewall is a *software* firewall installed on a "host" that provides firewall services for just that machine. A great example of this type of firewall is the Windows Firewall (see Figure 9.7). This makes the host-based firewall probably one of the most common types of firewalls you will encounter in your career as a network tech.

Building on the stateful firewall, firewalls that are application/context aware operate at layer 7 of the OSI model and use *Deep Packet Inspection (DPI)* to filter based on the application or service that originated the traffic. This makes context-aware firewalls invaluable in stopping port-hopping applications such as BitTorrent from overloading your network.

The entry-level or SOHO models usually have a fixed number of ports, often with a fixed-purpose function (like dedicated ports for WAN traffic). Enterprise-grade hardware (typically supporting 200+ users) often is built around the idea of a flexible system that supports having cards added for different interface types, which can also be reconfigured as the network changes. Once the hardware is plugged in, it's time to start configuring your firewall's settings.

One of the first modern techniques added to firewalls is *stateful inspection,* or the capability to tell if a packet is part of an existing connection. In other words, the firewall is aware of the packet's state, as it relates to other packets. This is an upgrade to the older stateless inspection model, where the firewall looked at each packet fresh, with no regard to the state of the packet's relation to any other packet.

Firewalls, no matter how advanced and aware they become, are still just one tool in the box that we use to protect our networks. That is why modern dedicated firewall/security appliances are built around providing unified threat management (UTM). UTM takes the traditional firewall and packages it with many other security services such as network-based IPS, VPN, load balancing, antivirus, and other features depending on the make and model.

Settings/Techniques

Now that we understand the different types of firewalls, let's look at ways to control them. Settings and techniques can really optimize your firewall, and keep your network safe.

Routed and Virtual Wire Firewalls

A common theme with network-based firewalls is how closely they are tied to routers. That's no coincidence, because firewalls often come with routers or ship with routing features, called *routed* firewalls. An alternative to traditional routed firewalls is called a *Virtual Wire* firewall. Virtual Wire (VWire) is a feature of firewalls from Palo Alto Networks that allows traffic to pass through the firewall with absolutely no routing or even layer-2 switching occurring on the packets.

Access Lists

Modern firewalls come with a massive number of features, and configuring them can be a daunting task for any network tech. But at its core, configuring a firewall is about defining which traffic can flow and which traffic shall not pass. This rule often takes the form of a humble access control list (ACL). An ACL is a rule applied to an interface that *permits* or *denies* traffic based on source IP addresses, destination IP addresses, protocols, ports, and so on.

Now that you know what an ACL is, let's take a look at one that you might find on a Cisco router or firewall:

```
access-list 10 deny 10.31.4.0 0.0.0.255
access-list 10 permit any
```

That looks rather cryptic at first glance, but what it's doing is very simple. The beginning of the first line, access-list 10, tells the Cisco IOS that we want to create an ACL, and its number is 10. The end of the first line, deny 10.31.4.0 0.0.0.255, is the actual rule we want the firewall to apply. In this case, it means deny (or *block* as CompTIA says) all traffic from the 10.31.4.0/24 subnet.

That's all well and good; any traffic coming from the 10.31.4.0/24 subnet will be dropped like a bad habit. But what's up with that second line? Well, that's there because of a very important detail about ACLs: they have an implicit deny any, or *automatically deny any packets that don't match a rule.* So in this case, if we stopped after the first line, no traffic would get through because we don't have a rule that explicitly permits it! So to make our ACL be a firewall instead of a brick wall, the last rule in this list will permit through any traffic that wasn't dropped by the first rule.

Once the ACL has been created, it must be assigned to an interface to be of any use. One interesting feature of ACLs is that they don't just get plugged in to an interface. You must specify the rules that apply to each *direction* the traffic flows. Traffic flowing through an interface can be thought of as either *inbound,* traffic entering from the network (inbound to the firewall), or *outbound,* traffic flowing from the firewall out to the network. This is an important detail because we will want to have different rules for traffic entering and leaving through an interface.

Firewalls and other advanced networking systems offer all sorts of filtering. Web filtering, for example, enables networks to block specific website access. Content filtering, in contrast, offers administrators to filter traffic with specific signatures or keywords. Schools often filter searches that use profane language, for example. Web/content filtering is a fairly standard network hardening technique. Other criteria to filter by include ports and IP addresses.

DMZ

The use of a single firewall between the network and the ISP in the example shown in Figure 9.8 is just one approach to firewall placement. That configuration works well in simple networks or when you want strong isolation between all clients on the inside of the firewall. But what happens when we have servers,

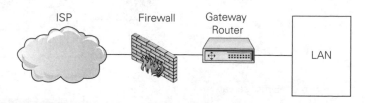

FIGURE 9.8 A network gateway

such as a web server, that need less restricted access to the Internet? That's where the concepts of the DMZ and internal/external firewalls come in.

A demilitarized zone (DMZ) is an area of the network carved out by a single or multiple firewalls to provide a special place (a zone) on the network for any servers that need to be publicly accessible from the Internet.

There's a good chance that you may have seen a DMZ setting on a SOHO router. This is generally not a good idea because it simply exposes a single system to the evils of the Internet. Just because you placed a server in the DMZ does not mean it shouldn't have or need firewall protection. It's important to understand that, unlike with the little SOHO gateway routers, all traffic destined for the DMZ in non-SOHO networks is still very much being looked at and filtered by the firewall.

The simplest type of DMZ is a single system that separates the public servers from the internal network. In this case, the public servers are all located on a separate security zone and network ID from the internal network (see Figure 9.9).

As you can see by looking at Figure 9.9, the DMZ isolates the public servers from our internal network. Of course, even with a well-configured firewall in front of your servers in the DMZ, the public nature of the DMZ means that the servers are under constant attack from the Internet. Should the worst happen and any of the machines in the DMZ become compromised (and I've seen how fast this can happen), the isolation provided by the DMZ means the hackers don't have a beachhead inside your internal network.

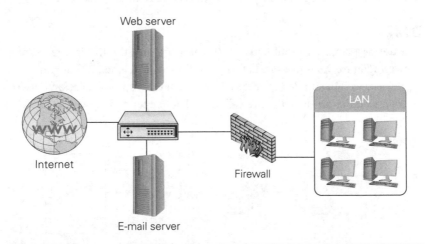

FIGURE 9.9   A simple DMZ using one firewall

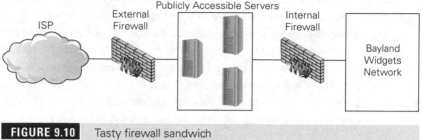

FIGURE 9.10   Tasty firewall sandwich

An alternative to the single-firewall DMZ design is to create a DMZ by using multiple firewalls to create a perimeter network. With a perimeter network, the two firewalls carve out areas with different levels of trust (see Figure 9.10). The firewall that sits between the perimeter network and the Internet is known as an external firewall and is responsible for bearing the brunt of the attacks from the Internet. This firewall still allows plenty of traffic through because behind it sit all the public-facing servers.

These servers are still publicly accessible, though, and are still more vulnerable to attack and takeover. That's where the internal firewall comes in; it sits between the perimeter network and the trusted network that houses all the organization's private servers and workstations.

 Objective 9.06   **Network Access Control Models**

Protecting network assets is more than a physical exercise. Physically speaking, we can harden a network by preventing and controlling access to tangible network resources through things like locking doors and video monitoring. Next, we will want to protect our network from malicious, suspicious, or potential threats that might connect to or access the network. This is called *access control* and it encompasses both physical security and network security. In this section, we look at some technologies and techniques to implement network access control, including user account control, edge devices, posture assessment, persistent and non-persistent agents, guest networks, and quarantine networks.

Network access control (NAC) is a standardized approach to verify that a node meets certain criteria before it is allowed to connect to a network. Many product vendors implement NAC in different ways. Network Admission Control (also known as NAC) is Cisco's version of network access control. Cisco's NAC can dictate that specific criteria must be met before allowing a node to connect to a secure network. Devices that do not meet the required criteria can be shunted with no connection or made to connect to another network. The types of criteria that can be checked are broad ranging and can be tested for in a number of ways. For the purposes of this text, we are mostly concerned about verifying that a device attempting to connect is not a threat to network security.

Posture Assessment

Cisco uses posture assessment as one of the tools to implement NAC. Posture assessment is a feature of certain advanced Cisco network appliances. A switch or router that has posture assessment enabled and configured will query network devices to confirm that they meet minimum security standards before being permitted to connect to the production network.

Posture assessment includes checking the type and version of anti-malware, level of QoS, type/version of operating system, and so on. Posture assessment can perform different checks at succeeding stages of connection. Certain tests can be applied at the initial physical connection.

After that, more checks can be conducted prior to logging in. Pre-login assessment may look at the type and version of operating system, detect whether keystroke loggers are present, and check whether the station is real or a virtual machine. The host may be queried for digital certificates, anti-malware version and currency, whether the machine is real or virtual, and a large list of other checks.

If everything checks out, the host will be granted a connection to the production network. If posture assessment finds a deficiency or potential threat, the host can be denied a connection or connected to a non-production network until it has been sufficiently upgraded.

Exam Tip

Although CompTIA uses the term "non-persistent agent" in its objectives, Cisco uses the term "dissolvable agent." You may see either term on the exam.

Guest Network

It may be desirable for an organization to provide a connection to the Internet as a service to visitors and clients. Envision a coffee shop that welcomes its patrons to check e-mail on their portable devices while enjoying an iced latte with two pumps of white cacao mocha. As you turn on your laptop to scan for Wi-Fi networks, two SSIDs appear. One SSID is labeled CustomerNet and the other is called CorpNet. Some might try to hack into CorpNet, but clearly the intent is for consumers to attach to CustomerNet and gain access to the Internet through that connection. The CustomerNet network is an example of a guest network.

A guest network can contain or allow access to any resource that management deems acceptable to be used by unsecure hosts that attach to the guest network. Those resources might include an Internet connection, a local web server with a company directory or catalog, and similar assets that are nonessential to the function of the organization.

In the preceding example, access to the guest network results from a user selecting the correct SSID. More in line with the goals of this book would be a scenario where a station attempts to connect to a network but is refused access because it does not conform to an acceptable level of security. In this case, the station might be assigned an IP address that only enables it to connect to the guest network. If the station needs access to the production network, the station could be updated to meet the appropriate security requirements. If it only requires the resources afforded by the guest network, then it's good to go.

Quarantined Network

Whenever a node is *denied* a connection to the production network, it is considered to be quarantined. It is common practice for suspicious nodes or nodes with active threats detected to be denied a connection or sent to a quarantine network.

So let's put it all together. An organization may have a multitude of production networks, a guest network, and a quarantine network. Who gets to go where? Stations that pass a profile query performed by an edge device with posture assessment features can connect to a production network. From there, access to the various networks and resources is determined by privileges granted to the login credentials.

Agents

Agents come in two flavors. The first is a small scanning program that, once installed on the computer, stays installed and runs every time the computer boots up. These agents are composed of modules that perform a thorough inventory of each security-oriented element in the computer. This type of agent is known as a *persistent agent*. If there is no agent to respond to a posture assessment query, the node is not permitted to connect to the production network.

Sometimes a computer needs to connect to a secure network via a website portal. Some portals provide VPN access to a corporate network, whereas others provide a less-robust connection. In either case, it is important that these kinds of stations meet the appropriate security standards before they are granted access to the network, just as a dedicated, onsite machine must. To that end, a posture assessment is installed at the endpoint. The endpoint in this instance is the device that actually creates a secure attachment to the production network. At the workstation, a small agent that scans only for the queried conditions is downloaded and run. If the query is satisfied that the station needing access is acceptable, connection is granted and the node can access the production network. When the node disconnects from the network and leaves the portal site, the agent is released from memory. This type of agent is known as a *non-persistent agent*.

 ## Basic Forensic Concepts

Computer forensics is the science of gathering, preserving, and presenting computerized data. Technicians are often first responders or supporters of first responders to a security incident and should follow good forensic practices.

First Responder

As mentioned earlier, first responders decide whether some event on the network qualifies as an incident the team should address, ignore, or escalate. They evaluate the scope and cause of the issue to prevent further disruption. Then, they resolve the cause, restore order to affected systems, and identify ways to prevent a recurrence. Most incidents are handled at this level. However, if an incident is so vast that the incident response team cannot stop, contain, or remediate it, disaster recovery comes into play.

Secure the Area

The first step for a first responder is to secure the area. In most cases, someone in authority has determined the person or persons who are allegedly responsible and calls you in to react to the incident. As a first responder, your job is to secure the systems involved as well as secure the immediate work areas.

The main way you secure the area is by your presence at the scene. If possible, you should block the scene from prying eyes or potential disturbance. If it's an office, lock the door, define the area of the scene, and mark it off in some way if possible.

Keep in mind that an incident is rarely anything as exciting (or scary) as catching a user committing a felony! In most cases, an incident involves something as simple as trying to determine if a user introduced malware into a system or if a user was playing *World of Warcraft* during work hours.

The rules for forensics still apply. If, however, you're responding to one of the more scary scenarios, it's important for you as a first responder to understand when you need to *escalate* an issue.

Document the Scene

Once you have secured the area, it's time to *document the scene.* You need to preserve the state of the equipment and look for anything that you might need to inspect forensically.

Although it's obvious you'll want to locate computers, switches, WAPs, and routers, be sure to take copious notes, paying particular attention to electronic media. Here are a few items you will want to document:

- Smartphones
- Optical media
- External hard drives
- Thumb drives
- Cameras
- VoIP phones

Evidence/Data Collection

With the scene secured and documented, it's time to start the *evidence/data collection.* The moment you take something away from an incident scene or start to handle or use any devices within the incident scene, there is a chance your actions could corrupt the evidence you are collecting. You must handle and document all evidence in a very specific manner.

Chain of Custody

Chain of custody, as the name implies, is the paper trail of who has accessed or controlled a given piece of evidence from the time it is initially brought into custody until the incident is resolved. From the standpoint of a first responder, the most important item to keep in mind about chain of custody is that you need to document what you took under control, when you did it, what you did to it, and when you passed it to the next person in line.

Data Transport

If you are transporting evidence, don't leave the evidence at any time. Delay your lunch break until after you hand the evidence over to the next person! Follow the proper procedures for *data transport* to avoid any problems with the evidence.

Forensics Report

The end result of your forensics is a forensics report. In general, this is where you report your findings, if any. A good forensics report will include the following:

- Examiner's name and title
- Examiner's qualifications
- Objective for the forensics
- Any case or incident numbers
- Tools used
- Where the examination took place
- Files found
- Log file output
- Screen snapshots

Legal Hold and E-Discovery

There are two places where the forensic reports (and forensic evidence) might be used. The first is legal holds. A *legal hold* is the process of an organization preserving and organizing data in anticipation of or in reaction to a pending legal issue. For example, a company might discover that your forensic report includes findings of criminal activity that require reporting to the authorities. In that case, the data and the reports must be preserved in such a way that, should a legal authority want access to that data, they can reasonably access it.

The second place forensic reports and evidence might be used is electronic discovery (or e-discovery). This is the process of actually requesting that data and providing it in a legal way.

CHECKPOINT

✔**Objective 9.01: Risk-Related Concepts** An incident is an event in which the security of an IT infrastructure is compromised. Organizations must have contingency plans to respond to an incident in such a way that the organization can continue to function. Incidents that take place within the organization that can be stopped, contained, and remediated without outside resources are handled by incident response planning. Disaster recovery deals with providing methods of recovering your primary infrastructure from a disaster. Disaster recovery starts with a plan and includes data backups. Business continuity planning prepares for a disaster that requires the business to continue functioning at remote sites.

✔**Objective 9.02: Common Network Vulnerabilities and Threats** Spoofing is the process of pretending to be someone or something you are not by placing false information into your packets. An attacker spoofs by replacing the attacker's MAC addresses, IP addresses, user names, e-mail addresses, and so forth with some other values. Abusing protocols is a common form of threat. A protocol is abused by forming communication in a way the protocol is not supposed to be used. ARP cache poisoning is a threat that confuses switches and nodes by sending false ARP comments to the system. ARP poisoning is a common method for man-in-the-middle attacks. Tools such as DHCP snooping and Dynamic ARP Inspection help negate ARP poisoning. A denial of service (DoS) attack is a targeted attack by one or more systems against a server or servers that provide some form of service on the Internet. A distributed denial of service (DDoS) uses a vast number of zombified systems (called a *botnet)* to attack a more robust target. In a man-in-the-middle attack, an attacker taps into communications between two systems, covertly intercepting traffic thought to be only between those systems, reading or in some cases even changing the data and then sending it on. *Brute force* means to try every permutation of some form of data in an attempt to discover protected information. Brute force is most commonly used on password cracking but can be used in other places such as guessing user names. Physical/local access threats are particularly dangerous because they take place inside your network. These threats include compromised systems, insider threats, VLAN hopping, and administrative access controls. Malware is probably the single greatest threat to our networks. Malware comes in a number of different forms, such as viruses, worms, macros, Trojan horses, rootkits, and adware/spyware. *Social engineering* is the process of using or manipulating people inside the networking environment to gain access to that network from the outside. *Phishing,* using false e-mails and websites to collect usernames and passwords, is a particularly notorious form of social engineering. Techniques such as tailgating can be used to gain physical entry into a secure location.

✔**Objective 9.03: Network Hardening Techniques**   *Anti-malware software* can be both sword and shield, working in an active seek-and-destroy mode and in a passive sentry mode. Switch port security can be accomplished through the combination of Dynamic ARP Inspection (DAI) and DHCP snooping. Other network hardening techniques include VLAN assignments, security policies, disabling unneeded services, using secure protocols, access control lists, WPA2, and 802.1 X.

✔**Objective 9.04: Physical Security Controls**   Security guards are multipurpose in that they can secure building access, secure individual room and office access, and perform facility patrols. The guard station can serve as central control of security systems such as video surveillance and key control. A *mantrap* is an entryway with two successive locked doors and a small space between them providing one-way entry or exit. Locking the door to the network closet or equipment room that holds servers, switches, routers, and other network gear goes a long way in protecting the network. IP cameras and closed-circuit televisions (CCTVs) are specific implementations of video monitoring. CCTV is a self-contained, closed system in which video cameras feed their signal to specific, dedicated monitors and storage devices. Door access controls are governed by a key, a badge, a key fob with a chip, or some other physical token. Proximity readers with RFID chips can authorize entry by checking a backend database. Biometric access calls for using a unique physical characteristic of a person to permit access to a controlled IT resource.

✔**Objective 9.05: Firewalls**   Firewalls are devices or software that protect an internal network from unauthorized access by acting as a filter. The network-based firewall is often implemented in some sort of hardware appliance or is built into the router that is installed between the LAN and the wilds of the Internet. A host-based firewall is a *software* firewall installed on a "host" that provides firewall services for just that machine. Firewalls that are application/context aware operate at layer 7 of the OSI model and use *Deep Packet Inspection (DPI)* to filter based on the application or service that originated the traffic. UTM takes the traditional firewall and packages it with many other security services such as network-based IPS, VPN, load balancing, antivirus, and many other features depending on the make and model.

✔**Objective 9.06: Network Access Control Models**   A switch or router that has posture assessment enabled and configured will query network devices to confirm that they meet minimum security standards before being permitted to connect to the production network. A guest network can contain or allow access to any resource that management deems acceptable to be used by unsecure hosts that attach to the guest network. It is common practice for suspicious nodes or nodes with active threats detected to be denied a connection or sent to a quarantine network. Stations that pass a profile query performed by an edge device with posture assessment features can connect to a production network. From there, access to the various networks and resources is determined by privileges granted to the login credentials.

✔**Objective 9.07: Basic Forensic Concepts**   Computer forensics is the science of gathering, preserving, and presenting computerized data. Technicians are often first responders or supporters of first responders to a security incident and should follow good forensic practices. In the event of an incident, be sure to secure the area, document the scene, collect evidence, and interface with authorities. First responders have to make immediate decisions on how to classify an event and what to do next. The area has to be secured and documented. The chain of custody is a log of anyone who has touched a piece of evidence. Care must be taken when transporting data that is evidence. The forensics report is used for legal holds and e-discovery.

REVIEW QUESTIONS

1. Dynamic ARP Inspection (DAI) depends on what to already be in place to successfully run?
   A. HTTPS
   B. DHCP snooping
   C. VPN
   D. IPsec

2. What does this single line access list do? access-list 52 deny 10.0.0.0 0.0.0.255

   A. Blocks all hosts from the 10.0.0.0/8 subnet

   B. Blocks some hosts from the 10.0.0.0/8 subnet

   C. Doesn't block any packets

   D. Blocks all packets

3. Which term describes the handling of evidence throughout a forensic investigation?

   A. Chain of custody

   B. Principle of Least Privilege

   C. E-discovery

   D. Forensics report

4. Which is arguably the most famous of all security policies, representing the document that pretty much everyone who works for any organization is required to read, and in many cases sign, before they can start work?

   A. MOU

   B. SLA

   C. VPN

   D. AUP

5. Which of these attacks does not depend on wireless technologies?

   A. Rogue AP

   B. Evil twin

   C. ARP cache poisoning

   D. Bluejacking

6. Which of the following is considered a secure protocol?

   A. FTP

   B. TFTP

   C. SLIP

   D. TLS

7. Which of the following attacks has nothing to do with technology?

   A. Social engineering

   B. DoS

   C. DDos

   D. War driving

8. How is a port closed?

    A. By stopping a running service

    B. By closing it through the firewall

    C. By configuring an access control list

    D. By running anti-malware software

9. Which of the following is considered an unsecure protocol?

    A. SSL

    B. Telnet

    C. IPsec

    D. SNMPv3

10. Which of the following statements regarding firewalls is true?

    A. A host-based firewall is implemented in software, whereas a network-based firewall is implemented in hardware.

    B. A host-based firewall is implemented in hardware, whereas a network-based firewall is implemented in software.

    C. Both host-based and network-based firewalls are implemented in hardware.

    D. Both host-based and network-based firewalls are implemented in hardware.

REVIEW ANSWERS

1. **B**   DHCP snooping and DAI use the same database.

2. **D**   The implicit deny any at the end of every access list will match all packets that are not blocked by the configured statement.

3. **A**   The chain of custody is a log of anyone who has touched a piece of evidence.

4. **D**   The Acceptable Use Policy applies to any type of employee, whereas the others are specialized documents.

5. **C**   Both wired and wireless clients can be victims of ARP cache poisoning. The other three attack types are specific to wireless clients.

6. **D**   Transport Layer Security is the only protocol listed that is secure.

7. **A**   Social engineering is the process of using or manipulating people inside the networking environment to gain access to that network from the outside.

8. **A**   An open port has a service listening on it. Firewalls don't close ports; they filter ports. Antivirus software doesn't close ports.

9. **B**   Telnet is highly unsecure, sending remote keystrokes in cleartext.

10. **A**   Host-based firewalls are of the software variety, whereas network-based firewalls are implemented through hardware.

The Complete Network

	NEWBIE	SOME EXPERIENCE	EXPERT
ETA	4 hours	2 hours	1 hour

This chapter puts major real-world elements into what we've been talking about so far, including categories of requirements, unified communication, specialized network devices, and industrial control systems.

Objective 10.01 Designing and Building a Network

Designing and building a network follows similar requirements, regardless of the scope of that network. The CompTIA Network+ exam objective 1.12 lists seven categories to consider:

1. **List of requirements**   Define the network's needs. Why are you installing this network? What primary features do you need?

2. **Device types/requirements**   What equipment do you need to build this network? How should you organize the network?

3. **Environment limitations**   What sort of building or buildings do you need to work with to install a network? Do you have access to the walls or ceiling?

4. **Equipment limitations**   Are you using existing equipment, applications, or cabling?

5. **Compatibility requirements**   What sort of compatibility issues do you have between old and new devices?

6. **Wired/wireless considerations**   What type of structured cabling do you need? Does this network need wireless? How do you connect to the Internet?

7. **Security considerations**   How will you deal with computer, data, and network security?

This list is workable, but seems a little too redundant in places. It also leaves out a few important considerations, such as costs vs. budget. Plus, although I've numbered them here, these steps might come in any order. Even though network security is in the sixth position, for example, you might make a decision concerning the firewall as early as Step 2. Don't be afraid to jump around a bit as needed to construct the network.

> **Exam Tip**
>
> This list happily ignores a few important issues, such as costs vs.
> budget, time to install, and so on. Although you should definitely
> consider these issues when constructing your own network, the
> CompTIA Network+ exam isn't very interested in them.

Using this list as a guideline, let's consider some of the pitfalls and issues that might pop up.

Define the Network Needs

Here are some examples of network needs that might be defined early: Individual offices need workstations that can do specific jobs. The company needs servers that can handle anything thrown at them. The buildings need internal cabling. The buildings need intermediate distribution frames (IDFs) to provide connections. The buildings need solid connectivity. The workstations and servers need appropriate operating systems. The network protocols need to be in place. Once the hardware and software inside the network works, then the network needs connectivity beyond. Today, that usually means connecting to the Internet, though private networks within organizations continue to operate.

Documentation

Right here at the beginning of the network development process you should begin what will be an immediate and continual process: documentation. Every well-designed and maintained network has every facet of that network detailed in documentation to support configuration management. Here are some of the areas of documentation:

- **Network diagrams** You need pretty seriously detailed diagrams that describe both the physical network components and the logical components too. For the physical, think cabling runs, server locations, and workstations; for the logical, think about VLANs and network segmentation.

- **Asset management** The network needs a detailed list of all the software owned by the company installed on workstations and servers. This includes versions, upgrade paths, and the like. There are many good programs to facilitate this process.

- **IP address utilization**   You need to know which device—physical or virtual—has which allocated IP address.

- **Vendor documentation**   It's important to have printed or electronic versions of essential details about the hardware and software systems in use by the company. This includes up-to-date contact information for representatives of the products employed.

- **Internal operating procedures/policies/standards**   Documenting network policies on every aspect of network behavior—from acceptable use of equipment to standards for high-grade passwords—needs to be done carefully and fully.

Network Design

Network design quantifies the equipment, operating systems, and applications used by the network. This task ties closely with the previously listed Steps 2 through 5 of designing a basic network.

You need to address the following equipment:

- Workstations
- Servers
- Equipment room
- Peripherals

Workstations

Most company workers need discrete workstations running a modern operating system such as Windows 8 or 10 or Mac OS X. An accounting department might run Sage 50 or QuickBooks Pro, the top competing applications. If they use the former, then clients and servers should run Windows; with the latter, I'd go with OS X.

The graphics folks—who do images, brochure layouts, and web design—have it a little easier today. With Adobe Creative Cloud dominating the graphics market, application choice is easy. The fact that Creative Cloud works equally well with Windows and OS X workstations means companies can choose the platform that most enhances worker productivity. (If most of your workers grew up in Windows, in other words, then choose Windows. If they all grew up with OS X, stick with OS X.)

The most entrenched platform-specific employees might be the more standard office workers, simply because Microsoft has traditionally updated Microsoft Office for the PC a year or two ahead of the OS X version.

Servers

The network needs servers. In a small company, you'd traditionally have one or two servers to handle network authentication, file storage and redundancy, and so on. Once you get into a bigger network, though, you'll find life easier with a more robust server solution where most (or even all) the server functions are virtualized. You can adapt the server infrastructure to accommodate multiple client types, for example, and run the necessary server functions:

- Network authentication
- Network management
- Accounting
- File management (including redundancy)
- Intranet services, such as internal wiki and document sharing (via Microsoft SharePoint, for example)
- Development environments (for product testing, web development, and so on)
- Software repositories (where programmers handle software development and version management)

You have a lot of flexibility here. By going virtual for some or all server resources, you can reduce your power usage and increase uptime. It's a win for everyone, including the accountants handling the bottom line.

Equipment Room

An equipment room provides a centralized core for the network. This is where the main servers live, for example, and where you implement features such as proper air flow, appropriate cable management, appropriate rack systems, and more.

Beyond a small office/home office (SOHO) setup, the equipment room would have much greater power needs and require better power management. A highly populated single floor-to-ceiling rack of servers, for example, can pull upward of 40 amps of power, enough to blow any standard circuit. Many routers and other equipment will run directly on DC rather than AC. To accommodate both higher-end and standard equipment, therefore, you would run the higher-amperage circuits and then install one or more power converters to change from AC to DC.

The more-demanding equipment room also requires more robust power. A single, decent uninterruptible power supply (UPS) might adequately handle brief power fluctuations for a single rack, for example, but won't be able to deal with a serious power outage. For that kind of power redundancy—keeping the lights on and the servers rolling—you'd need to connect a generator or two to the equipment room.

Peripherals

The peripherals—such as printers, scanners, fax machines, and so on—that a company needs to plan for and implement depend very much on what that company does in house. A company that produces its own brochures and fliers, for example, will need good, robust, color laser printers for its graphics folks. The company could house the printers in a central print room or attach them at various points in the network. The capability of the printers would fluctuate according to how many and what size documents they print.

Faxing might be handled by dedicated fax machines, or it could be a software function installed on the machines of the folks who need to fax regularly. All these features and peripherals would need to be unique to the company. (The foosball table, for example, simply must be a peripheral in my office.)

Compatibility Issues

You need to take compatibility issues into consideration when upgrading a network in an existing space. Several issues apply. It might make huge financial sense to leave installed CAT 5e runs in place, for example, and only upgrade to CAT 6a for additional runs. The older standard can handle Gigabit Ethernet just fine, after all, and that might be sufficient for now.

If you're upgrading some systems and not others, security can become a concern. In recent years, for example, as Microsoft has pushed later, more powerful operating systems, many businesses stubbornly continue to use Windows XP. Upgrading some systems to Windows 10 but leaving others running Windows XP presents a challenge. Microsoft isn't releasing security patches for the older OS anymore, which means Windows XP is more vulnerable by the day to hacking attacks.

If you find yourself having to deal with a mixed network of modern and legacy systems, you should isolate the legacy systems. Use VLANs to implement network segmentation and get those old systems out of the main network. These kinds of considerations vary by location and scenario, so keep this step in mind if you find yourself in an upgrade situation. (It's a helpful step to remember if you run into such scenarios on the CompTIA Network+ exam, too!)

Internal Connections

Now that you have an idea of your equipment and what you want to do with it, you need to get everything properly connected using structured cabling. You should also begin to install your 802.11 wireless network. Once you connect all your equipment, you're ready to configure your internal VLANs, IP address schemes, and so on.

Structured Cabling

Can buildings efficiently be wired with CAT 6a to all the workstations? That would provide Gigabit throughout, with all the cabling terminating in the main equipment room. To connect the buildings, a company could use faster pipes, thus providing adequate throughput for a lot of traffic. One option is fiber running some form of 10 Gigabit Ethernet, such as 10GBaseT. The fiber connections for all the buildings would terminate at intermediate distribution frames (IDFs), one in each building.

Wireless

A logical option is to provide high-speed wireless throughout a company's area. Multiple 802.11ac units should be installed within each building and outside as well, all controlled by a central (or unified) wireless controller. This controller would in turn connect to the primary equipment room to provide connectivity with the wired networks.

VLANs

To provide a properly segmented network, the various departments and components in the campus area network (CAN) need to be placed into unique virtual local area networks (VLANs). As you'll recall from Chapter 7, VLANs provide much better control over the network, with security and optimized performance.

Some of the VLANs are based on department. VLANs can be created for network services as well. The wireless network will get its own VLAN, for example, plus we could split it into multiple VLANs to provide support for separate private/public networks. That way, visitors will get access to what they need, but not to important internal systems. Phone connections (discussed in the next part of this chapter) will invariably have their own VLAN. The same is true of the industrial control systems that take care of the internal functions of the factory and warehouse. This gets complicated fast!

Network IP Address Scheme

Long before you start plugging in RJ45s, you need to decide on your internal IP addressing scheme. For most SOHO networks, this means picking an arbitrary, unique, internal private IP network ID and then preassigning static IP addresses to servers and WAPs. Plus, pick a DHCP server and preassign DHCP scope IP address ranges.

Setting up the IP addressing scheme beforehand saves you a lot of time and effort once you start installing the systems. Be sure to make multiple copies of this scheme. Print out a copy and put it in the equipment room. Also put a copy in your network documentation.

Exam Tip

The "Network+ Acronym List" includes the term *Network Access Control (NAC)*, which defines a newer series of protection applications that combine the features of what traditionally was done by separate applications. There is no perfect single definition for NAC. There are, however, certain functions that a NAC often does. A NAC usually prevents computers lacking anti-malware and patches from accessing the network. NACs also create policies (their own policies, not Windows policies) that define what individual systems can do on the network, including network access, segregation of portions of the network, and so on.

External Connections

No network is an island anymore. Each network needs an ISP so folks can Google and update their LinkedIn pages. In a SOHO network, you don't have to deal with many of the issues you'd see in larger networks. A typical home-type ISP (DSL or cable) should be more than enough for a SOHO network in terms of bandwidth.

On the other hand, a larger-sized business needs to be connected to the Internet all the time (or pay the price in lost business), so the company should consider a couple of options. First would be to have two ISPs, with the second ISP as a fallback in case the primary ISP fails. Another option is to pay up for a highly robust service such as a metro Ethernet line.

A metro Ethernet connection is usually a dedicated fiber line from the ISP to an office. By using Ethernet rather than one of the remote connectivity options (such as SONET or MPLS, which you read about in Chapter 8), the installation is less expensive and syncs with the local network more easily.

Objective 10.02 Unified Communication

Some years ago, TCP/IP-based communications began to replace the traditional PBX-style phone systems in most organizations. This switch enabled companies to minimize wire installation and enabled developers to get more creative with the gear. Technologies such as Voice over IP (VoIP) made it possible to communicate by voice right over an IP network, even one as big as the Internet. Today, TCP/IP communications encompass a range of technologies, including voice, video, and messaging. On the cutting edge (led by Cisco) is the field of unified communication (UC).

It Started with VoIP

Early VoIP systems usually required multiple cables running to each drop to accommodate the various services offered—one for data and the other exclusively for VoIP.

These drops would often even go to their own separate switches, and from there into separate VoIP gateways that would interface with old-school PBX systems or directly into the telephone network.

Travel Advisory

Many VoIP systems, such as Skype, are complete Internet services that rely on nothing more than software installed on computers and the computers' microphone/speakers. All of the interconnections to the PSTN are handled in the cloud. Although very popular for individuals, these systems, called unified voice services, are often considered unacceptable in office environments where people want a more classic "phone experience."

As you'll recall from Chapter 5, virtually all VoIP systems use the Real-time Transport Protocol (RTP) on TCP ports 5004 and 5005, as well as the Session Initiation Protocol (SIP) on TCP ports 5060 and 5061. This first-generation VoIP setup that required a separate wired network gave people pause. There really wasn't a critical need for physical separation of the data and the VoIP network, nor did these early VoIP systems handle video conferencing and text messaging. This prompted Cisco to develop and market its proprietary Cisco Unified Communications family of products.

Unified Communication Features

Of course, VoIP isn't the only communication game in town. As organizations were implementing VoIP, they realized a number of additional communications tasks would benefit from centralized management. Enter unified communication, which adds various additional services to the now-classic VoIP, including the following:

- Presence information
- Video conferencing/real-time video
- Fax
- Messaging
- Collaborate tools/workflow

Along with some other real-time communication-oriented tools, these are categorized as real-time services (RTS).

Most of these services should be fairly self-explanatory, but I'd like to elaborate on two of them. Presence information services simply refers to technologies that enable users to show they are present for some form of communication. Think of presence as a type of flag that tells others that you are present and capable of accepting other forms of communication (such as a video conference).

It's also very important to differentiate between video conferencing and real-time video. Video teleconferencing (VTC) is the classic, multicast-based presentation where one presenter pushes out a stream of video to any number of properly configured and authorized multicast clients. These clients do not have a way (normally) to respond via video.

Real-time video, in contrast, enables bidirectional communication via unicast messages. Real-time video offers both video and audio to communicate. Figure 10.1 compares the two types of video communication. Note that unicast traffic enables multiple unique signals.

UC Network Components

A typical UC network consists of three core components: UC devices, UC servers, and UC gateways. Let's take a quick peek at each of these.

A UC device is what we used to call the VoIP telephone. In a well-developed UC environment, the UC device handles voice, video, and more (see Figure 10.2).

A UC server is typically a dedicated box that supports any UC-provided service. In small organizations this might be a single box, but in larger organizations there will be many UC servers. UC servers connect directly to every UC device on the LAN. It's not uncommon to see all the UC servers (as well as the rest of the UC devices) on a separate VLAN.

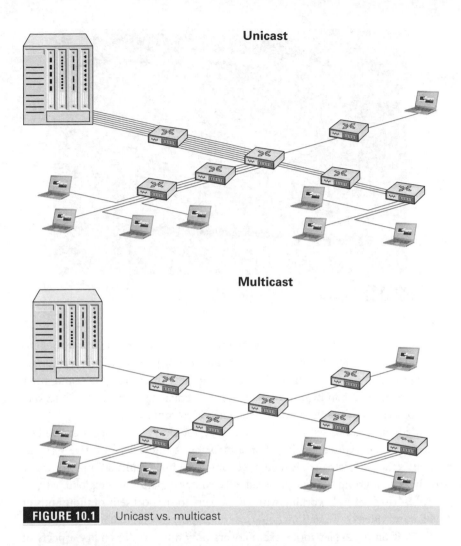

Unicast

Multicast

FIGURE 10.1   Unicast vs. multicast

A UC gateway is an edge device, sometime dedicated but often nothing more than a few extra services added to an existing edge router. That router interfaces with remote UC gateways as well as with PSTN systems and services.

VTC and Medianets

All forms of communication over IP networks have some degree of sensitivity to disruption and slowdowns, but video teleconferencing is particularly susceptible. No one wants to sit in on a video conference that continually

FIGURE 10.2   Cisco Unified IP Phone

stops and jitters due to a poor or slow Internet connection. Medianets help to eliminate or reduce this problem. A *medianet* is a network of (typically) far-flung routers and servers that provide—via quality of service (QoS) and other tools—sufficient bandwidth for VTC. Plus, medianets work with UC servers (or sometimes by themselves) to distribute video conferences.

Medianets can be wildly complex or very simple. A medianet could be two gateway routers with enough QoS smarts to open bandwidth for active VTCs as soon as they are detected. A medianet could be a huge multinational company with its own group of high-powered edge routers, spanning the globe with an MPLS-based VLAN, working with UC servers to support tens of thousands of voice and video conversations going on continually throughout its organization.

The CompTIA Network+ exam covers only a few rudimentary aspects of medianets, especially concentrating on a few protocols, so we don't need to dive too deeply. One aspect that the CompTIA Network+ exam does cover that is not too interesting is an early adoption of VTC using an ancient technology called ISDN.

ISDN vs. IP/SIP

Many organizations using VTC still rely on products based on the old Integrated Services Digital Network (ISDN) service. ISDN offers 128 Kbps bandwidth, which seems very slow by modern standards. But by using multiple

ISDN channels, a special VTC over ISDN standard called H.320 combined with aggressive compression enabled the VTC industry to roll out a number of not-too-shabby VTC systems all over the world. These were not based on IP addresses (so you couldn't connect via the Internet—which was okay back then because there wasn't an Internet), but they worked pretty well given the times.

With the Internet now dominant and IP/SIP-based VTC the norm, ISDN-based VTC is being replaced fairly quickly these days by high-speed Internet connections. However, it's important enough that CompTIA wants you to understand that ISDN-based VTC is still out there, and ISDN's 128 Kbps speed can be a real challenge to integrate into a typical high-speed Ethernet network.

QoS and Medianets

Medianets are all about the quality of service. VTC is the ultimate real-time application, and it needs a level of QoS that very few other applications need.

When we talk about QoS for medianets, we need to develop the concept of differentiated services (DiffServ). DiffServ is the underlying architecture that makes all the QoS stuff work. The cornerstone of DiffServ is two pieces of data that go into every IP header on every piece of data: DSCP (Differentiated Services Code Point) and ECN (Explicit Congestion Notification). These two comprise the Differentiated Services field (see Figure 10.3).

The six bits before the ECN portion (and right after the Header Length field in the IP packet) is the DSCP field. The first three DSCP bits are used for CoS, making a total of eight classes of service. A class of service (CoS) is just a value you may use (think of it as a group) to apply to services, ports, or whatever your QoS device might use. Figure 10.4 shows a sample from my home router. My router has four QoS priority queues, and I can assign a CoS to every port.

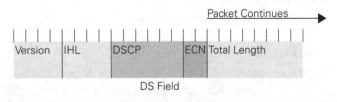

FIGURE 10.3   Differentiated Services field

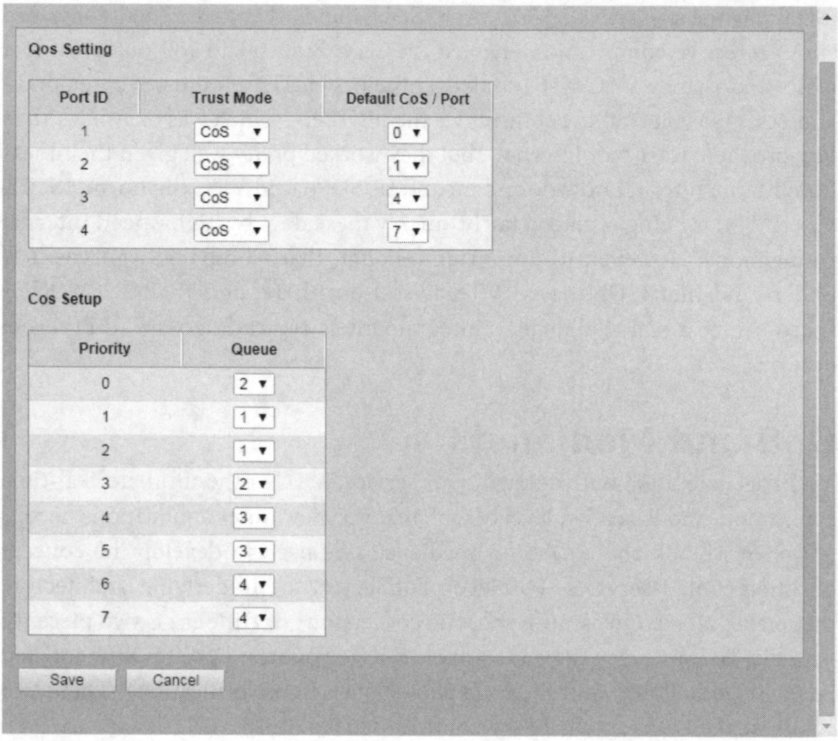

FIGURE 10.4   CoS settings on router

ECN is a two-bit field where QoS-aware devices can place a "congestion encountered" signal to other QoS-aware devices. The following four values may show in that field:

- **00**   Not QoS aware (default)
- **01**   QoS aware, no congestion
- **10**   QoS aware, no congestion
- **11**   QoS aware, congestion encountered

Exam Tip

The term *bandwidth shaping* is synonymous with traffic shaping. The routers and switches that can implement traffic shaping are commonly referred to as "shapers." The CompTIA Network+ exam refers to such devices as "bandwidth shapers." Additionally, the exam uses the term *packet shaper* to describe a traffic shaping device that controls the flow based on packet rules.

**Objective 10.03** # Specialized Network Devices

Think back to that device that most people call a "router." That little box, found in all our homes, does more than routing. It is also a NAT gateway. It is also a switch. It is also a DHCP server. It is also a DNS server. In this section, we look at the opposite of an "all-in-one device." We'll explore specialized devices, optimized to certain functions that improve network security and efficiency.

Intrusion Detection/Intrusion Prevention

Intrusion detection and intrusion prevention detect that something has intruded into a network and then do something about it. Firewalls, discussed in Chapter 9, are hardware or software tools that filter traffic based on various criteria, such as port number, IP address, or protocol. A firewall works at the border of your network, between the outside and the inside. (A host-based firewall, one installed on a single computer, similarly works on the border of that system.)

An intrusion detection system (IDS) is an application (often running on a dedicated IDS box) that inspects packets, looking for active intrusions. An IDS functions inside the network. A good IDS knows how to find attacks that a firewall might miss, such as viruses, illegal logon attempts, and other well-known attacks. Plus, because it inspects traffic inside the network, a good IDS can discover internal threats, such as the activity of a vulnerability scanner smuggled in on a flash drive by a disgruntled worker planning an attack on an internal database server.

An IDS in promiscuous mode inspects a copy of every packet on a network. This placement outside the direct flow of traffic has three effects. First, there's a slight delay between something malicious hitting the network and the detection occurring. Second, there's no impact on network traffic flow. Third, if the IDS goes down, traffic keeps flowing normally.

An IDS always has some way to let the network administrators know if an attack is taking place: at the very least the attack is logged, but some IDSs offer a pop-up message, an e-mail, or even a text message to your phone.

An IDS can also respond to detected intrusions with action. The IDS can't stop the attack directly, but can request assistance from other devices—such as a firewall—that can.

Modern IDS tools come in two flavors: network based or host based. A network-based IDS (NIDS) consists of multiple sensors placed around the

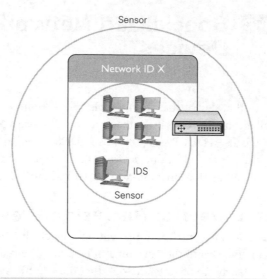

FIGURE 10.5 Diagram of network-based IDS

network, often on one or both sides of the gateway router. These sensors report to a central application that, in turn, reads a signature file to detect anything out of the ordinary (see Figure 10.5).

A host-based IDS (HIDS) is software running on individual systems that monitors for events such as system file modification or registry changes (see Figure 10.6). More expensive IDSs do all this and can provide a single reporting source—very handy when one person is in charge of anything that goes on throughout a network.

A well-protected network uses both a NIDS and a HIDS. A NIDS monitors the incoming and outgoing traffic from the Internet, whereas the HIDS monitors the individual computers.

An intrusion prevention system (IPS) is very similar to an IDS, but an IPS sits directly in the flow of network traffic. This active monitoring has a trio of consequences. First, an IPS can stop an attack while it is happening. No need to request help from any other devices. Second, the network bandwidth and latency take a hit. Third, if the IPS goes down, the link might go down, too.

Depending on what IPS product you choose, an IPS can block incoming packets on-the-fly based on IP address, port number, or application type. An IPS might go even further, literally fixing certain packets on-the-fly. As you might suspect, you can roll out an IPS on a network and it gets a new name: a network intrusion prevention system (NIPS).

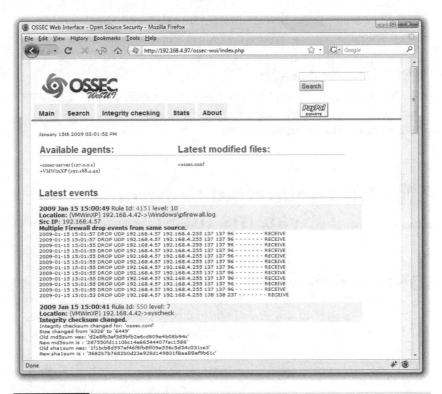

FIGURE 10.6   OSSEC HIDS

Exam Tip

The CompTIA Network+ exam can refer to an IDS system either by its location on the network—thus, NIDS or HIDS—or by what the IDS system does in each location. The network-based IDS scans using signature files, so it is a signature-based IDS. A host-based IDS watches for suspicious behavior on systems, so it is a behavior-based IDS.

Proxies

A forward proxy server acts on behalf of clients, getting information from various sources and handing that info to the clients. The sources (servers) don't know about the clients, only the proxy server. A reverse proxy server, in contrast, acts on behalf of its servers. Clients contact the reverse proxy server, which gathers information from its associated server(s) and hands that information to the clients. The clients don't know about the servers behind the scenes. The reverse proxy server is the only machine with which they interact.

VPN Concentrator

A VPN concentrator is a specific device designed to offer a highly secure VPN solution to an organization using the highest level of security technologies such as encryption and authentication services.

Objective 10.04 Industrial Control Systems (ICS)

Pretty much any industry that makes things, changes things, or moves things is filled with equipment to do the jobs that have to be done. From making mousetraps to ice cream, any given industrial plant, power grid, or pipeline is filled with stuff that needs monitoring and stuff that needs controlling.

Here are some examples of things to monitor:

- Temperature
- Power levels
- Fill quantify
- Illumination
- Mass

And these are some examples of the things to control:

- Heaters
- Voltage
- Pumps
- Retractable roofs
- Valves

In the early days of automation, you might have a single person monitoring a machine that produced something. When the temperature hit a certain point, for example, that person—the operator—might open a valve or turn a knob to make changes and keep the machine functioning properly. As machines became more complex, the role of the operator likewise changed. He or she needed to monitor more functions and, sometimes, more machines. Eventually, computers were brought in to help manage the machines. The overall system that monitors and controls machines today is called an *industrial control system (ICS)*.

ICS isn't a new concept. It has been around for over 100 years using technology such as telescopes and horns to monitor and using mechanisms and pneumatics to control from a distance. But ICSs really started to take off when computers were combined with digital monitors and controls. Over the last few years, many ICSs have taken on more and more personal-computer aspects such as Windows- or Linux-based operating systems, Intel-style processors, and specialized PCs. Today, ICS is moving from stand-alone networks to inter-connecting with the Internet, which brings up serious issues for security.

CompTIA has added ICS to the Network+ exam objectives and expects you to know that it exists. Plus, competent network techs know the basic ICS variations and the components that make up those systems.

DCS

An ICS has three basic components: input/output (I/O) functions on the machine, a controller, and the interface for the operator. Input and output work through sensors and actuators. Sensors monitor temperature, for example, and the actuator makes changes that modify that temperature. The controller, some sort of computer, knows enough to manage the process, such as "keep the temperature between 50 and 55 degrees Fahrenheit." The operator watches some kind of monitor—the interface—and intervenes if necessary (see Figure 10.7). Let's scale this up to a factory and add a little more complexity.

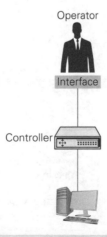

Operator

Interface

Controller

FIGURE 10.7   A simple ICS

What if you have multiple machines that accomplish a big task, like in a factory that produces some finished product?

The new widget at Bayland Widgets, for example, is produced in stages, with the machine at each stage needing monitoring and control. In the early days of computers, when computers were really expensive, the controller was a single computer. All the sensors from each of the machines had to provide feedback to that single controller. The controller would compute and then send signals to the various actuators to change things, thus managing the process (see Figure 10.8).

As computing power went up and costs when down, it made much more sense to put smaller controllers directly on each machine, to distribute the computing load. This is a *distributed control system (DCS)*. In a modern DCS, each of the local controllers connects (eventually) to a centralized controller—what CompTIA calls the ICS server—where global changes can be made (see Figure 10.9). Operators at the ICS server for Bayland Widgets, for example, could direct the controllers managing the robots to change production from green widgets to blue widgets.

Operators interact with controllers through a control or computer called a *human machine interface (HMI)*. Early HMIs were usually custom-made boxes with gauges and switches. Today, an HMI is most likely a PC running a custom,

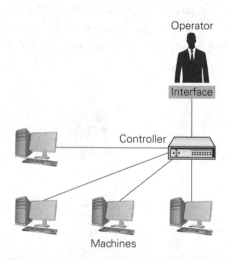

FIGURE 10.8   An early computer-assisted ICS

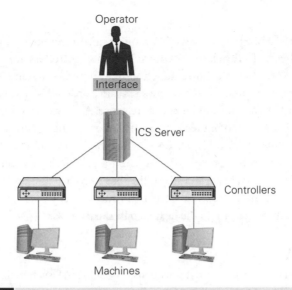

FIGURE 10.9	A simple DCS

touchscreen interface (see Figure 10.10). It's important to appreciate that HMIs are not general purpose. You wouldn't run Microsoft Office on an HMI, even if the PC on which it is built is capable of such things. It's very common for an HMI to show a single interface that never changes.

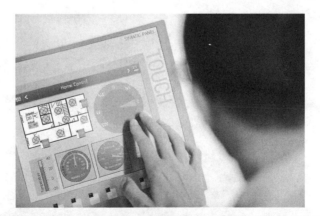

FIGURE 10.10	SIMATIC HMI Basic Panel with a touchscreen (© Siemens AG 2014, All rights reserved)

PLC

A DCS makes sense for a process that requires a continuous flow. The sensors provide real-time feedback to the controllers; the controllers are sophisticated enough to keep the machines functioning properly, making changes via the actuators. In a process that follows specific, ordered steps, in contrast, a different kind of system would make more sense. A classic programmable logic controller (PLC) is a computer that controls a machine according to a set of ordered steps (see Figure 10.11). Take, for example, a machine that produces cakes. Each step in the process of producing a cake follows a certain pattern (add ingredients, mix, bake, and so on) that has to go in order and in the proper timing. The PLC monitors sensors (such as timers and oven temperatures) and tells the machine when to do the next step in the process.

SCADA

A supervisory control and data acquisition (SCADA) system is a subset of ICS. Generally, a SCADA system has the same basic components as a DCS, but differs in two very important ways. First, a SCADA system is designed for large-scale, distributed processes such as power grids, pipelines, and railroads. Second, due to the distance involved, a SCADA system must function with the idea that remote devices may or may not have ongoing communication with the central control.

FIGURE 10.11   Siemens SIMATIC S7-1500 PLC (© Siemens AG 2014, All rights reserved)

Remote Terminal Unit

In general, a SCADA system is going to be a DCS using servers, HMIs, sensors, and actuators. The big difference is the replacement of controllers with devices called *remote terminal units (RTUs)*, which provide the same function as a controller, but have two major differences. First, an RTU is designed to have some amount of autonomy in case it loses connection with the central control. Second, an RTU is designed to take advantage of some form of long-distance communication such as telephony, fiber optic, or cellular WANs (see Figure 10.12). As you might imagine, the fear of interception is a big deal with SCADA systems these days, so let's discuss the need for network segmentation.

Segmentation and Industrial Control Systems

All forms of ICS are by definition closed networks. A *closed network* is any network that strictly controls who and what may connect to it. However, there are two places where we begin to see connectivity. In many SCADA systems, it is very convenient to use public wireless networks to connect RTUs, and,

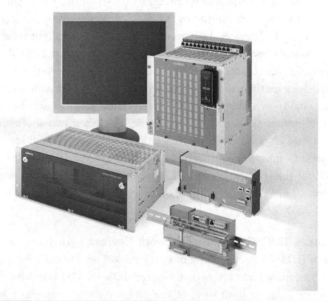

FIGURE 10.12 Substation automation and RTUs (© Siemens AG 2014, All rights reserved)

in some cases, we connect SCADA servers to the Internet to provide intranet access. The biggest single line of defense for these two scenarios is virtual private network connections. It's impossible to find any form of SCADA/ICS that doesn't use a VPN in cases where it must be open to the public Internet.

CHECKPOINT

✔**Objective 10.01: Designing and Building a Network**   With a list of requirements, define the network's needs. Identify device types, environment limitations, equipment limitations, compatibility requirements, wired/wireless considerations, and security considerations.

✔**Objective 10.02: Unified Communication**   Unified communication (UC) is the support of voice, video, and texting over IP networks. Unified communication is a natural evolution of VoIP technologies. VoIP uses Real-time Transport Protocol (RTP) on TCP ports 5004 and 5005, and Session Initiation Protocol (SIP) on TCP ports 5060 and 5061. UC improves over traditional VoIP by providing presence information, video conferencing/real-time video, fax, messaging, and collaborative tools/workflow. A UC network has UC devices, UC servers, and UC gateways. The most common UC protocols beyond RTP and SIP are H.323, which uses TCP port 1720, and MGCP, which uses ports 2427 and 2727. Video teleconferencing (VTC) is especially sensitive to network slowdowns. Medianets handle this problem using quality of service (QoS). Differentiated services are the underlying IP-level functions that make QoS work. There are two subfields in every QoS-aware IP field: DSCP (Differentiated Services Code Point) and ECN (Explicit Congestion Notification). DSCP is used to define a class of service (CoS) for the IP packet, while ECN is used to communicate congestion on sessions. The well-installed base of ISDN makes for a unique form of VTC called ISDN IP/SIP.

✔**Objective 10.03: Specialized Network Devices**   An intrusion detection system (IDS) inspects a copy of every packet on the network and actively monitors for attacks. A network-based IDS (NIDS) typically consists of sensors on one or both sides of the gateway router, whereas a host-based IDS (HIDS) consists of monitoring software installed on individual computers. An intrusion prevention system (IPS) proactively monitors for

---

attacks and then reacts if an attack is identified. An IPS sits directly in the flow of network traffic. A proxy server intercepts client requests and acts upon them, usually by blocking the request or forwarding the request to other servers.

✔**Objective 10.04: Industrial Control Systems (ICS)** An ICS consolidates the monitoring and control of a process into one or more control areas. An ICS has three basic components: input/output (I/O) functions on the machine, a controller, and the interface for the operator. A DCS has controllers distributed among the various machines to handle the I/O. The DCS controllers connect to the ICS server for managing global changes. The human machine interface (HMI) is how the ICS manifests itself to the operator(s) of the system. A programmable logic controller (PLC) has a parallel function to the controllers in a DCS, but works in a different way. A PLC controls a machine according to a set of ordered steps. A supervisory control and data acquisition (SCADA) system is designed for large-scale, distributed processes such as power grids. SCADA systems use remote terminal units (RTUs). An RTU uses some form of remote communication technology and is designed to have some amount of autonomy in case it loses connection with the central control. ICS/DCS/SCADA and other networks are traditionally good candidates for network segmentation.

REVIEW QUESTIONS

1. What is the first step in designing a network?
   A. Define a list of requirements.
   B. Determine the type of ISP you will use.
   C. Check the existing cable.
   D. Determine what security you need.

2. Which of the following is the most efficient method of transmission when more than one node (but not every single one) on a network needs certain packets?
   A. Unicast
   B. Broadcast
   C. Multicast
   D. Anycast

3. What are the parts of the DS field in IP packets? (Choose all that apply.)

    A. ToS

    B. DSCP

    C. CoS

    D. ECN

4. What is the term for the technology that brings together presence information, video conferencing/real-time video, fax, messaging, and collaborate tools/workflow?

    A. Unified communications

    B. Virtual private network

    C. Industrial control systems

    D. Programmable logic controller

5. Which of the following is a subset of an ICS that is designed for large-scale, distributed processes such as power grids, pipelines, and railroads, which must function with the idea that remote devices may or may not have ongoing communication with the central control?

    A. SCADA

    B. RTU

    C. DCS

    D. PLC

6. What is a network of (typically) far-flung routers and servers that provide—via quality of service (QoS) and other tools—sufficient bandwidth for VTC that work with UC servers (or sometimes by themselves) to distribute video conferences?

    A. ICS

    B. VPN

    C. VLAN

    D. Medianet

7. How does an IPS compare to an IDS? (Choose all that apply.)

    A. An IPS is more secure because it uses IPsec.

    B. An IDS is more secure because it uses L2TP.

    C. An IPS is inline with the traffic and can stop traffic before reaching other parts of the network.

    D. An IDS is out of band, but can notify another device, such as a firewall, to stop traffic.

8. Which of the following statements is true?

   A. All forms of ICS are considered open networks.

   B. All forms of ICS are considered closed networks.

   C. Some forms of ICS are considered open, and others are considered closed.

   D. No forms of ICS are considered closed networks.

9. In a distributed control system (DCS), what is the control or computer that operators interact with controllers through called?

   A. ICS

   B. PLC

   C. VPN

   D. HMI

10. Which of the following best describes a VoIP phone?

   A. UC gateway

   B. UC server

   C. UC device

   D. UC switch

REVIEW ANSWERS

1. **A**   Defining requirements is the first step in designing a network.

2. **C**   Multicast traffic can be pruned by the routers and switches, and is more efficient than sending individual unicast packets or broadcast packets to the entire network. Anycasting is where the same unicast IP address is shared by multiple nodes.

3. **B D**   Differentiated Services Code Point and Explicit Congestion Notification are the subfields of the Differentiated Services field in the IP packet.

4. **A**   Unified communications brings central management to collaborative technologies.

5. **A**   A supervisory control and data acquisition (SCADA) system is a subset of ICS that has the same general basic components as a DCS, but differs in two very important ways.

6. **D** A medianet could be two gateway routers with enough QoS smarts to open bandwidth for active VTCs as soon as they are detected, or a huge multinational company with its own group of high-powered edge routers, spanning the globe with an MPLS-based VLAN, working with UC servers to support tens of thousands of voice and video conversations going on continually throughout its organization.

7. **C** **D** An IPS is inline with the traffic, and an IPS is out of band.

8. **D** Industrial control systems by pure definition are closed systems.

9. **D** A human machine interface (HMI). Early HMIs were usually custom-made boxes with gauges and switches. Today, an HMI is most likely a PC running a custom, touchscreen interface.

10. **C** A VoIP phone is a UC device.

Troubleshooting Networks

	NEWBIE	SOME EXPERIENCE	EXPERT
ETA	4 hours	2 hours	1 hour

Did you ever watch the television show *ER?* It was a medical drama centering on a group of attractive doctors and nurses working in an emergency room. They spent much of their time casually checking up on patients and having witty conversations. But, at some point during every episode, something terrible happens and the ambulances pull up. People come crashing through the doors with a patient. Everyone starts shouting and the music gets very dramatic. It's an actual emergency and there is a life that needs saving!

A network tech is a little bit like an ER doctor, except you'll probably be fixing things by yourself, and all that shouting will be in your head. You won't always have a lot to do to keep a network running, but when something goes wrong and you see the server being wheeled through the doors on a gurney (if you happen to have a gurney, of course), you need to know how to troubleshoot the network. You'll also need to know the symptoms of hardware malfunctions and which tools to use to fix them. The dramatic music is optional.

 **Objective 11.01** Troubleshooting Methodology

Troubleshooting is a dynamic, fluid process that requires you to make snap judgments and act on them to try and make the network go. Any attempt to cover every possible scenario would be futile and probably not in your best interest, because any reference that tried to list every troubleshooting problem would be obsolete the moment it was created. If an exhaustive listing of all network problems is impossible, then how do you decide what to do and in what order?

Before you touch a single console or cable, you should remember two basic rules: To paraphrase the Hippocratic Oath, "First, do no harm." If at all possible, don't make a network problem bigger than it was originally. This is a rule I've broken thousands of times, and you will too. But if I change the good doctor's phrase a bit, it's possible to formulate a rule you can actually live with: "First, do not trash the data!" My gosh, if I had a dollar for every megabyte of irreplaceable data I've destroyed, I'd be rich! I've learned my lesson, and you should learn from my mistakes. The second rule is, "Always make good backups!" Computers can be replaced; data that is not backed up is, at best, expensive to recover and, at worst, gone forever.

Travel Advisory

In the late 1980s IBM actually tried to create documentation to cover every possible aspect of network troubleshooting via logical diagnostic diagrams—by the early 1990s the documents were over 1500 pages long and IBM simply gave up.

The CompTIA Network+ exam objectives contain a detailed troubleshooting methodology that provides a good starting point for our discussion. Here are the basic steps in the troubleshooting process.

Identify the Problem

First, *identify the problem*. That means grasping the true problem, rather than what someone tells you. A user might call in and complain that he can't access the Internet from his workstation, for example, which could be the only problem. But the problem could also be that the entire wing of the office just went down and you've got a much bigger problem on your hands. You need to gather information, duplicate the problem (if possible), question users, identify symptoms, determine if anything has changed on the network, and approach multiple problems individually. Following these steps will help you get to the root of the problem.

Gather Information, Duplicate the Problem, Question Users, and Identify Symptoms

Gather information about the situation. If you are working directly on the affected system and not relying on somebody on the other end of a telephone to guide you, you will *identify symptoms* through your observation of what is (or isn't) happening.

If you're troubleshooting over the telephone, you will need to *question users*. These can be *close-ended* questions, which is to say there can only be a yes-or-no-type answer, such as, "Can you see a light on the front of the monitor?" You can also ask *open-ended* questions, such as, "What have you already tried in attempting to fix the problem?"

One of the first steps in trying to determine the cause of a problem is to understand the extent of the problem. Is it specific to one user or is it network-wide? Sometimes this entails trying the task yourself, both from the user's machine and from your own or another machine.

For example, if a user is experiencing problems logging into the network, you might need to go to that user's machine and try to use his or her user name to log in. In other words, try to *duplicate the problem*. Doing this tells you whether the problem is a user error of some kind, as well as enables you to see the symptoms of the problem yourself. Next, you probably want to try logging in with your own user name from that machine, or have the user try to log in from another machine.

In some cases, you can ask other users in the area if they are experiencing the same problem to see if the issue is affecting more than one user. Depending on the size of your network, you should find out whether the problem is occurring in only one part of your company or across the entire network.

What does all of this tell you? Essentially, it tells you how big the problem is. If nobody in an entire remote office can log in, you may be able to assume that the problem is the network link or router connecting that office to the server. If nobody in any office can log in, you may be able to assume the server is down or not accepting logins. If only that one user in that one location can't log in, the problem may be with that user, that machine, or that user's account.

Exam Tip

The Network+ exam has lots of scenario questions that start with "User X is having a problem" or "Everyone on the network is having a problem." Use these clues to help you eliminate variables.

Determine If Anything Has Changed

Determine if anything has changed on the network recently that might have caused the problem. You may not have to ask many questions before the person using the problem system can tell you what has changed, but, in some cases, establishing if anything has changed can take quite a bit of time and involve further work behind the scenes. Here are some examples of questions to ask:

- "What exactly was happening when the problem occurred?"
- "Has anything been changed on the system recently?"
- "Has the system been moved recently?"

Notice the way I've tactfully avoided the word *you*, as in "Have *you* changed anything on the system recently?" This is a deliberate tactic to avoid any implied blame on the part of the user. Being nice never hurts, and it makes the whole troubleshooting process more friendly.

You should also *internally* ask yourself some isolating questions, such as "Was that machine involved in the software push last night?" or "Didn't a tech visit that machine this morning?" Note you will only be able to answer these questions if *your* documentation is up to date. Sometimes, isolating a problem may require you to check system and hardware logs (such as those stored by some routers and other network devices), so make sure you know how to do this.

Exam Tip
Avoid aggressive or accusatory questions.

Approach Multiple Problems Individually

If you encounter a complicated scenario, with various machines off the network and potential server room or wiring problems, break it down. *Approach multiple problems individually* to sort out root causes. Methodically tackle them, and you'll eventually have a list of one or more problems identified. Then you can move on to the next step.

Establish a Theory of Probable Cause

Once you've identified one or more problems, try to figure out what could have happened. In other words, *establish a theory of probable cause*. Just keep in mind that a *theory is not a fact*. You might need to chuck the theory out the window later in the process and establish a revised theory.

This step comes down to experience—or good use of the support tools at your disposal, such as your knowledge base. You need to select the most *probable* cause from all the *possible* causes, so the solution you choose fixes the problem the first time. This may not always happen, but whenever possible, you want to avoid spending a whole day stabbing in the dark while the problem snores softly to itself in some cozy, neglected corner of your network.

Don't forget to *question the obvious*. If Bob can't print to the networked printer, for example, check to see that the printer is plugged in and turned on.

Consider multiple approaches when tackling problems. This will keep you from locking your imagination into a single train of thought. Consider using the OSI seven-layer model as a troubleshooting tool in several ways to help with this process.

Here's a scenario to work through:

Martha can't access the database server to start her workday. The problem manifests this way: She opens the database client on her computer, then clicks on recent documents, one of which is the current project that management has assigned to her team. Nothing happens. Normally, the database client will connect to the database that resides on the server on the other side of the network.

Try a *top-to-bottom* or *bottom-to-top OSI model* approach to the problem. Sometimes it pays to try both.

7. Application: Could there be a problem with the API that enables the database application to connect to the database server? Sure.

6. Presentation: Could there be a problem with encryption between the application and the database server? Maybe, but Martha would probably see an error message rather than nothing.

5. Session: Could a database authentication failure be preventing access? Again, this could be the problem, but Martha would probably see an error message here as well.

4. Transport: Perhaps extreme traffic on the network could be blocking an acknowledgment segment? This seems a bit of a reach, but worth considering.

3. Network: Someone might have changed the IP address of the database server.

2. Data Link: The MAC address of the database server or Martha's machine might be blacklisted.

1. Physical: A disconnected cable or dead NIC can make for a bad day.

You might imagine the reverse model in some situations. If the network was newly installed, for example, running through some of the basic connectivity at layers 1 and 2 might be a good first approach.

Another option for tackling multiple options is to use the *divide and conquer* approach. As you gather information for troubleshooting, a general sense of where the problem lies should manifest. Place this likely cause at the appropriate layer of the OSI model and begin to test the theory and related theories at that layer. If the theory bears out, follow the appropriate troubleshooting steps. If the theory is wrong, move up or down the OSI model with new theories of probable causes.

On its face, divide and conquer appears to be a compromise between top-to-bottom OSI troubleshooting and bottom-to-top OSI troubleshooting. But it's better than a compromise. Divide and conquer is a time saver that comes into play as part of developing a theory of probable cause. If we arbitrarily always perform top-to-bottom troubleshooting, we'll waste a lot of time at layers 7 through 3 to troubleshoot Data Link layer and Physical layer issues.

Test the Theory to Determine the Cause

With the third step, you need to *test the theory to determine the cause,* but do so without changing anything or risking any repercussions. If you have determined that the probable cause for Bob not being able to print is that the printer is turned off, go look. If that's the case, then you should plan out your next step to resolve the problem. Do not act yet! That comes next.

If the theory is not confirmed, you need to *reestablish a new theory or escalate the problem.* Let's discuss what each of these means.

Reestablish a new theory is easy: go back to step two and determine a new probable cause. Once you have another idea, test it. The reason you should hesitate to act at this third step is that you might not have permission to make the fix or the fix might cause repercussions you don't fully understand yet. For example, if you walk over to the print server room to see if the printer is powered up and online and find the door padlocked, that's a whole different level of problem. Sure, the printer is turned off, but management has done it for a reason. In this sort of situation, you need to escalate the problem.

To *escalate* has two meanings: either to inform other parties about a problem for guidance or to pass the job off to another authority who has control over the device/issue that's most probably causing the problem. Let's say you have a server with a bad NIC. This server is used heavily by the accounting department, and taking it down may cause problems you don't even know about. You need to inform the accounting manager to consult with him or her. Alternatively, you'll come across problems over which you have no control or authority. A badly acting server across the country (hopefully) has another person in charge to whom you need to hand over the job.

Regardless of how many times you need to go through this process, you'll eventually reach a theory that seems right. *Once the theory is confirmed, determine the next steps you need to take to resolve the problem.*

Establish a Plan of Action and Identify Potential Effects

By this point, you should have some ideas as to what the problem might be. It's time to "look before you leap" and *establish a plan of action to resolve the problem.* An action plan defines how you are going to fix this problem. Most problems are simple, but if the problem is complex, you need to write down the steps. As you do this, think about what else might happen as you go about the repair. *Identify the potential effects* of the actions you're about to take, especially the unintended ones. If you take out a switch without a replacement switch at hand, the users might experience excessive downtime while you hunt for a new switch and move them over. If you replace a router, can you restore all the old router's settings to the new one or will you have to rebuild from scratch?

Implement the Solution or Escalate as Necessary

Once you think you have isolated the cause of the problem, you should decide what you think is the best way to fix it and then *implement the solution,* whether that's giving advice over the phone to a user, installing a replacement part, or adding a software patch. Or, if the solution you propose either requires more skill than you possess at the moment or falls into someone else's purview, *escalate as necessary* to get the fix implemented.

All the way through implementation, try only one likely solution at a time. Consider a problem that requires a patch. There's no benefit in installing several patches at once, because then you can't tell which one fixed the problem. Similarly, there's no point in replacing several items of hardware (such as a hard disk and its controller cable) at the same time, because then you can't tell which part (or parts) was faulty.

As you try each possibility, always *document* what you do and what results you get. This isn't just for a future problem either—during a lengthy troubleshooting process, it's easy to forget exactly what you tried two hours before or which thing you tried produced a particular result. Although being methodical may take longer, it will save you time the next time—and it may enable you to pinpoint what needs to be done to stop the problem from recurring at all, thereby reducing future call volume to your support team—and as any support person will tell you, that's definitely worth the effort!

Then you need to test the solution. This is the part everybody hates. Once you think you've fixed a problem, you should try to make it happen again. If you can't, great! But sometimes you will be able to re-create the problem, and then you know you haven't finished the job at hand. Many techs want to slide away quietly as soon as everything seems to be fine, but trust me on this, it won't impress your customer when her problem flares up again 30 seconds after you've left the building—not to mention that you get the joy of another two-hour car trip the next day to fix the same problem, for an even more unhappy client!

In the scenario where you are providing support to someone else rather than working directly on the problem, you should make *her* try to re-create the problem. This tells you whether she understands what you have been telling her and educates her at the same time, lessening the chance that she'll call you back later and ask, "Can we just go through that one more time?"

> **Exam Tip**
>
> Always test a solution before you walk away from the job.

Verify Full System Functionality and Implement Preventative Measures

Okay, now that you have changed something on the system in the process of solving one problem, you must think about the wider repercussions of what you have done. If you've replaced a faulty NIC in a server, for instance, will the fact that the MAC address has changed (remember, it's built into the NIC) affect anything else, such as the logon security controls or your network management and inventory software? If you've installed a patch on a client PC, will this change the default protocol or any other default settings that may affect other functionality? If you've changed a user's security settings, will this affect his or her ability to access other network resources? This is part of testing your solution to make sure it works properly, but it also makes you think about the impact of your work on the system as a whole.

Make sure you *verify full system functionality.* If you think you fixed the problem between Martha's workstation and the database server, have her open the database while you're still there. That way you don't have to make a second tech call to resolve an outstanding issue. This saves time and money and helps your customer do his or her job better. Everybody wins.

Also at this time, if applicable, *implement preventative measures* to avoid a repeat of the problem. If that means you need to educate the user to do or not do something, teach him or her tactfully. If you need to install software or patch a system, do it now.

Document Findings, Actions, and Outcomes

It is *vital* that you *document findings, actions, and outcomes* of all support calls, for two reasons: First, you're creating a support database to serve as a knowledge base for future reference, enabling everyone on the support team to identify new problems as they arise and know how to deal with them quickly, without having to duplicate someone else's research efforts. Second, documentation enables you to track problem trends and anticipate future workloads, or even to identify a particular brand or model of an item, such as a printer or a NIC, that seems to be less reliable or that creates more work for you than others. Don't skip this step—it *really* is essential!

 **Objective 11.02** Troubleshooting Tools

Troubleshooting tools come in two forms. First, there's the software tools, utilities like ping, which network techs use on a daily basis. Secondly, there's the physical hardware tools, like cable testers, that also see great usage out in the wild.

Software Tools

TCP/IP offers powerful troubleshooting utilities that all network techs should know. The CompTIA Network+ certification exam tests your knowledge of when to use each of the utilities discussed here, so be sure that you are familiar with these commands!

Travel Advisory

Case Matters With each of the command-line commands you're about to study, make note of the case for each command. With few exceptions, learn all commands in lowercase. Windows doesn't care that much, but every other operating system cares a lot, and running a command with the improper case will result in a failed command.

---

ipconfig and ifconfig

When troubleshooting a system connected to the network, the first thing you will most likely want to find out is whether the system has an IP address. The following commands can be used to determine the IP settings on the system.

ipconfig The *ipconfig* command is used in Windows to display the IP address information of the system. The following is a list of popular ipconfig commands:

- **ipconfig /all** Displays all TCP/IP settings and the MAC address
- **ipconfig /displaydns** Displays the DNS resolver cache
- **ipconfig /flushdns** Clears out the DNS resolver cache

ifconfig The *ifconfig* command displays or sets settings on a network card on a UNIX/Linux/OS X system. The following is a list of popular ifconfig commands:

- **ifconfig** Displays the network card and IP settings
- **ifconfig eth0 up** Enables the first Ethernet card
- **ifconfig eth0 down** Disables the Ethernet card

ping

The *ping* utility (for all operating systems) tests connections between two nodes. To test the connection between two nodes, sit at one of the systems and type in **ping** followed by the hostname or IP address of the other node. The ping utility uses Internet Control Message Protocol (ICMP) to send an ICMP Echo Request to determine whether the other machine can receive the test packet and reply to it. A node that can be reached will respond, and the ping utility will report success. The ping utility can also test for the availability of Internet-based services using fully qualified domain names (FQDNs), but note that some sites block ICMP Echo Requests to dissuade their sites from being used for testing—and some corporate Internet security systems also block ICMP Echo Requests to external sites. The output of the ping command looks like this:

```
C:\>ping 192.168.2.1
Pinging 192.168.2.1 with 32 bytes of data:
Reply from 192.168.2.1: bytes=32 time<10ms TTL=255
Reply from 192.168.2.1: bytes=32 time<10ms TTL=255
Reply from 192.168.2.1: bytes=32 time<10ms TTL=255
Reply from 192.168.2.1: bytes=32 time<10ms TTL=255
Ping statistics for 192.168.2.1:
Packets: Sent = 4, Received = 4, Lost = 0 (0% loss),
Approximate round trip times in milli-seconds:
Minimum = 0ms, Maximum =  0ms, Average =  0ms

C:\PING www.google.com
Pinging www.google.com [216.239.33.100] with 32 bytes of data:
Reply from 216.239.33.100: bytes=32 time=270ms TTL=49
Reply from 216.239.33.100: bytes=32 time=271ms TTL=49
Reply from 216.239.33.100: bytes=32 time=270ms TTL=49
Reply from 216.239.33.100: bytes=32 time=271ms TTL=49
Ping statistics for 216.239.33.100:

Packets: Sent = 4, Received = 4, Lost = 0 (0% loss),
Approximate round trip times in milli-seconds:
Minimum = 270ms, Maximum =  271ms, Average =  270ms

C:\ping www.madethisup.com
Unknown host www.madethisup.com.
```

You should read the messages ping reports back when it cannot reach another machine. They can contain important clues about the source of the problem.

If ping cannot turn a name into an IP address, for example, it will report back, "Unknown host" or some similar message. (The exact message returned by the ping command varies depending on the operating system.) If ping resolves an IP address but cannot reach the specified address, ping will display a different message, such as "Destination host unreachable." Keep the following points in mind when you receive such a message:

- **Unknown host**   This message means, "I don't know the IP address!" You probably specified an invalid/unused DNS name.

- **Destination host unreachable**   This message means, "I can't get to that IP address." In this case, you should check for possible routing problems—for example, have you specified a default gateway?

If a seemingly valid host is specified but that host doesn't appear to be responding, you will see a sequence similar to the following:

```
C:\> ping 192.168.2.223
Pinging 192.168.2.223 with 32 bytes of data:
Request timed out.
Request timed out.
Request timed out.
Request timed out.
Ping statistics for 192.168.2.223:
Packets: Sent = 4, Received = 0, Lost = 4 (100% loss),
Approximate round trip times in milli-seconds:
Minimum = 0ms, Maximum =  0ms, Average =  0ms
```

You need to know two switches for the ping command. The first is ping –t. The –t switch tells ping to run indefinitely in Windows (as opposed to only four times). In Linux, ping runs indefinitely by default. The second is ping -6. The ping command defaults to IPv4, but also functions well in an IPv6 network. In Windows, use the command with the -6 switch: ping -6. In UNIX/Linux, use ping6.

tracert

The *tracert* (or *traceroute* on UNIX/Linux/OS X systems) command traces the route between two hosts. The tracert command will send back a response with each router it hits. This enables you to determine if communication is slow because a link has gone down between your computer and the destination. If you know that three routers are normally between you and the destination, and the tracert returns six responses, you know that your packets are taking an indirect pathway (due to a link being down). The following listing shows a trace to the Total Seminars' web server from a machine in the UK (the –d switch tells tracert to display IP addresses without the corresponding domain names):

```
C:\> tracert -d www.totalsem.com
Tracing route to www.totalsem.com [64.226.214.168]
over a maximum of 30 hops:
1   <10 ms   <10 ms   <10 ms   192.168.2.1
2   80 ms    70 ms    80 ms    194.159.254.93
3   80 ms    90 ms    90 ms    194.159.254.100
```

```
4   90 ms   91 ms   90 ms   194.159.252.54
5   90 ms   100 ms  90 ms   194.159.36.234
6   90 ms   90 ms   90 ms   213.206.130.81
7   81 ms   90 ms   90 ms   213.206.128.41
8   130 ms  131 ms  120 ms  213.206.129.38
9   130 ms  120 ms  121 ms  80.77.64.33
10  200 ms  200 ms  201 ms  144.232.19.29
11  210 ms  210 ms  211 ms  144.232.19.98
12  210 ms  200 ms  211 ms  144.232.7.253
13  220 ms  211 ms  220 ms  144.232.9.198
14  220 ms  221 ms  220 ms  144.232.12.18
15  220 ms  221 ms  220 ms  160.81.204.10
16  220 ms  221 ms  220 ms  64.224.0.99
17  230 ms  221 ms  240 ms  totalsem.com [64.226.214.168]
Trace complete.
```

Exam Tip

The ping and traceroute commands are excellent examples of *connectivity software*, utilities that enable you to determine if a connection can be made between two computers.

Travel Advisory

The traceroute command defaults to IPv4, but also functions well in an IPv6 network. In Windows, use the command with the -6 switch: tracert -6. In UNIX/Linux, use traceroute6 (or traceroute -6 in some variants of Linux).

pathping

Microsoft has a utility called *pathping* that combines the functions of ping and tracert and adds some additional functions.

Here is some sample pathping output:

```
Tracing route to xeroxpaser.totalhome [182.168.4.17]
Over a maximum 30 hops:
  0  local-PC.totalhome [192.168.4.53]
  1  xrxphsr.totalhome [192.168.4.17]
Computing statistics for 25 seconds...
            Source to Here    This Node/Link
Hop  RTT    Lost/Sent - Pct   Lost/Sent - Pct Address
  0                                           local-PC.totalhome
                                              192.168.4.53]
                            0/ 100 - 0%   :
  1  0ms    0/ 100 - 0%     0/ 100 - 0%
                                              xrxphsr.totalhome
                                              192.168.4.17]

Trace complete
```

netstat

The *netstat* command (for all operating systems) enables a network tech to examine network statistics about a system. These statistics include information such as the ports listening on the system and any connections that have been established. The following is some output from the netstat command:

```
C:\>netstat
Active Connections
Proto  Local Address  Foreign Address  State
TCP   brian:1030   BRIAN:1274  ESTABLISHED
TCP   brian:2666   totalsem.com:pop3  TIME_WAIT
TCP   brian:2670   totalsem.com:pop3  TIME_WAIT
TCP   brian:2672   www.cnn.com:80  TIME_WAIT
TCP   brian:2674   www.nytimes.com:80  ESTABLISHED
TCP   brian:2460   MARSPDC:nbsession  ESTABLISHED
TCP   brian:1273   NOTES01:2986  TIME_WAIT
TCP   brian:1274   BRIAN:1030  ESTABLISHED
```

The netstat command can provide a wide range of information depending on the command-line switches used. Type **netstat /?** at a command prompt to list the optional command-line switches.

```
Displays protocol statistics and current TCP/IP network connections.
NETSTAT [-a] [-b] [-e] [-f] [-n] [-o] [-p proto] [-r] [-s] [-t] [interval]
  -a          Displays all connections and listening ports.
  -b          Displays the executable involved in creating each connection or
              listening port. In some cases well-known executables host
              multiple independent components, and in these cases the
              sequence of components involved in creating the connection
              or listening port is displayed. In this case the executable
              name is in [] at the bottom, on top is the component it called,
              and so forth until TCP/IP was reached. Note that this option
              can be time-consuming and will fail unless you have sufficient
              permissions.
  -e          Displays Ethernet statistics. This may be combined with the -s
              option.
  -f          Displays Fully Qualified Domain Names (FQDN) for foreign
              addresses.
  -n          Displays addresses and port numbers in numerical form.
  -o          Displays the owning process ID associated with each connection.
  -p proto    Shows connections for the protocol specified by proto; proto
              may be any of: TCP, UDP, TCPv6, or UDPv6.  If used with the -s
              option to display per-protocol statistics, proto may be any of:
              IP, IPv6, ICMP, ICMPv6, TCP, TCPv6, UDP, or UDPv6.
  -r          Displays the routing table.
  -s          Displays per-protocol statistics.  By default, statistics are
              shown for IP, IPv6, ICMP, ICMPv6, TCP, TCPv6, UDP, and UDPv6;
              the -p option may be used to specify a subset of the default.
  -t          Displays the current connection offload state.
```

```
interval    Redisplays selected statistics, pausing interval seconds
            between each display.  Press CTRL+C to stop redisplaying
            statistics.  If omitted, netstat will print the current
            configuration information once.
```

nbtstat

For backward compatibility with some truly ancient local area networking (LAN) applications, Microsoft implements the NetBIOS over TCP (NBT) protocol in Windows. This manifests in a couple of ways. First, every Windows PC has a distinct NetBIOS name. My computer's name, for example, is Mike7. Second, you can use a specific utility to interact with other Windows computers on a LAN.

The *nbtstat* (NetBIOS over TCP/IP statistics) command enables a network tech to check information about the NetBIOS names. This includes viewing the names that have been registered by the local system (nbtstat –n), viewing the names registered by a remote system (nbtstat –A), and viewing the NetBIOS name cache (nbtstat –c), which shows the NetBIOS names and corresponding IP addresses that have been resolved by a particular host.

Here's some sample output:

```
C:\>NBTSTAT -c
Node IpAddress: [192.168.43.5] Scope Id: []
NetBIOS Remote Cache Name Table
Name    Type   Host Address  Life [sec]
===================================================================
WRITERS    <1B>   UNIQUE   192.168.43.13   420
DAN        <20>   UNIQUE   192.168.43.3    420
VENUSPDC   <00>   UNIQUE   192.168.43.13   120
GLEN       <20>   UNIQUE   192.168.43.2    420
NOTES01    <20>   UNIQUE   192.168.43.4    420
```

When properly used, nbtstat helps network techs diagnose and troubleshoot NetBIOS problems, especially those related to NetBIOS name resolution.

Like netstat, nbtstat can provide a wealth of information using different switches. Here are some of the popular switches:

```
NBTSTAT [ [-a RemoteName] [-A IP address] [-c] [-n]
[-r] [-R] [-RR] [-s] [-S] [interval] ]
-a  Lists the remote machine's name table given its name
-A  Lists the remote machine's name table given its IP address
-c  Lists NBT's cache of remote [machine] names and their IP
addresses
-n  Lists local NetBIOS names
-R  Purges and reloads the remote cache name table
```

Exam Tip

Note that nbtstat enables you to purge and reload the NetBIOS name cache with the command nbtstat –R. Remember that, unlike most Windows command-line utilities, nbtstat is case-sensitive when it comes to its switches. Therefore, nbtstat –R and nbtstat –r are not the same command.

nslookup

The *nslookup* command provides a command-line utility for diagnosing DNS problems. All operating systems support this tool. Its most basic function returns the IP address, as shown here:

```
C:\>nslookup example.com
Server:  dns.example.com
Address:  192.168.31.211
Non-authoritative answer:
Name:  server1.example.com
Address:  192.68.67.12
```

The nslookup command also offers an interactive mode that enables you to specify a wide range of options as you diagnose and troubleshoot DNS issues. To see the full range of options, type **?** at the nslookup prompt in Windows:

```
>?
Commands:  (identifiers are shown in uppercase, [] means optional)
NAME   - print info about the host/domain NAME using
default server
NAME1 NAME2  - as above, but use NAME2 as server
help or ?  - print info on common commands
set OPTION  - set an option
all  - print options, current server and host
[no]debug  - print debugging information
[no]d2  - print exhaustive debugging information
[no]defname  - append domain name to each query
[no]recurse  - ask for recursive answer to query
[no]search  - use domain search list
[no]vc  - always use a virtual circuit
domain=NAME  - set default domain name to NAME
srchlist=N1[/N2/.../N6] - set domain to N1 and search list
to N1,N2, etc.
root=NAME  - set root server to NAME
retry=X  - set number of retries to X
timeout=X  - set initial time-out interval to X
seconds
type=X  - set query type (ex. A,ANY,CNAME,MX,NS,
```

```
PTR,SOA,SRV)
querytype=X  - same as type
class=X  - set query class (ex. IN (Internet),ANY)
[no]msxfr  - use MS fast zone transfer
ixfrver=X  - current version to use in IXFR transfer
request
server NAME  - set default server to NAME, using current
default server
lserver NAME  - set default server to NAME, using initial
server
finger [USER]  - finger the optional NAME at the current
default host
root  - set current default server to the root
ls [opt] DOMAIN [> FILE] - list addresses in DOMAIN (optional:
output to FILE)
-a  - list canonical names and aliases
-d  - list all records
-t TYPE  - list records of the given type
(e.g.A,CNAME,MX,NS,PTR etc.)
view FILE  - sort an 'ls' output file and view it
with pg exit  - exit the program
>
```

In UNIX/Linux/OS X, you get the detailed nslookup options by typing **man nslookup** from the terminal prompt.

Using command-line utilities such as ping, tracert, arp, netstat, nbtstat, and nslookup, an experienced network tech can diagnose most TCP/IP problems quickly and begin working on solutions. If two hosts can ping each other by IP address but not by name, for example, the wise network tech knows to leave the routers alone and concentrate on name resolution issues instead.

To function effectively as a network tech, you need to learn TCP/IP. Supported by all operating systems, the TCP/IP suite provides excellent tools for integrating multiple operating systems within the same network. Its importance will continue to grow as the Internet continues to increase its importance in both business and everyday life.

arp

The *arp* utility, found in all operating systems, helps diagnose problems associated with the Address Resolution Protocol (ARP). CompTIA refers to the output of the arp command as the MAC address lookup table, while most folks would just call it the arp cache or arp table. TCP/IP hosts use arp to determine the physical (MAC) address that corresponds with a specific logical (IP) address. The arp utility, when used with the –a option, displays any

IP addresses that have been resolved to MAC addresses recently. Here's an example from Windows:

```
C:\>arp -a
Interface: 192.168.43.5 on Interface 0x1000002
Internet Address   Physical Address   Type
192.168.43.2   00-40-05-60-7f-64   dynamic
192.168.43.3   00-40-05-5b-71-51   dynamic
192.168.43.4   00-a0-c9-98-97-7f   dynamic
```

Looking Glass Sites

Sometimes you need to perform a ping or traceroute from a location outside of the local environment. *Looking glass sites* are remote servers accessible with a browser that contain common collections of diagnostic tools such as ping and traceroute, plus some Border Gateway Protocol (BGP) query tools.

Most looking glass sites allow you to select where the diagnostic process will originate from a list of locations, as well as the target destination, which diagnostic, and sometimes the version of IP to test. A Google search for "looking glass sites" will provide a large selection from which to choose.

Protocol Analyzer

Protocol analyzers monitor the different protocols running at different layers on the network. A good protocol analyzer will give you Application, Session, Transport, Network, and Data Link layer information on every frame going through your network. Even though the CompTIA Network+ exam places protocol analyzers in a hardware category, they aren't necessarily always hardware. Some of the best and most useful protocol analyzers, such as Wireshark, are software.

Use a protocol analyzer when being able to see the data on the network will help you answer these questions: Is something trying to start a session and not getting an answer? Maybe a DNS server isn't responding. Is some computer on the network placing confusing information on the network? Is a rogue DHCP server sending out responses to DHCP requests? In the same vein, a protocol analyzer helps you determine slowdowns on a network by giving you an idea of excess or unexpected traffic.

Wi-Fi Analyzer

A wireless analyzer, or Wi-Fi analyzer, is any device that looks for and documents all existing wireless networks in the area. Wireless analyzers are handy tools that are useful for diagnosing wireless network issues and conducting site surveys. You can get dedicated, hand-held wireless analyzer tools or you can run site survey software on a laptop or mobile wireless device.

Speed-Test Sites

Most techs use one of several speed-test sites for checking an Internet connection's throughput, such as MegaPath's Speakeasy Speed Test (www.speakeasy .net/speedtest).

Now that we've seen some software tools that can provide great troubleshooting help, let's now take a look at some hardware tools.

Hardware Tools

Testing for physical problems, layer-1 issues, require specialized hardware tools. Grab your toolbox, and let's explore some of the more commonly used tools.

Line Testers

Line testers are relatively simple devices used to check the integrity of telephone wiring. Use a line tester to check a twisted pair line to see if it is good, dead, reverse wired, or if there is AC voltage on the line.

Light Meter

The extremely transparent fiber-optic cables allow light to shine but have some inherent impurities in the glass that can reduce light transmission. Dust, poor connections, and light leakage can also degrade the strength of light pulses as they travel through a fiber-optic run. To measure the amount of light loss, technicians use an optical power meter, also referred to as a light meter.

The light meter system uses a high-powered source of light at one end of a run and a calibrated detector at the other end. This measures the amount of light that reaches the detector.

Tone Locators and Toner Probes

Even in the best of networks, labels fall off ports and outlets, mystery cables disappear behind walls, and new cable runs are added without documentation. To help you figure out which end belongs to a cable when you are working with a stack of cables, you can use tone locators. A *toner* is a generic term for two separate devices that are used together: a tone generator and a tone probe. These two devices are often referred to as *Fox and Hound,* the brand name of a popular toner made by Triplett Corporation. The tone generator connects to a cable with alligator clips, tiny hooks, or a network jack, and it sends an electrical signal

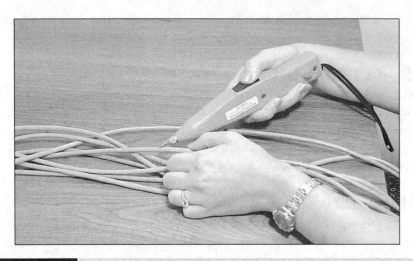

FIGURE 11.1 A tone locator in use

along the wire at a certain frequency. A tone probe emits a sound if it comes close to the cable to which the tone generator is connected (see Figure 11.1).

To trace a cable, you connect the tone generator to it and then move the tone probe next to all the possible cables. The tone probe makes a sound when it is next to the right cable. More advanced toners include phone jacks, enabling the person manipulating the tone generator to communicate with the person manipulating the tone probe: "Jim, move the tone generator to the next port!" Some toners have one probe working with multiple generators. Each generator emits a different frequency, and the probe emits a different sound for each frequency. Good toners cost around US$75. Bad toners can cost less than US$25, but usually don't work very well. If you want to support a network, you'll need to own a toner.

Together, a good, medium-priced cable tester and a good toner are the most important tools used by folks who support, but don't install, networks. Be sure to add a few extra batteries—avoid the frustration of sitting on the top of a ladder holding a cable tester or toner that has just run out of juice!

Cable Testers

As the name implies, cable testers test cables. But before we can talk about cable testers, we have to determine what makes a cable bad. When troubleshooting cables, ask the following questions:

- How long is this cable?
- Is it over its rated length?

- Are any of the wires broken?
- If there is a break, where is it?
- Are any of the wires shorted together?
- Are any of the wires not in the correct order?
- Is there too much electrical or radio interference from external components?

Cable testers are designed to answer some or all of these questions, depending on the amount of money you are willing to pay. The low end of the cable-tester market consists of devices that test only for broken wires; these testers are often called *continuity testers*. Some cheap testers will also test for improperly wired cables, such as having the wires in a different order at either end, or they may test for shorts in the cable (see Figure 11.2).

Exam Tip

A *certifier* is a normal cable tester that will also report on characteristics such as speed and duplex settings. You might see this on the CompTIA Network+ exam as a *cable certifier*.

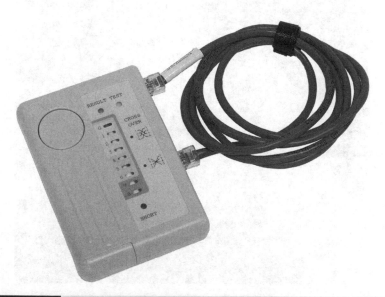

FIGURE 11.2   A simple cable tester

These cheap testers usually require you to insert both ends of the cable into the tester. That can be a little bit tough if the cable is already installed in the wall! A number of testers come in two parts so that you can connect the tester to a cable in the wiring room while taking the other part of the tester to the wall jack (located elsewhere) for that cable.

Medium-priced testers add the ability to tell you the length of the cables by switching the mode of the tester to what is usually known as the "length" mode. They also tell you where a break or short is located in a cable. These are generically called *time-domain reflectometers,* or *TDRs* (see Figure 11.3). *Optical time-domain reflectometers* (OTDRs) serve the same purpose as TDRs, but are used for fiber-optic cabling.

The medium-priced testers have a small loopback device that gets inserted into the far end of the cable, enabling the tester to work with installed cables. This is the type of tester that you want. With a basic unit, you can plug in both ends of a patch lead, and the tester will check for correct wiring and open or

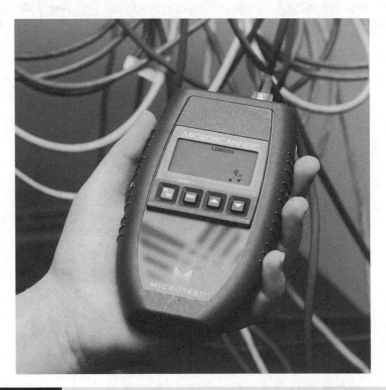

FIGURE 11.3   Time-domain reflectometer

short circuits. If you are testing a wall port, you generally fit a loopback plug into the socket at the other end to complete the circuit and enable testing.

A combination of troubleshooting methodology and test equipment will enable you to determine whether a particular cable is bad. In most trouble-shooting situations, you will use other clues to determine whether you have a hardware or software problem. In the "I can't log in" scenario, for example, if you have determined that everyone else in the area can log in and that this user can log on from another location, you have narrowed the problem either to a configuration or hardware issue. If all network activity is broken (that is, if nothing is available on the network, or you can't ping the default gateway), you may choose to test cables by connecting the PC to the server. This is not the only option, but it is one variable that can be tested and eliminated.

> **Travel Advisory**
>
> When troubleshooting network problems, don't forget to check the simple stuff first—you can save yourself a lot of time. For example, make sure that cables are physically connected, or verify that the printer is online before trying more complicated solutions.

Multimeters

A multimeter, shown in Figure 11.4, can be used to test a cable or bus segment for open or short circuits by testing an electrical characteristic called *resistance*, which is measured in *ohms*. A good cable will have close to zero resistance (0 ohms) between its ends (pin 1 to pin 1 on a UTP cable). A faulty or broken cable will show a higher-than-normal resistance—anything above a few ohms to infinity.

> **Exam Tip**
>
> A multimeter and a voltage event recorder can measure voltage.

Certifiers

The process of verifying that every cable run meets the exacting TIA/EIA stand-ards requires very powerful testing tools, generally known as *cable certifiers* or just *certifiers*. Cable certifiers can do the high-end testing as well as generate a

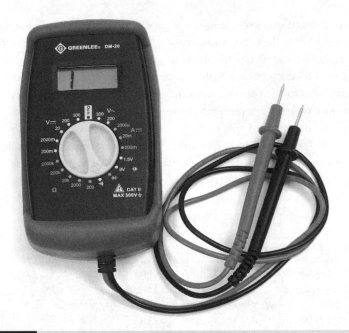

report that a cable installer can print out and hand to a customer to prove that the installed cable runs pass TIA/EIA standards.

> **Exam Tip**
>
> A certifier is a normal cable tester that will also report on characteristics such as speed and duplex settings. You might see this on the CompTIA Network+ exam as a cable certifier.

Objective 11.03 Troubleshooting Wireless Issues

Wireless networks are pretty magical when they work right, but the nature of no wires often makes them vexing things to troubleshoot when they don't. As with any troubleshooting scenario, your first step in troubleshooting a wireless network is to break down your tasks into logical steps. First, figure out the scope of the wireless networking problem.

Signal Loss

802.11 is a collection of standards that deal with radio frequencies that have limited ranges. If the WAP doesn't have enough power, you'll have signal loss and you won't be able to access the wireless network. There are a number of issues that cause power levels to drop too low to connect beyond the obvious "you're too far away" from the WAP. If you lack enough signal power, you have five choices: get closer to the WAP, avoid dead spots, turn up the power, use a better antenna, or upgrade to a newer 802.11 version (such as 802.11n or 802.11ac) with features that enable power to be used more efficiently.

Interference

Radio frequency interference (RFI) is an equally big problem when it comes to wireless network slowdowns. The 802.11 standard is pretty impressive in its ability to deal with noisy RF environments, but there's a point where any environment gets too noisy for 802.11. Interference comes from a number of sources, but basically we can break them down into two categories: RFI from non-Wi-Fi sources and RFI from Wi-Fi networks.

Non-Wi-Fi sources of RFI include lighting and low-power RF devices such as Bluetooth, wireless phones, and microwaves. In general these devices can work nicely with 802.11 networks, but too many devices, especially devices too close to 802.11 equipment, can cause problems. The only way to eliminate this type of interference is to shut down or move the devices.

When it comes to 802.11-based interference, we are looking mainly at other WAPs generating signals that interfere with ours. The most common problem is that the limited number of 2.4-GHz channels and their natural overlap makes it easy to form overlapped channels.

A few years ago you could jump from one channel to another, using the classic channels 1, 6, or 11 in the United States, but today the most common method is to simply abandon the 2.4-GHz channel by avoiding 802.11g and head over to more modern 802.11 standards that use the 5-GHz band. The fix to interference (other than avoiding RF reflective surfaces) is to scan for RF sources using some form of RF scanner/analyzer. We measure RFI with the signal-to-noise ratio (SNR). AirMagnet Wi-Fi Analyzer Pro is a popular tool that reports SNR. Use a channel that's not overwhelmed.

Overlapping Channels

If you're working with one of the older 802.11 versions using the 2.4-GHz channel, you may have problems with overlapping channels. All 2.4-GHz channels overlap with their nearest channel neighbors. For example, channel 3 overlaps with channels 1, 2, 4, and 5. Some folks make the mistake of configuring an SSID and setting each WAP only one channel apart. This will lead to connection problems, so always try to stick to using channels 1, 6, and 11 only.

Mismatched Channels

Mismatched channels, when the client is set to use a different channel than the one configured on the access point, may still take place. However, automatic channel selection is now the norm, and mismatched channels are extremely rare. If you suspect this is a problem, set your wireless device to auto channel selection.

Device Saturation

An individual WAP has a very specific amount of bandwidth that depends on the version of 802.11 and the way it is configured. Once you hit the maximum bandwidth, you're going to have network slowdowns as the overworked WAP tries to handle all the incoming wireless connections.

We overwork WAPs in many different ways, but one of the most common is by attaching too many devices to a single SSID over time, what's called *device saturation*. Avoid device saturation by adding more capacity. Careful placement of extra WAPs in high-demand areas is a huge step in the right direction. Usually the best, but most expensive, method is to upgrade your hardware: leaping from the 802.11g standard to the 802.11ac standard alone makes a massive difference in eliminating device saturation.

Bandwidth Saturation

Speaking of 802.11ac, the biggest single issue causing device saturation is the imbalance of many devices using the 2.4-GHz band and only a few devices using the 5.0-GHz band. In almost every midsized or larger wireless network, the 2.4-GHz band is simply filled to capacity, even with careful use of multiple channels, SSIDs, and VPNs. We call this *bandwidth saturation,* and it's a huge issue with 802.11 networks. There is no answer other than to move to the 5.0-GHz band using primarily 802.11ac.

Untested Updates

802.11 is an ever-evolving standard, and manufacturers learned a long time ago to work hard to ensure their devices could evolve with the standard. This means that anyone supporting any 802.11 network is going to find themselves continually updating client firmware/software and WAP firmware. These updates are almost always good, but you need to stay aware of problems.

First, always research and test any update—especially firmware updates, because they aren't too easy to reverse. Untested updates that go into your production network can potentially wreak havoc. If at all possible, run updates on a test network first.

Wrong SSID

It's easy to access the wrong SSID. Some 802.11 clients are notorious for moving their list of discovered SSIDs in such a way that you think you are clicking one SSID when you are actually accidently clicking the wrong one. The only fix to this is to practice diligence when logging onto a new SSID. For example, who hasn't seen SSIDs such as the infamous "attwifi"? This SSID is AT&T's attempt to use all of their clients as hotspots. Sadly, it's a simple process to create an evil twin SSID (described in the upcoming section "Rogue Access Point") to mimic the attwifi SSID and get otherwise unsuspecting people to log into it. Manually entering an SSID can obviously result in a typo. Luckily, in these cases your typo won't accidently land you onto another SSID. You'll just get an error.

Power Levels

Increasing the power is actually not that hard to do, depending on the wireless device. Most WAP manufacturers set their radio power levels relatively low out of the box. A few manufacturers—a great example is Cisco on their high-end WAPs—enable you to increase or to decrease the power. Sadly, very few low-end/SOHO devices have a method to increase radio power using the OEM interface, other than installing third-party firmware updates such as DD-WRT or Tomato.

Open Networks

Open (non-encrypted) 802.11 networks are the bane of users and administrators. The two biggest challenges are how to avoid unintentionally logging into an open network with an SSID identical to one you have in another location, and how to provide security in an open network environment.

It's very common for your wireless device to access open networks with WAPs that use manufacturer default SSID names such as Linksys or D-Link. The danger with these is that bad guys know that most wireless devices, once they have created a profile to connect to one of these default, open SSIDs, will then automatically connect to them again should they ever see one—and bad guys love to use this as a tool to attack these devices.

The second issue with any open wireless is that all of the data is transferred in the clear. It's easy for bad guys to listen in on your transmissions. The only way to avoid this is either to use a VPN or to use a web browser add-on, such as HTTPS Everywhere, that tries to connect you via HTTPS to every web page.

Rogue Access Point

A rogue access point (rogue AP) is simply an unauthorized access point. Rogue access points have tortured every wireless network since the day Linksys came out with the first cheap wireless router back in the early 2000s. Most rogue APs aren't necessarily evil: often they're just a user wanting to connect to the network who innocently installs a WAP in a handy location into the wired network. Evil rogue APs are far more nefarious, acting as a backdoor to a network or a man-in-the-middle attack, grabbing user names and passwords, among other items. The most infamous form of rogue AP is called an *evil twin,* which is a rogue AP that intentionally mimics an existing SSID in order to get people to connect to it instead of the proper WAP. Evil twins work best in unsecured networks such as those you see in airports and hotels.

Wrong Antenna Type

Too many 802.11 installations ignore the antennas, dropping in WAPs using their default antennas. In most cases the omnidirectional antennas that come with WAPs are very good—which is why they are so often the default antennas—but in many cases they are simply the wrong antenna type and need to be replaced. If you're losing signal, don't forget to consider if the antenna is wrong for the wireless setup.

Incompatibilities

Incompatibilities are related to untested updates in that they tend to appear at the same time an update appears. Make sure you are extremely clear on backward compatibility of different 802.11 versions. Also be aware that even in the same type of network there might be incompatibilities. A few years ago I bought what I thought was a dual-band (2.4- and 5.0-GHz) 802.11n WAP. I invested serious money in upgrading my 802.11n NICs in a few clients to accept dual-band. Sadly, it wasn't until I was installing the new WAP that I read in the instructions that the WAP only supported one of the two bands at a time, and was totally incompatible with my new, expensive wireless NICs. Ouch! Too bad I didn't test the WAP before I tried to run it in my production environment.

Wrong Encryption

The term *wrong encryption* can mean one of two things: either you've connected manually to a wireless network and have set up the incorrect encryption type, or you've entered the wrong encryption key. Entering the wrong encryption key is the classic no-errors-but-won't-work issue. In older operating systems, you often would only get one chance to enter a key, and if you failed your only clue was that your client got an APIPA address. Pretty much every wireless NIC is set to DHCP, and if you don't have the right password your client won't get past the WAP to talk to anything on the network, including the DHCP server. Symptoms include not being on network, a continual prompting for a password, and an APIPA address. The solution is simple. Just enter the correct password.

Bounce

Another issue that causes WAPs to be overworked is bounce, which occurs when a signal sent by one device takes many different paths to get to the receiving systems. These multiple signals are hard for an 802.11 receiver to modulate. We minimize this issue first by trying to reduce anything that might reflect a signal. Secondly, we use WAPs with multiple antennas in a process called *multipath*.

MIMO

The 802.11n specification requires all but handheld devices to use multiple antennas to implement a feature called *multiple in/multiple out (MIMO)*, which enables the devices to make multiple simultaneous connections called *streams*. With up to four antennas, 802.11n devices can achieve amazing speeds. They also can implement channel bonding to increase throughput even more. (The official standard supports throughput of up to 600 Mbps, although practical implementation drops that down substantially.)

AP Placement

All wireless access points have antennas that radiate the 802.11 signal to the clients, so the optimal location for a WAP depends on the area you want to cover and whether you care if the signal bleeds out beyond the borders. You also need to use antennas that provide enough signal and push that signal in the proper direction.

Antenna Placement

Optimal antenna placement varies according to the space to fill and security concerns. You can use site survey and wireless analyzer tools to find dead spots and odd corners. Use the right kind of antenna on each WAP to fill in the space.

WAP antennas come in many shapes and sizes. In the early days it was common to see WAPs with two antennas. Some WAPs have only one antenna, and some (802.11n and 802.11ac) have more than two. Even a WAP that doesn't seem to have antennas is simply hiding them inside the case.

Three basic types of antennas are common in 802.11 networks: omnidirectional, unidirectional, and patch.

In general, an omnidirectional antenna radiates outward from the WAP in all directions. For a typical network, you want blanket coverage and would place a WAP with an omnidirectional antenna in the center of the area. This has the advantage of ease of use—anything within the signal radius can potentially access the network.

When you don't necessarily want to broadcast to the world, you can use one or more directional antennas to create a nicely focused network. A unidirectional antenna, as the name implies, focuses a radio wave into a beam of sorts.

Patch antennas are flat, plate-shaped antennas that generate a half-sphere beam. Patch antennas are always placed on walls. The half-sphere is perfect for indoor offices where you want to fill the room with a strong signal but not broadcast to the room behind the patch.

An antenna strengthens and focuses the RF output from a WAP. The ratio of increase—what's called *gain*—is measured in decibels (dB). The gain from a typical WAP is 2 dB, enough to cover a reasonable area, but not a very large room. Increasing the signal requires a bigger device antenna. Many WAPs have removable device antennas. To increase the signal in an unidirectional and centered setup, simply replace the factory device antennas with one or more bigger device antennas. Get a big enough antenna, and you can crank it all the way up to 11!

AP Configuration

With most home networks, you can simply leave the channel and frequency of the WAP at the factory defaults, but in an environment with overlapping Wi-Fi signals, you'll want to adjust one or both features. Using a wireless analyzer, you can see current channel utilization and then change your channel to something that doesn't conflict. To adjust the channel, find the option in the WAP configuration screens and simply change it.

With dual-band 802.11n WAPs, you can choose which band to put 802.11n traffic on, either 2.4 GHz or 5.0 GHz. In an area with overlapping signals, most of the traffic will be on the 2.4-GHz frequency because most devices are either 802.11b or 802.11g. You can avoid any kind of conflict with your 802.11n devices by using the 5.0-GHz frequency band instead.

Thin Client/Thick Client/LWAPP

Any WAP that you can access directly and configure singularly via its own interface is called a *thick client*. A WAP that can only be configured by a wireless controller is called a *thin client*. For years, these centralized configuration methods were proprietary for each wireless manufacturer, making for little or no cross-brand interoperability. This incompatibility in thin and think clients was a common wireless issue back in the day. Today, most manufacturers use the Lightweight Access Point Protocol (LWAPP) to ensure interoperability. Given LWAPP's broad acceptance, most WAPs will accept commands from any wireless controller.

Environmental Factors

Wireless networking range is hard to define. You'll see most descriptions listed with qualifiers such as "around 150 feet" and "about 300 feet." Wireless range is greatly affected by environmental factors. Interference from other wireless devices and solid objects affects range.

A *dead spot* is what it sounds like—a place that should be covered by the network signal but where devices get no signal. Dead spots just happen in a wireless network due to environmental factors. When installing a network you must watch out for concrete walls, metal (especially metal studs), and the use of special RF-blocking window film. The solution is more careful planning of WAP placement and realizing that even in the best-planned environment it is not at all uncommon to move WAPs based on the need to clear dead spots.

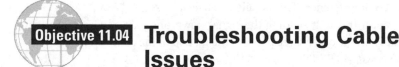 **Objective 11.04** # Troubleshooting Cable Issues

While working through the process of finding a problem's cause, you sometimes need tools. These tools are the software and hardware tools that provide information about your network and enact repairs. The trick is knowing when and how to use these tools to solve your network problems.

Shorts/Opens

A broken cable might have an open circuit, where one or more of the wires in a cable simply don't connect from one end of the cable to the other. The signal lacks continuity. Also, a cable might have a short, where one or more of the wires in a cable connect to another wire in the cable. (Within a normal cable, no wires connect to other wires.) A cable tester can tell you if there is a continuity issue.

Incorrect Termination

If the installation is new and unproven, a perfectly fine network device might be unreachable because of interface errors, meaning that the installer didn't install the wall jack correctly. The resulting incorrect termination might be a mismatched standard (568A rather than 568B, for example). The cable from the wall to the workstation might be bad or might be a crossover cable rather than a straight-through cable. Try another cable.

Crosstalk

The cable might experience *crosstalk,* where the electrical signal bleeds from one wire pair to another, creating interference. Crosstalk poses a threat to properly functioning cable runs. Today's UTP cables consist of four pairs of wires, all squished together inside a plastic tube. When you send a signal down one of these pairs, the other pairs pick up some of the signal. This is called crosstalk.

Every piece of UTP in existence generates crosstalk. Worse, when you crimp the end of a UTP cable to a jack or plug, crosstalk increases. A poor-quality crimp creates so much crosstalk that a cable run won't operate at its designed speed. To detect crosstalk, a normal-strength signal is sent down one pair of wires in a cable. An electronic detector, connected on the same end of the cable as the end emanating the signal, listens on the other three pairs and measures the amount of interference. This is called *near-end crosstalk (NEXT).*

If you repeat this test, sending the signal down one pair of wires, but this time listening on the other three pairs on the far end of the connection, you test for *far-end crosstalk (FEXT).*

EMI/RFI

Outside invisible forces can cause problems with copper cabling. You've read about electromagnetic interference (EMI) and radio frequency interference (RFI) previously in the book. EMI and RFI can disrupt signaling on a copper cable, especially with the very low voltages used today on those cables. These are crazy things to troubleshoot.

Distance Limitations

UTP cabling cannot meet the needs of every organization. The 100-meter distance limitation of UTP-based networks is inadequate for networks covering large buildings or campuses.

Attenuation/dB Loss

Attenuation is the weakening of a signal as it travels long distances. As a cable run gets longer, the attenuation increases, and the signal becomes more susceptible to crosstalk. A tester must send a signal down one end of a wire, then the next, and then repeat this process for every pair in the UTP cable.

Bad Wiring/Bad Connector

If your problem system is clearly not connecting, eliminate the possibility of a failed switch or other larger problem by checking to make sure other people can access the network, and that other systems can access the shared resource (server) that the problem system can't see. Make a quick visual inspection of the cable running from the back of the PC to the outlet.

Finally, if you can, plug the system into a known-good outlet and see if it works. A good network tech always keeps a long patch cable for just this purpose. If you get connectivity with the second outlet, you should begin to suspect bad wiring in structured cable running from the first outlet to the switch. Or, it could be a bad connector. Assuming the cable is installed properly and has been working correctly before this event, a simple continuity test will confirm your suspicion in most cases.

Split Pair

Is the signal from any of the pairs in the same cable interfering with another pair? This common problem in UTP installations is called a split pair. A variety of cable testers, including time domain reflectometers and optical time domain reflectometers, can be used to test for split pairs as well as other issues discussed earlier (continuity, shorts, attenuation, and crosstalk).

TX/RX Reversed

Make sure you insert the wires according to the same standard (TIA/EIA 568A or TIA/EIA 568B) on both ends of the cable. If you don't, you might end up swapping the sending and receiving wires (known as TX/RX reversed) and inadvertently creating a crossover cable.

Incorrect VLAN Assignment

If you configure a switch port for VLAN 101, when in fact it should be configured for VLAN 102, the machine connecting to that switch port will not have access to the resources associated with VLAN 102. This could mean a sales employee might not have access to sales resources, but might actually get access to management resources.

Cable Placement

The right patch cables need to be plugged into the right ports. If a patch cable is placed into a port associated with a different VLAN that a user should be on (the accounting VLAN instead of the marketing VLAN, for instance), users will not have access to resources they need. Such cable placement errors show up pretty quickly and are readily fixed. Keep proper records of patch cable assignments and plug the cables into the proper ports.

SFP/GBIC Transceiver Problems— Cable Mismatch

Just like with copper wire, various imperfections in the media—the glass fiber, in this case—cause signal loss over distance. A lot of factors come into play. Broken cables or open connections obviously stop signals. The typical transceivers, small form-factor pluggable (SFP) or gigabit interface converter (GBIC), can have problems. When you're checking for a bad SFP/GBIC, you'll need to check both the connector and the cable going into that connector. Either or both could cause the signal loss.

Physical or Signal Mismatch Fiber networks have a relatively small number of connectors but offer a pretty wide variety of signal types that use those connectors. These variations come into play in several ways. First, just because you can connect to a particular SFC or GBIC, that doesn't mean the signal will work. Plugging a generic SFC into a Cisco switch might work in a physical sense, but if the switch won't play with anything but Cisco technology, you'll get a mismatch.

Likewise, you can find fiber connectors such as SC and LC that will attach to single-mode or multimode fiber. Plugging a single-mode cable into a switch that expects multimode? Such a cable mismatch or fiber mismatch means your network—at least that portion of it—won't work.

Wavelength Mismatch

Different runs of fiber use different wavelength signals. You might be able to plug an LC connector into a switch just fine, for example, but if the signal starts at 1310 nm and the switch expects 1530 nm, that sort of wavelength mismatch will stop the transmission cold.

Connector Issues

A dirty connector can cause pretty serious signal loss with fiber. It's important not to smudge the glass! When you think about fiber-optic cables, you need to remember that the part that carries the signal is really tiny, only a few microns. When you're connecting two pieces of fiber, even a small connector mismatch in either the cladding (the outside) or the core (the inside) can cause serious losses.

Bend Radius

Every piece of fiber has a certain bend radius limitation. If you bend a fiber-optic cable too much, you get light leakage, which means that part of the signal goes out the cable rather than arriving at the end. That's not a good thing.

Distance Limitations

Finally, check the coupler if one is used to extend a cable run. *Couplers* are small devices with two female ports that enable you to connect two pieces of cable together to overcome distance limitations. UTP couplers are most common, but you can find couplers for every type of network: fiber couplers and even coaxial or BNC couplers. The plastic UTP couplers are relatively easily broken if exposed to humans.

Objective 11.05 Troubleshooting Network Issues

Incorrect configuration of any number of options in devices can stop a device from accessing resources over a LAN. These problems can be simple to fix, although tracking down the culprit can take time and patience.

Incorrect IP Configuration/Gateway

Aside from obvious physical problems, other hands-on problems you can fix manifest as some sort of misconfiguration. An incorrect IP configuration, such as setting a PC to a static IP address that's not on the same network ID as other resources, would result in a "dead-to-me" network. A similar fate would result from inputting incorrect default gateway IP address information. The system will go nowhere, fast. The fix for these sorts of problems should be pretty obvious to you at this point. Go into the network configuration for the device and put in correct numbers.

Broadcast Storms

A *broadcast storm* is the result of one or more devices sending a nonstop flurry of broadcast frames on the network. The first sign of a broadcast storm is when every computer on the broadcast domain suddenly can't connect to the rest of the network. There are usually no clues other than network applications freezing or presenting "can't connect to..." types of error messages. Every activity light on every node is solidly on. Computers on other broadcast domains work perfectly well.

The trick is to isolate; that's where escalation comes in. You need to break down the network quickly by unplugging devices until you can find the one causing trouble. Getting a packet analyzer to work can be difficult, but at least try. If you can scoop up one packet, you'll know what node is causing the trouble. The second the bad node is disconnected, the network returns to normal. But if you have a lot of machines to deal with and a bunch of users who can't get on the network yelling at you, you'll need help. Call a supervisor to get support to solve the crisis as quickly as possible.

Switching Loops

Also known as a bridging loop, a *switching loop* is when you connect and configure multiple switches together in such a way that causes a circular path to appear. Switching loops are rare because all switches use the Spanning Tree Protocol (STP), but they do happen. The symptoms are identical to a broadcast storm: every computer on the broadcast domain can no longer access the network.

The good part about switching loops is that they rarely take place on a well-running network. Someone had to break something, and that means someone, somewhere is messing with the switch configuration. Escalate the problem, and get the team to help you find the person making changes to the switches.

Duplicate IP

Incorrect configuration of any number of options in a device can stop that device from accessing resources over a LAN. These problems can be simple to fix, although tracking down the culprit can take time and patience.

One of the most obvious errors occurs when you're duplicating machines and using static IP addresses. As soon as you plug in the duplicated machine with its duplicate IP address, the network will howl. No two computers can have the same IP address on a broadcast domain. The fix for the problem— after the face-palm—is to change the IP address on the new machine either to an unused static IP or to DHCP.

Speed/Duplex Mismatch

CompTIA continues to include speed and duplex mismatch as a common network issue, although that's not how networks work today. Every NIC, switch, and router features autosensing and autonegotiating ports. You plug two devices in and, as long as they're not otherwise misconfigured, they'll run at the same speed—most likely at full duplex. It's important to note that if the speeds on the two NICs are mismatched, the link will not come up, but if it's just the duplex that's mismatched, the link will come up but the connection will be erratic. Look for this "common error" on the exam, but not in the real world.

End-To-End Connectivity

The end-to-end principle meant originally that applications and work should happen only at the endpoints in a network. In the early days of networking, this made a lot of sense. Connections weren't always fully reliable and therefore were not good for real-time activity, so the work should get done by the computers at the ends of a network connection. The Internet was founded on the end-to-end principle.

With modern networks such as the Internet, the end-to-end concept has had to evolve. Clearly, anything you do over the Internet goes through many different machines. So, perhaps end-to-end means that the intermediary devices simply don't change the essential data in packets that flow through them.

Add in today, though, the fact that plenty of intermediaries want to do a lot of things to your data as it flows through their devices. Thieves want to steal information. Merchants want to sell you things. Advertisers want to intrude on your monitor. Government agencies want to control what you can see or do, or simply want to monitor what you do for later, perhaps benign purposes. Other intermediaries help create trust bonds between your computer and a secure site so that e-commerce can function.

That dynamic between the fundamental principle of work only happening on the ends of the connection and all the intermediaries facilitating, pilfering, or punctuating is the current state of the Internet. It's the basic tension between ISP companies that want to build in tiered profit structures and the consumers and creators who want Net Neutrality.

From a technician's standpoint, there's not a lot you can do. So, why would CompTIA put end-to-end connectivity as a common network issue in the Network+ exam objectives?

As a common issue, end-to-end connectivity refers to connecting users with essential resources within a smaller network, such as a LAN or a private WAN. In such a scenario, the job of the tech is to ensure connections happen fully. Make sure the proper ports are open on an application server. Make sure the right people have the right permissions to access resources and that whitelist and blacklist ACLs are set up correctly.

Hardware Failure

A hardware failure can certainly make a network device unreachable. Fall back on your CompTIA A+ training for troubleshooting. Check the link lights on the NIC. Try another NIC if the machine seems functional in every other aspect. Also, ping the localhost.

Misconfigured DHCP

Misconfigurations of server settings can block all or some access to resources on a LAN. Misconfigured DHCP settings on a host above can cause problems, but they will be limited to the host. If these settings are misconfigured on the DHCP server, however, many more machines and people can be affected.

Misconfigured DNS

A misconfigured DNS server might direct hosts to incorrect sites or no sites at all. Misconfigured DNS settings on a client will stop name resolution altogether and cause the network to appear to be down for the user.

You'll be clued into such misconfiguration by using ping and other tools. If you can ping a file server by IP address but not by name, this points to DNS issues. Similarly, if a computer fails in discovering neighboring devices/nodes, such as connecting to a networked printer, DHCP or DNS misconfiguration can be the culprit. To fix the issue, go into the network configuration for the client or the server and find the misconfigured settings.

Incorrect Interface/Interface Misconfiguration

One common issue with network appliances is technician error. By default, for example, NAT rules take precedence over an appliance's routing table entries. If the tech fails to set the NAT rule order correctly, traffic that should be routed to go out one interface—such as to the DMZ network—can go out an incorrect interface—such as to the inside network.

Users on the outside would expect a response from something but instead get nothing, all because of a NAT interface misconfiguration.

Interface Errors

If the installation is new and unproven, a perfectly fine network device might be unreachable because of interface errors, meaning that the installer didn't install the wall jack correctly. The resulting incorrect termination might be a mismatched standard (568A rather than 568B, for example). The cable from the wall to the workstation might be bad or might be a crossover cable rather than straight-through cable. Try another cable.

Simultaneous Wired/Wireless Connections

Tina has a wireless network connection to the Internet. She gets a shiny new printer with an Ethernet port, but with no Wi-Fi capability. She wants to print from both her PC and her laptop, so she creates a small LAN: a couple of Ethernet cables and a switch. She plugs everything in, installs drivers, and all is well. She can print from both machines. Unfortunately, as soon as she prints, her Internet connection goes down.

The funny part is that the Internet connection didn't go anywhere, but her simultaneous wired/wireless connections created a network failure. The wired and wireless NICs can't actually operate simultaneously and, by default, the wired connection takes priority in the order in which devices are accessed by network services.

To fix this problem, open Network Connections in the Control Panel. Press the ALT key to activate the menu bar; then select Advanced | Advanced Settings (see Figure 11.5). Change the connection priority in the Advanced Settings

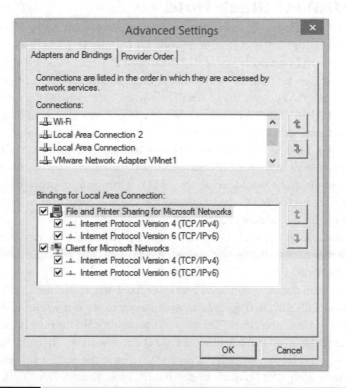

| **FIGURE 11.5** | Network Connections Advanced Settings |

options by selecting the one Tina wants to take priority and clicking the up arrow to move it up the list.

Discovering Neighboring Devices/Nodes

Similarly, if a computer fails in discovering neighboring devices/nodes, such as connecting to a networked printer, DHCP or DNS misconfiguration can be the culprit. To fix the issue, go into the network configuration for the client or the server and find the misconfigured settings.

Power Failure/Power Anomalies

A power failure or power anomalies, such as dips and surges, can make a network device unreachable. We've addressed the fixes for such issues a couple of times already in this book: manage the power to the network device in question and install an uninterruptible power supply (UPS).

MTU/MTU Black Hole

Back in the dark ages (before Windows Vista), Microsoft users often found themselves with terrible connection problems because IP packets were too big to fit into certain network protocols. The largest Ethernet packet is 1500 bytes, so some earlier versions of Windows set their Maximum Transmission Unit (MTU) size to a value less than 1500 to minimize the fragmentation of packets.

The problem cropped up when you tried to connect to a technology other than Ethernet, such as DSL. Some DSL carriers couldn't handle an MTU size greater than 1400. When your network's packets are so large that they must be fragmented to fit into your ISP's packets, this is called an *MTU mismatch*.

As a result, techs would tweak their MTU settings to improve throughput by matching up the MTU sizes between the ISP and their own network. This usually required a manual registry setting adjustment.

Around 2007, Path MTU Discovery (PMTU), a method to determine the best MTU setting automatically, was created. PMTU works by adding a new feature called the "Don't Fragment" (DF) flag to the IP packet. A PMTU-aware operating system can automatically send a series of fixed-size ICMP packets (basically just pings) with the DF flag set to another device to see if it works. If it doesn't work, the system lowers the MTU size and tries again until the ping is successful. Imagine the hassle of incrementing the MTU size manually. That's the beauty of PMTU—you can automatically set your MTU size to the perfect amount.

Unfortunately, PMTU runs under ICMP; most routers have firewall features that, by default, are configured to block ICMP requests, making PMTU worthless. This is called a *PMTU* or *MTU black hole*. If you're having terrible connection problems and you've checked everything else, you need to consider this issue. In many cases, going into the router and turning off ICMP blocking in the firewall is all you need to do to fix the problem.

Missing IP Routes

An access control list (ACL) might include addresses to block that shouldn't be blocked or allow access to network resources for nodes that shouldn't have it. A misconfiguration can lead to missing IP routes so that some destinations just aren't there for users.

NIC Teaming Misconfiguration

Manufacturers came up with ways to use multiple NICs in tandem to increase bandwidth in smaller increments—what's called *link aggregation* or *NIC teaming*. Numerous protocols enable two or more connections to work together simultaneously, such as the vendor-neutral IEEE 802.3ad specification Link Aggregation Control Protocol (LACP) and the Cisco-proprietary Port Aggregation Protocol (PAgP). Let's focus on the former for a common network issue scenario.

To enable LACP between two devices, such as the switch and file server, each device needs two or more interconnected network interfaces configured for LACP. When the two devices interact, they will make sure they can communicate over multiple physical ports at the same speeds and form a single logical port that takes advantage of the full combined bandwidth (see Figure 11.6).

Those ports can be in one of two modes: active or passive. Active ports want to use LACP and send special frames out trying to initiate creating an aggregated logical port. Passive ports wait for active ports to initiate the conversation before they will respond.

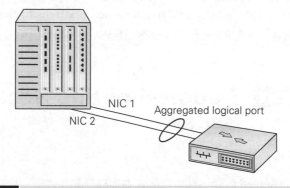

NIC 1
NIC 2
Aggregated logical port

FIGURE 11.6 LACP

So here's the common network error with LACP setups: An aggregated connection set to active on both ends (active-active) automatically talks, negotiates, and works. One set to active on one end and passive on the other (active-passive) will talk, negotiate, and work. However, if you set both sides to passive (passive-passive), neither will initiate the conversation, and LACP will not engage. Setting both ends to passive when you want to use LACP is an example of NIC teaming misconfiguration.

Multicast vs. Broadcast

NIC teaming provides many more benefits than just increasing bandwidth, such as redundancy. You can team two NICs in a logical unit, but set them up with one NIC as the primary (live) and the second as the hot spare (standby). If the first NIC goes down, the traffic will automatically flow through the second NIC. In a simple network setup for redundancy, you'd make one connection live and the other a standby on each device. Switch A has a live and a standby, Switch B has a live and a standby, and so on.

The key here is that multicast traffic to the various devices needs to be enabled on every device through which that traffic might pass. If Switch C doesn't play nice with multicast and it's connected to Switch B, this can cause multicast traffic to stop. One "fix" for this in a Cisco network is to turn off a feature called IGMP snooping, which is enabled by default on Cisco switches. IGMP snooping is normally a good thing, because it helps the switches keep track of devices that use multicast and filter traffic away from devices that don't.

The problem with turning off IGMP snooping is that the switches won't map and filter multicast traffic. Instead of only sending to the devices that are set up to receive multicast, the switches will treat multicast messages as broadcast messages and send them to everybody. This is a NIC teaming misconfiguration that can seriously degrade network performance.

A better fix would be to send a couple of network techs to change the settings on Switch C and make it send multicast packets properly.

Objective 11.06 # Troubleshooting Security Issues

The very nature of networking makes networks vulnerable. By definition, a network must allow multiple users to access serving systems. At the same time, the network must be protected from harm. Doing so is a big business and part of risk management. Troubleshooting security issues is crucial to keeping the bad guys out and letting the good guys in.

Misconfigured Firewall

The firewalls used in modern networks are essential and flexible tools that are critical for securing our networks. Yet, this flexibility means a misconfigured firewall becomes more likely, and with it a security breach. You should be familiar with a couple issues that can crop up: misconfigured ACLs and misconfigured applications.

When you're troubleshooting hardware firewalls, a common place for misconfigurations to pop up is in the ACLs. Because of "implicit deny," all nonmatching traffic is blocked by default. Therefore, if a newly installed firewall refuses to pass any traffic, check to see if it's missing the "permit any" ACL statement. Furthermore, make sure that no statements were added sequentially after the "permit any" ACL statement, because they will never be reached.

The other source of firewall misconfigurations you should know about concerns applications. With firewalls, "application" means two different things depending on whether you are configuring a network-based firewall or a host-based firewall.

With a network-based firewall, "application," in most situations, can be read as "protocol" or even "port." ACLs on modern firewalls may filter by protocols as well as addresses and ports; therefore, a careless entry blocking an application/protocol/port may inadvertently drop access to an entire class of applications on the network.

With a host-based firewall, "application" has its traditional meaning. A host-based firewall is aware of the actual applications running on the machine it's protecting, not just the traffic's protocol. With this knowledge, the firewall can be configured to grant or deny traffic to individual applications, not just protocols, ports, or addresses. When you're dealing with a misconfiguration here, symptoms are most likely to pop up when an application has been accidently added to the deny list. When this happens, the application will no longer be able to communicate with the network. Fortunately, on a single system the fix is easy: open the firewall settings, look for the application's name or executable, and change the deny to allow.

Malware

The term *malware* defines any program or code (macro, script, and so on) that's designed to do something on a system or network that you don't want to have happen. Malware comes in many forms, such as viruses, worms, macros,

Trojan horses, rootkits, adware, and spyware. We'll examine all these malware flavors in this section.

Virus

A virus is a program that has two jobs: to replicate and to activate. *Replication* means it makes copies of itself, often as code stored in boot sectors or as extra code added to the end of executable programs. A virus is not a stand-alone program but rather something attached to a host file, kind of like a human virus. *Activation* is when a virus does something like erase the boot sector of a drive. A virus only replicates to other applications on a drive or to other drives, such as thumb drives or optical media. It does not replicate across networks. Plus, a virus needs human action to spread.

Worm

A worm functions similarly to a virus, but it replicates exclusively through networks. A worm, unlike a virus, doesn't have to wait for someone to use a removable drive to replicate. If the infected computer is on a network, a worm will immediately start sending copies of itself to any other computers it can locate on the network. Worms can exploit inherent flaws in program code like buffer overflows, where a buffer cannot hold all the data sent to it. Worms, unlike viruses, do not need host files to infect.

Macro

A macro is any type of virus that exploits application macros to replicate and activate. A macro is also programming within an application that enables you to control aspects of the application. Macros exist in any application that has a built-in macro language, such as Microsoft Excel, that users can program to handle repetitive tasks (among other things).

Trojan Horse

A Trojan horse is a piece of malware that looks or pretends to do one thing while, at the same time, doing something evil. A Trojan horse may be a game such as poker or a free screensaver. The sky is the limit. The more "popular" Trojan horses turn an infected computer into a server and then open TCP or UDP ports so a remote user can control the infected computer. They can be used to capture keystrokes, passwords, files, credit card information, and more. Trojan horses do not replicate.

Rootkit

For a virus or Trojan horse to succeed, it needs to come up with some method to hide itself. As awareness of malware has grown, anti-malware programs make it harder to find new locations on a computer to hide. A rootkit takes advantage of very low-level operating system functions to hide itself from all but the most aggressive of anti-malware tools. Worse, a rootkit, by definition, gains privileged access to the computer. Rootkits can strike operating systems, hypervisors, and even firmware.

Adware/Spyware

There are two types of programs that are similar to malware in that they try to hide themselves to an extent. *Adware* is a program that monitors the types of websites you frequent and uses that information to generate targeted advertisements, usually pop-up windows. Many of these programs use Adobe Flash. Adware isn't, by definition, evil, but many adware makers use sneaky methods to get you to use adware, such as using deceptive-looking web pages ("Your computer is infected with a virus—click here to scan NOW!"). As a result, adware is often considered malware. Some of the computer-infected ads actually install a virus when you click them, so avoid these things like the plague. *Spyware* is a function of any program that sends information about your system or your actions over the Internet. The type of information sent depends on the program. A spyware program will include your browsing history. A more aggressive form of spyware may send keystrokes or all of the contacts in your e-mail. Some spyware makers bundle their product with ads to make them look innocuous. Adware, therefore, can contain spyware.

Dealing with Malware

You can deal with malware in several ways, including anti-malware programs, training and awareness, patch management, and remediation.

At the very least, every computer should run an anti-malware program. If possible, add an appliance that runs anti-malware programs against incoming data from your network. Also remember that an anti-malware program is only as good as its updates, which should literally be nightly updates! Users must be trained to look for suspicious ads, programs, and pop-ups, and understand that they must not click these things. The more you teach users about malware, the more aware they'll be of potential threats. Your organization should have policies and procedures in place so everyone knows what to do if they encounter malware. Finally, a good tech maintains proper incident response records to see if any pattern to attacks emerges. He or she can then adjust policies and procedures to mitigate these attacks.

DoS

A *denial of service (DoS)* is a targeted attack by one or more systems against a server or servers that provide some form of service on the Internet. A *distributed denial of service (DDoS)* uses a vast number of zombified systems (called a *botnet)* to attack a more robust target. ACLs and firewalls go a long way toward stopping a DoS.

Unneeded Running Services

Unneeded running services give attackers opportunities to attack by exploiting open ports and propagating malware. Shut them down. Any open ports on a system give attackers a potential attack vector. Close the ports by shutting down the associated service.

ICMP-Related Issues

Many years ago, ping had a bug that allowed malicious users to send malformed ping packets to a destination. This "ping of death" would cause the recipient computer to crash. This issue was long ago fixed, and you'll only hear this term from ancient techs—and you'll see it on the CompTIA Network+ exam.

CompTIA uses the term *unreachable default gateway* as an ICMP-related issue. If you ping the default gateway and get a "Destination host unreachable" response, you could infer that the default gateway is unreachable.

Unpatched Firmware/OS

Unpatched firmware presents a little more of a challenge. Most firmware never needs to be or gets patched, but once in a while you'll run into devices that have a discovered flaw or security hole. These you'll need to patch.

The process of patching device firmware varies from device to device, so you'll need to do some research on each. In general, you'll download a patch from the manufacturer and run it on the device. Make sure you have good power before you start the patch. If something goes wrong in the update, you'll brick whatever device you're trying to patch. There's no undo or patch rollback with firmware, so patch only when necessary.

Legacy systems are a different issue altogether. By "legacy" I mean systems that are no longer supported by the OS maker and are no longer patched. In that case, you need to consider the function of the systems and update them if possible. If updating is not possible, you need to isolate the legacy systems behind some type of firewall that will give them the support they need. Equally, you need to be extremely careful about adding any software or hardware to the systems because doing so might create even more vulnerabilities.

Malicious Users

Much more worrisome than accidental accesses to unauthorized resources are those who consciously attempt to access, steal, and/or damage resources. CompTIA calls these folks "malicious users," but they go by many names, often including the term "actors." Malicious actors may represent an external or internal threat.

What do malicious users want to do? If they are intent on stealing data or gaining further access, they may try packet sniffing. This is difficult to detect, but as you know from previous chapters, encryption is a strong defense against sniffing. One of the first techniques that malicious users try is to probe hosts to identify any open ports. Many tools are available to poll all stations on a network for their up/down status and for a list of any open ports (and, by inference, all closed ports too). Angry IP Scanner is a great tool for troubleshooting hosts, but it can be used for these types of malevolent activities.

Trusted and Untrusted Users

A worst-case scenario from the perspective of security is unsecured access to private resources. A couple of terms come into play here. There are trusted users and untrusted users. A *trusted user* is an account that has been granted specific authority to perform certain or all administrative tasks. An *untrusted user* is just the opposite: an account that has been granted no administrative powers.

Trusted users with poor password protection or other security leakages can be compromised. Untrusted users can be upgraded "temporarily" to accomplish a particular task and then forgotten.

Consider this situation: A user accidently copied a bunch of files to several shared network repositories. The administrator does not have time to search for and delete all of the files. The user is granted deletion capability and told to remove the unneeded files. Do you feel a disaster coming? The newly created trusted user could easily remove the wrong files. Careful management of trusted users is the simple solution to these types of threats.

Authentication Issues

Identification is saying you are someone. Authentication is proving it. The authentication process, therefore, needs to be carefully controlled or else someone could actually prove that they are you.

Default Settings, Passwords, Accounts, and Groups

Some configurable devices, such as multilayer switches, have default passwords and default settings, both of which can create an inadvertent insider threat if not addressed. People sometimes can't help but be curious. A user might note the IP address of a switch on his network, for example, and run Telnet or SSH "just to see." Because it's so easy to get the default passwords/settings for devices with a simple Google search, that information is available to the user. One change on that switch might mean a whole lot of pain for the network tech or administrator who has to fix things.

Tight control of user accounts helps prevent unauthorized access or improper access. *Unauthorized access* means a person does something beyond his or her authority. *Improper access* occurs when a user who shouldn't have access gains access through some means. Often the improper access happens when a network tech or administrator makes a mistake.

Dealing with such authentication issues is pretty straightforward. Before bringing any system online, change any default accounts and passwords. This is particularly true for administrative accounts. Also, disable or delete any "guest" accounts.

Watch out for other default user accounts and groups—they can grant improper access or secret backdoor access to your network! All network operating systems have a default Everyone group, and it can easily be used to sneak into shared resources. This Everyone group, as its name implies, literally includes anyone who connects to that resource. Some versions of Windows give full control to the Everyone group by default. All of the default groups—Everyone, Guest, Users—define broad groups of users. Never use them unless you intend to permit all those folks to access a resource. If you use one of the default groups, remember to configure it with the proper permissions to prevent users from doing things you don't want them to do with a shared resource!

AAA

Implementing AAA, as discussed in Chapter 9, brings a number of challenges. For example, configuring a switch for AAA—especially the first time—almost guarantees that you'll run into plenty of TACACS+/RADIUS misconfiguration issues. Although it's impossible to name every possible misconfiguration issue, here are three common ones:

- **Failing to point the switch to the correct RADIUS/TACACS+ server**   You need to give the switch the right IP address. It's a simple issue, but one that often happens.
- **Improperly configuring the correct authentication method for the switch**   If you configure the switch for EAP-PEAP and the server is expecting EAP-TLS, it won't work properly. If you want to use a certificate-based authentication, you'll need a valid certificate that the server can use.
- **Failing to give the switch proper security policies on the server**   In this case, the switch won't be allowed to do its job.

Again, the list of misconfiguration issues setting up AAA is vast. The secret to dealing with these problems is locating and reading errors that come up on the switch and the AAA server. If a switch can get to the AAA server, then all the errors you need to know will be neatly listed for you on the server itself. How these errors manifest varies by the brand of AAA server you use. For example, Microsoft's RADIUS server (called Network Policy and Access Services) places all authentication errors in the Event Viewer. It's going to take some research and practice on your part, but once you have your misconfiguration issues handled, most AAA systems tend to run invisibly for years. (CompTIA drops the + symbol when discussing TACACS.)

One of the really cool things about switch- and router-level authentication is the ability to fall back or fail over to a "next method" of authentication. You can configure as many fallback methods as you like, as long as the method is supported by the switch you configure. The system attempts to authenticate using the first method in a list. If that first method isn't available (for instance, if the RADIUS server is down), the system reverts to the second method in the list, and so forth.

ARP Issues

The problem with Address Resolution Protocol (ARP) is that there is no security. Any device that can get on a LAN can wreak havoc with ARP requests and responses. For example, ARP enables any device at any time to announce its MAC address without first getting a request. Additionally, ARP has a number of very detailed but relatively unused specifications. A device can just declare itself to be a "router." How that information is used is up to the writer of the software used by the device that hears this announcement. Fifteen years ago ARP poisoning caused a tremendous amount of trouble. The nature of ARP means it still has the same ARP issues today.

Banner Grabbing/OUI

Having found an open port, another way for a malicious user to gain information and additional access is to probe a host's open ports to learn details about running services. This is known as *banner grabbing*. For instance, a host may have a running web server installed. Using a utility such as Telnet or Netcat, a malicious user can send an invalid request to port 80 of the server. The server may respond with an error message indicating the type and version of web server software that is running. With that information, the malicious actor can then learn about vulnerabilities of that product and continue their pursuit. The obvious solution to port scanning and banner grabbing is to not run unnecessary services (resulting in an open port) on a host and to make sure that running processes have current security patches installed.

In the same vein, a malicious user may attempt to exploit known vulnerabilities of certain devices attached to the network. MAC addresses of Ethernet NICs have their first 24 bits assigned by the IEEE. This is a unique number assigned to a specific manufacturer and is known as the *organizationally unique identifier (OUI)*, sometimes called the *vendor ID*. By issuing certain ICMP messages such as broadcasted ARP and RARP packets, a malicious user can collect all of the OUI numbers of the wired and wireless nodes attached to a network or subnetwork. Using common lookup tools, the malicious user can identify devices by OUI numbers assigned to particular manufacturers, such as those assigned to Apple and used in a certain generation of iPad.

Domain/Local Group Configurations

The CompTIA Network+ objectives call the proper setup of groups "domain/local group configurations." Kind of a mouthful, but it gets the point across.

A user account is just information: nothing more than a combination of a user name and password. Like any important information, it's critical to control who has a user account and to track what these accounts can do. Access to user accounts should be restricted to the assigned individuals (no sharing, no stealing), and those accounts should have permission to access only the resources they need, no more. This control over what a legitimate account can do is called the principle of least privilege approach to network security and is, by far, the most common approach used in networks.

Tight control of user accounts helps prevent unauthorized access or improper access. Unauthorized access means a person does something beyond his or her authority to do. Improper access occurs when a user who shouldn't have access gains access through some means. Often the improper access happens when a network tech or administrator makes a mistake.

Disabling unused accounts is an important first step in addressing these problems, but good user account control goes far deeper than that. One of your best tools for user account control is to implement groups. Instead of giving permissions to individual user accounts, give them to groups; this makes keeping track of the permissions assigned to individual user accounts much easier.

Once a group is created and its permissions are set, you can then add user accounts to that group as needed. Any user account that becomes a member of a group automatically gets the permissions assigned to that group.

Objective 11.07 Troubleshooting WAN Issues

Competent network techs can recognize and deal with typical remote connectivity issues in a WAN setting. Sometimes the problem lies well beyond the job description, but that's when the tech knows to escalate the problem. This section deals with the CompTIA Network+ WAN problem areas.

Loss of Internet Connectivity

Given that the core reason to use all these forms of remote connectivity is to get to the Internet in the first place, I don't look at loss of Internet connectivity as a problem. It's more a symptom. Be sure to watch for WAN scenarios on the CompTIA Network+ exam that really aren't always WAN scenarios.

If you want to connect a computer to the Internet, that computer needs a legitimate IP address, subnet mask, default gateway, and DNS address. These needs don't change whether you connect through a Gigabit Ethernet wired network or through a cable modem. Use the utilities already covered in the book in such a scenario, such as ping, ipconfig, netstat, nslookup, and so forth, to verify that the device has a solid IP connection.

Interference

Interference at the WAN level—at least that CompTIA Network+ techs can fix—generally implies the connection between the LAN and the WAN. The point at which the ISP's responsibility ends and the customer's begins is the *demarc*. On the customer side, the customer premises equipment (CPE) can create problems. In a busy office building, for example, new installations or connections can add electromagnetic interference (EMI) and create disturbances. New things added to old environments, in other words, can create interference in existing networks.

When my company changed locations, for example, the building we moved into had several offices, connected to Internet and corporate WANs with several dedicated T1 lines. With the local cable company offering 100 Mbps connections, we opted to have cable installed in the building for us (T1 at 1.5 Mbps, not so much). If the cable company had not been careful or used properly shielded boxes and cables, this could have wreaked havoc on the other folks in the building.

In a consumer space, the CPE doesn't run into interference that would block connectivity at the demarc, unless you overly broaden the term "interference" to include "failure." Then you can point to the "modem" as the only major failure culprit.

Once you go to the ISP side of the demarc, there's not much interference involved, especially with existing, previously well-functioning networks. Again, WAN interference only happens if you extend the definition to include failure. Then storms, downed power lines, extraterrestrial activity, and so on can cause problems.

In a home network, there are only two times you should worry about interference in a WAN outside the demarc: during installation and when changing the connection in any way. Every form of remote connection has very clear interference tolerances, and you should have the installation tech verify this. Cable and DSL self-installations are a big issue here because most people don't have access to the tools necessary to confirm their PSTN or coax cabling. If I'm installing a new DSL or cable modem, I refuse the self-install option and gladly pay the extra money to verify my cabling can handle the connection.

It's incredibly easy to introduce interference into an otherwise perfectly functioning wired WAN connection by adding splitters, noisy devices, splices, and so on. This is especially true for tech folks (such as your humble author) who have learned this the hard way. In general, be conservative when disturbing your WAN connection and be ready to call support if needed.

> **Exam Tip**
>
> The best way to think of a demarc is in terms of responsibility. If something breaks on one side of the demarc, it's your problem; on the other side, it's the ISP/phone company's problem.

Interface Errors

CompTIA loves to use the term *interface errors* as a catchall to describe the many connections between your computer and the remote connection that enables you to get to the Internet. Think about a typical office environment. When you use DSL or cable or any other form of remote connection, it's very easy to forget all of the LAN connections that make connectivity possible. It's plausible, if you're anything like me, that you'll call an ISP such as Comcast or AT&T and complain, only to find that you don't have a patch cable plugged into the right connection on the back of the computer. Before you blame Comcast or AT&T for losing your connection, make sure to verify that everything on your end is in order. Is the computer properly connected to the LAN? If you are using a router, is it providing good IP information? Can you access the router and see if it is reporting that it has a proper upstream connection? Before you blame the WAN interface, always first confirm everything on the LAN.

It doesn't really matter what type of remote connection you use. There's always a modem. Be careful here: "modem" is the term I use for any box that sits in your location and connects your LAN to the WAN, even if your ISP calls it something more lofty, such as cable modem, router, or customer premises equipment (CPE). Everything said here that references "modem" works for whatever CPE device your ISP provides.

The modem's job is to connect your LAN to the WAN, so by definition it's going to have at least two interfaces: one to the LAN and one to the WAN. First of all, familiarize yourself with the lights on your modem, preferably before you have problems. Any modem is going to have a power LED, link LEDs to both the LAN and the WAN, and some form of activity LED. Study them first when you're looking for interface issues. In almost every case of a bad interface, you'll verify connections and reset the modem.

Be warned that a bad NIC can also generate this "can't see the network" problem. Use the utility provided by your OS to verify that the NIC works. If you've got a NIC with diagnostic software, run it—this software will check the NIC's circuitry. The NIC's female connector is a common failure point, so NICs that come with diagnostic software often include a special test called a *loopback test,* which sends data out of the NIC and checks to see if it comes back. Some NICs perform only an internal loopback, which tests the circuitry that sends and receives, but not the actual connecting pins. A true external loopback requires a loopback plug inserted into the NIC's port (see Figure 11.7). If a NIC is bad, replace it—preferably with an identical NIC so you don't have to reinstall drivers!

At either end of a T1 line, you'll find an unassuming box called a Channel Service Unit/Digital Service Unit (CSU/DSU). The CSU/DSU has a second connection that goes from the phone company (where the boxes reside) to a customer's equipment (usually a router). A T1 connection is point-to-point—you cannot have more than two CSU/DSUs on a single T1 line.

DNS Issues

That said, there is one specific DNS issue that comes up in WANs: choosing what DNS server to use. Every ISP has its own DNS server(s) and, in almost every case, your modem is going to propagate those DNS settings down to every device in your LAN. In most cases there isn't any problem with this, but

FIGURE 11.7 Loopback plug

there are two cases where you might want to consider manually adding DNS to your local devices or your local router. First, an ISP's DNS servers can fail.

Second, some ISPs notoriously use DNS helpers, DNS servers that redirect your browser to advertising when you type in an incorrect URL. So, get yourself a fast public DNS IP address—I love the Google 8.8.8.8 and 8.8.4.4 addresses—and at the very least load one of those as a secondary DNS server.

Split Horizon

When a router learns a route through a certain interface, it will not communicate that route out the same interface. Routing Information Protocol (RIP) has been gone a long time, but for some reason CompTIA keeps split horizon on the objectives. This is not a real-world issue; it's only a CompTIA Network+ exam issue.

Router Configurations

Router configuration issues can be a bit trickier. The ways to mess up a router are many.

Routing Protocols

You can specify the wrong routing protocol, for example, or misconfigure the right routing protocol.

ACLs

An access control list (ACL) might include addresses to block that shouldn't be blocked or allow access to network resources for nodes that shouldn't have it.

Missing Routes

A misconfiguration can lead to missing IP routes so that some destinations just aren't there for users. Improperly configured routers aren't going to send packets to the proper destination. The symptoms are clear: every system that uses the misconfigured router as a default gateway is either not able to get packets out or not able to get packets in—or sometimes both. Web pages don't come up, FTP servers suddenly disappear, and e-mail clients can't access their servers. In these cases, you need to verify first that everything in your area of responsibility works. If that is true, then escalate the problem and find the person responsible for the router.

tracert/traceroute

The key tool for determining a router problem beyond your LAN is tracert/traceroute.

Run traceroute to your default gateway. If that fails, you know you have a local issue and can potentially do something about it. If the traceroute comes back positive, run it to a site on the Internet. A solid connection should return something like Figure 11.8. A failed route will return a failed response.

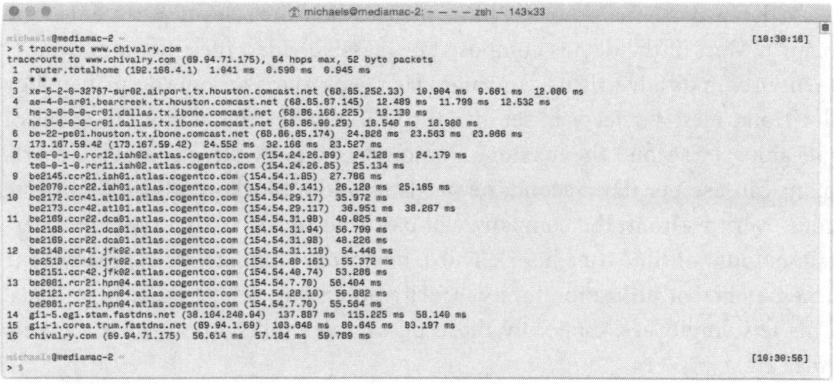

FIGURE 11.8   Good connection

CSU/DSU

Many routers feature two ports on one router, with the dual links providing redundancy if one link goes down. The CSU part of a CSU/DSU protects the T1 or T3 line and the user equipment from lightning strikes and other types of electrical interference. It also stores statistics and has capabilities for loopback testing. The DSU part supplies timing to each user port, taking the incoming user's data signals and converting the input signal into the specified line code and then framing the format for transmission over the provided line.

Copper Line Drivers/Repeaters

Creative companies invented methods to use unshielded twisted pair (UTP) cabling to connect runs longer than Ethernet's 100-meter limit. These devices were called copper line drivers/repeaters, essentially special boxes at each end of the run to manage the much amplified signal. Line drivers enabled installers to avoid using fiber, which was wildly more expensive at the time.

Company Security Policy

Implemented company security policies can make routine WAN connectivity actions completely fail. Here's a scenario: Mike is the head of his company's IT department and he has a big problem—the amount of traffic running between the two company locations is on a dedicated connection and is blowing his bandwidth out of the water! It's so bad that data moving between the two offices will often drop to a crawl four to five times per day. Why are people using so much bandwidth?

As he inspects the problem, Mike realizes that the sales department is the culprit. Most of the data is composed of massive video files the sales department uses in its advertising campaign. He needs to make some security policy decisions. First, he needs to set up a throttling policy that defines in terms of megabits per second the maximum amount of bandwidth any single department can use per day. Second, he needs to add a blocking policy. If anyone goes over this limit, the company will block all traffic of that type for a certain amount of time (one hour). Third, he needs to update his company's fair access policy or utilization limits security policies to reflect these new limits. This lets employees, especially those pesky sales folks, know what the new rules are.

CHECKPOINT

✔**Objective 11.01: Troubleshooting Methodology** Follow the troubleshooting process to find solutions for your network's issues. Begin by identifying the problem. Establish a theory of probable cause, and then test that theory to determine if you were right. Once you've found the cause, establish a plan of action and identify potential effects. Test your solution or escalate the issue to someone else, if needed. Before leaving your client, verify full system functionality, implement preventative measures, and document the outcome.

✔**Objective 11.02: Troubleshooting Tools** Valuable logical networking tools include ipconfig, netstat, ifconfig, ping, tracert, nslookup, arp, pathping, looking glass sites, Wi-Fi analyzers, and protocol analyzers. Valuable physical networking tools include line testers, certifiers, multimeters, cable testers, light meters, and toner probes.

✔**Objective 11.03: Troubleshooting Wireless Issues** Common wireless issues include signal loss, interference, overlapping channels, signal-to-noise-ratio, device saturation, bandwidth saturation, untested updates, wrong SSID, power levels, open networks, rogue access points, wrong antenna types, incompatibles, wrong encryption, bounce, MIMO, AP placement and configuration, environmental factors, and more.

✔**Objective 11.04: Troubleshooting Cable Issues** Cable-related issues include shorts, opens, incorrect termination, crosstalk, distance limitations, attenuation, bad connectors, bad wiring, split pairs, cable placement, and more.

✔**Objective 11.05: Troubleshooting Network Issues** Network-related issues include incorrect IP configuration, broadcast storms, switching loops, speed and duplex mismatch, incorrect VLAN assignment, hardware failure, misconfigured DNS, misconfigured DHCP, and more.

✔**Objective 11.06: Troubleshooting Security Issues** Security-related issues include misconfigured firewall, malware, denial of service, unpatched firmware/OSs, malicious users, authentication issues, and more.

✔**Objective 11.07: Troubleshooting WAN Issues** WAN-related issues include loss of Internet connectivity, DNS issues, interference, router configurations, customer premises equipment, company security policies, satellite issues, and more.

REVIEW QUESTIONS

1. Which of the following is the final step of the troubleshooting model?

   A. Establish a theory of probable cause.

   B. Test the solution.

   C. Document your findings.

   D. Establish a plan of action.

2. In the event of a T1/T3 issue, which of the following should you inspect first?

   A. DNS server

   B. DHCP server

   C. CSU/DSU

   D. Switch

3. Which of the following are open-ended questions? (Select all that apply.)

   A. "Has anything been changed on the system recently?"

   B. "Can you see a power light on the monitor?"

   C. "What lights can you see on the monitor?"

   D. "What happens when you move the mouse?"

4. Which of the following is most likely responsible for a user having an authentication issue and not being able to remotely connect to the company network?

   A. TFTP misconfiguration

   B. RADIUS misconfiguration

   C. DHCP misconfiguration

   D. DNS misconfiguration

5. A user plugged into a certain switch port can't communicate with other nodes on his network. You change the port, and now he can communicate. What was the likely problem?

   A. Incorrect IP assignment

   B. Incorrect gateway assignment

   C. Incorrect DHCP server assignment

   D. Incorrect VLAN assignment

6. Which of the following tools can identify a cabling fault due to an overlong segment?
   A. Multimeter
   B. TDR
   C. Tone locator
   D. Punch-down tool

7. Which of the following is not related to signal bleeding?
   A. SSID
   B. NEXT
   C. FEXT
   D. Crosstalk

8. Which of the following is used to test fiber-optic cabling?
   A. Multimeter
   B. Butt set
   C. OTDR
   D. TDR

9. Which of the following is not an issue related to an open Wi-Fi network?
   A. Rogue AP
   B. Evil twin
   C. Crosstalk
   D. No encryption

10. Which of the following utilities can show you exactly where a problem in communication might be?
    A. ping
    B. netstat
    C. tracert
    D. arp

REVIEW ANSWERS

1. **C** Once you have solved the problem, always document your findings so that you or someone else may more quickly come to a solution the next time.

2. **C** CSU/DSU devices translate between the LAN and WAN.

3. **C** **D** Any question that cannot be answered with a "yes" or "no" is an open-ended question.

4. **B** RADIUS servers manage remote access.

5. **D** The cable was originally plugged into a port that wasn't on the same VLAN as other devices on the subnet.

6. **B** A TDR can accurately measure segment length. A multimeter can't.

7. **A** The Service Set Identifier is the name of a wireless network.

8. **D** An optical time-domain reflectometer (OTDR) tests fiber-optic cabling.

9. **C** Crosstalk deals with signals in the wires of cables.

10. **C** The tracert/traceroute utility identifies all hops between a source and destination.

Network
Management

	NEWBIE	SOME EXPERIENCE	EXPERT
ETA	4 hours	2 hours	1 hour

A modern network doesn't behave properly without regular (and sometimes irregular) intervention from network technicians. Techs need to install network management tools and then deploy other tools to monitor, troubleshoot, and optimize networks over time. Because IP networks dominate today, we have a standard set of free tools to accomplish these goals.

This chapter looks first at network policies and procedures. Documentation between a company and another company, such as a service provider, sets the expectations between the two organizations. After those agreements are in place, electrical, physical, and installation safety details should be determined. Emergency procedures and HVAC configurations should be constructed. After these topics are explored, the chapter continues the progression of setting up network management by exploring segmentation, patching, and updating. Then, wireless configuration and management is explored, followed by network monitoring, change, and configuration management.

Objective 12.01 Network Policies and Procedures

When you're dealing with a service provider, or another company that has a relationship with yours, expectations need to be clearly documented before the relationship is formed. Nothing should be left to chance with safety, in terms of electrical safety, physical safety, and installation safety. Emergency procedures and HVAC configurations are also very important considerations, long before any packets are sent across your network!

Standard Business Documents

Dealing with third-party vendors is an ongoing part of any organization. When you are dealing with third parties, you must have some form of agreement that defines the relationship between you and the third party. The CompTIA Network+ exam expects you to know about four specific business documents: a service level agreement, a memorandum of understanding, a multi-source agreement, and a statement of work.

Service Level Agreement

A *service level agreement (SLA)* is a document between a customer and a service provider that defines the scope, quality, and terms of the service to be provided.

SLAs are common in the IT world, given the large number of services provided. Some of the more common SLAs in the IT world are provided by ISPs to customers. A typical SLA from an ISP contains the following:

- **Service provided**   Defines the minimum and/or maximum bandwidth and describes any recompense for degraded services or downtime.
- **Equipment**   Defines what equipment, if any, the ISP provides. It also specifies the type of connections to be provided.
- **Technical support**   Defines the level of technical support that will be given, such as phone support, web support, and in-person support. This also defines costs for that support.

Memorandum of Understanding

A *memorandum of understanding (MOU)* is a document that defines an agreement between two parties in situations where a legal contract wouldn't be appropriate. An MOU defines the duties the parties commit to perform for each other and a time frame for the MOU. An MOU is common between companies that have only occasional business relations with each other. For example, all of the hospitals in a city might generate an MOU to take on each other's patients in case of a disaster such as a fire or tornado. This MOU would define costs, contacts, logistics, and so forth.

Multi-source Agreement

Manufacturers of various network hardware agree to a *multi-source agreement (MSA)*, a document that details the interoperability of their components. For example, two companies might agree that their gigabit interface converters (GBICs) will work in Cisco and Juniper switches.

Statement of Work

A *statement of work (SOW)* is in essence a legal contract between a vendor and a customer. An SOW defines the services and products the vendor agrees to supply and the time frames in which to supply them. A typical SOW might be between an IT security company and a customer. An SOW tends to be a detailed document, clearly explaining what the vendor needs to do. Time frames must also be very detailed, with milestones through the completion of the work.

Electrical Safety

Electrical safety in a networking environment covers several topics: the inherent danger of electricity, grounding, and static.

As you'll recall from Science 101, electricity can shock you badly, damage you, or even kill you. Therefore, keep the networking closet or room clear of clutter, and never use frayed cords. Use the same skills you use to avoid getting cooked by electricity in everyday life.

It is very important with networking to use properly grounded circuits. This is more a data safety issue than a personal safety issue. Poorly grounded circuits can create a ground loop—where a voltage differential exists between two parts of your network. This can cause data to become unreadable. Improper grounding also exposes equipment to more risk from power surges.

Electrostatic discharge (ESD)—the passage of a static electrical charge from one item to another—can damage or destroy computing equipment. It's important to wear a properly connected anti-ESD wrist strap when replacing a NIC or doing anything inside a workstation.

The risks from ESD get a lot smaller when you stop opening up computing machines. Routers, switches, and other networking boxes are enclosed and thus protected from technician ESD. Even when you insert a module in a router or switch, the rack is metal and protected, and the box should be attached to the rack and thus grounded too.

Physical/Installation Safety

IT techs live in a dangerous world. We're in constant danger of tripping, hurting our backs, and getting burned by hot components. You also need to keep in mind what you wear (in a safety sense). Let's take a moment to discuss these physical safety issues and what to do about them.

If you don't keep organized, hardware technology will take over your life.

Cable messes such as these are dangerous tripping hazards. Although I may allow a mess like this in my home office, all cables in a business environment are carefully tucked away behind computer cases, run into walls, or placed under cable runners. If you see a cable that is an obvious tripping hazard, contact the person in charge of the building (CompTIA calls these folks "building services") to take care of it immediately. The results of ignoring such hazards can be catastrophic.

Another physical safety issue is lifting equipment. Computers, printers, routers—everything we use—all seem to come to us in heavy boxes. Remember, never lift with your back; lift with your legs, and always use a hand truck if available. You are never paid enough to risk your own well-being. Lifting is an important consideration in an important part of a network tech's life: working with racks.

Rack Installation and Maintenance

Installing components into a rack isn't too challenging of a process. Standard 19-inch equipment racks are designed to accept a tremendous amount of abuse, making it sometimes far too easy for people to use them in ways where failure is almost a guarantee. In general, you need to keep in mind three big areas when using rack-mounted equipment: power, mounting, and environment.

The placement of a rack should *optimize the airflow* in a server area. All racks should be placed so that components draw air in from a shared cool row and then exhaust the hot air into a hot row.

Follow standard safety practices when installing gear, especially if you use power tools. *Tool safety* means, for example, using the properly sized screwdriver head, wearing safety goggles when cutting wires, and not using a band saw to miter joints. The usual practices will get you through any exam question as well as keep you safe in the workplace.

Finally, follow the guidelines in the material safety data sheet (MSDS) for the racks and network components to determine best practices for recycling and so forth. An MSDS details how you should deal with just about any component, including information on replacement parts, recycling, and more.

Emergency Procedures

A final step in managing risk in any company is to have proper *emergency procedures* in place before the emergencies happen. The CompTIA Network+ exam competencies list five essential aspects that should be covered:

* Building layout
* Fire escape plan
* Safety/emergency exits
* Fail open/fail close
* Emergency alert system

HVAC

The heating, ventilation, and air conditioning (HVAC) system should be optimized to recirculate and purify the hot air into cool air in a continuous flow. What's the proper temperature and humidity level? The ideal for the room, regardless of size, is an average temperature of 68 degrees Fahrenheit and

~50 percent humidity. A proper *fire suppression system*—one that can detect fire, cut power to protect sensitive equipment, displace oxygen with fire-suppressing gasses, alert relevant staff, activate sprinklers in a pinch, and so on—is an absolute must for any server closet or room. You need to get any electrical spark out quickly to minimize server or data loss.

Objective 12.02 Network Segmentation, Patching, and Updating

It's pretty easy to say that a network failure isn't a happy occurrence. On the lowest end, losing your network in your home is going to make someone very unhappy when they can't watch the latest episode of *Orange Is the New Black* on Netflix. Taking it to the other extreme, many industrial control systems (ICSs) are incredibly crucial for the needs of everyday living. From the distributed control systems (DCSs) that run an oil refinery to the SCADA systems keeping our electrical infrastructure up and running, the potential downside of a catastrophic failure is far worse than that of missing a show!

Segmentation, which means to logically and/or physically split up a network, is usually associated with security. It can also be done to reduce network congestion and limit network problems. We segment to optimize performance. We segment to be in compliance with standards, laws, or best practices. We also segment for easier troubleshooting.

One of the best tools to help us understand network segmentation is the OSI seven-layer model, in particular the first three layers:

- **Layer 1 (Physical)**   Physically separating your network from every other network. This is also known as an *air gap*.
- **Layer 2 (Data Link)**   Separating a physically connected network into separate broadcast domains. Think VLANs here.
- **Layer 3 (Network)**   Separating broadcast domains by blocking IP routes.
- **Above layer 3**   VPNs, separate SSIDs, separate Windows domains, and virtualization.

Exam Tip

Network segmentation is done for security, performance optimization, load balancing, and compliance.

Segmentation and Industrial Control Systems

All forms of ICS are by definition closed networks. A *closed network* is any network that strictly controls who and what may connect to it. However, there are two places where we begin to see connectivity. In many SCADA systems, it is very convenient to use public wireless networks to connect Remote Terminal Units (RTUs), and, in some cases, we connect SCADA servers to the Internet to provide intranet access. The biggest single line of defense for these two scenarios is the use of virtual private network connections. It's impossible to find any form of SCADA/ICS that doesn't use a VPN in cases where it must be open to the public Internet.

VLANs

To provide a properly segmented network, various departments and components need to be placed into unique *virtual local area networks (VLANs)*. As you'll recall from Chapter 7, VLANs provide much better control over the network, with security and optimized performance.

Some of the VLANs are based on department. The quality assurance (QA) lab doesn't need access to all the same resources as the accounting folks, and vice versa. The testing lab tests software and firmware and has very different needs than other departments.

But take the network segmentation a step further and also create unique VLANs for network services. The wireless network will get its own VLAN, for example, plus we could split it into multiple VLANs to provide support for *separate private/public networks*. That way, visitors will get access to what they need, but not to important internal systems.

Phone connections invariably will have their own VLAN. The same is true of the industrial control systems that take care of the internal functions of the factory and warehouse. This gets complicated fast!

Legacy Systems

If you find yourself having to deal with a mixed network of modern and legacy systems, you should isolate the legacy systems. Use VLANs to implement network segmentation and get those old systems out of the main network.

Honeypots and Honeynets

As described in Chapter 9, a firewall is a bidirectional "filter" system that can prevent access into a network or out of a network. It's a good system, but nothing is foolproof. Any high-value network resource provides sufficient motivation for a nefarious actor to work through the hoops to get at your goodies. Remember that malicious hackers have three primary weapons to gain access to computer assets: expertise, time, and money (to pay others with more expertise and to buy time).

To protect our network from expert hackers with too much time on their hands, we layer roadblocks to exhaust their time. We upgrade those roadblocks, and add more where practical, to defeat a hacker's expertise. We can also use something from our own arsenal that works in conjunction with our roadblocks: a detour.

Have you ever seen one of those sports-type movies where a ragtag team of misfits is playing a pro team? In the beginning of the game the pros are beating the brains out of the misfits. Then, when the misfits have had enough of a drubbing, the captain calls a play to "Let 'em through." The bad guy comes through and gets a pasting or two of his own. The network security equivalents to "Let 'em through" are honeypots and honeynets.

Now, "letting them through" is about choices. A network administrator may elect to make access to honeypots and honeynets an easy thing. Or, the network administrator may lay them out as a reward to a hacker after breaking through the normal protection barriers. This is a choice that depends on a lot of variables. In either case, a *honeypot* is a computer that presents itself as a sweet, tempting target to a hacker but, in reality, is a decoy. Honeypots can be as simple as a "real" network machine with decoy files in it. A text file called PASSWORDS.TXT with fake contents makes for an enticing objective.

Of course, there are much more sophisticated products that can run on a computer as a program or within a virtual machine. These products can mimic all of the features of a real computer asset, including firewalls and other roadblocks to keep a hacker occupied and wasting time on a resource that will yield no value in the end.

Scale up a honeypot to present a complete network as a decoy and you have a *honeynet*. A honeynet, like a honeypot, could be built by constructing an actual network, but that wouldn't be very cost effective. Honeynets can run on a single computer or within a virtual machine and can look like a simple network or a vast installation.

Honeypots and honeynets are useful tools not just in their diversionary value, but in that they can also monitor and report the characteristics of attacks that target them.

When you are deploying honeypots and honeynets, it is critical that they be segmented from any live or production networks. Pure isolation is the ideal goal. Network segmentation can be achieved by creating a disconnected network or assigning the honeypots/honeynets to an isolated VLAN.

Patching and Updates

When we talk about patching and updates, we aren't just talking about the handy tools provided to us by Microsoft Windows or Ubuntu Linux. Almost every piece of software and firmware on almost every type of equipment you own is subject to patching and updating: printers, routers, wireless access points, desktops, programmable logic controllers (PLCs), and so on. Everything needs a patch or update now and then.

Operating System Updates

OS updates are easily the most common type of update. Individuals install automatic updates on their OSs with impunity, but when you're updating a large number of systems, especially critical nodes such as servers, it's never a good idea to apply all OS updates without a little bit of due diligence beforehand. Most operating systems provide some method of network server–based patching, giving administrators the opportunity to test first and then distribute patches when they desire.

All systems use device drivers, and they are another part of the system we often need to patch. In general, we only apply *driver updates* to fix an incompatibility, incorporate new features, or repair a bug. Because device drivers are only present in systems with full-blown operating systems, all OS-updating tools will include device drivers in their updates. Many patches will include feature changes and updates, as well as security vulnerability patches.

Feature Changes/Updates

Feature changes/updates are just what they sound like: They add new functionality to the system. Remember back in the old days when a touchscreen phone only understood a single touch? Then some phone operating system came out to provide multitouch. Competitors responded with patches to their own phone OSs that added the multitouch feature.

Major vs. Minor Updates

All software of any complexity has flaws. For example, hardware changes, exposing flaws in the software that supports that hardware; newer applications create unexpected interactions; security standards change over time. All these factors mean that responsible companies patch their products after they release them. How they approach the patching depends on scope: *major vs. minor updates* require different actions.

Vulnerability Patch

When a major vulnerability to an OS or other system is discovered, vendors tend to respond quickly by creating a fix in the form of a *vulnerability patch.* If the vulnerability is significant, that patch is usually made available as soon as it is complete. Sometimes, these high-priority security patches are even pushed to the end user right away.

Less significant vulnerabilities get patched as part of a regular patch cycle. You may have noticed that on the second Wednesday of each month, Microsoft-based computers reboot. Since October of 2003, Microsoft has sent out patches that have been in development and are ready for deployment on the second Tuesday of the month. This has become known as *Patch Tuesday.* These patches are released for a wide variety of Microsoft products, including operating systems, productivity applications, utilities, and more.

Firmware updates are far less common than software updates and usually aren't as automated (although a few motherboard makers might challenge this statement). In general, firmware patching is a manual process and is done in response to a known problem or issue. Keep in mind that firmware updates are inherently risky, because in many cases it's difficult to recover from a bad patch.

Upgrading vs. Downgrading

Patches, whether major or minor, require thorough testing before techs or administrators apply them to clients throughout the network. Sometimes, though, a hot fix might slip through to patch a security hole that then breaks other things inadvertently. In those cases, by following good patch management procedures, you can roll back—the Windows terminology—or downgrade by removing the patch. You can then push an upgrade when a better patch is made available.

How to Patch

In a network environment, patching is a routine but critical process. Here are a few important steps that take place in almost every scenario of a network patch environment:

- **Research** As a critical patch is announced, it's important to do some research to verify that the patch is going to do what you need it to do and that people who have already installed the patch aren't having problems.
- **Test** It's always a good idea to test a patch on a test system when possible.

- **Configuration backups** Backing up configurations is critical, especially when backing up firmware. The process of backing up a configuration varies from platform to platform, but almost all PCs can back up their system setups, and switches and routers have well-known "backupconfig"-style commands.

Objective 12.03 Wireless Configuration and Management

Installing and configuring a Wi-Fi network requires a number of discrete steps. You should start with a site survey to determine any obstacles (existing wireless, interference, and so on) you need to overcome, and identify the best location for your access points. You'll need to install one or more access points, and then configure both the access point(s) and wireless clients. Finally, you should put the network to the test, verifying that it works as you intended.

Site Survey

The first step of installing a wireless network is the site survey. A *site survey* will reveal any obstacles to creating the wireless network, and will help determine the best possible location for your access points. The main components for creating a site survey are a floor plan of the area you wish to provide with wireless and a site survey tool such as Fluke Network's AirMagnet Survey Pro. Wireless survey tools help you discover any other wireless networks in the area and will integrate a drawing of your floor plan with interference sources clearly marked. This enables you to get the right kind of hardware you need and makes it possible to get the proper network coverage.

Discovering any wireless network signals other than your own in your space enables you to set both the SSID and channel to avoid networks that overlap. One part of any good site survey is a wireless analyzer. A *wireless analyzer* or *Wi-Fi analyzer* is any device that looks for and documents all existing wireless networks in the area. Wireless analyzers are handy tools that are useful for diagnosing wireless network issues and conducting site surveys. You can get dedicated, hand-held wireless analyzer tools, or you can run site survey software on a laptop or mobile wireless device. Wireless survey tools such as AirMagnet Survey Pro always include an analyzer as well.

Wireless networks send out radio signals on the 2.4-, 5.0-, or 60-GHz spectrum using one of a number of discrete channels. In early wireless networks, a big part of the setup was to determine the channels used nearby in order to avoid them. In more modern wireless networks, we rarely adjust channels manually anymore. Instead, we rely on powerful algorithms built into WAPs to locate the least congested channels automatically. The bigger challenge today is the preexistence of many Wi-Fi networks with lots of clients, creating *high device density environments*. You need a wireless solution that handles many users running on the few wireless frequencies available.

Plenty of tools such as AirMagnet Survey Pro support a wireless survey. All good survey utilities share some common ways to report their findings. One of the most powerful reports they generate is called a *heat map*, which is nothing more than a graphical representation of the RF sources on your site, using different colors to represent the intensity of the signal.

As you read about the many speeds listed for 802.11, you need to appreciate that wireless networking has a tremendous amount of overhead and latency. WAPs send out almost continuous streams of packets that do nothing more than advertise their existence or maintain connections. Wireless devices may sometimes stall due to processing or timeouts. The end result is that only a percentage of the total throughput speed is actually achieved in real data bits getting to the applications that need them. The *actual* number of useful bits per second is called the *goodput* of the wireless network.

Like 802.11g, 802.11n WAPs can support earlier, slower 802.11b/g devices. The problem with supporting these older types of 802.11 is that 802.11n WAPs need to encapsulate 802.11n frames into 802.11b or 802.11g frames. This adds some overhead to the process. Worse, if any 802.11b devices join the network, traffic drops to 802.11b speeds. (802.11g devices don't cause this behavior on 802.11n networks.)

To handle these issues, 802.11 WAPs can transmit in three different modes: legacy, mixed, and greenfield. These modes are also sometimes known as connection types.

Legacy mode means the 802.11n WAP sends out separate packets just for legacy devices. This is a terrible way to utilize 802.11n, but it has been added as a stopgap measure if the other modes don't work. In *mixed mode*, also often called *high-throughput* or 802.11a-ht/802.11g-ht, the WAP sends special packets that support the older standards yet also can improve the speed of those standards via 802.11n's wider bandwidth. *Greenfield mode* is exclusively for 802.11n-only wireless networks. The WAP will only process 802.11n frames. Dropping support for older devices gives greenfield mode the best goodput.

Power over Ethernet

Wireless access points need electrical power, but they're invariably placed in strange locations (such as ceilings or high up on walls) where providing electrical power is not convenient. No worries! Better WAPs now support an IEEE standard (802.3af) called *Power over Ethernet (PoE)*, which enables them to receive their power from the same Ethernet cables that transfer their data. The switch that connects the WAPs must support PoE, but as long as both the WAP and the switches to which they connect support PoE, you don't have to do anything other than just plug in Ethernet cables. PoE works automatically. As you might imagine, it costs extra to get WAPs and switches that support PoE, but the convenience of PoE for wireless networks makes it a popular option.

The original PoE standard came out in 2003 with great response from the industry. However, its popularity showed a big problem: the original 802.3af standard only supported a maximum of 15.4 watts of DC power, and many devices needed more. In 2009, 802.3af was revised to output as much as 25.5 watts. This new PoE amendment to 802.3 is called 802.3at, PoE plus, or PoE+.

Bring Your Own Device

Everybody seems to have a smartphone, a tablet, and laptop. These devices rival desktop PCs in sheer computing power and functionality. Integrating them into a corporate network, along with gaming devices and media devices, like Apple TV, can present administrative challenges.

In truth, corporations have included mobile devices into their networking experience for a number of years. The BlackBerry Enterprise Service (BES) software enabled corporations to issue BlackBerrys to users and retain control over how those users could use those mobile devices on their network. This enabled users to get and synchronize company e-mail, calendars, and more with mobile devices and workstations. Because of central control, network admins could allow or deny mobile devices access to network features, what's called *on-boarding and off-boarding mobile devices.*

SSID Broadcasting

The primary way we locate wireless networks is by using our clients to scan for SSIDs. All wireless networks have a function to turn off the SSID broadcast. You can choose not to broadcast the SSID, but this only stops casual users—sophisticated wireless intruders have tools to detect networks that do not broadcast their SSIDs. Turning off the SSID broadcast forces users to configure the connection to a particular SSID manually.

> **Exam Tip**
>
> The signal strength is a measurement of how well your wireless device is connecting to other devices.

MIMO

The 802.11n specification requires all but handheld devices to use multiple antennas to implement a feature called *multiple in/multiple out (MIMO)*, which enables the devices to make multiple simultaneous connections called *streams*. With up to four antennas, 802.11n devices can achieve amazing speeds. They also can implement channel bonding to increase throughput even more. (The official standard supports throughput of up to 600 Mbps, although practical implementation drops that down substantially.)

802.11ac is a natural expansion of the 802.11n standard, incorporating even more streams, wider bandwidth, and higher speed. To avoid *device density* issues in the 2.4-GHz band, 802.11ac only uses the 5.0-GHz band.

With multiple WAPs in an Extended Service Set (ESS), clients will connect to whichever WAP has the strongest signal. As clients move through the space covered by the broadcast area, they will change WAP connections seamlessly, a process called *roaming*. Multiple User MIMO (MU-MIMO) uses multiple antennas, boosting performance.

VLAN Pooling

One of the big challenges to larger enterprise networks is the large number of clients that might be on a single SSID at any given moment. As the number of devices grows, you get a huge amount of broadcasts on the network.

The traditional method to reduce this is to divide the wireless LAN (WLAN) into multiple broadcast domains and use routers to interconnect the domains. In many cases, though, the needs of the wireless network require a single domain; instead, we create a pool of VLANs for a single SSID and randomly assign wireless clients to one of the VLANs. This is called *VLAN pooling*.

Wireless Bridges

Dedicated wireless bridges are used to connect two wireless networks together, or to join wireless and wired networks together in the same way that wired switches do. You can also use wireless bridges to join wireless networks with other networked devices, such as printers.

Wireless bridges come in two different flavors: point-to-point and point-to-multipoint. Point-to-point bridges can only communicate with a single other bridge and are used to connect two wireless network segments. Point-to-multi-point bridges can talk to more than one other bridge at a time and can connect multiple network segments.

Objective 12.04 Network Monitoring

The biggest trick to monitoring a network is to start by appreciating that even the smallest network has a dizzying amount of traffic moving though it every second. Even more, this traffic is moving through all kinds of different aspects of the network—from individual interfaces coming from a single NIC in a system, to everything moving through a massive router on the edge of your infrastructure.

To be able to do the monitoring, the troubleshooting, and the optimizing necessary to keep our networks in top shape, we need the right monitoring tools at the right places looking for the right things.

Packet Analyzers

Various names are used to describe utilities that analyze packets: *packet sniffer, packet analyzer, protocol analyzer,* and *network analyzer.* There's so much overlap here! That can be attributed to the fact that so many packet analyzers come with sniffers as well. Bottom line, don't rely on the name of the monitoring tool to determine all it can do. Read the tech specs.

A packet analyzer is a program that reads captured files from packet sniffers and analyzes them based on our monitoring needs. A good packet analyzer can file and sort a capture file based on almost anything and create an output to help us do monitoring properly. A typical question a packet analyzer might answer is, "What is the IP and MAC address of the device sending out DHCP Offer messages and when is it doing this?"

Plenty of protocol analyzers are available out there, but you'd be hard pressed to find a network administrator/technician/whatever who isn't familiar with the powerful and free Wireshark. It was originally written by Gerald Combs, who still maintains the program with the help of hundreds of contributors. Wireshark is the perfect prototype of a protocol analyzer. (And it's also specifically mentioned in the CompTIA Network+ objectives. Know this amazing tool!)

When you stop the capture, you'll see something like Figure 12.1. Wireshark's screen breaks into three parts. The top part is a numbered list of all the packets

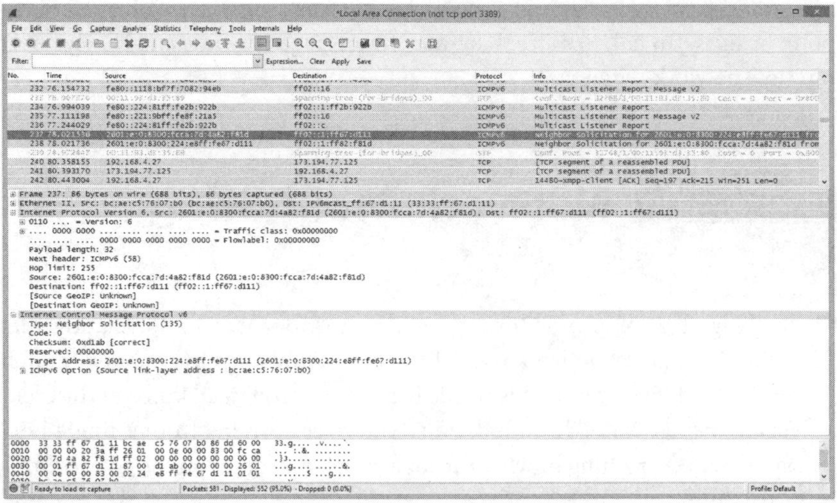

FIGURE 12.1   Wireshark capturing packets

in the capture file, showing some of the most important information. The second part is a very detailed breakdown of the packet that is currently highlighted in the top pane. The bottom pane is the hex representation and the ASCII representation of whatever part of the second pane is detailed.

The downside to a capture is that Wireshark is going to grab everything unless you filter the capture or filter the capture file after the capture. In many cases, you'll find yourself doing both. The filter is the real challenge to Wireshark because it uses its own wonky syntax. Figure 12.2 shows a filter added to a capture file to only show DHCP packets. Note that the filter doesn't actually say "DHCP." Wireshark uses the term *bootp* (note that it needs to be lowercase, because Wireshark is case sensitive).

Interface Monitors

If you want to know how hard your network is working, turn to an interface monitor. Interface monitors track the bandwidth and utilization of one or more interfaces on one or more devices. Think of them as the traffic monitors for your network. A typical question you might ask an interface monitor is, "How hard is the Gigabit Ethernet port 17 on our backbone switch working right now, in megabits per second?"

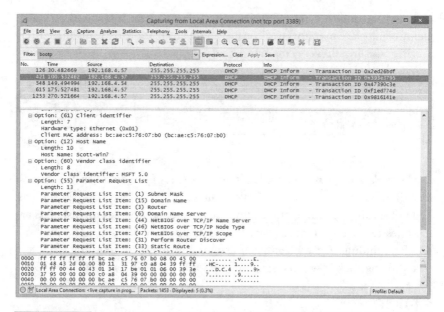

FIGURE 12.2 Wireshark filter

Interface monitors track the quantity and utilization of traffic through a physical port or ports on a single device. Interface monitoring will consist of, among other items, the following:

- **Speed and duplex** At what speed is the port set to run? What duplex is the port running?

- **Utilization** How much of the total bandwidth of the port is being used?

- **Packet drops** A port will drop a packet for one of two reasons: an error or a discard.

- **Errors** How many packets per second are errors? A port treats a packet as erroneous if the packet is malformed or unreadable.

- **Discards** How many frames are discarded per second? A *discard* is when a port intentionally drops a well-formed frame. A discard is not an error. There are many reasons for a port to discard a frame. If a port is trunking VLANs 1 and 2 and it gets a frame for VLAN 3, the port will discard the packet.

- **Interface resets** Is the interface being reset at any time? If so, how often is this taking place?

Interface monitors started as manufacturer-specific tools, and although plenty of interface monitors work on just about any platform, the manufacturer-specific ones are still very common.

Exam Tip
The Cisco Network Assistant (CNA) software enables you to monitor Cisco routers and switches.

Network analyzers and packet flow analyzers can discover the busiest machines on the network, potentially sources of overall network slowdowns. Top talkers are the computers sending the most data, whereas top listeners are the ones receiving the most data. If a company is worried about a malware problem, finding that the computer assigned to Joe in Accounting is the top talker might track down that spam infestation.

SNMP

A quick Google search for network monitoring tools finds literally hundreds of products out there, ranging from complex and expensive to simple and free. One thing most of them have in common is the underlying protocol that enables them to work. The Simple Network Management Protocol (SNMP) is the de facto network management protocol for TCP/IP networks (and it comes dragging in a truckload full of jargon terms to describe the various components).

An SNMP system—which creates a managed network—consists of at least three components:

- SNMP manager
- Managed devices
- Management information bases

The SNMP manager requests and processes information from the managed devices. The SNMP manager runs specialized software called a *network management station (NMS)*. Managed devices run specialized software called *agents* that are designed to respond to requests from SNMP managers. Managed device types include workstations, printers, video cameras, routers, switches, and more.

The kind of information the SNMP manager can get from managed devices varies, primarily because SNMP is an *extensible protocol,* meaning it can be adapted to accommodate different needs. Developers create software that queries almost any aspect of a managed device, from current CPU load on a workstation to how much paper is left in a printer. SNMP uses management information bases (MIBs) to categorize the data that can be queried (and subsequently analyzed).

Once set up properly, an SNMP managed network runs regular queries to managed devices and then gathers that information in a format usable by SNMP operators. An SNMP system has up to eight core functions (depending on the version of SNMP), of which four merit discussion here: Get, Response, Set, and Trap. The common term for each of these functions is protocol data unit (PDU).

When an SNMP manager wants to query an agent, it sends a Get request, such as *GetRequest* or *GetNextRequest*. An agent then sends a Response with the requested information. An NMS can tell an agent to make changes to the information it queries and sends, called variables, through a Set PDU, specifically *SetRequest*.

An agent can solicit information from an NMS with the Trap PDU. An agent can send a *Trap* with or without prior action from the SNMP manager, at least from SNMPv2 to the current SNMPv3.

SNMP systems can use many additional utilities developed over the years. Some can automate various tasks. The snmpwalk utility, for example, tells the SNMP manager to perform a series of Get commands. Note that the CompTIA Network+ objectives shorten this utility name to *Walk*.

The manager software has the capability to send *alerts*, messages directly sent to the techs when their intervention is required. These alerts can have a variety of forms, such as Short Message Service (SMS) and e-mail. SNMP has three major versions. SNMP version 1 (SNMPv1) appeared in three requests for proposals (RFPs) all the way back in 1988. SNMPv2 was a relatively minor tweak to version 1. SNMPv3 added additional security with support for encryption and robust authentication, plus it provided features to make administering a large number of devices easier. SNMP uses User Datagram Protocol (UDP) ports 161 and 162 for unsecure communication. The NMS receives/listens on port 162. The agent receives/listens on port 161. When security is added via Transport Layer Security (TLS), the standard ports used are 10162 and 10161, respectively.

NetFlow

Packet flow monitoring, accomplished with a set of tools related to general packet sniffers and analyzers, tracks traffic flowing between specific source and destination devices. Cisco developed the concept of packet flow monitoring and subsequently included it in routers and switches. The primary tool is called NetFlow.

NetFlow has been around for quite a while and has evolved into a powerful tool that just about every Cisco house uses. It's important to appreciate that NetFlow is similar to SNMP but different. NetFlow is based on the idea of flows that you define to track the type of traffic you wish to see.

A single flow is a flow of packets from one specific place to another. Each of these flows is then cached in a flow cache. A single entry in a flow cache normally contains information such as destination and source addresses, destination and source ports, the source on the device running that flow, and the total number of bytes of that flow.

Analyzing the flow data enables administrators to build a clear picture of the volume and flow of traffic on the network. This in turn enables them to optimize the network (by adding capacity where needed or other options).

Most of the heavy lifting of NetFlow is handled by the NetFlow collectors. NetFlow collectors store information from one or more devices' NetFlow caches, placing it into a table that can then be analyzed by NetFlow analysis tools.

There are many different companies selling different tools, and which tool you should choose is often a matter of features and cost. Figure 12.3 shows a screenshot of a popular tool called LiveAction.

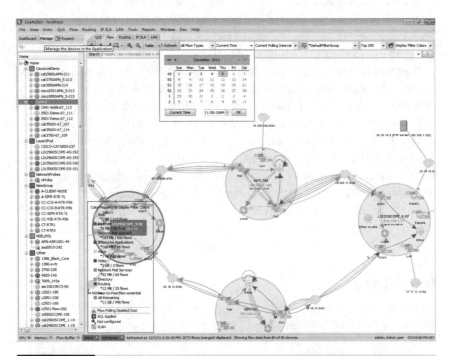

FIGURE 12.3   LiveAction in action!

Cisco's NetFlow started the idea of traffic flows that can then be collected and analyzed. Just about every other form of competing flow-monitoring concept (names like sFlow, Netstream, and IPFix) builds on the idea of the flow.

Performance Monitors

A performance monitor tracks the performance of some aspect of a system over time and lets you know when things aren't normal. Performance monitors are usually tied to a particular operating system or application, as the performance monitoring requires very detailed understanding of the low-level aspects of the system. A typical question you might ask a performance monitor is, "How many hits per hour occurred on my web server over the last two weeks?"

The two most common performance monitoring tools are Windows Performance Monitor (PerfMon) and Linux's syslog. Although they perform the same job, I want to introduce both tools to you because they do that job very differently—and use very different terms to describe the same things. As we next look at certain aspects that are common to any good performance monitor, I'll use the terminology for both tools.

> ### Exam Tip
>
> The term *performance monitor* is not an industry term but instead just a handy way to discuss several utilities with similar functions that are listed in the CompTIA Network+ objectives. Also, PerfMon is a unique Linux tool for performance monitoring. It just happens to share the same name as the Windows Performance Monitor.

SIEM

Security information and event management (SIEM) is used to monitor and manage networks. SIEM is an industry-standard term, but many products of various types are marketed as SIEM solutions. SIEM is a mashup of two processes: security event management (SEM) and security information management (SIM).

As the name would imply, SIEM is a two-part process that begins with the security event monitoring component. SEM is based on real-time monitoring of security events. The SEM framework calls for monitoring the entire enterprise, often through edge devices at monitor points, then saving the logged events to a location that supports single viewpoint review and analysis of the events. In addition to active event monitoring, another task of SEM is to collect and centralize otherwise disparately located security and event logs.

Once logs are created and saved, the second part of SIEM, security information management, kicks in: here, the log files are reviewed and analyzed by automated and human interpreters.

SIEM systems are complex solution suites that are found in large enterprise environments. Depending on the organization, they may be self-implemented and managed or may be administered under contract by a vendor in the form of a managed security service provider (MSSP).

Power and Environmental Monitors

In Chapter 2, we discussed the importance of an uninterruptible power supply (UPS), a battery backup that plugs into the wall. A good UPS acts as a *power monitoring tool* so it can report problems when any fluctuations occur in the electrical supply. All UPS boxes can provide security from power spikes and sags.

The temperature in the telecommunications room should be maintained and monitored properly. If you lose the air conditioning, for example, and leave systems running, the equipment will overheat and shut down—sometimes with serious damage. To prevent this, all serious telecommunications rooms should have temperature monitors as part of their rack monitoring system.

Likewise, you need to control the level of humidity in a telecommunications room. You can install environmental monitors that keep a constant watch on humidity, temperature, and more, for just a few hundred dollars. The devices cost little in comparison to the equipment in the telecommunications room that you're protecting.

Baselines

The only way to know when a problem is brewing on your network is to know how things perform when all's well with the network. Part of any proper performance monitor is the facility to create a baseline: a log of performance indicators such as CPU usage, network utilization, and other values to give you a picture of your network and servers when they are working correctly. A major change in these values can point to problems on a server or the network as a whole.

All operating systems come with some form of baseline tools. Performance Monitor is the common tool used to create a baseline on Windows systems.

Performance monitoring software enables techs to create baselines when the network is functioning correctly. If complaints about network performance come in from one portion of the network (Accounting, for example), that same software can be used to compare current network performance with the historical, normal performance. If there's a discrepancy, the techs can turn to other tools—packet flow analyzers and interface monitors—to figure out if the issue is excess traffic, failing devices, failing interfaces on a device, or an overworked bottleneck (a spot where traffic slows precipitously).

Log Management

Any system that generates electronic log files has two issues. The first is security. Log files are important for the information they provide. The second is maintenance. Log files are going to continue to grow until they fill the mass storage they are stored on. The job of providing proper security and maintenance for log files is called *log management.*

Logs often contain private or sensitive data and thus must be protected. Access to active logs must be carefully controlled. It's very common to give read access rights only to specific users, to make sure only the correct users have access to the log files. In many cases, it's not uncommon for the logging application to have only write access to the files—it's not a good idea to give root access to critical log files.

Generally, log files by default simply grow until they fill the space they are stored on. To prevent this, it's common to make log files *cyclical*—when a file grows to a certain size, it begins to cycle. *Cycling* just means that as a new record appears in the file, the oldest record in the file is deleted. It's also common for log files to be re-created on a time basis. Depending on the utility, you can set a new log file to be created daily, weekly, hourly—whatever is most convenient for the administrators. These files can then be backed up.

There are many laws today that require the retention of log files for a certain period of time. It's important to check with your legal department to see if any files need to be kept longer than your standard backup time frames.

Modern networking tools enable skilled network administrators to manage complex networks fairly easily, after those tools have been set up properly. The tools used must be customized for the network. Plus, the various tools aren't really interchangeable. Just like you wouldn't use a hammer when you need to turn a screw, you wouldn't use a packet analyzer when you want to check toner levels in a laser printer.

Companies dedicate an area in the main office as a *network operations center (NOC)*, a centralized location for techs and administrators to manage all aspects of the network. From that NOC, they can use various programs on the SNMP-managed network to query devices. A graphing program could create graphs that display any set of the data received.

Graphing programs such as Cacti can show everything about a specific switch, for example, to determine utilization of that switch in many aspects— that is, how well it handles its current workload. Figure 12.4 shows Cacti with

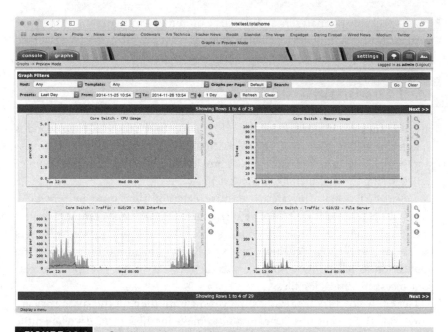

FIGURE 12.4   Cacti showing switch utilization graphs

four graphs depicting network device CPU utilization, memory usage, traffic (bandwidth usage) on the WAN interface, and traffic to the file server.

With a different query, Cacti can graph available storage on a file server or even wireless channel utilization.

Cycling through the various network monitoring tools enables network administrators to see very quickly if a specific server or other device has problems. They could analyze the campus Wi-Fi network and spot a problematic WAP. Going a little further up the food chain, a company could add Nagios, a monitoring application, to their network. Nagios can have systems proactively send alerts via SMS or e-mail when problem areas are detected. If the *link status*—signifying how good the connection is between two systems—between the two access servers connecting the main office and the factory goes red, that's a whole different level of priority than if Kitty the art printer runs low on toner, right?

Programs such as Cacti enable you to see very quickly essential facts about your network hardware. You can see available storage, network device CPU usage, network device memory usage, and more. With wireless-aware tools, you can quickly spot problems with wireless channel usage or channel saturation. These tools are a tech's friend!

Change and Configuration Management

An IT infrastructure is an ever-changing thing. Applications are updated, operating systems change, server configurations adjust; change is a tricky part of managing an infrastructure. Change needs to happen, but not at the cost of losing security. The process of creating change in your infrastructure in an organized, controlled, safe way is called *change management.*

Change management usually begins with a change management team. This team, consisting of people from all over your organization, is tasked with the job of investigating, testing, and authorizing all but the simplest changes to your network.

Change Request

Depending on the organization, this can be a highly official document or, for a smaller organization, nothing more than a detailed e-mail message. Whatever the case, you need to document the reason for this change. A good change request will include the following.

Type of Change

Software and hardware changes are obviously part of this category, but this could also encompass issues such as backup methods, work hours, network access, workflow changes, and so forth.

Configuration Procedures

What is it going to take to make this happen? Who will help? How long will it take?

Rollback Process

If this change in some way makes such a negative impact that going back to how things were before the change is needed, what will it take to roll back to the previous configuration?

Potential Impact

How will this change impact the organization? Will it save time? Save money? Increase efficiency? Will it affect the perception of the organization?

Notification

What steps will be taken to notify the organization about this change?

Dealing with the Change Management Team

With your change request in hand, it's time to get the change approved. In most organizations, change management teams meet at fixed intervals, so there's usually a deadline for you to be ready at a certain time. From here, most organizations will rely heavily on a well-written change request form to get the details. The approval process usually consists of considering the issues listed in the change request, but also management approval and funding.

Making the Change Happen

Once your change is approved, the real work starts. Equipment, software, tools, and so forth must be purchased. Configuration teams need to be trained. The change committee must provide an adequate maintenance window: the time it will take to implement and thoroughly test the coming changes. As part of that process, the committee must *authorize downtime* for systems, departments, and so on. Your job is to provide *notification of the change* to those people who will be affected, if possible providing alternative workplaces or equipment.

Documenting the Change

The ongoing and last step of the change is documentation. All changes must be clearly documented, including but not limited to:

- Network configurations, such as server settings, router configurations, and so on
- Additions to the network, such as additional servers, switches, and so on
- Physical location changes, such as moved workstations, relocated switches, and so on

Every well-designed and maintained network has detailed documentation of every facet of that network *to support configuration management*. Here are some of the areas of documentation:

- **Network diagram** You need pretty seriously detailed diagrams that describe both the *physical* network components and the *logical* components, such as VLANs, too.
- **Asset management** The network needs a detailed list of all the software owned by the company installed on workstations and servers. This includes versions, upgrade paths, and the like. There are many good programs to facilitate this process.

- **IP address utilization** You need to know which device—physical or virtual—has which allocated IP address.

- **Vendor documentation** It's important to have printed or electronic versions of essential details about the hardware and software systems in use by the company. This includes up-to-date contact information for representatives of the products employed.

- **Internal operating procedures/policies/standards** Documenting network policies on every aspect of network behavior—from acceptable use of equipment to standards for high-grade passwords—needs to be documented carefully and fully.

Port Mirroring

Many managed switches have the capability to copy data from any or all physical ports on a switch to a single physical port. This is called *port mirroring*. It's as though you make a customized, fully configurable promiscuous port. Port mirroring is incredibly useful for any type of situation where an administrator needs to inspect packets coming to or from certain computers.

There are two forms of port mirroring: local and remote. Local port mirroring copies data from one or more ports on a single switch to a specific port on that switch. To monitor this data, you have to plug directly into the switch with ports being monitored. Remote port mirroring enables you to access data copied from one or more specific ports on a switch without plugging directly into that switch.

802.1X Configuration

Configuring a switch for authentication, authorization, and accounting (AAA) is arguably one of the most complex configuration jobs a network tech may ever face. Before you get anywhere near the switch, you'll need to make a number of decisions, such as the version of AAA you want to use (RADIUS or TACACS+), the type of 802.1X authentication methods you will use (passwords, certificates, retina scanners?), deciding on and setting up the authentication database system, and opening up security policies to make sure it all works. This list is long, to say the least.

Once your AAA infrastructure is set up, you then configure a AAA-capable switch to support one or more methods of authentication. This is complicated too! Ten flavors and "subflavors" of authentication are supported by Cisco, for example, ranging from simple passwords to a local database to a RADIUS server and a TACACS+ server.

Configuring a switch for AAA—especially the first time—almost guarantees you'll run into plenty of TACACS+/RADIUS misconfiguration issues.

CHECKPOINT

✔**Objective 12.01: Network Policies and Procedures** A service level agreement (SLA) is a document between a customer and a service provider that defines the scope, quality, and terms of the service to be provided. A memorandum of understanding (MOU) defines the duties the parties commit to perform for each other and the time frame. Manufacturers of various network hardware agree to a multi-source agreement (MSA), a document that details the interoperability of their components. A statement of work (SOW) is in essence a legal contract between a vendor and a customer. An SOW defines the services and products the vendor agrees to supply and the time frames in which to supply them. Electrical safety in a networking environment covers several topics, including the inherent danger of electricity, grounding, and static. Physical/installation safety must strictly be adhered to. A final step in managing risk in any company is to have proper *emergency procedures* in place before the emergencies happen. The heating, ventilation, and air conditioning (HVAC) system should be optimized to recirculate and purify the hot air into cool air in a continuous flow.

✔**Objective 12.02: Network Segmentation, Patching, and Updating** Security isn't the only reason we segment networks. We also reduce network congestion and limit network problems through segmentation. We segment to optimize performance. We segment to be in compliance with standards, laws, or best practices. We also segment for easier troubleshooting. Almost every piece of software and firmware on almost every type of equipment you own is subject to patching and updating: printers, routers, wireless access points, desktops, programmable logic controllers (PLCs), and more.

✔**Objective 12.03: Wireless Configuration and Management** The first step of installing a wireless network is the site survey. A site survey will reveal any obstacles to creating the wireless network, and will help determine the best possible location for your access points. Better WAPs now support an IEEE standard (802.3af) called Power over Ethernet (PoE), which enables them to receive their power from the same Ethernet cables that transfer their data. Multiple in/multiple out (MIMO) enables the devices to make multiple simultaneous connections, called streams. VLAN pooling involves creating a pool of VLANs for a single SSID and randomly assigning wireless clients to one of the VLANs. Dedicated wireless bridges are used to connect two wireless networks together, or to join wireless and wired networks together in the same way that wired switches do.

✔**Objective 12.04: Network Monitoring** Packet analyzers such as Wireshark capture and analyze packets. Interface monitors track the bandwidth and utilization of device interfaces. Simple Network Management Protocol (SNMP) is the de facto network management protocol for TCP/IP networks. Packet flow monitoring—accomplished with tools such as NetFlow—tracks traffic flows between specific source and destination devices. Performance monitors track how the system is running over a certain time frame and let you know when things aren't normal. The job of providing proper security and maintenance for log files is called log management.

✔**Objective 12.05: Change and Configuration Management** The process of creating change in your infrastructure in an organized, controlled, and safe way is called change management. All changes must be clearly documented. Port mirroring is incredibly useful for any type of situation where an administrator needs to inspect packets coming to or from certain computers. Configuring a switch for AAA is arguably one of the most complex configuration jobs a network tech may ever face.

REVIEW QUESTIONS

1. Which of the following is not an SNMP utility?
   A. Trap
   B. Get
   C. Walk
   D. Run

2. Which of the following is not related to interface monitoring?
   A. Shorts
   B. Speed
   C. Duplex
   D. Drops

3. When employees bring their own devices to work, the administration can deny devices from accessing the network. What is this called?

   A. On-boarding

   B. Off-boarding

   C. On-loading

   D. Off-loading

4. When should operating system updates be deployed in a company setting?

   A. Automatically

   B. After testing

   C. Only on the second Tuesday of each month

   D. Whenever desired

5. Which of the following documents is usually signed by an ISP and its customers?

   A. SLA

   B. MOU

   C. MSA

   D. SOW

6. Which of the following aggregates and analyzes logs?

   A. SMTP

   B. SNMP

   C. SIEM

   D. SFTP

7. What details how you should deal with just about any component, including information on replacement parts, recycling, and more?

   A. MSDS

   B. MSDN

   C. SSH

   D. MOU

8. What is a honeypot?

   A. A secure server

   B. A gateway

   C. A machine with fake data

   D. A VPN mechanism

9. What is the last step of change management?

    A. Approval from manager

    B. Implementing the changes

    C. Documentation

    D. Testing

10. What is the most famous packet sniffer used today?

    A. Process Monitor

    B. Wireshark

    C. SNMP

    D. netstat

REVIEW ANSWERS

1. **D** Run is not an SNMP utility. The other three do exist.

2. **A** Shorts are a problem with cables, not interfaces.

3. **B** Off-boarding is where administrators deny users' devices to connect.

4. **B** On production networks, it is imperative to test updates before they are deployed, because they could be problematic in terms of compatibility with other components of your network.

5. **A** A service level agreement (SLA) is a document between a customer and a service provider that defines the scope, quality, and terms of the service to be provided.

6. **C** Security information and event management (SIEM) is used to monitor and manage the network.

7. **A** The material safety data sheet (MSDS) must be read and understood in the event of an emergency.

8. **C** Honeypots are machines with fake data that are placed as roadblocks for the hackers.

9. **C** Documentation is always the last step, so that if something similar occurs in the future, there's a repository to go to.

10. **B** Wireshark is the most famous packet sniffer.

Career Flight Path

CompTIA Network+ certification generally serves as the follow-up to the immensely popular CompTIA A+ certification and is an important cornerstone for any number of career flight paths. Many IT companies see CompTIA Network+ certification as the foundation for networking expertise. After CompTIA Network+, you have a number of certification options, depending on the types or specific brands of network hardware you choose to support. Look at these three in particular:

- CompTIA Certifications
- Microsoft Certifications
- Cisco Certifications

CompTIA Certifications

CompTIA Security+ is a great starting point to learn about network security. CompTIA Security+ certification covers a wide range of security topics and technologies and is a great next step after you obtain your CompTIA Network+ certification. Another great CompTIA certification to pursue is CompTIA Linux+.

Microsoft Certifications

Microsoft offers several certifications of their own, including, Microsoft Certified Solutions Associate (MCSA), Microsoft Certified Solutions Expert (MCSE), and Microsoft Certified Solutions Developer (MCSD).

These certifications deal with operating systems, servers, databases, and development.

Cisco Certifications

Cisco offers five levels of network certification.

- The entry level consists of CCENT and CNT.
- The associate level includes Cisco Certified Design Associate (CCDA) and varieties of the popular Cisco Certified Network Associate (CCNA), with specializations in Routing and Switching among many others.
- The professional level includes Cisco Certified Design Professional (CCDP)and varieties of Cisco Certified Network Professional (CCNP).
- The expert level includes Cisco Certified Design Expert (CCDE) and varieties of the Cisco Certified Internetwork Expert (CCIE).
- The architect level consists just of the Cisco Certified Architect (CCAr) certification.

About the CD-ROM

The CD-ROM included with this book comes with

- A video from author Mike Meyers introducing the CompTIA Network+ certification exam
- A link to the Total Tester practice exam software, which includes over 100 practice exam questions
- A link to over 20 sample simulations from Total Seminars' Total Sims
- A link to over an hour's worth of episodes from Mike Meyers' CompTIA Network+ Certification Video Training series
- Links to a collection of Mike's favorite tools and utilities for network troubleshooting
- An electronic copy of the book in PDF format

Playing the Mike Meyers Introduction Video

If your computer's optical drive is configured to auto-run, the menu will automatically start upon inserting the CD-ROM. If the auto-run feature does not launch the CD-ROM, browse to the disc and double-click the **Launch.exe** icon.

From the opening screen you can launch the video message from Mike by clicking the **Mike Meyers Introduction Video** button. This launches the video file using your system's default video player.

System Requirements

The software requires Windows XP or higher, in addition to a current or prior major release of Chrome, Firefox, or Internet Explorer. To run, the screen resolution must be set to 1024 × 768 or higher. The PDF files require Adobe Acrobat, Adobe Reader, or Adobe Digital Editions to view.

Total Tester Exam Software

Total Tester provides you with a simulation of the CompTIA Network+ exam. The exam can be taken in either Practice mode or Exam mode. Practice mode provides an assistance window with hints, references to the book, explanations of the correct and incorrect answers, and the option to check your answers as you take the test. Exam mode provides a simulation of the actual exam. Both Practice mode and Exam mode provide an overall grade and a grade broken down by certification objectives.

The link on the CD-ROM takes you to a Web download page. Click the download and follow the prompts to install the software. To take a test, launch the program and select **Network Demo** from the Installed Question Packs list. You can then select Practice Mode, Exam mode, or Custom Mode. (In Custom mode, you can select the number of questions and the duration of the exam.) After making your selection, click **Start Exam** to begin.

Assessment Test

In addition to the sample exam questions, the Total Tester also includes a Network+ Assessment test to help you assess your understanding of the topics before reading the book. To launch the Assessment test, click **Net+ Assessment** from the Installed Question Packs list. The Network+ Assessment test is 50 questions and runs in Exam mode. When you complete the test, you can review the questions with answers and detailed explanations by clicking **See Detailed Results**.

TotalSims for Network+

The CD-ROM contains a link that takes you to Total Seminars Training Hub. Select **TotalSims for Network+ N10-006**. The simulations are organized by topic, and there are over 20 free simulations available for reviewing topics referenced in the book, with an option to purchase access to the full TotalSims for Network+ N10-006 with over 120 simulations.

Mike's Video Training

The CD-ROM comes with links to training videos, starring Mike Meyers. On the main page of the CD-ROM, click the **Software and Videos** link and then select **Mike Meyers Video Training Online**. Along with access to the videos, you'll find an option to purchase Mike's complete video training series.

Mike's Cool Tools

Mike loves freeware/open source networking tools! Most of the utilities mentioned in the text can be found via the CD-ROM. On the main page of the CD-ROM, click the **Software and Videos** link and then select **Mike's Cool Tools Online**. This will take you to the Total Seminars website, where you can download Mike's favorite tools.

PDF Copy of the Book

The entire contents of the book are provided as a PDF file on the CD-ROM. This file is viewable on your computer and many portable devices. Adobe Acrobat, Adobe Reader, or Adobe Digital Editions is required to view the file on your computer. The CD-ROM includes a link to Adobe's website, where you can download and install Adobe Reader.

> **Note**
>
> For more information on Adobe Reader and to check for the most recent version of the software, visit Adobe's website at www.adobe.com and search for the free Adobe Reader or look for Adobe Reader on the product page. Adobe Digital Editions can also be downloaded from the Adobe website.

To view the PDF copy of the book on a portable device, copy the PDF file to your computer from the CD-ROM, and then copy the file to your portable device using a USB or other connection. Adobe offers a mobile version of Adobe Reader, the Adobe Reader mobile app, which currently supports iOS and Android. For customers using Adobe Digital Editions and an iPad, you may have to download and install a separate reader program on your device. The Adobe website has a list of recommended applications, and McGraw-Hill Education recommends the Bluefire Reader.

Technical Support

Technical support information is provided in the following sections by feature.

Total Seminars Technical Support

For questions regarding the Total Tester software, the operation of the CD-ROM, the Mike Meyers videos, or Mike's Cool Tools, visit www.totalsem.com or e-mail support@totalsem.com.

McGraw-Hill Education Content Support

For questions regarding the PDF copy of the book, e-mail techsolutions@mhedu .com or visit http://mhp.softwareassist.com.

For questions regarding book content, e-mail customer.service@mheducation .com. For customers outside the United States, e-mail international_cs @mheducation.com.

Index

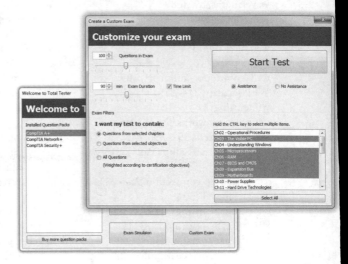